UFF
2-V-20
RING RING.
CABO

1st Edition: December, 2009

4927 Southfork Drive
Lakeland, Florida 33813
www.instituteofspanish.com
T. 863-646-5141

All paintings & vignettes: © Carlos Luna
www.carlosluna.com
Edition: Dr. Norma de la Torre, Teresa Vázquez Martínez
& Stephen Osthoff
Art Direction: Eduardo Sarmiento
www.eduardosarmiento.com

Library of Congress
ISBN: 978-0-9825558-0-4

Printed in China

To my parents
Dr. Luis J. Vázquez and Mrs. María Teresa García de Vázquez

My parents-in-law
Rev. Gerardo Martínez and Teresa H. Martínez

and to Lizette, Alexis, Peter, Lauren, Antonio and Colton
For being my inspiration

Acknowledgements

It has taken over two years to compile, edit and translate the stories in this book. It is the contribution of many individuals, family members and other good friends of mine, who have granted me the right to publish, and even film, their personal stories. It has been our common purpose to leave testimonies of our exodus, so that other generations learn to appreciate freedom. My deepest gratitude also goes to everyone that, so unselfishly, collaborated. Muchas gracias for cheering me on to the finish line.

I want to thank my **mother** *and* ***father*** *for having the courage and fortitude of character to make the decision to uproot and bring our family to freedom. Thank you for ensuring that Lourdes and I, as well as our children, enjoy the fruit of free-will. You have been a perfect example of what good parents should be, and this lesson we, and our children will carry on. This book is as much your accomplishment, as it is mine.*

My dear husband **Carlos**, *thank you for loving me unconditionally and providing all the emotional and financial support I have needed. Thank you for reading every story and giving me your opinion and much required attention. You are the best!*

To my loving daughters **Lizette** *and* **Alexis Martínez**. *Thank you for being my inspiration, for helping proofread, for understanding my work commitments and always giving me a 100% of your love, respect and support. Thank you for being successful and autonomous young ladies. I am so proud of you!*

Lizette, thanks for giving me my precious **Antonio**.

My sister **Lourdes**, *my biggest fan and personal cheerleader. Thank you for always being there every step of the way, and for thinking that most of the things I do are great... It is you who is great!*

This book could not have been done without the constant help and support of my loyal Peruvian friend and colleague, **Karen Gallardo Heverling**. *There are no words to express my gratitude for your unconditional dedication. Thank you for editing, translating and proofreading every single page! You are now almost a Cuban! We shall make you an Honorary Cuban.*

I would like to extend a very special thanks to **Gay Finkleman**, *President and CEO of Ginnie Publishing, Inc., and life story writer, who was instrumental in the launching of this book. Thank you, Gay!*

Dr. Norma de la Torre, *my life-long friend; my first teacher in the United States, to whom I promised I would write this book 38 years ago. Thank you for giving me the gift of innumerable hours of support. It has been a privilege to work with you by my side…in person and on the telephone…even in the middle of the night! Thank you for being you, but above all, for the great influence you have had in my life.*

To my dearest friend and colleague, Prof. **Stephen Osthoff** *for proofreading every single story and making sure the English version was not "Cubanized." Thanks for being like a brother to me.*

A very special thank-you to so many friends and family who have helped me on this project: **Claudia Luna**, **Pam Matheny**, **Sandra Hudson**, **Ami Scroggin**, **Dr. Luis J. Vazquez**, *and many others who have so graciously read and edited stories. My best friend,* **Dr. Solange Pendas** *as well as* **Rosa D. Hernández** *and* **Mark Kaylor**, **Esq. Emily Soto**, **Daniel Stetson** *and* **Carolyn Jackson** *for sharing great ideas and suggestions. Thanks to* **Wayne Kline** *for always watching out for my business success. To my wonderful graphic designer,* **Ed Sarmiento**, *for your talent, friendship, and also for being my personal GPS when I was lost in the Miami traffic.*

I must also mention, **Lizette**, **Alexis**, **Ana**, **Alex**, **Abby**, **Maya**, **Isaac** *and* **Adam Martinez**, **Ami, Sam Scroggin**, **Peter Petriw**, **Lauren Farrell**, *as well as my best little friend* **Natham Gimness**, *for being our successful and independent first generation Cubans; thus honoring the sacrifices made by their grandparents when they left their country.*

Most of all, I thank God for the many blessings I have received throughout my live. In this particular occasion, for putting a person of the caliber of our internationally renowned Cuban artist, **Carlos Luna**, *in my path. It is an ineffable honor for me to have your work represented in this book.* **Carlos**, *thank you for the privilege of having my name along side of yours!*

Contents

10 Preface • *Dr. Norma de la Torre*

12 Foreword • *Dr. José Manuel García*

14 Introduction • *Teresa Vázquez Martínez*

22 My Crocodile-shaped Island • *Teresa Vázquez Martínez*

DECADE OF THE 60's

42 Invaded by Our Own People • *Felipe & Alicia Olivera*

46 I Did Not Know How to Swim:
A Story of Stoicism • *Dr. Sergio & Mirtha Vallejo*

52 I Saw It Coming • *Dr. Pedro Almazán*

58 A True Act of Love • *Rosa Delfín Hernández*

64 I Believe in Miracles! • *Dr. Ramón Rodríguez-Torres*

70 A Legacy of Faith. The Story of Rev. Gerardo
& Teresa Martínez • *Teresa Hidalgo de Martínez*

76 A Lesson of Patriotism • *Martha Espinosa Laurent*

84 Cuban Treasures • *Ana María Guitérrez Myers*

92 Five Dollars and a Box of Cigars • *Roberto & Viviana Pedroso*

98 A Lost Opportunity, a Lesson Learned • *Dr. Jorge González*

DECADE OF THE 70's

104 Five Years of Loneliness • *Loly Garriga*

110 Building the Future • *Eduardo Tapia*

114 Memoirs of an Ice Cream Lady • *Dania Frías de Pendas*

120 The Interrupted Youth
of Yara Borges Guzmán • *Dr. Norma de la Torre*

DECADE OF THE 80's

128 Memories of a Political Prisoner • *Pedro Ramiro Machín*

144 My Memories of El Mariel • *Dr. José Manuel García*

150 I Reached My Goal • *Acela (Carito) Lumpuy*

158 My Escape Through Honduras • *Dr. Manuel Martínez*

DECADE OF THE 90's

166 I Will Always Be With You • *Carlos Luna*

176 Everything Was a Lie • *Eduardo Fernández*

DECADE OF THE 2000

182 The Soul of the Song • *Ivelisse de la Fe*

190 I Come From All Places • *Eduardo Sarmiento*

BORN IN USA

196 He Made It Come True!
The Story of Eddy García • *Teresa Vázquez Martínez*

202 That Mysterious Island • *Rick García*

GALLERY

208 Paintings by Carlos Luna

Dr. Norma de la Torre

Preface

Dr. Norma de la Torre

For the first time, and in her own words, Teresa Vázquez Martínez, tells us about the intense trauma she suffered when her parents decided to flee Cuba with their two daughters: Teresa, and Lourdes, her sister. She also narrates about the difficulties her family confronted in order to leave the island; about their arrival to this land of freedom, and how they were able to -successfully- rebuild their lives so drastically interrupted by Castro's Revolution.

At the same time, the author includes in this book, the odyssey that another twenty-four families went through. These families, as her own, had to abandon their country of origin- and their worldly possessions- to "start at zero" in a foreign land with a different culture, language, fragrances and flavors to those of their homeland. Each family is a true example of Success in Exile.

Most of the stories have been written by their protagonists. Others are based on Mrs. Martínez's interviews or films of the families portrayed. All of the stories include personal and/or family photographs.

In this important work, Teresa Martínez also interjects a series of statistics, plus other relevant data of Cuba prior to the Marxist-Leninist government of Fidel Castro, accompanied by an analysis of the exodus that has occurred in the fifty years of oppression and misgovernment the island has suffered. In addition, this book embodies a colorful gallery of several paintings of our world-renown Cuban artist, Carlos Luna who, through his unique art, gives us a visual testimony of the customs of the island, and the tragedy of the Cuban people.

This book proves, once more, the ingenuity and the talent of its author, an illustrious exiled who is today a prominent figure in her community. She represents a legitimate glory for all the Cuban exiles, as well as those from other countries, wherever they are.

Foreword

Dr. José Manuel García

I can honestly say that this is one of the most interesting, compelling and inspiring books that I have read. This important testimonial portrays the reality of the Cuban exiles through their own voices. It reaches into the deepest corners of our souls, making us reflect about who we are, what we want, and where are we going. At the same time, it drives us to look differently at everything we had taken for granted when we lived in a free country.

Like many other Cuban emigrants, my family and I arrived in the United States of America as part of the 1980 Cuban exodus known as the Mariel boatlift fleeing a tyrannical dictatorship in search of a better life. Just a few days before our arrival to this land, my father was arrested by the soldiers of Castro's regime, and just a few days later, our ship began to sink during the voyage in the treacherous waters of the Florida straits; however, our hopes and our dreams of freedom conquered all obstacles.

Teresa Martinez, the author of this fascinating memoir, also came to United States fleeing the cruel dictatorship that changed her life and that of her family. Her story is a vivid example of how, with perseverance and dedication, all dreams can become true in this land of opportunity. Teresa, after a successful career as an educator, was also able to achieve great success in the business world and has dedicated part of her life to help the Hispanic community and many other groups of immigrants to fulfill their dreams. Today, Teresa is a distinguished individual with a powerful presence in Central Florida, where she is the producer/host of a very important and popular program on a local television network.

This book, which is the realization of a dream for its author, will undoubtedly become an important contribution to the study of immigration in the United States. It can be used as a reference text in the field of ethnic studies. It is another example of Teresa's talent and once again, demonstrates her deep moral commitment to other inmigrants.

As head of the Foreign Languages Department at Florida Southern College, and a critic of Hispanic Literature, I can honestly say that books such as this one are only possible when their authors share the same experiences as their interviewees.

The text, in spite of placing great emphasis on the political and economic reality of Cuban exiles, could also become a motivational tool for other immigrants who strive to reach their goals and realize their dreams. This book can serve as a reminder to the immigrants' children, so that they can become aware of their parent's struggles and sacrifices of leaving everything behind to come to another country in search of better opportunities and a better life.

Statue of José Martí. Cienfuegos, Cuba

Statue of Liberty. New York, USA

Introduction

Teresa Vázquez Martínez

WHO ARE THE CUBANS

The Cuban community in the United States has had a notable influence on the economic, political and social development of this country, especially in Miami, New Jersey, New York, California and Texas. We feel proud of what has been accomplished as a nation of Cubans in exile, of the struggles we have had to overcome to insure the well being and liberty of our families. It is also our deepest desire to preserve our history, our culture and our triumphant spirit to transmit it to new generations who need to know where they come from, why they are here, and the sacrifices undertaken by their predecessors, so that they can enjoy life in the land of opportunities.

Cuban exiles have the highest income per capita of all the minorities in the United States, as well as the highest level of education. We have been described as the foreign-language-speaking group that has had the fastest mobilization towards a middle class in the history of the United States. Over the years, we have made enormous contributions to the American culture for the benefit of all.

Cuban-American entertainers such as Celia Cruz, Gloria and Emilio Estefan, Desi Arnaz, Andy Garcia, Christina Saralegui, Cameron Diaz, Carmen Electra, Jon Secada, Christina Milian, Willy Chirino, Lissette Álvarez, Albita, Olga Guillot, Enrique Chia, and many others have climbed far up the ladder of success. Many have been actively involved in politics, even elected to United States Congress, such as Ileana-Ros-Lehtinen, Lincoln and Mario Diaz-Balart from Florida; Senator Robert Menendez from New Jersey; Bob Martínez, fortieth Governor of Florida, and Mel Martínez who was the first Hispanic to serve as Director of the Republican Party of the United States.

Jorge Mas Canosa (1939–1997) was an activist best known for his strong opposition to Fidel Castro and for his leadership of the

Cuban-American National Foundation. In the field of business, Roberto Goyzueta became Chairman, Director, and Chief Executive Officer (CEO) of The Coca-Cola Company from August 1980 until his death in October 1997. Raul Alarcon was President and CEO of Spanish Broadcasting Systems. Ralph Alvarez was President and COO of McDonalds. Others include the Bacardi and Fanjul families.

It is important that our story be told, that it is shared. We come from a beautiful land, a land that in the years before Castro, was the third economic power in all of Latin America. We are the sons and daughters of the "Pearl of the Caribbean," the land of sugar, tobacco and rum. We are charismatic, innovative, and extroverted. We have an enterprising spirit and a proud character that will always help us to overcome obstacles, and that has made us a prominent part of American Society.

My deepest gratitude to the families who kindly offered their personal stories to ensure that our new generations, who have had the privilege of being born in freedom, know that it is important to appreciate it, to love the land that took us in, and to be proud of their roots. Also to our North American friends, as well as those from other parts of the world, know that we are thankful to the countries that took us in with open arms. We hope you understand from the testimonials in this book what can easily happen to a country that is not vigilant of its freedom.

Cuban Exodus

We Cubans who have arrived in the United States of America are known for our progress, innovation and the insatiable desire to achieve success. In addition to being immigrants, we are exiles. We were forced to flee the island Christopher Columbus once described as "The most beautiful land human eyes have ever seen." Five decades have gone by since that fateful New Year's Day in 1959, and during that time, there have been four main exodus:

THE FIRST EXODUS (1959 - 1962)

Most of the first exiles that arrived in Miami in 1959 were followers of Fulgencio Batista. Soon after, entrepreneurs and professionals whose properties and businesses had been confiscated by the new Cuban government began to arrive. They thought the situation could not last long and believed they would be able to return in a not-too-distant future. Some began to plan the invasion of the Bay of Pigs with the help of the United States, but it resulted in a total failure. Shortly after, Castro aligned himself with the Soviet Union and declared himself a Marxist-Leninist, thus ensuring Russian protection for his new Communist Government.

Within this exodus we must also recognize Operation Peter Pan, coordinated by the USA Department of State, the CIA, the Archdiocese of Miami, and a group of Cuban exiles. During this time, more than 14,000 children were sent from Cuba to the United States by their parents, who opposed the revolutionary government, and feared the rumors that their children could be sent to student camps in the Soviet Union. With the help of Monsignor Bryan O. Walsh, children were received by their relatives, friends of their families or host families all over the country.

THE FREEDOM FLIGHTS (1965 - 1974)

The discontent continued in Cuba because of freedom of expression, religion and financial and political difficulties. All the private business entities were confiscated by the "people"(the government), and private property ceased to exist. There were more imprisonments and executions, some of them public, because of political disagreement. Due to the anti-Castro pressure, Fidel opened the Port of Camarioca for those who wished to leave the country to be rescued by their exiled relatives. President Lyndon Johnson opened the famous "Freedom Flights." Hundreds of thousands of Cubans arrived in Miami on these flights. Others left via Spain or Mexico. It is estimated that during this particular exodus, more than 450,000 Cubans left the island.

Most of these Cubans had to leave the country without any belongings. They could only take the most urgent necessities and those things that the Castro government could not take from them: love for God, love for family, perseverance, dignity and their education. They arrived without their credentials or university documentation which were needed for revalidation of their careers. They did not have credit to obtain commercial loans, nor anyone to back them or co-sign for them. The most prestigious professionals, business owners, blue collar workers, everyone had to wash dishes in restaurants, work in gas stations, clean offices or do any honest type of work that was available. Thousands of professional women, or those who, due to their social level, had never worked in Cuba, were now working as seamstresses in factories or as housemaids. Gradually, they rebuilt their lives and enjoy what we describe today as a success in exile.

THE MARIEL (1980)

In April 1980 a bus full of people wanting political asylum, crashed the entrance door of the Peruvian Embassy in Havana. During the shooting that followed, two guards were injured and Fidel, furiously, gave orders to remove the security post at the entrance of the embassy. In just a few hours, more than 10,000 Cubans sought asylum at the embassy. Frantic, Castro opened the Port of Mariel and announced that anybody wishing to leave the island could do so. Immediately, a fleet of Cubans-Americans went to rescue their families while some others went looking for the opportunity to make money. This was known as the "Freedom Flotilla." Between April and September of that year, approximately 125,000 Cubans arrived in Florida.

A large percent of those new refugees were laborers and farmers. In fact, they were part of the Cuban population for which the revolution was carried out in the first place. By this time Castro had already reached an agreement with President Jimmy Carter to free the political prisoners and allow them to leave the country. Fidel took advantage of this opportunity to empty his prisons and mental asylums. Now it was not only the upper and middle classes that were fleeing from the clutches of communism. Although among the Marielitos arrived worthy professionals and thousands of honorable families, criminals and mentally ill Cubans wandered the streets of Miami tarnishing the good standing that had cost so much effort to build.

THE RAFTERS (1993 - 1995)

The Cuban economy continued to worsen, and with the collapse of the Soviet Union in 1991, it reached deplorable conditions. Fidel was feeling the pressure of an unhappy country, and once again, in a furious tantrum, he declared that anyone who would like to leave the island could do so. Since there was no means of transportation, thousands of Cubans threw themselves on the mercy of the sea in makeshift rafts or anything that would keep them afloat on the high seas. They preferred to run the risk of drowning or being devoured by sharks, rather than staying in their country and living under the oppression of the Castro regime. The waters of the Florida Straits became the grave for thousands of unknown Cubans, many of them women and children.

THE AGREEMENT

Finally, there was an agreement between the United States and Cuba to grant visas to 20,000 Cubans per year. This was known as the Visa Lottery, that is still in place. To this day, thousands of Cubans come to Florida searching for freedom. Those who dare to cross the Florida Straits can only stay in the United States if they touch American soil. This is known as the "Wet Feet vs. Dry Feet Law". If the Coastguard finds them in the water, the law is applied and they are sent back to Cuba. Meanwhile, we never hear of anyone, from anywhere in the civilized world, seeking political and/or economical asylum in Cuba.

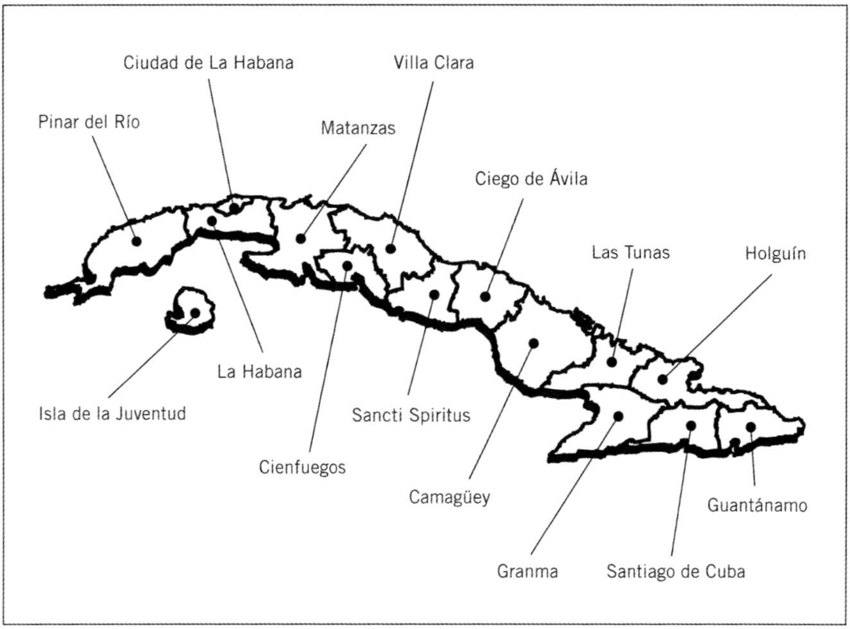

Actual map of Cuba

ISLAND OF CUBA

The Republic of Cuba is part of an archipelago of the Caribbean Sea. Its main island, known as the Island of Cuba, is the largest of the Greater Antilles and is recognizable –at a bird's eye view– by its crocodile shape. Also forming part of this archipelago is the *Isla de la Juventud,* (*Youth Island*) known as *Isla de Pinos* (*Pine Island*) until 1978, and another 4,195 keys or small islands. Cuba is located near Mexico and the United States, only 90 miles from Key West. Cuba is home to over 11 million people and is the most populated insular nation in the Caribbean.

Cuba's name comes from the word *cubao* in the Taino language which translates to: "*Where fertile land is abundant*" or *coabana,* which means "*Great place.*"

Some Facts about Cuba before Castro

• In 1958 Cuba was the third economic power in Latin America after Venezuela and Brazil due to its gold reserves, dollars and securities in precious metals. Cuba's inflation was the lowest in the region with 1.4%. (The medium was Mexico with 7.8% and the highest was Bolivia with 63%) The Cuban peso was equal in value to the US dollar and at times even surpassed it.

• In the area of health, Cuba occupied the third place in Latin America after Uruguay and Argentina with 128 physicians and dentists per 100,000 inhabitants. The infant mortality was the lowest in the region.

• In 1958 Cuba was the first producer of cobalt in Latin America and the second producer of nickel worldwide.

• In fresh fish consumption, Cuba held first place with 5.6 pounds per capita followed by the United States with 5.4. In calorie consumption, Cuba occupied third place in Latin America with 2,682 surpassed only by Argentina with 3,106 and Uruguay with 2,991.

• In the 1950's Cuba had an excellent educational system and an impressive literacy rate. Cuba was also the country with the largest percentage of public expenditure for education in Latin America.

• Cuba held first place in Latin America and fifth in the world in television sets per capita. The country had 58 newspapers in circulation. Cuba also held eighth place in the world in the number of radio stations.

• In cars per capita, Cuba occupied third place. New cars arrived in Cuba before they did in Miami.

• Life in Cuba was comparable to that of the United States but more relaxed.

These facts can be found in the following sources: *UN Statistical Yearbook; the Statistical Abstract for Latin America; and the Bureau of Inter-American Affairs, U.S. Department of State, Contacto Magazine, Cuban Facts, Wikipedia Free Encyclopedia.*

Dr. Luis J. Vázquez & María Teresa García Vázquez

My Crocodile-shaped Island

Teresa Vázquez Martínez

> *Liberty, Sancho, is one of the most precious gifts that heaven gave to men; we cannot compare the treasures contained in the earth or the sea with her: for liberty, as well as for honor, one could and should, risk life.*
> MIGUEL DE CERVANTES SAAVEDRA

Life was beautiful on my crocodile-shaped Island…the crystal clear waters of Varadero Beach, the majestic palm trees that stood tall and proud in the tropical vegetation of the mountains and valleys. I can still close my eyes and see my sister Lourdes and me crossing the palm-trunk bridge over the Guásima Creek (a short cut through a tropical forest) to go visit our Uncle Filo and Aunt Mercedes in the country. His house, where our mother grew up, was a quaint wooden house surrounded by fruit trees and with a large well where they gathered the water supply. My memories are endless: the smell of tobacco leaves permeated the walls of the warehouse, the sugar cane fields seemed to go on forever, and my favorite place… the "monte," the deep woods where my cousin Nancy and I would escape to go sit under the mamoncillo tree. There, we would tell each other our deepest and darkest secrets and dreams. We were seven and ten years old. Nancy was, and still is, my favorite cousin, my confidant. Once in a while my uncle would come by on his horse and scare us to death. All the children loved to spend the summers at Uncle Filo's house at La Guásima. It was like Old McDonald's farm with a variety of animals and the freedom to run and play in the fields without a care in the world.

Back in our town, Esperanza, Las Villas, we lived in a very convenient location. Most of our closest relatives lived on Barnada Street. We were surrounded by the love of both sets of grandparents on each side of our home, as well as aunts, uncles and several cousins. In the afternoons we would go from house to house to see who had the tastiest food for the evening and have a taste. At night, everyone sat outside in the wooden rocking chairs on the front porches to greet the neighbors as they went by. It was an excellent form of entertainment and fellowship, not to mention keeping up with the town's latest gossip. Our father, Dr. Luis J. Vazquez, had his office adjacent to our home. He was always around, coming in and out of the house in between patients to go get a cup of coffee, or to get a whiff of the spices that were being prepared in the kitchen. Sometimes it was just to keep in touch with what we were doing or simply to steal a kiss from Mom. I can still smell the fresh scent of his well pressed linen doctor's gown. He always dressed in white, as did all the doctors on the island. Our colonial style home had a large beautifully tiled courtyard in the center, large enough for Lourdes and me to ride our bikes around or sit with our friends on the swing. Each room of our house opened to this courtyard, so our mother or the hired help could always keep an eye on us. Barnada Street was in the center of town. There we had the Catholic Church and the Central Park where all the youth gathered in the evenings. There was a "glorieta," (a central square) where bands usually played on the weekends. Young men and women walked in opposite directions at night wearing their best outfits and admiring each other. When a young man stopped a young lady, there were plenty of park benches to sit and talk or start a great romance. There were lots of flamboyant trees that provided fabulous shade during the day and, when these trees bloomed, they would turn bright orange. There was always a lot of fun activity in the park.

On the corner was La Central, Uncle Carlos' grocery store where my parents met. My Mother, María Teresa García, was a beautiful woman with the typical hourglass figure. Dad was a rather thin, blonde-haired, young man who was home for vacation from medical school. Mom was spending a few days with her sister, Lidia, and Lidia's husband, Carlos, taking care of their children, Carlitos and Manolo. Dad went crazy over her! As soon as he graduated, Dad and my mom got married and also settled on Barnada Street. La Central was also a meeting place where people would go to buy their groceries and to sit and have a drink, some coffee or a great sandwich. There was always a delightful aroma of roasting pork. They made the most fabulous pork sandwiches and churros calientes in the world. Manolo and I used to go there after school to get a small bottle of Coca-Cola®, and drop in two Chiclets® to watch it bubble up. It is a shame I was only able to enjoy those Cokes during first grade. Aunt

Lidia had the beauty salon next to their home. It was always full of ladies doing their hair, their nails, having coffee, sharing the town's news and having fun. Several ladies worked for my aunt and they were like part of the family. At the other end of the street was La Maravilla, a clothing store with anything you could possibly need. It was a fun life. We never needed an alarm clock because we slept with the windows open. Consequently, we woke up to the sounds of neighbors greeting each other, the milkman, a car horn or a friendly rooster.

During the summers the whole family would go to the beach house at El Salto. Year after year we would meet with the same friends and go swimming in the morning and have fresh fish for lunch. We had to wait for hours to swim again because "swimming after eating" was believed to "stop digestion." We would play games or fight over the hammock. We waited for evening to arrive so that our grandfather would take us crab hunting using a broom stick with a nail at the end and a flash light. Mom and Dad would also take us to Varadero for one or two weeks during the summer. That was some beach!

My favorite time of the year was Christmas. The park and streets were decorated, and the rest of the family would come to visit from Havana. We all gathered at Rosita's house (my paternal grandmother) and had the traditional roast pork, black beans and rice, plus all the trimmings. On the 25th there was always a dance and New Year's celebration was at Carlos and Lidia's house. At 12:00 midnight we would eat the traditional 12 grapes and throw a bucket of water out the front door to start the year clean and fresh… this was hilarious! We also danced until sunrise.

I was a small child then, yet these memories and smells are very fresh in my mind. Even today, five decades later, I still have dreams about being there, in my beautiful home. I always remember the butterfly flowers at grandmother Rosita's house, next to the mint bush, which emitted a fragrance that was very typical of her courtyard. The aroma of the fresh mint leaves in the "mojitos" I enjoy so much these days, always transports me to my grandmother's courtyard.

As children, we were not aware of the political situation. I later understood that we were living under a dictatorship, and most Cubans wanted to be free from the oppression of Batista's government. I only remember that we were happy, we were pampered by our family and by the women that worked for us in our home. We had everything we wanted. I was only four years old when Dad bought his Pontiac. I liked it so much that he went and bought me a red toy car that I could even drive. I was the most pampered little girl on the block!

My first memory of the revolution is a wounded soldier that came to my father's office for medical care. Shortly after that, on New Year's Day 1959, while celebrating at my Aunt Lidia's house, the news came that Fulgencio Batista had fled the island. Ignorant of the fate that awaited the country, most Cubans went out on the street celebrating New Year's Day, the new government, and democracy… in a nutshell, a fictitious freedom. This freedom would turn out to be the destruction of many households and the heartbreak of millions, who had to uproot their families and leave the island, many to never ever see it again.

My father had a large bird cage with several quails on the patio of our home. In the emotion of the moment, he opened the cage to set them free as well. "Enjoy freedom," he said. The next morning most of the quails were back roosting on top of the cage and some had gone back inside. I guess they were smarter than we were about what had just happened to our island.

A couple of days later, several rebels came to my house asking for the car keys as the car was needed for the revolution; they wanted to go to Havana to march in the manifestation. When Dad refused to give them the keys to his brand new Pointiac, they became verbally abusive, calling him an "esbirro" (someone against the cause), but Dad refused saying that he was a medical doctor and needed his car to serve his patients, and that he personally had done more for the revolution than they had, as he had contributed money and medication for the rebels in the Escambray, and he could prove it. My father would send medication for sick and wounded soldiers via the town's priest. The angry men calmed down a bit and decided to take my aunt Nonín's car instead. Dad found it fifteen days later in awful condition.

Soon came the expropriation of private property. Fidel had his own definition of socialism – a society controlled by him. My father had gone to Havana when the militia came to confiscate his medical practice, the rental homes and anything we owned. That same day La Central, Lidia's Beauty Salon and La Maravilla were confiscated as well. In one afternoon all the businesses in the area were taken over by the government, the doors closed and sealed. I remember Uncle Carlos, a strong, handsome man, sitting on his rocking chair, crying like a baby for hours and hours. He had worked very hard, day and night, to build La Central into the successful business it was. Now there was nothing else he could do; they had to go work for the government. There was no other option.

My father arrived from Havana late that night, and my mother did not say anything; she just wanted to spare him the pain as much as possible. The next morning Mom brought him his espresso coffee, sat by the bedside and, in between tears, informed him that there was no office for him to go to work, or patients to see. There was a big sign glued to the office door that said, "Confiscated, Property of the Revolution." My father, self-assured, asked her not to cry, that God would open other doors. When the officer came back to inform him of where he was going to work, Dad refused by saying,

"I am sorry, but I will not work for Communists."

Furiously, the officer replied, "Then you will not work, but you will have to speak to the Director of Public Health."

Dad went to see him. The director informed him that he was going to work 24 consecutive hours every other day. Angrily my father answered,

"Why don't you go ahead and put a bullet in me instead of killing me with those hours? I refuse to work!" Later he admitted that when he was walking to his car, his legs were shaking. He knew that was not the right way to speak to a communist government official.

Dad was loved by his patients; he was also needed in the town. We feared for his life, but the government left him alone. We never lacked money as he discreetly continued seeing patients. People paid him under the table; others would bring chickens or vegetables. We had a large backyard with lots of chickens! They became Lourdes'

Grandmother María & Teresa Vázquez

Dr. Vázquez, grandmother Rosita & family

Carlos & Teresa Martínez

favorite toys, and at one time, she had them trained to sit in the chicken coop and stay perfectly still as she read stories to them. She would even make them walk in an almost straight line. If she could do that at the age of seven or eight...imagine what she can do now.

The private school I attended was to suffer the same fate. I remember a lady and a man dressed in green coming to our classroom and talking to us,

"Do you believe in God?"

Confused we replied, "Yes."

They smiled and asked, "Have you ever seen Him? Touched Him? Talked to him and had Him respond?"

"No," we said quite confused.

"So, why are you so sure He exists? Why don't we do a test and see what happens? Close your eyes and pray with all your heart that God sends you some ice cream. Oops, what a shame, you must have not prayed hard enough; let's try it again."

"I know why we can't have ice cream," a classmate emphatically declared. "It would melt!" Then they had us pray with all our hearts' desires for a cookie, a toy, and other things. With disappointment, we realized that our Lord was ignoring our requests, which were quickly fulfilled by Castro. Brainwashing at its best! They marched us to the public school that same day. Parents started worrying about the way in which the government was starting to exercise control over their children. They were afraid they were going to lose parental rights. Many families could not leave immediately, so they started to send their young children to the United States through "Operation Peter Pan." I was horrified. This operation was coordinated by the United States government, the Roman Catholic Archdiocese of Miami, and certain Cubans. Between 1960 and 1962, over 14,000 children were sent alone from Cuba to Miami by their parents. With the help of Monsignor Bryan O. Walsh, the children were placed with friends, relatives and families who took them in all over the United States. Many of them waited several years before they were able to reunite with their parents.

To ensure that the whole island was under vigilance against contra-revolutionary attacks, they formed the Revolutionary Defense Committees (CDR). Every block of every street throughout the whole country would have a family who voluntarily offered its service to spy on their neighbors. Any activity would be investigated and, if it was considered improper, reported to Government Security (G-2). Improper activities, for example, would be having more food than was allocated. One day my father bought a big chunk of cheese from a farmer. That afternoon two policemen carrying guns and wearing all the communists' insignias came to arrest him. Why? Because he had bought cheese from a farmer! We were living under socialism, and no one was to have more than the other. Dad refused to be escorted to the police like a common criminal and promised to go turn himself in, but first he wanted them to see the cheese. Since it had been divided in equal parts among the family, the piece that was left in the refrigerator was so small that they just gave him a warning.

My parents decided it was time to leave. Dad started gathering the family trying to get everyone to leave Cuba at the same time. There were so many of us, that the necessary paperwork, the pictures for the passports, everything was taking a long time to prepare. Meanwhile a law was implemented that boys between the ages of fifteen and twenty-one could not leave until they had served in the military service. By the time we presented our request to leave, it was too late. Most doctors had already left, and there was now a new law requiring professionals to serve two years of forced labor before they were able to leave the country.

Soon after receiving the request, two officers came to our house to do a complete inventory of our home; everything to the last detail!

Everything was listed and given a number. At the time of our departure, they would go over the list, and if anything was missing, our permission would be denied. The inventory also included our car; it had to be in working order. Of course, the bank accounts also had to have the same balances as they did on that humiliating day. We were now "Gusanos" (worms), and they didn't show much respect to those who turned their back on the new "Cuba, free territory of America." Although we knew that the permission would not arrive very soon, Mom had a suitcase ready to go with a change of clothes for each of us...nothing else! That was the allotment. I can't imagine how much Mom must have worried knowing that we were growing kids and everything was rationed.

There was a lot of vigilance; as a matter of fact, I hear that things have gotten worse since then. There was a time when we could hear people walking on top of our roof during the evenings. From the roof they could keep an eye on us. It was quite scary. When we would hear the thump, thump, thump, Lourdes and I would start crying and shaking. It would go on for a while and then stop and start again. My parents would ask, "Who is there?" but no one would answer. Dad went to the Police Department to express his concern; the Chief of Police assured him, "Don't worry Dr. Vázquez, we will make sure to send two policemen tonight to protect your family. Don't worry."

Teresa, Carlos, Alexis & Lizette Martínez Candela

Our prowler went away for a while. About two weeks later, the sounds started again. Dad went again to see the police and they offered to help, but this time Dad told the officer, "I am going to help you. I have x-ray equipment. Consequently, I have access to 220-volt electricity in my home. I already fixed a booby trap on the roof. If the prowler comes tonight, I will call you tomorrow to pick up the body." Our thumper never came back!

Food was rationed to 2 oz. of meat per family member every two weeks. The cost was $0.40 per pound at the government store. But the black market will always exist in oppressed countries. Dad would go to farmers and buy meat for $10 a pound whenever possible. We just had to be very careful about getting it from the car to the house without being caught by our friendly neighbor. Another doctor had just purchased meat from a Guajiro (farmer) and told Dad where to find it, but he warned him to be careful. Coming back with quite a few pounds of beef in the car, the police stopped him,

"Stop in the name of the Revolution. We are going to inspect your car and it better be clear!" When they discovered the fresh chunk of beef, they said, "You are under arrest! You also need to tell us who sold this meat to you!"

Dad calmly answered, "OK, but first call your Chief of Police and let him know what is happening. I am not moving from here until he arrives."

Two years before, the man who was now Chief of Police was a farmer with very limited income. He had a seven-year-old daughter who had lost her eyesight. The doctors had diagnosed that she would never see again. Dad was a well known pediatrician, so they brought the girl to him for a second opinion. He hospitalized her and took a personal interest in the case. He spent many hours next to the child's hospital bed until finally, her eye sight came back. There was no charge for his time and care because he knew the family could not afford it. When the girl's father insisted on paying, Dad said, "Your baby's eyesight is more than enough payment for me."

The grateful father shook Dad's hand and uttered, "Thank you Dr. Vazquez. If there is ever something I can do for you, please count on me." Now years later, he was standing in front of this "meat buying criminal," the same doctor who once saved his daughter's sight. "I can't do anything to this doctor." Then he turned to my father and said, "Just this time you can take the meat with you, but don't ever come back around here." My dad got home with his meat, and feeling well paid for curing the girl.

Mom's brother, Ricardo, was already living in the United States since before the Revolution. Once in a while he would send a package with a few things. He always sent Chiclets®, something we no longer had in Cuba, and it was just simply "cool" to chew. To receive one of those treasures was like winning the lotto. Sometimes we would receive a letter with a stick of gum taped to it. Lourdes and I would cut it into pieces and put them in a very safe place. The important thing was to smell and look like we had the precious and rare delicacy. If someone ever shared a tiny slice with you, wow, that was a true blue friend!

Mom never had to work in Cuba. Regardless of Communism, we had a good life thanks to my father's efforts. I guess I can say that we were privileged "gusanos." Dad had not worked legally for six years. He was quite a stoic man, and he continued refusing to work for the government. Although there was a two-year forced labor law for professionals who wanted to leave the country, he had a heart condition that kept him from field work.

One day the head of the health department told him that he wanted to help. He knew that we wanted to leave the country and could not escape the two years of forced labor, and he was going to make him an offer my father could not refuse; to work as a pediatrician at the children's hospital in Esperanza. Dad accepted. After working for a few months, two soldiers came to arrest him. Why? They had heard that he had made a tasteless joke about the government. When they had him detained, one of the hospital administrators came by and said, "What are you doing to Dr. Vazquez? He is a good guy! Let him go, I will become responsible for his actions." Dad realized that they just wanted to intimidate him.

During all this time we continued living with the fear of something breaking or being stolen from our home. Mom continued to worry about having a suitcase ready for us with clothes that would fit. Everything was rationed and we could only buy clothes, shoes, and other necessities once a year with our rationing book. When it was time for clothes or shoes to come to the stores, people would form lines that would go on for days to make sure they would get the right sizes or get to what they wanted before it was gone. This is something that is still in practice today.

Every year schools would take students out to camp in the fields to help the Revolution through farm work and training. We would go to a destination, usually far from home to avoid the interference of worried parents. Once there, we usually participated in constructing rudimentary quarters including our own bunk beds out of potato sacks, and our own bath areas. Parents could visit on Sundays if they could find transportation. I remember that, as kids, we really didn't mind. We had fun regardless. We would get up at sunrise, put on our boots and uniforms, pledge the flag, march to the fields to cut sugarcane or plant or pick watermelons. We would march back tired and thirsty to have anything but a delicious lunch. After a short nap, we went back to the fields, and later we went to class. We also learned to deal with firearms in order to protect our country. It was mandatory six-week training. Our parents suffered the most as they didn't really know what we were doing, nor were they able to keep us from going.

As a teenager, it was difficult to think about leaving the country, saying goodbye to family and friends to never, ever be able to come back, not even to visit. Once we left, we were expatriated. We had been waiting for eight years, and it really didn't feel like we were going to get permission. I had a boyfriend, and I didn't really want to leave to go to an unknown land where I didn't know anyone. They didn't teach English in the public schools, so our parents made us take private lessons every week. The famous, old prim and proper Professor Curi would come to our house to torture us with long verb conjugations and sentence repetition. Even on hot summer days, he always wore a three-piece suit, and he wore round glasses and carried a cane. Dad also made us sit and listen to American stations on a short wave radio (something that was considered an illegal activity). I would listen every day, and the only thing I understood was "Publix, where shopping is a pleasure."

In February of 1970, a lady, who had been Dad's patient as a child, came looking for him. She had a very ill daughter and her treating doctors had not been able to make a diagnosis. The child was getting worse by the minute and the mother was desperate. At first Dad refused to see the child. He knew that this lady was married to a high-ranking government official, and he was not allowed to see patients privately. It could be a trap. She insisted, crying and begging for his help, until he said, "Bring her to me. I will do whatever is in my power to help you."

"Oh, thank you doctor! She said as she hugged him. "You will never know how grateful I am." Dad discovered that the child simply had pneumonia. Soon she was well and enjoying life. The extremely grateful mother continued to ask, "How much do I owe you for saving my daughter's life?"

"You don't owe me anything," my father would say, it is my duty as a doctor to help cure the ill and it has been my pleasure to help you."

But the mother insisted on more than one occasion, "Please doctor, tell me how I can repay you, I have to do something."

Then Dad looked straight into her eyes and with a very serious tone said, "You know what I want."

A few days later, a highly decorated officer knocked at our door late at night. He entered our home quickly, as if hiding from meddlesome eyes, and uttered, "I am very grateful to you for my daughter's health. You will be leaving the country in a few days. I will make sure that there is no inventory check. Feel free to take out anything you want from your house, as long as you do it discreetly. Have a nice trip!"

My sister and I were not aware of this officer until years later. We do remember Mom, Dad and Aunt Lidia exchanging things over the back-yard fence during the night. I even remember them exchanging a mattress, which they covered in a black sheet so no one could see it. Mom was also throwing canned food over the fence. We thought our parents had gone crazy!

A couple of weeks later, on April 2, on my way home from school, I stopped at the park to talk to some friends. My best friend Miriam came running with tears in her eyes, "Hurry, she said, they are about to close your home. Your telegram has arrived." I dropped my books and ran, my heart beating uncontrollably. I was about to face the moment of truth. We were leaving the island, to never come back. The officers did not check the inventory, but they did ask my parents to repay $2,000 pesos they had withdrawn from their own bank account the day before requesting permission to leave the country. My father paid them and was still able to give his mother $20,000 pesos he had earned secretly seeing patients.

Three days later, the whole town seemed to be gathered on Barnada Street to say goodbye. I had spent the night at Lidia's house, holding my cousin Nancy close to me. How was I going to say goodbye to my dearest cousin? In the morning, I heard Lidia crying out loud, asking Our Lady of Charity, "Why, dear Virgin, why?" It was time to say goodbye to everyone I had grown up with. I felt as if my heart were bleeding; it was hard to breathe; I felt incapable of hugging or saying anything to anyone. I asked Nancy to go get something from our grandmother's house. She knew I didn't have the strength to say goodbye to her; she looked at me, sadly smiled and left. I asked Mom for everyone to get in the car and leave the door open for me. My

Lourdes Vázquez & her children Peter & Lauren

plan was to dash out and close the car door, but my grandmother Maria, crying, grabbed my arm and said, "I'll never see you again." I just pushed her aside, an action I had to live with for many years. Carlos, Lidia and Manolo took us to the Varadero Airport. No one said a word during the trip. I don't remember much about the flight except the plane taking off. I looked down and saw Manolo waving goodbye with one hand and drying his tears with the other. I was totally numb.

Arriving at Miami, a not-too-friendly immigration officer informed us that we were being sent to Michigan. I remember Dad getting furious and demanding to stay in Miami where we had family. "We just left a communist country to come to freedom. If we are going to be forced to go to Michigan, just send us back to Cuba!"

After a while, we were being greeted by Uncle Ricardo, Aunt Aida, and our cousins Ricky and Eddy. It was the first time that Lourdes and I met them face to face, but soon they became like parents and brothers to us. They lived in Hialeah in a three bedroom, one bath house. Now there were eight of us waiting our turn to use the restroom every morning. What a fiasco that was!

My cousin Ricky, who was about my age, invited me to go to the mall with his friends the day after we arrived. As usual, I asked Dad if I could have some money. With a serious look, he took $3 dollars out of his pocket, looked into my eyes and said, "Here is one dollar, please don't spend it unless it is for an emergency. This is all we have." He had never talked so seriously to me. That was the day I matured. Soon I began to work, and I have never stopped.

Some of his patients, who now lived in Florida, found out, through the newspaper, about our arrival and collected about $1000 to help us get started. At that time, that was quite a sum of money. Immediately he bought a nice used Ford Falcon for $300. We lived happily at my uncle's home for a few months, surrounded by their love and kindness. Such acts of unconditional family love can only be repaid by paying it forward.

For the first time in her life Mom had to look for employment. She went to work as a seamstress in a garment factory, as did many other Cuban ladies. Dad went to work at a clinic, as an assistant, not as a doctor. He spent every minute he could studying to pass his Foreign Medical Graduate and later the Medical State Board. He seemed to be aging quickly, but he passed the exams on the first try, unlike many other doctors who had serious difficulties with them.

The first day I attended Hialeah Junior High School, I was very lucky to meet Emily Alemán, a Cuban classmate, who is still one of my best friends, and Norma de la Torre, my favorite teacher, who inspired me to study to become an educator and who is still a very

Alexis Martínez, grandfather Vázquez & Lizette Martínez Candela

important person in my life. It was to her I promised to write this book in 1971, and I am honored to be doing it with her help today. I made many friends in Hialeah and adapted to my new life quite well. I was happy.

Once my father passed his exam, he was offered an Internship at Polk General Hospital in Bartow, Florida. When we arrived at Bartow, I found it nothing like Miami. It was a small town with oak trees full of moss that seemed to be crying along with me. We lived in a one bedroom, one bath duplex. No one spoke Spanish, and their English had a Southern accent. I did not understand a word they said. I hated Bartow with a purple passion! I was frustrated with school, with everything. One day, Mary Jane Driesler, the duplex owner, saw me crying. For many months she devoted her evenings to teach me English and to get me acquainted with the North American way of life. Another beautiful act of unconditional love!

Soon we met other Cubans like the Almazáns who became like part of our family. Martha, their older daughter, became my best friend, and years later I became godmother to her first daughter. She is my first daughter's godmother as well. Little by little everything changed. Bartow took us in with open arms. We will never forget the kindness and beautiful acts of love this town showed. My dad opened his medical practice there, and we were able to rebuild our lives.

In 1973, I met Carlos Martinez while having lunch with Martha at the newly built McDonalds in Bartow. He came in with his lifelong best friend, Steve, now Dr. Stephen McNutt, a well known endodontist, who decided to introduce us since we were the only Cubans around. Carlos and I had a lot in common, including the cars we were both driving, a Chevy Nova. We fell in love and married in 1975 at the tender age of twenty. We have practically grown up together, happily studying, working and raising our daughters Lizette and Alexis.

Then a miracle happened. In 1980 the Cuban crops failed and the government decided to allow the "worms" to travel to Cuba for the nominal fee of $1,500 for a fifteen minute flight. My father invited me to go with him. I remember the plane had a door tied with a rope. My prayers were answered as I finally got to properly hug my grandmothers goodbye. I was able to enjoy seeing my friends and relatives again, as well as talk for hours on end with my cousin Nancy. It was hard to see my beautiful home in ruins. The beautiful roman columns that decorated the front porch, had crumbled and now were just the structural frames. Everything seemed so dilapidated from twenty years of negligence. The stores were empty. I made a comment about how bad the situation was for the country, and my cousin asked me to be quiet. She said, "You can't speak like that, Tere! Do you want to go jail? Remember that here, even the walls have ears." I had forgotten where I was. I was accustomed to the freedom of speech I enjoy in the United States of America. Although it was good to go back to my island, when we arrived at Miami, I wanted to kiss the ground. I suffered from depression for quite a while. I felt enormously guilty for having so much while my people in Cuba had so little. Why was I so lucky?

After faithfully working for many years, my father retired, for the third time, in 2008 as Medical Director of the ROHR Home, an elderly care facility in Polk County. Dad is now 87 years old, and sometimes we laugh when we say that he started with pediatrics and ended with geriatrics. He says there is not too much of a difference.

My parents recently celebrated their 57th wedding anniversary. They are the proud grandparents of four grandchildren and two beautiful great-grandchildren. We have all been blessed by their influence and the lessons they taught us on how to stand firm for our freedom and for what we consider honorable.

My sister Lourdes and I have enjoyed a wonderful life. She has been in the cosmetic industry for the last thirty years, working with dynamic individuals of the Estee Lauder Corporation. She is currently Florida's West Coast Account Executive for the prestigious company, Christian Dior. She has two children, Peter and Lauren, and a beautiful grandson, Colton. I became a teacher and entrepreneur. I founded the Institute of Spanish Communication, Inc. in 1989. It has allowed me and my family to experience the meaning of the great American Dream for over 20 years. I am also the producer and host of Comunidad Viva, a local television program. My husband Carlos is a Clinical Specialist, working with medical devices used by patients in need of heart transplants. Carlos has even had the honor of working with the world-renowned Dr. DeBakey. Our daughters, Lizette and Alexis, are both college graduates with a bright future ahead of them.

My parents were able to help my cousin Manolo escape while he was working as a doctor in Nicaragua. Manolo, in turn, was able to get his brother and his family out of Cuba, as well as his parents Carlos and Lidia. My dear cousin Nancy was also able to escape, as did many other relatives. They all enjoy a great life in the United States. We still have relatives in Cuba, and we help them to the best of our ability.

Life in Cuba continues to get worse. Food is still rationed to 3 pounds of rice per person per month, 1 pound of beans, 4 pounds of sugar, 1 pound of salt per family, 1 bun of bread per person per day. Milk is reserved only for children up to 7 years of age, or for those who are 65 and over or ill. Meat is very scarce, 3 ounces per person per month for those who are ill, usually chicken. The rest of the population enjoys ground soy once in a while. Those who have access to "converted dollars" can purchase chicken legs or an occasional thigh. I have been told that the chicken breasts are not for sale. The government either keeps the best food for tourism or for export. The citizens have to sacrifice for their country. I guess that is why in an island known for excellent fishing, seafood is only sold to those who suffer from cholesterol or diabetes.

The ration for a family of three is one tube of toothpaste per month and ½ bar of soap per person. There is no deodorant, no toilet paper, no shampoo; only 10 sanitary napkins a month for a lady's monthly needs. Everything is rationed or non-existent at stores for Cubans who live on the Island, especially those who live in rural areas. At the same time, there are other stores stocked with almost anything anyone could possibly need but at prices only accessible for tourists. These stores sell exclusively in converted dollars known as "chavitos", whose value is only 80% of a US dollar. For years Cuban

Giuseppe Candela, Tere, Antonio & Lizette Candela & Carlos Martínez

residents were not allowed to enter such stores, nor were they allowed in tourist hotels and restaurants. This changed when Fidel gave up his power to his brother Raul. Since 2009, the Cuban residents can buy whatever they want as long as they can pay with the "almighty dollar."

Another progress is that Cubans on the island are able to have cell phones and some computer equipment. Salaries have remained the same. According to recent information, most professionals such as doctors, engineers, and lawyers have a standard socialist salary of less than $300 pesos per month. Some specialists might earn between $500 and $700 pesos per month. Regular workers earn between $150 and $250 pesos per month. The exchange rate is $25 pesos to $1.00 US dollar making these salaries equal to $6 to $30 dollars per month, plus a 20% discount of exchange. Only 1.5% of the population has a salary of about $6,000 pesos or higher; these are high ranking government officials. If the tourist store's items, at regular prices, are compared to United States currency, a package of toilet paper costs about 10% of a common worker's salary. Consequently, it is not common to find such a luxury in the bathrooms of most Cuban homes. (In case you are wondering what do they use, the Gramma, the only newspaper in circulation, actually has a good purpose!). Of course, some people have families in the United States who send help, and tourism has created hospitality opportunities for friendly and charming Cubans to make a good living helping generous and compassionate tourists. One of these extra dollar income opportunities began when Cubans were allowed to work in Cuban hotels and restaurants that were designed for tourists only.

As far as health care, Cuba enjoys international fame for its "fabulous" health system. Many doctors are ready, willing and able to go practice medicine in third world countries which are better off than Cuba. These physicians work hard for the right to stay in a different country or to escape to freedom. This is why they have acquired a positive international reputation.

Cuba has fabulous hospitals for tourists. People from all over the world go there to get treatment and plastic surgery at reduced prices. The embargo does not affect tourists or high ranking government officials. For a while, there was a doctor and two nurses for every 120 families. There is no doubt that the attention to the patient has been good. But the physicians lack medicine and equipment. Preventive medicine is rarely practiced in Cuba, one of the most "advanced" medical countries in Latin America. Cubans have to go to undesirable and prehistoric hospitals not even fit for rats. In 2008 one of my relatives had to be hospitalized for a surgical procedure. She was told to make sure to bring her own sheets, pillow, robe, food, and especially a bucket, cup and soap for bathing and flushing the toilet. In order to get water, she had to go to the only working faucet in the entire building. She also had to wait a couple of months until the hospital got some sutures to close her wound. Where is the equality in this socialist system? What kind of advances have taken place in five decades of communism in the medical system in Cuba?

Now, my husband and I are the about the same age as my parents were when they left Cuba. We have two wonderful daughters, Lizette and Alexis, who have grown up knowing that the "sky is the limit", and Antonio, our first grandchild, who is our new motivation. We have had family and personal success, but we still have things to accomplish. I often wonder what we would do if this country experienced a change in government, and we were faced with similar circumstances as our parents. It is unimaginable for me to leave everything and have to go to another country, with empty pockets, where we would have to start from zero with a different language and a different culture. I often wonder if we would have the same courage, determination and perseverance as our parents had to ensure our freedom.

One day, hopefully in the near future, I would like to take my children to my crocodile-shaped island to soak up their cultural roots, to swim in the crystal clear waters of Varadero, to cross over the palm-tree bridge over the creek of La Guásima. I want them to run free through the fields and to taste the tropical fruits from Uncle Filo's trees. There they will see the tall and majestic palms that have for centuries withstood the constant barrage of tropical depressions, storms and hurricanes, the Caribbean breeze; and above all, Castro's fury. If the palms could talk...!

Felipe & Alicia Olivera

Invaded by Our Own People

Felipe & Alicia Olivera

To accomplish great things, we must not only act,
but also dream; not only plan, but also believe.
ANATOLE FRANCE

I was born in Havana and came to the United States on October, 1961...alone. This was approximately two years after Fidel Castro took over our country.

I came simply because my parents decided I should. The political situation was quickly deteriorating. I had just started at the university. Those years that I thought would be so happy and important were abruptly crushed. It had always been my dream to study architecture, but I was not even able to finish the first semester. All my hopes and dreams vanished.

Some of the students at the university who were against Castro's revolution were in constant danger and persecution due to their ideas and activities. They were arrested and taken to prison. After a quick trial, they were sent to "El Paredón" (the firing wall.) No questions asked.

This was the case with my sister's brother-in-law, a young man in his twenties who was executed for being involved in a student movement against the revolution.

My family underwent persecutions and abuses. One night at three o'clock in the morning, the secret police invaded our home looking for some kind of evidence that could also connect any of us, to this case. My brother-in-law, who lived there with my sister, was a prime target. It was a horrible experience that I will never forget. I was a young girl and the policemen, carrying machine guns, scandalously entered my bedroom. I was awakened by these men screaming and talking to us as if we were criminals. That was when I understood the seriousness of the situation and my parent's decision to send me to the United States.

I agreed to say goodbye to my parents and the whole family. I thought that it would only be for a few months and that I would come back to my native land in the near future. I could not have been more mistaken. I was not afraid to leave Cuba because I thought of it as an adventure. It was, however, very painful when I had to say goodbye to my wise grandmother. With tears rolling down her cheeks, she looked into my eyes and said, "I will never see you again." I did not believe it at that moment, but she was right. She passed away soon after. My parents were not able to leave Cuba for another five years. Those were the longest five years of my life.

I don't remember much about my trip from Cuba. My mind erased those painful moments. I do remember arriving at the home of my parents' friends. I did not know them, and although they were very kind, I felt terribly lonesome and sad. I was a young lady living in a foreign country without any family or friends. My country had been invaded by our own people…Cubans like us.

I began to take the necessary steps to bring my family to the United States. My five-year-old niece came over through an organization dedicated to the rescue of Cuban children from the possibility of being sent to Russia. Shortly after, her parents, my sister and her husband, arrived. This was a blessing for me as I started to feel once more the support of my family.

I decided to learn English and soon began studying at the university. I earned a degree in education. This was not easy, partly because of the language barrier, but I was determined to do it. Many years went by before I received my degree, but to my surprise and joy, I had found a new vocation. I worked for twenty glorious years as a Spanish and mathematics teacher in Lakeland, Florida.

Although I did not get to study architecture, God blessed me with my husband Felipe, a Cuban exile like me, who, with much sacrifice, became an engineer and has accomplished a fabulous career as a builder of luxury homes. Felipe left Cuba in 1960, right after completing his first year of mechanical engineering at the University of Villanueva in Havana. At 19 years old he arrived in Miami with a tourist visa, a suitcase with a few items, a couple of engineering books, and five dollars in his pocket. Felipe was also the first in his family to leave Cuba.

The day after he arrived, he rode along with a friend who drove a bread delivery truck to grocery stores. At each delivery stop, Felipe hopped down and inquired about a job opportunity. At the end of the day, he had two job offers. The next day, he was hired at a supermarket to mop the floors before it opened, and then as a bag boy the rest of the day. That was his first real job since he had never worked in Cuba. He has not stopped working ever since.

In January of 1961, he was accepted to the School of Engineering at the University of Miami. With the help of a student loan and working while he studied, he obtained his mechanical engineering degree from this prestigious university.

Shortly after his graduation, he found an engineering position, and we got married. A few years later, he invested in a coin laundry business, which he kept for five years. He was the owner, the maintenance man, and the repairman. A few years later in 1972, he obtained his general contractor's license and began to build a few homes while he was still working as a Senior Project Engineer. After several years of keeping up with two and sometimes three jobs, Felipe decided to sell the coin laundry business, leave his engineering position and concentrate all his efforts on the construction business.

Today, in partnership with our son and son-in-law, the company builds approximately twenty upscale custom homes per year, as well as commercial and professional buildings. Olivera Construction, Inc. is recognized as one of the top construction companies in the area. Many of the homes have been honored with numerous awards.

Hard work and honesty, combined with a Christian family life in this country of opportunities, is what has made our life a success in exile. Our family is our pride and joy. We have three children, eight grandchildren and wonderful relatives and friends.

After forty-nine years in the United States, we feel very much at home. Both my husband and I are eternally grateful to this country for the doors that have been opened for us, and the help we received in rebuilding our lives.

Still we long for our little island. The memories are many: we love our music, our culture, and the way we enjoyed our lives. We still feel very Cuban in our hearts, and we would love to visit and savor again all we lost; but first, Cuba needs to be free.

I think that our generation was the one that suffered the least, as we were able to reconstruct our lives by means of our education, hard work and sacrifices. It was our parents who were affected the most since it was too late for them to start over. Even so, they were happy and quite content to be together once more as a family, which is after all, the essence of being Cubans.

Vallejo family

I Did Not Know How to Swim: A Story of Stoicism

Dr. Sergio Vallejo

To do anything in this world worth doing,
we must not stand back shivering and thinking of
the cold and danger, but jump in, and
scramble through as well as we can.
SYDNEY SMITH

In the middle of the night, dressed in black and scared to death, we escaped the guards and the machine guns that patrolled the coast of Matanzas. It was the evening of July 29, 1968, when we left on a manmade float.

We were a group of thirteen people, including four children and four women, trying to flee from Cuba. Some were known to me, others were not. Supposedly a boat would come to our rescue three miles off the coast. Praying for this to be so, some of us pushed the float while others, with a rope tied to their waists, pulled it while they swam without looking back.

Once in the boat, we started to paddle and to struggle against the giant waves, all the while bailing out the water that constantly invaded our boat. We had brought along some drinking water, condensed milk and a compass. There were critical moments during our journey. We were exhausted, some of us started to hallucinate. It took us 30 hours until we finally arrived at a sand bar on the Southside of Isla Morada in the Florida Keys. It was 3:00 a.m. on the 31st. I did not know how to swim, but my desperation and my faith in God gave me the strength to reach freedom.

We waited until daylight to put the boat back on the water and started to paddle towards the bridge. Fishing boats were coming in with their catch. One of them approached us and offered help. With my poor English I let him know that we were a group of Cubans who had escaped the communist island and that we had to go before the immigration authorities of the United States.

From Isla Morada a police car took us to Key Marathon and then to the refuge offices of the House of Liberty at the Miami Airport. Our clothes were torn and we were barefooted. I held tightly to my medical bag. Inside I had brought information about the public health system in Cuba, my stethoscope, my otoscope and my prescription pad. That was the only thing I brought with me, and I keep it as a symbol of the sacrifice I had to make.

The next day my brother, who lived in Miami, went to the House of Liberty to pick me up. I immediately established contact with other doctors from Matanzas, who were able to get me a job in Winfield Hospital, Kansas. I took the Foreign Board Exam, the Kansas State Board and others and passed them all. In 1970, with my wife and children already at my side, we moved to Lakeland, Florida where we have lived and I have practiced medicine for many years.

Not a day goes by that I don't think about my childhood in Cuba. We were five brothers and sisters. My father worked all his life in the Bank of Canada in Santiago de Cuba. With much sacrifice, I was sent to study medicine at the University of Havana. In Cuba it did not matter what your financial position was; if you wanted to study to have a better life, you could do it. A career in medicine cost $60 pesos per year, and if you graduated with honors with a Bachelors degree, medical school was free. There were wonderful private colleges, but public education was just as good and was attainable for everyone. Cuba was a paradise we did not appreciate.

With Castro, everything changed. When I graduated from Medical School, I was sent to practice rural medicine. When I expressed my desire to leave the country, I was informed that as long as my medical services were needed, the government would not grant me permission to leave. Since I manifested my intention of going to the United States, I was considered "un gusano," a worm, and I was punished in every imaginable way. It was very difficult to tolerate the humiliations: the unending work hours, the lack of freedom, the inability to treat my own patients as I saw fit. In addition, we didn't have basic necessities: enough food, shoes for the kids, and medicine. My situation became dangerous since I rebelled on a daily basis expressing out loud what I thought of the communist government. I could not wait any longer. My only alternative was to flee my country. Even though I was conscious of dangers the ocean presented, I knew that if I succeeded, I would be finally free.

That is the reason I left on a manmade float, leaving my family in Cuba and not knowing what would become of them. That was the most difficult decision I have ever had to make in my life, but it was also the best. If I was taken to prison or executed, then there would have been no hope for my family, like the families of many others who dared to express their opinions against the regime.

I left my country looking for freedom so that our children would have the opportunity for a better life. Our lives have been a complete realization of success and happiness. Our children have received a good education; they are respected professionals. Our grandchildren will also enjoy wonderful opportunities to fully develop in life.

Someday I would like to visit my parents' graves and my house in Cuba. I would like to enjoy the beaches again, see the fields, the colonial buildings, the grand avenues and the University of Havana. But to return while the Castro regime that destroyed the Pearl of the Caribbean as we knew it...Never, never ever!

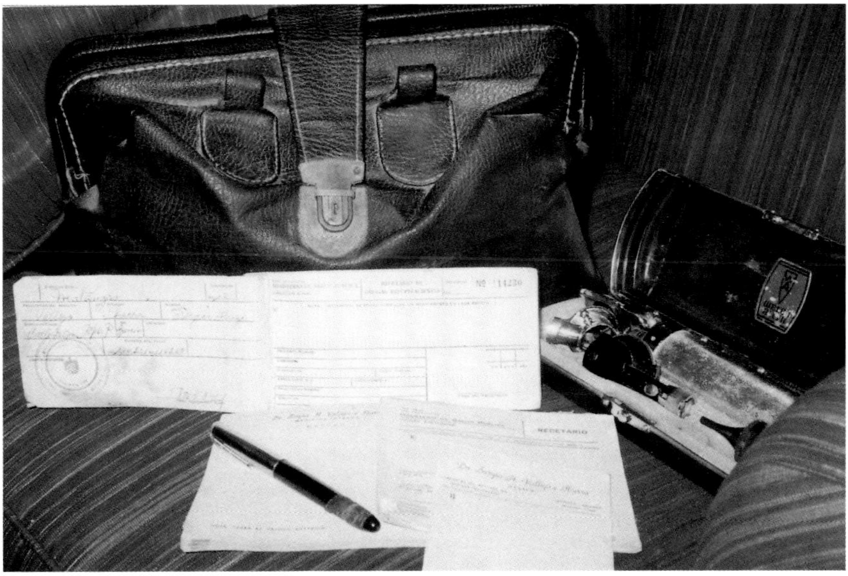

The only belongings Dr. Sergio Vallejo brought from Cuba

Dr. Pedro & Alicia Almazán

I Saw It Coming

Dr. Pedro Almazán

Life is not that which one lived, but that which one remembers, and how one remembers to tell it.
GABRIEL GARCÍA MÁRQUEZ

Our family left Cuba in 1962 for the same reason over three million compatriots left. Cubans were born to be free. We like to sing and dance and openly express our opinions. We are friendly, open people; we project happiness, solidarity, and we are full of charisma. We should not have to live oppressed, subjugated and subdued under a regime led by one man who decided to take control of the island and its people.

Once Fidel took power, he carried out his plan of becoming the Commander and Chief. Then he aligned Cuba with the Soviet Union and began seizing private property. He took control of the farms, hotels, restaurants, schools, and more.... all in the name of the "People," yes, they began confiscating everything from everyone -from the richest to the poorest. The government became the only employment agency. The biggest tragedy was that the masses did not realize the plans of the victorious and charismatic leader of the Revolution. When the government nationalized the largest industries, the masses thought they deserved it because the owners and administrators were making too much money. Then the government started confiscating the smaller industries, but this was still supported by the people. The small business owners didn't think that they were going to be affected, that the government only would take over the big corporations. Little by little Fidel took over the private sector and most Cubans started waking up. This is why it was called "the Revolution of the Callus" because no one complained until the government stepped on their toes! The situation, for those of us who realized what was happening, could not have been more tragic.

In 1959, I realized that we were in for trouble. I had my private practice for ten years after graduating as a veterinarian from the *University of Havana* in 1952. I was a large animal veterinarian, and in those days, worked for families who had ranches and cattle. Their land had been in their families for many years. Unfortunately I was able to witness what was coming because they started confiscating the land and ranches first. People in the cities had no idea of what was happening. One day, while I was on a ranch taking care of the animals, four or five Jeeps full of soldiers with machine guns arrived. They told the landlord that their property now belonged to "the people" and since they ran their business out of their home, the "people's government" were now going to put them out in the street. The owners begged,

"Please let me get at least some clothes or something from my home."

"No, you can't take anything; everything inside belongs to the people."

I remember the second farm the government confiscated in my presence. They took everything the family owned: their home, furniture, clothes, trucks, cars, everything. They did not let them take anything at all. Why should they? In their eyes, this family had made too much money in the past, and that was not fair! We were now a socialist country where everybody had to be equal… equally poor.

I was working for this unfortunate family that day. When I went to my Jeep, they decided to confiscate it as well. I became very angry and let them know that this was not my farm. I was a veterinarian and they were my clients; this was my own personal Jeep. They had no right to take it from me. In an authoritarian tone, I told them I was a personal friend of Fidel Castro, and I would call him and get it taken care of. After carefully examining my identification, they let me go. Of course, I was not Fidel's friend…I couldn't possibly be. I took my clients with me, as they had to find refuge with their relatives in Cienfuegos, the city where I was from. They were now homeless. They were punished for being successful.

One of the reasons communism does not prosper is because independent individuals do not follow such a system. This is why most of them left or tried to leave the country during the early years of communism. Although many Cubans have had to stay in a system that they realize is unfair, they know that if they protest or express an unfavorable opinion, they will be punished, so they are quiet and everything goes on.

Cuba suffered a "brain drain" in the 60's. At the time, the government empowered the masses, those who had little education were given high authority. Now all of a sudden they saw themselves in a much higher position. Their egos were fed, and they were "Fidelists," indeed. They would scream: "Viva Fidel!" All they had to do was agree with the system to have a salary. It didn't matter if they worked or not, if they really knew what they were doing, or abused their new power. This was communism. Everything was changing... for the worst.

That is why I decided to leave Cuba. I saw my clients lose their ranches where I had worked for ten years. These were ranches and farms that had been started by their grandfathers. The children and the whole family worked day and night until they had a prosperous business. They had cattle, plants and livestock. Then I saw how Fidel's people, who did not have any idea what they were doing, were destroying the land, planting something that would never produce in that type of soil. It was a tragic situation, a destruction of decades of work and dedication.

I went home one day and told my wife Alicia, "Get ready, we have to get out of here." I knew what was happening and what was coming. My lifelong friends in the city didn't believe what was taking place in the country, what I was witnessing with my own eyes. They would say, "No, no... 'the horse' (Fidel) spoke last night and he didn't say anything like that... you are wrong!" I could not convince them that he was just a gifted speaker who could mesmerize a crowd.

Soon all veterinarians had to work for the government, which formed cooperatives that paid low salaries to the veterinarians to care largely for the state's cattle. I refused to work for Castro. I could not see large animals anymore, so I took care of small animals, family pets and whatever I could do to make a living while getting ready to leave the island.

Our daughter Martha was seven years old. The schools were starting to brainwash kids to fit in the communist mold. There were rumors that the textbooks were being changed to reflect a different version of our history. I was afraid that soon they were going to say that Christopher Columbus came from Russia! Our beloved daughter might turn out to be a Marxist-Leninist! Peter, our three-year-old son, would be going to school soon, and Alicia and I would not have a choice about their education. It was really time to go.

We left on one of the last "Freedom Flights" three years after Castro tried to take control of our lives. I arrived in Miami with my wife, my children and not a cent in my pocket. I did not have a dime to make a phone call, and if I did...who was I going to call?

Suddenly, a miracle happened! My ex-brother-in-law, Rolando Gonzalez, happened to be at the airport that night for some reason. He saw us and with a big smile asked,

"What are you doing here?"

"What do you think?" I said as we hugged.

He took us to his small apartment where we stayed for a while. He helped us and tried to get me a job, but there was no real opportunity there. I worked in Miami for two months for a salary of $1.15 per hour. I asked the government to relocate us anywhere in the country where I could have a job that would allow me to support my family. We were sent to New Mexico were I worked in a cattle feed lot, vaccinating and roping cattle. I was a peon, but I was happy peon. I was a professional going through a transition, and I was studying to rebuild our lives. It was just a matter of time and dedication.

In 1963, I found a job with the Department of Agriculture of the State of Virginia where I worked for two years in the laboratory. I will always be grateful to all of the people I worked with for the help they gave me. In 1965, I went to work for the federal government for the USDA as a meat inspector veterinarian. It was in 1966 that I was able to validate my veterinarian license and became a Veterinary Supervisor for the Meat Inspection Program. In 1968, I was transferred to Florida by the USDA to work at the old Kaplan Industries slaughterhouse in Bartow. I held several positions during thirty years, among them, President of the National Association of Federal Veterinarians in 1997 (NAFV). I retired in 1999.

We have been very happy in Bartow. In the 70's, there was a small group of Cubans in the area, mainly doctors, that were doing their internships at the *Polk General Hospital*, engineers that came to work at *Davy McKee Corporation*, or simply families that came to this beautiful area because their families or friends were living here. We used to gather at my home and tried to keep our culture alive. We danced the cha-cha-cha, did the conga, cooked our traditional food and supported each other. We had a great time. Our American neighbors admired our spirit. I helped start "Spanish Night" at the *Bartow Country Club* where we shared our culture, our food and the typical dances with all of the club's members. This night became very popular.

At Christmastime, we started lighting up our house to show our grateful spirit for being able to celebrate this holiday season (Cubans back home were no longer allowed to celebrate this religious holiday). The neighborhood seemed so dark to me. I decided to "Cubanize" it! I started urging neighbors to decorate their homes, synchronizing Christmas lights along the street and playing music of the season. It started with two or three houses the first year, and then it gradually grew. George Street earned the nickname "Christmas Tree Lane" and the city named me "The Santa Claus of South Bartow". *The Chamber of Commerce* gave me the *Spirit of Bartow Award.* Today, thirty six years later, people come from surrounding cities to see the light show, which encompasses many neighborhoods. Sometimes there are over one thousand cars per night, bumper to bumper traffic. I had to design a route, marked by green arrows, to help alleviate the traffic. We also have horse-drawn carriage tours and hayrides!

My wife Alicia always dreamed of having a boutique, and in 1974 we opened the doors of *Alicia's*, a fine clothing store, where she happyly worked for many years. She has been able to bring most of her family to the United States. We also opened *Pedro's Cuban Sandwich Shop*, across the street from the boutique, in downtown Bartow.

Now we are enjoying retirement. I remain active in the community. I am the President of the *Polk County Republican Club.* We have been blessed to have the opportunity to live our lives in a country where a person can make any dream come true as long as he or she is willing to work hard with enthusiasm and dedication. Our children, Martha and Peter, are both married and have given us four wonderful grandchildren and a great-grandchild. We are proud of their accomplishments and their successes. We thank God everyday for our blessings. We miss our beautiful island, the *Pearl of the Caribbean,* but we found our second home in the United States.

Hernández family in Birmingham, Alabama 1998

A True Act of Love

Rosa Delfín Hernández

There are two lasting bequests we can give our children.
One is roots. The other is wings.
HODDING CARTER, JR.

Today I know it was truly an act of "tough love" for my parents, but at the time in 1961, I was bitter and I pleaded with them many times. I was nineteen, I felt helpless. It was really traumatic. Our parents had made the decision to send my younger brother, Ramón, and me to the U.S.

We were born and raised in Cienfuegos, on the south side of the island and very close to the Bay of Pigs. Our father was an insurance agent, and we lived a very comfortable and happy life. I had never lived anywhere other than with my parents and brother in our lovely home. I knew all the children at school, all our neighbors and everyone in our church community. My comfort and safety were just a given. The idea of leaving everything I had ever known would have been terrible enough if the whole family was going into exile together; but since our parents were unable to leave Cuba, Ramón and I would go alone to a strange country. I did not comprehend what the danger might be.

Our parents, Olivia and Ramón Delfín, worried more and more about us children. Thousands of Cubans had already left, most going to Miami. Then in April 1961 several thousand Cuban exiles from the United States, backed by the CIA, invaded the Bay of Pigs in an attempt to overthrow the Castro regime. Castro's army easily crushed the invasion, and over 1,100 prisoners were captured. This event, happening so close to us, convinced our parents that they must get us out of the country and to safety in the United States. Among the exiles at that time were many members of religious orders who were feeling pressure under the communist-inspired government although it was not until December of that year that Fidel

Castro officially aligned himself and his government with the USSR and the communist bloc. During the summer of 1961 a group of twenty-four nuns from my school, Sisters of the Sacred Heart, were planning to leave, and they told us that they had room and were willing to take Ramón and me with them to the U.S.

I was distraught. I argued my case without any success. I could not imagine leaving my home, my friends, and my parents. I did not understand how my mother and father could make the decision to force us to leave. I had always found safety in family and the community, and I could not understand how safety might lie in a foreign country, far from everything I had ever known.

On the day of our departure from Havana airport, I was terrified. There were soldiers with guns everywhere. When the guards questioned me, I just kept repeating what my father and the Sisters had instructed me to say. When asked over and over, "Why do you want to leave Cuba?" I replied stony-faced, although my heart was breaking, "I am going to the U.S. to enter a convent and become a nun." I was terrified of the soldiers. I wanted to cry, but I wouldn't. I couldn't let them see me crying. My brother Ramon had been attending Los Maristas, a catholic school for boys, and he said that he was going to finish the school year with his teachers and to keep me company. Finally they let us through and we boarded the plane, exiled from our homeland.

It was such a difficult adjustment when we arrived in the United States and went to live with friends of our parents in Pennsylvania, a cold and strange place to young Cubans. I spoke little English when I arrived and I was often homesick and lonely.

Then the next year, when I was studying at St. Joseph's College in Philadelphia, I met a Villanova student, Andy Hernández, an exile from Havana. He, too, was homesick although his story of emigration was different from mine. Andy and one of his friends had been arrested by the G-2 (the government police) in September of 1960 in Havana because a friend of Andy's had mentioned that Andy had a gun in the car. The boys were in a countryside restaurant where a farm worker who had wanted a ride to Havana turned the licence plate number to the police. The two young men spent two days in jail. After they were released, the friend was later re-arrested, and the police were now looking for Andy. Andy never took the risk of going home to sleep after he heard the police were after him again. His parents had not sent him away, as I felt that mine had, but Andy knew that he must leave for his own safety. He stayed with relatives

Residence of Delfín family, Cienfuegos, Cuba

in Havana that night, then went to the airport the next morning, October 27, 1960.

In September the government, in an effort to stop the flow of people leaving the country, had passed a law that all tickets sold for trips outside the country had to be paid for with foreign currency. A travel agent, sympathetic to the cause of the refugees, had stamped every ticket his agency had with a date prior to the new law. Andy left Cuba, with a round trip ticket from Havana to New Orleans, New York, Miami, and back to Havana. He had one suitcase and $5 in his pocket with which to start a new life.

We fell in love and were married on September 5th, 1964, two years after we first met. When our lives were blessed with the birth of our son, Andy, Jr., I began to understand how much love a parent can have for a child, and how difficult some choices can be. I began to heal and to understand my parents.

With a master's degree in chemical engineering, ten years after his frightening trip to the States, Andy had the opportunity to work in Florida. He first worked as a chemical engineer, then in sales, and finally as a Director of Business Development in Latin America. Andy later made the move from corporate work to real estate, and he was the president of Century 21, A.H. Realty, in Lakeland and Winter Haven. On three different ocassions since 1999, A.H. Realty was named number one in sales in Central Florida out of 150 Century 21 agencies. Andy has served on the Board of the Greater Lakeland Chamber of Commerce, and he was President of the Board of Trustees for Polk Museum of Art and at the Imperial Symphony Orchestra. He was also the President of the Parrish Council at Resurrection

Rosa, Ryan, Nicolás & Andy Hernández

Catholic Church Parrish for two years. He is on the Board of Directors of the Lakeland Regional Medical Center and Santa Fe Catholic High School, Alabama. He is now the President of MidFlorida Real Estate Sales, LLC., a branch of Mid Florida Credit Union.

I have always wanted to give back to the community that had welcomed me, as an exile. I became active in many groups in my new hometown, but my family has always come first. Andy, Jr. and his wife Lisa live in Alabama. Our two grandsons, Nicholas and Andy, make our lives so full. My family is the most important thing to me. They make me so happy.

I didn't want to leave Cuba, but now that I am a mother, I know that I would do the same thing my parents did. Although the separation from our family was difficult and painful for Ramon and me, I know that the choice they had to make, and the separation, was even more difficult for them than for us, and that it was the right decision.

P.S. Rosa Delfín Hernández has distinguished herself by her volunteer service to Lakeland in many capacities, and most notably as President of the Polk Museum of Art's, 36 member board of trustees. In October 2009 The Polk Museum of Art awarded Rosa the Harrison-Hooks Lifetime Achievement Award, she is a member of the Florida House Council in Lakeland and an holds a seat on the Florida House Board of Trustees in Washington. Her brother Ramón Delfín lives in Coral Gables, Florida and is the International Director of an international packing company.

Dr. Rodríguez-Torres & Guly

I Believe in Miracles!

Dr. Ramón Rodríguez-Torres

There are only two ways to live your life.
One is as though nothing is a miracle,
the other is as though everything is a miracle.
ALBERT EINSTEIN

After my graduation as a medical doctor from the University of Havana Cuba, in 1951, and after finishing a specialty in internal medicine and cardiology in 1953, I decided to open a medical practice in Havana. Soon after, I realized that the Health Medical Organization in Cuba, similar to what we know in the United States as HMO, did not accept elderly patients because they were considered high risk from an economic point of view. Consequently, I took it upon myself to create a private clinic with excellent care that would accept senior citizens. After recruiting a group of highly skilled physicians, who shared my vision, we created "Clínica F y 25" a fabulous clinic which opened in El Vedado, Havana in 1954. Since we were the only medical center with these characteristics, our patient membership grew in such a way, that two years after our inauguration, we had to build two extra floors to better serve our patients.

In 1957, I won a scholarship provided by the British Government to study Cardiology at Manchester University and at The National Heart Hospital in London. During my stay in England, several of the "Clínica F y 25" physicians helped Castro's guerrillas in Sierra Maestra, Oriente, Cuba. When I returned to the island at the end of 1958, I was informed that the clinic was helping the revolutionary movement and that one of our physicians had decided to join the guerrilla group in the mountains of Sierra Maestra.

On January 1st, 1959, after the fall of Fulgencio Batista's government, Castro's guerillas established themselves as the new government. Therefore, some of the clinic's physicians were able to occupy high positions in the new government, Minister of Health,

Chief of the Health Care System for the city of Havana, for example. During that time, I was offered a position as a professor at the University of Havana. Although I had always dreamed of reaching such a high level in my career, I did not accept. Those positions had always been obtained through competition with other candidates, not by political favors.

That year was critical for all of us who had democratic principles. Thousands of Cubans were executed or sentenced to long terms in prison for simply disagreeing with the Castro's communist regime. In February 1960 one of my colleagues invited me to a dinner party at her home. Apparently she thought I agreed with the new government's doctrine. At 11:00 p.m., Fidel Castro arrived and began to explain what the Revolution was going to create in Cuba; and the significant "changes" that were going to take place in the country. I couldn't believe my ears! I went home around 2:30 a.m. I couldn't sleep the rest of the night thinking about everything that I had heard that evening. The following morning, I made one of the greatest mistakes of my life. I called an emergency meeting at the Clinic to inform my partners of the necessity to do something immediately; otherwise, Cuba was going to suffer for a very long time. At the end of my presentation, no one said a word, except for someone who was like a brother to me. He came up and handed me a small red book and said, "All you have to do is read this book, you will change your mind. " The book was "The Guerrilla Warfare of Mao Tse Tung." At that point, I understood that my days in Cuba were numbered that I should leave as soon as possible.

Although I was quite fortunate that my "friends" did not report me to the new government for not sharing their doctrine, from that day on, our home would be searched at odd hours of the night by government officials who were trying to find anything that could be legally incriminating against the regime. After many months of, anxiety, anguish, and trials and tribulations, I was able to obtain permission to leave the country. Making the decision to leave my country and losing everything that I had created was not the most difficult for me, it was leaving the rest of the family, and the people I loved so much. In October, we decided that I would leave alone; my wife, two children and my parents would leave 48 hours later. This way if the government officials changed their minds and denied my departure, Guly, my wife, would not be faced with the decision of having to travel alone with the kids. At the airport, security took everything I was carrying except for $5.00 and two changes of clothes.

Rafael, Dr. Rodríguez-Torres, Raymond, Guly & Raúl.

I had decided to go to Puerto Rico because at that time, a physician's starting salary for an intership in the United States was $50 dollars a month, while in Puerto Rico was $150. When the plane took off for Miami and from there for Puerto Rico, my mind started wandering, "What am I going to do with only $5.00? – I don't know anybody in that country!" I wondered if I should spend that evening at a bench at the airport or if I should go to a park. Finally my plane landed in San Juan at 9:00 p.m.

Rodríguez-Torres family

I have always been a Christian and consequently, I believe in miracles. That night, God showed me his omnipotence. As I was getting off the plane, I saw an English friend I had met in London. I will never forget the question he asked me, "WHAT ARE YOU DOING HERE, RAMON?" He was a businessman who was successfully working in Puerto Rico.

After I explained my situation, he invited me to his home where I was able to spend the night. The following morning my friend helped me rent a house, buy furniture, and food. When my wife and children arrived the following day, they had a home waiting for them. Tell me now... do you believe in miracles? I DO!

After my friend and I finished making all the arrangement for the home, I decided to go on my own to see the Minister of Health to inquire about a job. I knew it would be difficult since getting an appointment with a minister in any country takes months, even if you are lucky. Apparently, that was not the case that day, since the Health Minister not only received me, but he also gave me a job in a district hospital. Some would call these coincidences, good luck; I personally call them "Miracles."

One year later, we moved to New York where I was appointed as Assistant to the Director of Pediatric Cardiology at the State University of New York. After twelve years, I became the director of the department and pediatric professor. I had reached my goal. I had maintained my principles, and God had given me the opportunity to live and work in a free country: THE UNITED STATES OF AMERICA.

When the Medical College of Ohio opened, I had the honor of becoming Professor and Chairman of the Department of Pediatrics, with all the emotions and opportunities of starting and establishing a new department.

Five years later, and after I was offered the position of Chief of Pediatric Staff at Michigan State University, I decided to accept the position as Chief of Medical Staff at the Miami Children's Hospital in Florida, a position that I held for fifteen years until my retirement on June 30th of 1996.

In my work with children, as well as adults, I have been able to treat many of my countrymen. I have always advised them the same thing Guly and I taught our children; never let go of your principles and don't be afraid of the truth. People that work and persevere reach their goals of SUCCESS IN EXILE; it does not matter where they are from or where destiny takes them.

Teresa Hidalgo de Martínez & Reverendo Gerardo Martínez †

A Legacy of Faith. The Story of Rev. Gerardo & Teresa Martínez

Teresa Hidalgo de Martínez

They can burn the churches and the synagogues, they can destroy all the Sacred Texts, but they will never be able to keep the grandmothers from telling their stories to their grandchildren… so there can always be hope for freedom.
ANONYMOUS

My husband, Rev. Gerardo Martínez, was the pastor of the Methodist Church in Guayabo, Mayarí in the province of Oriente. In 1958 during the height of Castro's Revolution, we were transferred to the Methodist Church of Guantanamo. The pastoral house was right next to the church, and right behind it was the Barracks of Batista's guards. From our kitchen we could see the armed soldiers walking back and forth in the attic, and we could sense the stress and tension inside. On the next street there was a police station which was attacked almost nightly by the rebels who would kill the policemen and take their firearms. It was a frightening environment, especially because we had two small children and one on the way.

During those days the revolution had strengthened. All roads and streets to leave the city were closed, and some of them had been dynamited. No one could be out of their homes after 5:00 p.m. At night the police did not want anyone to turn on the front lights of their homes. We were terrified when we heard the sounds of gun shots. My small children and I would hide under the bed. Gerardo did not seem to pay much attention to the gunfire. He went about his business as usual.

Suddenly, one Saturday night while he was preparing the next morning's sermon in the front office, we heard a gunshot. The bullet came through the window, went right over my husband's head, and hit the wall. He quickly turned off the light and went to finish in the kitchen under a lamp's dim light. The situation was getting extremely difficult. Everyone was afraid to leave his home, and finding food was becoming a problem. We spent fifteen days eating cornmeal.

On December 28, 1958, Rebeca was born. I was not able to go to the hospital since it was not safe to leave our home. I also did not want to leave the kids. A member of our church who was a mid-wife came and stayed with me until the baby was born. My husband went out to the market to see if he could find anyone who would sell him some meat. He was able to buy a duck and since I was out of commission, he had to cook it himself. The poor man had never cooked before in his life, much less plucked a duck; there were feathers everywhere, but the meal turned out to be delicious.

On January 1st, 1959, the Revolution finally triumphed. I remember the people celebrating in the streets, thinking this day marked the salvation and independence of Cuba. Others were worried and feared for the freedom of Cuba, among them Gerardo, who had never trusted Fidel and his people. He was right.

The next day the rebels entered the city and wanted to take over police headquarters. The chief of police was not willing to give it up, and the rebels promised that if the police officers came out without a fight, they would pardon them. The police surrendered, and the rebels made them get in the back of a cattle truck. The real plan was to take them to be executed in front of a firing squad. The policemen soon realized what was happening and tried to fight. The rebels then started shooting and killed them all right there in the street.

A young man, who was the president of the church's youth group, came to Gerardo and with a smile on his face said, "Reverend, I saw how those policemen were killed; they fell like flies. I even spit on one of them."

With a look of disgust, my husband said, "You did that? Well, then, I want you to resign as president of the youth immediately."

"Why Reverend?" He said in shock.

"Because you did not feel compassion for those men, and no one has the right to take the lives of his brothers. Only God has the right to call us home." The young man did not appreciate Gerardo's reaction and left quite angry.

As a Methodist Minister, Gerardo could not agree with the atrocities that were happening all around us, and he started preaching against the executions and the actions that were being taken by the Revolution. Many of our members were in favor of the Revolution at that time and began to complain to our superintendant who quickly called him and said, "Gerardo, I know that you are doing the right thing, but for the safety of your family, I am going to transfer you."

In June of 1959, we moved to Báguanos, a town known for its sugar mill. This was a small but beautiful and friendly town and my husband had to tend to several other churches in the area.

The manager of the sugar mill was a very educated man who had been in charge of the mill for many years, but he was not in favor of Fidel. He was replaced with someone who had not even completed second grade but was in full agreement with Fidel's policies. Consequently, the sugar mill's production started to decrease, and soon the entire mill shut down. The manager and two soldiers came to our home to ask for our Jeep to go to the sugarcane fields to check what the workers were doing.

"I am very sorry" said Gerardo," right now I am leaving for a church program. I can't give it to you."

The manager turned to one of the soldiers and said, "Write down that Reverend Martinez refuses to collaborate with the revolution." A few months later they came again to ask for the Jeep to take some weapons to the fields but Gerardo responded, "I am very sorry, but this car belongs to the church, and it can only carry Bibles not guns." This was unacceptable and things became uncomfortable for us.

Martínez family

Monday morning when he was outside the church, a few soldiers came. "How can I help you," he asked.

"We understand that you were preaching about Uncle Sam yesterday."

"Yes, I told my congregation that the missionaries had come from the United States to speak about Christ, not about Uncle Sam, but please come to my office so you can read my sermon." They came in, read it, and apologized. During all this time we had not considered leaving the country. We never expected that this situation would last very long. The nice and serene life of our island had changed to one of atrocities and fear. How could this possibly last?

The Báguanos church had a school that taught kindergarten through eighth grade. One morning Gerardo went to open the school and found several armed soldiers with machine guns who said that the school had been taken over by the Revolution and that if he insisted on opening it, he would be taken prisoner. That was the day we decided that it was time to leave the country. We realized that the situation in Cuba was now hopeless.

We began to prepare our passports, get vaccinations and do everything that was required to leave the country. We waited and waited and had almost lost all hope of leaving when on January 4, 1962, my cousin, who worked at the post office, brought the telegrams. We had 72 hours to get out of Cuba. It was 10:00 a.m. and that day Gerardo was in Holguin in a church meeting. I called him. "Get everything ready." He said. "We are leaving the house this afternoon."

A Jamaican lady, who helped me around the house, helped me prepare two suitcases with clothing for the six of us. At 3:00 p.m., that afternoon, we said goodbye to some of our friends and left Báguanos. No one in our family knew anything. On the way to Havana, we stopped at my parents' home. This was one of the saddest days of my life as my father hugged me and said that this would be the last time we would see each other, and so it was. He passed away a few years later.

We left Cuba on the January 6th, the day of the Epiphany. This is the day when gifts are given, and we had been given the gift of freedom. We moved to Chicago, Illinois, and my husband went to work for Abbott Laboratories. In 1965 he received a call from the Bishop of the Methodist Church to informing us that we were needed in Florida.

Gerardo resigned from a distinguished position at Abbott and went to work as the pastor of the Methodist Church in Zolfo Springs,

Florida. The congregation consisted mainly of Mexican immigrants who needed a Spanish speaking pastor. While he worked in the church, he also studied for the seminary at Duke University in North Carolina during the summers. Later, he also attended Emory University in Atlanta, Georgia. After graduating with a theology degree, the Florida Methodist Conference sent us to Nicaragua where Gerardo worked as the Director of Community Development for Alfalit, a non-profit literacy organization which, based in faith, teaches needy adults around the world to read and write.

In 1974 we were sent to Costa Rica, where Gerardo became the General Director of Alfalit International. From there, he directed the entire Alfalit organization in Latin America. He frequently traveled and was able to carry out the Lord's work, helping innumerable individuals to better their lives.

In 1979, we came back to the United States to work in the United Methodist Church of Coral Way, Miami, Florida. There we enjoyed thirteen unforgettable years working with a growing congregation. Gerardo became an elder of the United Methodist Florida Conference in May of 1991. He worked his last years in the Methodist Church in Tampa. He retired after fifty years of service to the church. My husband went to be with the Lord on May 27th, 2003, leaving behind his four children, ten grandchildren and a great-grandson, a legacy of Christian faith and love.

We have always been grateful to the United States for taking us in and for opening the doors to so many wonderful opportunities. Our children Santiago, Carlos, Gerardo and Rebeca have been able to study and develop their talents as dignified and responsible citizens. We are also grateful to the United Methodist Church to which we devoted our lives.

We still dream of a not-so-distant day when Cuba will be free and sovereign once again, even if many of us will not be here to witness it.

Dr. Madelyn Espinosa Buttler, Miriam Espinosa Martínez & Martha Espinosa Laurent

A Lesson of Patriotism

Martha Espinosa Laurent

Teaching is not a profession; it is a passion.
ANONYMOUS

The morning bell rang. As usual, the school principal's voice came over the intercom asking us to stand for the pledge of alliance. As we repeated in unison, "I pledge alliance to the flag of the United States of America...," I realized that some of my students' hands had not risen to cover their hearts, while others simply uttered the words by inertia. It was then when I decided to take a few minutes of the Spanish class to teach them a little bit about the history of my country, Cuba, with the hopes of awaking in them a bit more appreciation for theirs.

"Do you think you are privileged because you live in a democratic country?" The students looked at me without a response."How many of your parents are business owners?" Some raised their hands. "Do you plan to be a business owner someday?"

"When was the last time you ate a big juicy steak, chicken, fish, a hamburger, any kind of meat?"

"Why are you asking these questions, Mrs. Laurent?"

"Why? I would like to share some of my life experiences with you."

I was only four years old when my parents decided that we had to flee Cuba, the country where I was born. Fidel Castro had taken over the government, and we were now a communist country. This meant that there should be an equal distribution of wealth and social equality. Nevertheless, this is usually a theory; in our country this meant that the government would have absolute power. The government took over all private properties, and even our lives.

Like many other families that requested permission to leave the country, we underwent a meticulous inventory of everything we had in our home. The armed soldiers told my parents that they would do a inventory the day we got our permission approved. Everything had to be intact. When the day finally arrived, eight years later, they did just that. Then, the heartless soldiers closed the door to our home and sealed it with a sign that read, "Property of the Cuban Government." We were never to go back to the home where we had grown up.

During the beginning of Castro's government, I remember my mom trying to prevent my sister and me from listening to the horrible news that came over the public system address at the plaza near our home, "Paredón… (Firing wall) Paredón! We could hear the loud voice again and again during the public trials where the alleged counterrevolutionaries were sentenced to death. She would make us cover our ears or send us to our rooms. Nevertheless we would hear the stories that adults and children would tell about the shooting executions that took place in the afternoons at the walls surrounding the city cemetery. These victims: sons, husbands, parents, brothers, friends… people from our town, became a show for the blood thirsty crowds. Their only crime was to protest against a government that had taken their properties, or to openly disagree with the communist regime.

One of the most vivid memories of my childhood is the day we went to the jail to visit my uncle Oscar. It was a hot, steamy day, and my father was holding my hand. The high-perched guard despotically yelled out my uncle's name and touched his shoulder with a long stick, "Oscar, your brother and nieces are here to see you." I can still recall the impression that it caused me to see my uncle in a prisoner's uniform which exposed parts of his chest because it was a few sizes too small for him. The prisoner longed to be allowed a visit from a loved one.

"What did Uncle Oscar do?" I asked my father.

"Your uncle did not do anything wrong," my father tried to assure me. "A neighbor reported him because he butchered one of his own cows…that is considered illegal now. He butchered it to eat the meat and to share it with the whole family. Your uncle is an wonderful person."

I also remember a day, when a sea of green camouflaged, uniformed soldiers rampaged through our home yelling, "Where are you hiding that man?" They were looking for one my father's friends who had returned for the Bay of Pigs invasion and had escaped the claws of the government. They knew of the friendship that existed between the two of them, and someone had told the officials that he was hiding in our home. That is the reason why they felt they had the right to barge into our home and verbally attack us. My mother was pregnant with my younger sister, Madelyn, at the time. I was holding her hand while she took me with her to the toilet to wretch from both morning sickness and fear. "Gusanos" had no human rights. We did not deserve respect or consideration.

Communism also brought rationing at all levels. Each family was assigned a ration book which determined the amount of food and provisions that each family was allowed based on the number and condition of each family member. For example, milk was only for children or the elderly above a certain age. I suppose that the communist government decided that the rest of the population no longer needed calcium. Food was rationed by ounces per person. What a different experience from shopping at a supermarket. How lucky we are to be able to go into a mall and buy whatever we please!

The same thing happened with everything else. When word got out that a shipment of shoes from Russia was coming in, people flocked to the streets to stand in line to wait for their turn to buy those shoes, even if they were horribly ugly and of poor quality. Family members held their treasured place in line for hours and hours until another family member could take their place. They were there for days, morning, afternoon and night. Most of the time, by the time it was their turn, their size would have run out. It was the same thing when a shipment of clothes and other items arrived.

Later on they decided that it would be easier to distribute personal items at the level of a "neighborhood committee." These committees were headed by an openly communist family who assumed the responsibility of gathering representatives from different families in the neighborhood with the sole purpose of assigning tickets to buy clothes, shoes, material or anything of personal use. I attended some of these meetings with my oldest sister and will never forget seeing an elderly lady plead her case as to why she needed undergarments more than anyone else in the room. Although these meetings' purpose was to carry out a coordinated effort to distribute goods fairly, its principal function was to be the eyes and ears for anything suspicious which could be interpreted as a counter revolutionary act.

I was twelve years old when, finally in 1966 after waiting for quite a few years, my family was able to leave Cuba. Those were years in which even living in our home had turned into a terrible stress; we were always afraid of being heard saying something against the government or that something in the inventory would be lost. If we did any of these things, our dream of escaping communism would be compromised.

We were leaving via Mexico one of two ways that could be taken to leave Cuba legally. My father was able to obtain visas from a former client who used his contacts to gain access to the Mexican Embassy. Because we were so young, my sister Madelyn and I thought that we were going on a short trip. We would soon find out that it was the trip of no return. My older sister, Miriam, knew that this trip would mean saying goodbye forever to the rest of our family, her childhood friends and all the hopes and dreams that a fifteen year old holds in her heart. My parents knew that they would leave behind everything that they had worked for: their home, their possessions, their savings, their family heirlooms and their families. They knew that they had to leave Cuba to ensure that we would have freedom–the most cherished of possessions.

The day of our departure, Madelyn and I held on to our favorite dolls, but the guards at the airport abruptly took them from us and pulled their heads off to ensure that our parents had not hidden any money, or jewelry inside of them. Of course, they didn't care about the psychological effect that this might have on two little girls. My parents also feared that we would be subjected to a body search which might include the removal of all our clothes. We finally got on board the plane to Mexico—now exiles. For a period of three months, my father, Dr. Jorge Espinosa, my mother, Matilde, my sisters, Miriam, Madelyn and I lived in modest neighborhood in Mexico City in a small room of the Hotel Pal, The hotel was a favorite among Cubans making the journey to the United States because it had the bare essentials required for an extended stay at a low cost. The majority of them had to depend on their families in the United States to send money to survive, as Cubans could not legally work in Mexico. We were merely surviving, until my father could get all of the paperwork necessary for our departure to the United States.

The memory of that hotel room is still fresh in my mind. The room served as a bedroom for all of us at night and as a living area during the day. There was a small bathroom and a miniscule kitchen. Not long after our arrival, an old friend of our family, who had married a Mexican man and had lived in Mexico for years, offered to take my fifteen-year-old sister to live with her in her beautiful house where she would have her own room. My parent's agreed. Soon afterwards, Señora Lola found my sister a job as an extra in a Cantinflas movie.

When we arrived in Miami, life was quite different. It was time to mature. My mother went to work for the first time outside the home. She had to take three buses to go to work as a seamstress in a clothing factory. She worked with many other Cuban exiles that, like Mom, never would have imagined they would find themselves in such a situation. She worked from Monday to Friday and also brought sewing home so that she could make extra money on the weekend. Miriam worked in the same factory as my mother. She and I helped take care of our younger sister, Madelyn. My father, in spite of being a veterinarian, took a job in the Everglades as a laborer. He would leave in the early hours of Monday morning. During the week he lived with some cowboys in a trailer, where he was also the cook. Somehow, he found time to stay in touch with what was going on in his profession. At his age, it was very strenuous doing ranch work. Therefore, when he heard that the federal government was in need of meat inspectors, and they had developed a program to train foreign veterinarians, he researched it.

He bought a plane ticket to Tallahassee and went to the office of the Department of Agriculture and applied. A few weeks later he was accepted to an intensive training program for meat inspectors in the state of California. After two months he returned with his license in hand and a job as a veterinarian meat inspector in Sylvester, a small town in southern Georgia.

Once my father began this job, things began to look up for us from the economic stand point, but it was not all happiness since the rest of the family was in Miami and Sylvester was almost eight hours away. Dad took this trip south to see us every two weeks. On one of those trips, we received an alarming phone call from the police very late at the night. Mom, who did not speak English, handed the

Dr. Jorge Espinosa † & wife Matilde †

Ana María Gutiérrez Myers

Cuban Treasures

Ana María Gutiérrez Myers

Education consists of teaching men,
not what they should think, but how to think.
ANONYMOUS

"What are we taking with us from Cuba today?" Papi asked.

We were at the Havana airport, and he was trying to distract us from the marauding soldiers and their machine guns and the blaring PA system that barked, it seemed like every five minutes, demanding a departing family, like us, to report to "headquarters" – a terrifying threat to our hopes of leaving Cuba. I was fourteen, my sister was 12 and my brother was 8.

We laughed at his question, thinking this was another of his usual jokes. Yet we always replyed,

"Nothing," said my sister dejectedly, acknowledging our absent luggage with a glance around us. She was wearing a red wool gabardine suit with a pleated skirt and a white silk blouse made by our seamstress according to an old Vogue sewing pattern. For a long time, Mami had saved up our rationing cards that allotted the amount of material we could purchase to make clothing in anticipation of our departure. With these, she bought the best Chinese wool and silk available. Mami wanted it to be obvious that we were not, by our dress or our behavior, gusanos, the adjective that Fidel Castro used to describe the "worms" that left his island.

"Not any of my toys," pouted my little brother, probably remembering his truck collection and his plastic zoo, which had been left inside his toy box back in Holguin, our proud city in Oriente Province.

"You are just trying to make us laugh, Papi," I said, thinking of my boyfriend who, just a few nights before, had hugged me and timidly kissed me goodbye. The ring he had given me as a gift by which to remember him, I had reluctantly entrusted to my grandmother's care. I stared sadly at my naked hands.

"No, I'm not joking, think," he said earnestly. "We are taking the most important things with us." Again, he posed his question. I panicked then, thinking that my parents had recklessly decided to smuggle jewelry and gold coins by swallowing them. I had heard other families tell horror stories of guards searching the body cavities of children and parents alike, exposing and humiliating them as examples to onlookers who might have the same idea. I looked searchingly at Mami.

"He is not talking about material things," she responded, as if reading my mind. "We are leaving with the clothes and shoes we are wearing – only what we are allowed." She said this loudly, looking around. "I hope someone will have some old clothes, or, at least some clean underwear to give us when we get there. We'll need them!" We all giggled when she pinched her nose.

"Think." Papi insisted on getting an answer to his question. "Everything that is most important to us, we have here with us." He gestured with his hands at the seats we occupied. All around us, other families were talking and hoping that their names would not be called for another grueling interrogation.

"OK," I said, finally getting the point. "We have each other. We're taking our family."

"Very good, Ana Maria!" He beamed proudly at me. He looked so handsome, wearing his finest suit and tie, his thin mustache trimmed neatly over his mouth. I remembered his face just two years before, in April of 1961, when he had been taken in the early morning and marched to prison, after he had been accused of cooperating with the Bay if Pigs Invasion. For six weeks we'd had no idea where he had been taken, or even whether he was alive or dead.

"But that isn't true!" interjected my sister angrily. "What about the rest of our family? They are all staying here!" The image of my Abuela Felisa's anguished face reappeared in my mind, and I felt again the fierce way she had held me the day we had said goodbye.

"That's true," Mami agreed with optimism in her voice. "But as soon as we have jobs in America, we'll be able to send for them."

We were leaving Cuba that day. Our dreams of freedom were finally being realized. Still, why did I feel so sad?

"OK," Papi was ready to continue his game. "Any other ideas?" I looked at my little brother who was fidgeting impatiently because he wasn't scoring any points in Papi's game. "No, Papi, just tell us, please!"

"OK, we are bringing our family, he repeated." He looked proudly at Mami and at each of us, and then he had that familiar twinkle in his eyes, "We have slipped through Fidel's fingers, and he's going to be furious!" Grinning, he continued, "We're also smuggling our memories! Think of all the days we have enjoyed together: birthday parties, baptisms, and communions at our church. We have school recitals, Christmases at your abuelos', summers at the beach, and days on the boat.

Suddenly, the not-so-long-ago events and the warm, smiling faces of those we were leaving behind, flooded my mind, as if they were the *comparsa* during the Cuban carnivals we celebrated during Mardi Gras. This memory came complete with songs, crashing waves, sunshine, and aromas of roast pork, fried plaintains, churros and rum.

"No one can inventory those moments or force us to leave them behind," Papi laughed triumphantly. I remembered the last day in Holguin, just a few days before, when I saw the guards pasting an official document over the door of our house. Our house, furniture, books, and toys had disappeared forever behind that door.

It didn't seem to me that Papi was very sad about leaving behind the only life we had ever known. "Mami, our children don't

Father, Ana María, Liliam, Mother & Guillermo

know how to play this game very well! They don't have even the slightest idea of the treasures that we are taking with us!" Papi loved teasing us, and it was clear that he was enjoying himself then. "I think maybe they left their brains in the house in Holguin, behind those sealed doors!"

"Well, the other treasure," Mami said, following Papi's lead, insisting that they shouldn't give up on us, "is something that we are taking inside our heads."

"Our brains!" shouted my little brother, using Papi's idea of a few seconds before. He couldn't wait to contribute to the game. My sister and I burst into laughter.

"He's right," said my mother, shooting us a threatening look. My brother sat down proudly in his seat. "But what is it that your Papi and I have in our brains that will be so important for us in the United States?"

When we stared blankly at her for a few seconds, she continued. "What we know, what we have studied." She said this slowly. "We'll have our training. When we get to the United States, we won't have a dime. We are going to depend on other people to live for the first few weeks, maybe months. We are going to have to stay with Tio Carlos in Miami until Papi and I can find jobs. But do you know what is going to enable us to find those jobs? The fact that I am a teacher and Papi a pharmacist is another great treasure we are smuggling out of Cuba. "This," she put her hands on her head, "is portable! No one can take it away from us. Our education is going to make it easier to find well-paying jobs. When we get those jobs, we'll be able to buy a house, a car, food and clothes. We'll also be able to get the rest of the family out of Cuba. We will also be able to send you three to college when the time comes." When she said that, she smiled. My father's eyes filled with tears. Maybe he was thinking about how proud my mother had always been of her teaching career. Most women in Holguin did not attend college and the fact that Mami had a degree from the University of Havana as well as a Doctorate and was an admired professor had always made her feel very happy with herself.

"In America," said Papi, almost crying. "We will have the freedom to make our dreams come true. The United States will give us the opportunities. We will be able to make decisions about our own lives." When he said the next words, he lowered his voice. "Without the government telling us what we can and cannot do. That is the beauty of that country. That is where we will be free." We knew not to add anything more to what he had just said. We suspected that there were "ears" all around us listening. We had learned that anything we might say against the revolution could get our parents arrested. So, we continued our game without drawing any attention to ourselves.

"There is something else that we are taking with us without anyone knowing it." My mother took advantage of the silence to make her statement. "It's the most important of all of our treasures."

Again, we didn't have a clue.

"God," she said simply, with a prayerful gesture. "It's our faith." It is what our parents passed down to your Papi and to me, and it is what we want you to take with you to the United States. When you have children someday, we hope that faith is the gift that you give them. Without faith in God, nothing else exists. With faith, we have everything. As she said this, she sighed and looked at us lovingly, satisfied that she had completed the lesson.

While she spoke, I thought about the illegal short-wave radio that Papi kept hidden under his bed in Holguin. Papi always turned on the air conditioner to prevent the sounds of that radio from being heard outside the house. The government had banned listening to any station on short-wave radios because it was considered an act against the Revolution. The neighbors who were members of the Committee for the Defense of the Revolution would denounce anyone they discovered violating this law. We had always listened to "The Voice of the Americas" and I clearly recalled a recent program that had aired a trial of a group of young Cubans that were accused of being against the Revolution. The prosecution had requested that they say they believed in the Revolution. They had refused and in the moment before they were executed by a firing squad, they shouted, "Viva Cristo Rey! – Long Live Christ the King - as they breathed their last breath. This was the faith that Mami was talking about.

A few minutes later, our flight was announced. We didn't have any baggage, but we had it all.

The Courtyard of My Childhood

Ana María Gutiérrez Myers

Dedicated to my Daughter, who shares my dream

Endlessly brilliant May afternoon,
lifetime of memories.
Prickly bramble agonizing on iron bars
defends boarded windows.
Tangled.
Cicadas serenade
in accelerating assonance.
A rocking chair sways, off-balance
in the breeze, at the front door of my home.
Childhood,
forgotten and raped
by History.

Militiamen, invaders
divide the streets of my town.
After school my friend walks home
to shouts of "kill them,"
her father's blood paints her door.

Comrades! Revolution! Slaughter!

Still my misplaced dreams linger,
pinned to May afternoons
unforgotten:
Held in my mother's embrace,
and in the fragrance of jasmine,
in roses offered to Mary;
youthful kisses, strummed guitars;
family, teachers and friends,
memorized gerunds and verbs.

For what?

Lives discarded while in motion,
songs accompanied
by shrapnel,
sounds of everlasting laughter
resonating through the bramble.

So much hope wilted.

In the late breeze
a cadence echoes
numbly, through the Island,
warm, hushed, somber voices…

"…and from me they took
my bracelet."
"they took my toys."
"I left all my brothers there…"
"… I left my soul."

When I rummage and remember
In the attic of my youth,
the dreams are ageless,
fresh, church bells strident,
hands feel soft, lips are warm,
my skates abandoned in haste
their wheels still spinning,
are waiting;
my dolls—ignorant
to absence–
hold out their
arms

Half-opened windows,
the sun zigzagged on the floor
my wish
unchanged,
marking time,
in the courtyard of my youth.

Roberto & Viviana Pedroso

Five Dollars and a Box of Cigars

Roberto Pedroso

Everyone loves life, but a brave an honorable man appreciates honor the most.
WILLIAM SHAKESPEARE

I left Cuba for the last time in 1960. The reason I say the last time is because, even after being in the United States, I was still able to return to Cuba for Christmas holidays and summer vacations. However, having to leave Cuba under duress, fearing for my life and for my family that stayed behind, was an overpowering experience.

I remember the summer of 1960. I was working at a chemical plant in a small city named Sagua la Grande, located three hundred kilometers east of Havana, where my home was. The chemical plant had been confiscated by Castro's government. One day, the plant administrator, appointed by the government, came to me and said,

"When are you going to stand guard over the plant at night, as other employees are doing?"

"I don't know what you're talking about." He was carrying a machine gun and tossed it to me, saying,

"Here! grab this and let me teach you how to handle it so you can stand guard over the plant tonight." I let the gun fall to the ground and said,

"I do not plan to cooperate with you people tonight, tomorrow night, or any other night. "

"Well, we'll have to see about that, but I should tell you that the Sagua's Police Captain's nickname is Rocky Marciano because he hits very hard."

That night, before going to bed, I stopped at a small cafe to drink a Cuban coffee and smoke an American cigarette. By the way, I paid the huge amount of three cents for the coffee and two cents for the cigarette. Waiting for me at the café was a man whom I had befriended at the chemical plant. He had participated in the revolution against Batista but was very disappointed by the direction the revolution had taken. He wanted to warn me that Castro's police were waiting for me at the boarding house where I was staying. They were going to arrest me and submit me to interrogation. In Castro's Cuba, you never knew whether you were going to endure or even survive an interrogation. I got in my car, drove to Havana, and took the first plane out of Cuba going to the United States.

When I left Cuba, I had five dollars in my pocket, which was all the money one was allowed to take out of the country at that time. Today, you are lucky if you manage to leave alive! However, they also allowed taking a small suitcase with three changes of underwear, three shirts, one pair of pants, and a simple watch because Castro's police would confiscate fancy ones at the airport. After considering the options, I decided to buy a box of Cuban cigars at the Havana airport. As soon as the plane landed in Miami, I hitched a ride to a tobacco shop downtown and sold them the cigars I had bought. I had paid ten cents each and sold them for one dollar each. That's how I got started in this country, with fifty dollars I obtained by selling a box of Cuban cigars.

I left Miami hitching several rides to Atlanta. There I found a job and continued my engineering education. Needless to say, I had to work my way through college because I didn't have anyone to help or support me. Work was my only source of income.

My college education was briefly interrupted by my participation in the failed Bay of Pigs invasion against Fidel Castro. In 1960 I spent Christmas holidays with my parents, who were living in Miami at the time. They had left Cuba in October 1960 because they suffered constant harassment by Castro's police due to my refusal to cooperate with the Communist Revolution. On New Year's Eve, a Cuban friend of mine asked me if I was planning to join the training camps for the Cuba invasion. I responded that I had no idea such plans existed, but that I would think about it. I did think about it, and decided I would join the camps.

I went back to Atlanta, picked up all my belongings, and returned to Miami. My parents were surprised to see me back in Miami and asked me why I had returned. When I informed them of my decision, they were despondent and tried to convince me not to participate in this activity. I told them that Cuba needed soldiers to liberate it, and engineers to help rebuild it.

I signed up at a small office in Miami that was being operated by Cubans and by an agency of the United States government. I was asked what I was doing, and I responded that I was studying engineering. I was then asked if I knew and understood vectors (direction of a force), and I responded positively. I was then asked if I could swim, and I responded that I could swim well and was able to swim long distances. Then I was told that I would be a navigator for one of the boats that would participate in the invasion, and that I would be transported to one of the training camps shortly thereafter. I was warned that, if captured by Castro's forces during the invasion, "the Secretary would disavow your actions." About a week later, I was driven to a motel on Big Pine Key, in the Florida Keys. Together with several other Cuban compatriots, we were trained by "Tom, Dick and Harry." "Tom" taught us weaponry, "Dick" taught us navigation, and "Harry" brought food and other essentials every week from Key West. Each of us was provided with a 45-caliber handgun and either a Thompson or an M-1 machine gun. We were also provided with a 57mm recoilless rifle.

We traveled twice to Cuba in an unmarked rescue boat belonging to the United States. This boat was equipped with two 50-caliber machine guns and we used it to deliver weapons wrapped in waterproof cloth that were dumped at specific locations in the Caribbean. We also traveled to Havana Bay once to transport two men that would infiltrate the island in order to sabotage Castro's facilities. Finally, on April 19, 1961, we traveled to the north coast of Cuba to pick up invaders that had escaped the persecution that resulted from the failed invasion. I was not harmed or captured, and so I returned to Atlanta to continue my engineering education at Georgia Tech.

That was the last time I was in Cuba since my wife Viviana and I have lived in the United States, except for five and a half years when we worked in Venezuela. Throughout the years, my work has taken me to many other parts of the world, and I have been able to see that there is no other country like this one, a land of opportunity in which it is possible to work hard and make something out of yourself.

Even though I am now a U.S. Citizen and owe a great debt of gratitude to the people of the United States, I still love my native country. The future will inevitably bring changes, and I hope they result in a united, prosperous and happy Cuba.

Viviana Pedroso

When asked, "What was the hardest thing for you in leaving Cuba?" I answer that it was leaving behind a lifestyle that I will cherish forever.

During my childhood my family and I lived at my grandparents' home, an old mansion in El Vedado. It not only had many rooms, but was always full of relatives, joy and love. During my teenage years we moved to the Biltmore subdivision, where my parents, grandparents and all my uncles bought an entire block so that all houses would be adjacent and we would share a common backyard.

My father was a physician in Cuba and a professor at the University of Havana. He was a man who loved his country and passionately believed in democracy. His conscience wouldn't let him ignore the plea of his students, some of whom were part of the counter-revolution against Castro. They would seek his help, whether in healing wounds from tortures inflicted by Castro's men, or due to their desperate need to escape the island.

For two years Dad was able to escape the enemy and help the cause. However, since January 1960, Castro's men, armed with machine guns and rifles, came on several occasions to our home looking for my father. Dad escaped from Cuba on March 13, 1960. Mother joined him in June. The situation in Cuba was deteriorating by the day, and thus plans began for my sister and me to join them in New York.

On November 8, 1960, my sister and I arrived at the Idlewild Airport, now JFK, in New York. I was fifteen years old, and had just been separated from the rest of my family not knowing if I would ever see them again. I cried during the entire trip, from the moment our plane took off from Rancho Boyero until it landed at Idlewild. The worst part was the agony of waiting as we went through customs. However, when at last I felt my parents' arms around me, I understood the meaning of the phrase "home is where your heart is."

In spite of the pain and sorrow in our hearts for leaving our other family members behind, we were able to survive that period of time in New York due to my parents' faith, perseverance and outlook on life. My parents were incredible people. They taught us to laugh at the adversities of life, to smile like we mean it, to sing as if the world couldn't hear how terribly we sang, to dance, dance and dance like there was no tomorrow, to cry as if we were a river, to love as if we had never been hurt, and to hope for tomorrow with a passion for today.

My husband and I and both our families came to this country as exiles, yet we felt welcomed from the very beginning. We have been given many opportunities, the same ones offered to anyone born in the United States. And although the reasons that bring people to the United States are different, in order to succeed in this country you have to work hard! That's why the favorite expression of Cuban immigrants upon arriving here is, "It's not easy!" Success can only be achieved through faith, hope and determination. Disillusionment can only be conquered by being grateful and working hard. One must never forget that we have been welcomed in this country with open arms; we have been given more than we probably deserved.

As an adult I came to realize that my self-confidence, faith, and positive frame of mind come from the nourishment of my parents' love and affection. Success is a journey not a destination... and the journey is our effort.

González family

A Lost Opportunity, a Lesson Learned

Dr. Jorge González

When we miss an opportunity, we gain a lesson.
ANONYMOUS

The morning sun blazed through the window of the living room of our modest new home. My father had always made sure that our home had a pool, at least ever since I was stricken with Poliomyelitis when I was a toddler and physicians recommended that I perform water exercises. This new home was in Miami, and the year was 1963. I was ten and my brother was twelve, and we lay on the floor paging through Sunday's Miami Herald hoping my father would hold off on his eagerness to discuss politics and world events until we had finished reading all the sports news that interested us.

"Uh huh," I stammered, as my older brother and I respectfully glanced up at our father who was interrupting our search. He loved to read the Sunday newspaper cover to cover before we kids even got up so he could discuss politics and life with us. Unfortunately, we were too young to appreciate the opportunity. As time passed, we learned more and more about our father and his dreams and his courage.

Although we enjoyed our lives in Miami, I often thought back to my pre-school days in Cuba. I remembered our beautiful home in Biltmore, a modern subdivision in Malecón, Havana, where we had a large home with a pool and live-in maid's quarters. In my mind I can see Mother assisting our housekeeper preparing breakfast and welcoming our grandmother and aunt from next door and my uncle who lived nearby. Our house was always full of activity, family and visitors sharing food and gaiety in the Latin tradition. My three younger sisters were always in the midst of the activity, as well.

In Cuba, my father had run his family-owned and very successful lumber and hardware company. Fearing the unrest and violence he was seeing in Cuba, he sent my mother and us five children—my brother and me and our three sisters—to Mexico City to live in an apartment near my father's sister. My father stayed in Havana running the business that he had inherited from his father. Soon after the Bay of Pigs invasion, a military Jeep drove up to the store. A captain and four military men approached my father and asked him who owned the business. My father replied that he did, and the captain promptly told him that the business was being confiscated, but that he could stay and run the business for the government.

"If I'm not the owner, I'm not staying," my father said, and the captain asked for the keys and the combination to the safe. Castro had been taking over businesses, one category at a time, starting with the media. Now it was apparently time to take over the building supply industry. In less than five minutes, and without any compensation whatsoever, my father lost everything that he had worked for, and his father before him.

Luckily for my father, he had kept his visa to Mexico updated, so he returned to our Havana home, closed it up, and flew to Mexico City to be with all of us. Of course, he had to leave all of our material possessions and knew that our house would soon be ransacked and taken over as new government property.

I recall another time when the government took someone's house. One day when I was six years old, my mother suggested we go outside and see what all the commotion was about. There was a motorcade driving up to our neighbor's home. Previously, our neighbor, a general in Batista's Army, had disappeared practically overnight on December 31, 1959, after Castro took over Cuba. There was almost a "free for all" dash by people from neighboring areas who came to steal things from the abandoned house. Now the government owned our neighbor's house and the motorcade was bringing the new Russian president, Mikoyan, to stay next door. I actually got to see the heavily-guarded Castro when he stepped out of the car to escort his comrade guest into what was now a huge guest house belonging to the Cuban government.

We left Cuba in 1960. In Mexico City, my father entered into several business ventures. He was bright, had good business sense, and was multi-lingual. His father—my grandfather—was a Spaniard, and when my father graduated from high school, he was sent to England to a one-year business school so that he could also learn English. When my grandfather died, my father, his sisters and his mother together inherited the lucrative business. He was always the CEO and was able to develop other successful businesses.

In 1962 the family moved to Miami. With a partner, my father operated a chicken hatchery in the Dominican Republic, buying eggs from Miami, shipping them to the Dominican Republic, and then selling the hatched baby chicks to the farmers. He sold out his share to his partner and tried another business venture in the Dominican Republic. It involved buying corn from the farmers, having the corn shucked, and selling it back to the farmers as feed. During this time in the summer of 1969, my father was in a terrible auto accident in the Dominican Republic, badly fracturing both his legs. He had been commuting between Miami and the Dominican Republic, but because of his lengthy recovery from the accident, he quit the commute and by 1971 had moved to Miami permanently. He opened a building supply business there, much like what he had had in Havana. After several years of hard work, the business became a success.

While my father was working hard at his business in Miami, I was working hard at school. In my first year of school in the U.S., I was having a difficult time learning English. I don't know why, but it seemed all my siblings learned English fairly easily, and I was having so much trouble. However, in the sixth grade I had a wonderful teacher, Mrs. Shefsky, who took a special interest in helping me learn the language after school. She became a good friend of the family helping my mother get into a home-based cosmetic business.

Although I had been attending a good public elementary school, in eighth grade I began going to a Catholic school and in ninth grade I was enrolled in a private Catholic prep high school for boys. This was a big sacrifice for my parents, but our education and ability to succeed was very important to them. Following high school, I went to the University of Miami for my undergraduate degree and then graduated from the University of Miami School of Medicine. I then went to the University of Alabama in Birmingham where I completed a residency in Internal Medicine and a Fellowship in Cardiology.

Another wonderful blessing of my move to Birmingham was meeting my wife. Leah is an American who had recently graduated as a registered nurse. We met while she was working in the hospital at the same time that I was there working on my internal medicine residency. My plan had been to return to Miami to make my mark in combine research and academic career. However, it was then the early 80's, and my wife was hesitant to move to Miami to start a family because of the city's bad reputation for its crime rate. Also, Leah felt that moving to

Loly & Dr. Alex Garriga

Five Years of Loneliness

Loly Garriga

Time is too slow for those who wait, too swift for those who fear,
too long for those who grieve, too short for those who rejoice,
but for those who love, time is eternity.
HENRY VAN DYKE

We Cubans have many stories about the circumstances that surround our departures from our beloved island. We could fill thousands of pages with those anecdotes: experiences, the motives, the pain and the cost of wanting to live in freedom. Without exception, everybody paid a price. However, many stories have remained silent and forgotten. Those stories were the most tragic and costly ones because those Cubans paid with their own lives. They were not able to savor freedom and tell their stories. Our prayers and admiration are with them.

My family was one of the lucky ones. This is our story.

We arrived at the main entrance to the Varadero Airport on August 28th, 1969. It was a hot summer afternoon, and although it was 6:00 p.m. the sun shined high in the blue sky. We were sweating heavily because of the heat and the nervousness that we felt. Our two daughters, Beatriz, fifteen months old, and Vivian, five years old, perceived our anxiety, and their faces reflected uncertainty and fear.

The four of us walked into a big room where two officers were standing behind a counter, meticulously checking our documentation. The heat was more intense inside this room which did not have a fan or air conditioning. Impatience was taking hold of us while we were anxiously awaiting the decision of the authorities. Finally, the officer who was holding the documents addressed Alex, "Are you a doctor?"

"Yes"

"Do you know that people like you who abandon their country are considered traitors to the Revolution?

Alex and I exchanged looks not knowing what to answer. Once again the man addressed us in a mocking tone, "You can't leave;

your departure has not been authorized by the Provincial Regional Public Health."

Alex tried to explain that he had gotten permission from the office of National Public Health, and that should be enough. The officer could not disguise his dislike for Alex's insistence about his authorization to leave the country. The officer talked to another official, gave him the documents for his perusal, and told Alex,

"You have to stay here, and if you want your daughters and wife to leave, sign this power of attorney."

Alex took the paper; his hands were shaking, and we looked at each other trying to find strength and support. My eyes were filling with tears while begging Alex not to sign, to let me wait with him so that we could all leave together; but he had already made his decision for our own safety. He signed and turned in the document. Sarcastically the officer gave us an order,

"Go ahead and give each other a parting kiss and say goodbye."

We looked deeply into each other's eyes, my husband's image becoming blurry through my uncontrollable tears. Our daughters could not understand what was about to happen. We had to control our emotions for them. Our cries and sobs were not going to change our situation; we had to be strong and face the consequences. We hugged each other tightly, our bodies trying to melt with one another; we could not believe that in just a few seconds there would be such emptiness, the absence of a loved one which would last an eternity. Alex was abruptly escorted out of the room.

Desperation had taken hold of me, and without being able to avoid it, I started to sob. Vivian and Betty began to cry as well, and in an instant, a officer grabbed me by the arm and warned me,

"Go to the patio until you get hold of yourself."

Everything around us was darkness; only the light of passing cars would shed some light on the patio. We were there for a long time until finally they ordered us to come in so they could check what was in our luggage. We were not carrying much, but everything was thoroughly checked. They even checked the seams and hems of our clothes to ensure that we were not hiding any valuables. They had taken an inventory of our jewelry, but regardless of that fact, they examined them again. I was wearing my wedding ring which was taken from me. I do not know where I found the strength and courage, but I asked the man to give it back. I insisted that as a jewel per se, it did not have much value, but it held precious memories. I think I softened his heart because without thinking, he gave it back to me.

That night was endless and so were the thoughts in my mind. I could not stop wondering what fate was waiting the next day. A new life was about to start for us in an unknown country far away from what we loved the most: our land, our customs, our loved ones. That was the price we had to pay in exchange for the freedom that we yearned for. That was the punishment that was being imposed upon us.

We arrived in New York. My parents were already there, and we would have shelter and the support of our family. Years of struggle, instability and sadness lay ahead of us.

More and more we needed the presence of the father, the husband. I worked hard to keep our home functioning as normally as possible. I did not want my daughters to be victims of emotional traumas; I wanted their lives to develop as best as possible given our current circumstances.

After five long years, Alex was finally able to leave Cuba. On August 24, 1974, we were reunited at the John F. Kennedy airport. We all went to meet him. His eyes were shining as he hugged us. We were all overwhelmed with emotion. That much desired moment had finally arrived; our lives would make sense once again. The years of separation had made us stronger, wiser and more mature. Now we really appreciated the most important things in life: our family, our values and the love that helped us conquer a very difficult trial imposed upon us.

Yet, we had ground to cover. We had won the first part of our journey; now we had to face the future, to reach the goal of revalidating his medical license so he could practice medicine in the United States. Eagerly, he tried to get a job, but he was overqualified for most jobs. He was an anesthesiologist, and soon we realized that once he was asked about his background and experience, he was rejected.

Alex decided that learning English was a top priority. He enrolled in an intensive class and got a job in a jewelry factory. He didn't earn much, but he felt useful knowing that he was contributing to the expenses. Once he finished the intensive English course, he started preparing for the exams that would revalidate his medical degree. He would study long hours in the living room of our small apartment in Queens. To concentrate, he had to have peace and quiet, and the children had to cooperate. When they got home from school, they had to go to the one and only bedroom in the apartment. They would do their homework and entertain each other until dinner and then they would go back to their "jail" to sleep. We spent many weeks in the same routine until a colleague called and convinced Alex to move to Miami where they were offering more courses to prepare for the exams. Miami also offered more opportunities for Cuban exiles.

In September 1975 we moved to Miami. I got a job as a medical secretary and Alex as a medical assistant in a hospital. He worked weekends and studied during the week. In March 1977 Alex took the State Medical Board Exam. A few weeks later, he was certified to practice medicine. Thirteen years had gone by since he had made the decision to leave his cherished island. The land of opportunity had opened her doors to us.

Today, three decades later, after a long journey, Alex still practices medicine in Lakeland, Florida. We have found in this country everything that we had dreamed of: freedom, happiness, prosperity and SUCCESS IN EXILE.

My Cuba of Yesteryear

Loly Garriga

My Cuba of yesteryear, the one I remember,
The one that happily sings the danzón in my heart,
The one with blue skies and her ardent sun,
And clear nights lighted by the moon over the Malecón.

The one with eternal summers and fragrant springs,
Where the flowers are always blooming
For the lover to offer to his beloved one,
As proof of his pure and eternal love.

The one with serene beaches and white sands,
With crystal clear waters painted in blue hue,
Where the waves caress the shores,
And the seagulls soar under the brilliant sun.

The one with majestic palm trees, that proudly stand tall
Wishing to reach the distant sun,
That with its soft rays embraces the green fields,
Bathing them in Cuban warmth.

When nostalgia invades my soul, in this cruel exile,
Far from the country that saw me born
I see my hopes to return to my land, die,
Because the Cuba in my heart exists only in years bygone.

Tapia family

Building the Future

Eduardo Tapia

Educate the children. Educate them about tolerance, solidarity. Transmit to them the most important thing we have: cultural heritage.
JOSEFINA ALDECOA

In 1968, feeling the oppression of the communist regime, my wife Zenia and I decided to leave the country of Cuba with our daughters Jacqueline, Patricia and Zenia. The girls were very young– one of them was a newborn– and we wanted them to grow up in a free democratic country. I was an engineer, and I knew that if I wanted to leave the country, I would have to submit to a minimum of two years of forced labor. This was one of the prices professionals had to pay if they wanted to leave Cuba. In my case, it turned out to be forty-nine months. During that time I was only allowed to visit my family once in awhile.

My forced labor was in the fields cutting sugarcane and planting and fertilizing the plants. It was like a concentration camp where we were obligated to work twelve hours a day. The bosses would get us up before sunrise and transport us like animals, in a horse-drawn wagon, to where the job was. We would come back after sunset, about four hundred tired and sweaty men, to await our turn for one of the four showers. The food was horrendous and there was very little of it. If we had not eaten the sugarcane we were cutting or the wild fruit we found, we would have died. Our mistreated bodies wanted to rest, but in these shelters there were only three-level iron bunk beds that would actually cause more pain than rest, and the mosquitoes would drive us insane at dusk.

Mistreatment was evident. They would only allow us to go home every two weeks for less than thirty hours and then only if we would comply with all our duties and, above all, if we did not protest. Many of my co-workers were punished by having visits to their families suspended or by delaying permission to leave the country. This treatment against professionals, whose only crime was to want to live in a country where their families could have free will, was highly abusive. It was a high price to pay.

When I had been in this oppressive situation for about two years, the government had the gall to offer me a good position working as an engineer for them. In order to take the position, I would be required to waive my rights to leave the island. Of course I totally refused. Then one day when we arrived from work, an army truck was waiting for me. As soon as I got down from the wagon, one of the guards told me to pick up all my belonging because I was being transferred. They took me to a jail for common criminals in a remote area. Soon an officer who was the warden of the prison came to me and with a humiliating and degrading tone said, "I have been told that you are an engineer. You are going to build us a cafeteria for the prisoners, and you will not leave here until you finish." They put two prisoners to work for me and allowed me to sleep in the infirmary. Luckily, I didn't spend a lot of time there because, after finishing the foundation, they ran out of construction materials, and they sent me back to my camp.

Finally in 1972 we received permission to leave the country via Spain. Our family, together and more willing than ever, was leaving to go to a country where we didn't know anyone, but we had faith in God who had never failed us. I remember that trip to Madrid very well. Everything had been taken from us at the airport, even my wife's wedding ring. Where were we going to sleep that night?

As soon as we arrived, I began to look for a job. Three days later, I was working for an engineering firm. A year after that, I was in charge of a group of twenty-four engineers. These were successful years. I worked with dedication and devotion and had the opportunity to travel abroad and continue studying at the university. We were happy in Spain. However, our parents and siblings had gone to live in the United States and wanted us near them.

In 1974 we arrived at the New York airport. My brother had told me he would be waiting there, but when I didn't see him, I got extremely nervous and started perspiring profusely. A Spanish-speaking worker noticed my anxiety and asked, "Do you have a problem?" I needed to use the pay phone but did not have a dime to my name to make a phone call because I had not been able to exchange my Spanish currency for US dollars. The good-hearted man gave it to me.

My brother soon arrived and informed me that he had sent my resume to several companies. Wellman Lord, an engineering firm in

Lakeland, Florida was waiting for my call. I didn't speak English very well, but I called anyway. They asked me when I could come for an interview. "Tomorrow" I said. I worked there for ten years. Later, I worked with the Public Works Department in Hillsborough County for twenty-three years. I was the Director of Solid Waste, County Engineer, and Storm Water Manager.

In 1977, Tapia Construction, a family owned and operated company, opened its doors in Lakeland. Since then we have built more than five hundred luxury homes to client specifications. On more than eight occasions we have had the honor of receiving the "Home of the Year Award" for our style, beauty and originality. I believe that I was successful because I always had the vocation of an engineer, and now I am actually getting paid to do something I love. Besides, every time I look back, I realize that the experiences I had during my last four years in Cuba make everything else now seem so easy!

I am very grateful to be able to live in the United States, a country where hard work and honesty continue to be the basis of personal and social progress. This is why all of us immigrants have the responsibility to give back a part of what has been given to us.

As for me, I have the honor to be a Chancellor for the Knights of Columbus and the President of the Hispanic Club of Lakeland, whose main objectives are to raise funds to help needy families, to offer scholarships to deserving students, and to propagate Hispanic culture. The Hispanic Club of Lakeland has given twenty-three scholarships in the last ten years.

I always tell immigrants that this is a great nation, full of opportunities. We all arrive without anything other than the desire to prosper and work hard. At first it might seem difficult, but if they work hard, they will find SUCCESS IN EXILE.

Mario Pendas, Solange, Danita & Dania Frías de Pendas

Memoirs of an Ice Cream Lady

Dania Frías de Pendas

The future of a child is always the master piece of the mother.
NAPOLEÓN

"A chocolate ice cream, please."

"And for me, vanilla and a strawberry fruit bar for my sister."

Children would always run to me with a smile when they heard the typical music coming from my cart. Some of them spoke to me in Spanish, but the majority spoke English. I immediately learned all the necessary vocabulary to communicate with them without any problem at all.

The Cubans who arrived in this country at the beginning of the Revolution never looked back. We forgot about our comfortable past and accepted any job we considered honorable enough to earn an honest living. I bought an ice cream cart and went out to sell ice cream in the streets of Tampa, satisfying the wishes of hundreds of children and ensuring the future and education of my own.

Day after day, I drove the same route, smiling for my clients and remembering my own childhood in Havana, a time during which I never thought I would ever work outside my home. I had always planned to stay home to raise my children and be there for them at all times. I was a pampered child, the youngest of nine brothers and sisters. When I was still a high school student, some of my brothers were already successful professionals and business owners. Little by little they opened their restaurant/cafeterias in Havana until they had eleven "Mi Buchito Oriental." I used to love to go eat their famous fried rice, smell the spices coming from the kitchen, and the aroma of brewing coffee and to enjoy the cordial and friendly environment of loyal clients, who would come to savor the Cuban coffee and share the daily events with their friends. Those were prosperous and happy days; our future seemed so secure.

Unfortunately, the only constant thing in life is change, and Fidel Castro's government made sure to change our lives radically. At the beginning of the 60's he started confiscating all of the restaurants. One by one the government took all of our properties and took control of our destiny. If we wanted to work, we could, as long as we worked for Fidel for a miserable salary. We were now a communist country. We were all equally poor; we were all at the mercy of a diabolical genius that controlled and continues controlling the masses.

"We have to go to the United States," I would repeat daily. I remember the family meetings in which we planned means of escape from that nightmare. Mario and I had recently married and were not ready to be apart. Mario did not have anyone to claim him immediately. The plan was that my brothers would leave first and then claim us. Some of my brothers were able to leave legally. Felipe, Rafael and Fernando were not able to leave then. Being young, brave and full of pride, they dared to try escape in a boat. They were caught and sent to political prison.

The entire island of Cuba became a jail. It was not possible to leave the country freely. The simple fact of appearing to have ideas opposed to the Communists was reason enough to be sentenced to prison or even to be executed. The Communists started to open prisons everywhere; they needed to control the opposition.

My brothers went to La Cabaña, a place where the political prisoners lived in horrible conditions. It was the ruins of an ancient fortress that had been built by the Spaniards during colonial times. It didn't even have running water. Once a month, the government would allow us to take our relatives a bag with certain items that were approved by the regime such as powdered milk, guava paste and banana chips. The prisoners were suffering from constipation due to the bad nutrition they received. One of my sisters who lived in the United States sent a laxative (Ex-lax) in the form of chocolate. Since this was not on the approved list, my other two brothers and I decided to unstitch the hem of the food bag, put the Ex-Lax tablets inside the hem, and sew it back up. The day we took the bag, the guards decided to do a meticulous inspection and unfortunately they discovered our plan. I sincerely hope they ate the "chocolate!"

They took away the bags that we had filled and punished my three brothers as if they had been guilty of our actions. Immediately, I identified myself as being responsible for hiding the tablets and told them that my brothers Ciro and Ramón, who were with me, had no idea of what I had done. They were waiting for their permission to leave to the United States; any accusation could cost them their permission to leave Cuba. For my "crime," I spent twelve hours detained in a cellar, totally isolated, not knowing what was going happen to me, thinking about when I would see my family again, and if it was going to affect my husband's work and many other disturbing thoughts. Thanks to the Lord, Mario, who at that time had a good job building the CUJAE (Jose Antonio Echeverria University City) had connections in the government and begged for our daughter's sake. The guards let me go home. From then on, I was marked and had to watch my every step.

After innumerable psychological and physical tortures in the Cabaña, my brothers were separated. Felipe was sent to one of the concentration camps in Mijial, Oriente. Rafael went to Puerto Boniato for refusing to work and for not wearing the blue common prisoner's uniform. These prisoners were known as "The planted ones" (Los plantados). Fernando went to Tacotaco in Pinar del Rio, where we could visit him once a month. It was not easy to go see him due to the lack of transportation to the prison. We also carried food bags on foot uncertain if the guards would let us bring in the few items that we were able to get with much difficulty. We were not allowed to bring cooked food into the prison. The food they were served was atrocious, and my brother was suffering from malnutrition.

I was pregnant with my daughter Solange when we had the opportunity to buy beef on the black market (beef wasn't and still isn't available with the ration book). If caught, it could cost the buyer and the seller up to 30 years in jail. Since I was wearing maternity clothes, I took the risk and did something quite daring. During one of our visits, I took three cooked and cut steaks hidden inside my brassiere. I would watch the guards. and when they were not looking, I would take a piece of steak and feed it to my brother. He would not chew when the guards were looking. If he was caught, his visits would be automatically cancelled, and I would go straight to jail. When I think about it now, I realize we will do anything for our loved ones, without taking into consideration the consequences. If we had been discovered, Solange would have been born in prison.

After two years, my brothers were set free and were able to leave the country. Eventually, we were also able to leave sponsored by them. We went to Spain with just the clothes we had on and a change of clothes for our daughters Danita and Solange. I remember it was snowing when we arrived, and we felt cold and alone. Where were we going to go now? Where were we going to get the next meal for the girls? We had nothing nor did we know anyone in Spain. We were totally at the mercy of our Lord!

"Mayito!... Mayito!"

I thought I heard someone calling my husband when we were at the airport in Madrid.

"Mayito, someone is calling your name!"

"You are hallucinating, who could be calling me here?"

We did not know a soul in Spain and only his friends and family called him Mayito; everyone else knew him as Mario. It was evident that I was hallucinating, like a thirsty soul in the dessert, when he sees an oasis.

"Mayito!...Mayito!" This time the voice was louder, clearer.

"Yes, Mayito, I hear a voice calling your name, listen, I am not crazy!"

"Mayito, it's me! Your cousin Marta, praise the Lord, I have been able to find you. Welcome to Spain!"

It seemed like an appearance of the Virgin Mary herself! Marta was in Spain and we did not know it. She had read the names of the Cubans that were arriving in the newspaper, among them, ours. It was a true miracle of God, something for which, I will be eternally grateful. The next day, she bought coats and clothes for the girls and helped us get settled.

A few weeks later, on December 31, 1970, we were at the Barajas airport in Madrid getting ready to go to Costa Rica sponsored by our friends Pancho and Dulce. When we heard the loud speakers announce, "It's 12:00 midnight, Happy New Year!" We embraced as a family and thanked God for being together and safe. It was a hug of freedom, fraternity and love.

Pancho and Dulce were influential people, and consequently, Mayito was able to get a job in an engineering firm, and, miraculously, they also were able to help us become Costa Rican residents in only 46 days. We were soon able to travel to the United States with tourist visas. Once at the Miami Airport, through the glass windows, I saw my whole family: my mother, brothers, nieces and nephews and other family members, welcoming us. Finding myself once again in my mother's arms was the most emotional moment of my life.

That is how we eventually arrived in Tampa, and I found my job as an ice cream lady. My husband's salary was not enough to pay for the education that I wanted for my girls. I had studied in La Inmaculada, a Catholic school in Havana, and I wanted them to attend a catholic school as well. I was willing to work day and night to make it happen. "Why are they going to accept the daughters of an ice cream lady when they have a waiting list for the children of doctors and professionals?" I would often hear, but I would not give up and would not tire of going to the school to try to enroll them. For two weeks I sat on the floor in front of the rectory of the Saint Lawrence School until I accomplished my goal. After they graduated from Tampa Catholic High School, they went to college while we devoted ourselves to the jewelry business. This business allowed us to achieve a good financial status, and be at home for our children. We were also able to invest in apartments and houses. We are able to live off their rents today.

Danita, our oldest daughter, graduated with a master degree in Electrical Engineering at twenty years of age. She worked for General Electric for many years until the birth of her first child. Today she enjoys a successful career as a real estate agent, selling over twenty five million dollars worth of properties in Central Florida during 2008, in spite of a declining economy.

Today Dr. Solange Pendas is a surgical oncologist and the Director of the Breast Cancer Department at Lakeland Regional Cancer Center. Her work has been recognized by the National Accreditation of Breast Cancer Center Programs. She has studied and worked under the masters of her field and published numerous research papers in her relentless pursue for the cure.

All of my brothers have achieved the American Dream in Miami where they have become successful in exile. I have been able to make a living from my home, ensuring the education I always wanted for my children. I enjoy their successes, and I am the proud grandmother of five wonderful grandchildren for whom, from time to time, I buy an ice cream when the ice cream lady comes by.

Yara Borges Guzmán, two months before being imprisioned

The Interrupted Youth of Yara Borges Guzmán

1938 - 2008

Dr. Norma de la Torre

There is not anything on earth, as far as I know,
that compares to the happiness of regaining our lost freedom.
MIGUEL DE CERVANTES SAAVEDRA

Abruptly, in the middle of a lecture by one of the professors of the School of Medicine in the distinguished University of Havana, the double doors of the classroom flew open. This was most extraordinary; something unheard of since, once the doors of any classroom in the university were closed for a lecture or class, those doors remained closed for the entire period unless a very serious emergency occurred. That very seldom happened; therefore, all the students, as well as the professor, were in shock. No one dared to say a word. Boisterously, the feared Militia of the Revolutionary Government stormed into the place. Without excuses of any kind, without preambles, and without addressing anyone in particular, one of the guards asked, "Who is Yara Borges Guzmán?" Yara stood up and said, "I am." Immediately two guards placed themselves on each side of her, grabbed her by the arms and took her outside. All of this happened without ever acknowledging the professor in charge.

Yara was taken from there to the Central Police Station where she was thrown into one of the holding cells. No one advised her parents of the situation nor the events that took place at the university. Some of Yara's classmates and friends, in spite of the risk they were taking for doing so, had the integrity to inform her parents of what had happened. Yara's parents immediately went to the police station in question; but they were not allowed to see her, nor were they informed of the reasons for her detention.

A few days later, Yara and other people arrested in different raids of the militia, were taken in front of a revolutionary tribunal to be tried for the serious crime of counter- revolution, which was a type of generic charge, brought against anyone that disagreed with the postulates of Fidel Castro's Revolution. Without witnesses for the prosecution, and without defense attorneys (Who dared?), the Tribunal proceeded to try them.

When it was Yara's turn to be tried, the prosecutor addressed her icily, accusing her in a bullish manner of distributing "subversive propaganda" against the Revolution at a well-known entertainment park in Havana called Conney Island. When asked what she had to say about the charges, Yara responded,

"I was not distributing any counter-revolution propaganda in that park or anywhere else, for that matter."

"Then what were you doing there?"

"I was playing with the mini-cars."

Exasperated and almost out of control, the prosecutor said to the judge, "I have no other questions for this woman."

Without hesitation or any more interaction, the judge produced a loud thump with the gavel, saying in a stormy manner, "Sentenced to ten years in prison!"

And this was how Yara Borges Guzmán was condemned on March 21 of 1961 under Cause No.102/61 to ten years of horrific physical and mental torture, . She was then 22 years old with a brilliant mind and a promising future, but nothing promising could coexist with the cruel and tyrannical regime of Fidel Castro.

Yara was born in Havana on November 4, of 1938. She completed her first nine years of education in the School of the Sacred Heart, a Catholic school, where she received a Christian foundation that accompanied her throughout her entire life. That, probably, prepared Yara for what fate had in store for her.

After completing the eighth grade and passing the entrance test, she was admitted into the prestigious Baldor Institute, where she graduated with a Bachelor of Science degree. Soon after, she started her studies in the School of Medicine at the University of Havana to fulfill her dream of becoming a medical doctor. Yara was in the middle of the third year of her studies when it was perversely cut short by the Revolution.

Yara was outstanding in her studies and excelled in sports. She won several swimming championships in both the Havana and Marianao Yatch Clubs. She also loved to write. Many of her articles were published in different well-known magazines in Havana, among them the renowned "Revista Carteles."

Now in political prison, Yara was assigned to Cell Block "D," the most feared of all cell blocks, where the women who refused to go to "rehabilitation" were assigned. This so-called "re-habilitation" consisted in declaring publicly that "one was wrong," that the Revolution was the "salvation of all the Cuban people." Those who did not accept the "rehabilitation" were considered rebels and given the nickname "las plantadas" which could be loosely translated as "the planted ones." This was a belittling term to imply than those "planted ones" would not move forward, as they were still living in "the old infamous regime that the Revolution had conquered."

During the ten years that Yara endured in jail, she was transferred several times from one prison to another. Each new prison was worse than the one before. As always, she and the other women that were transferred with her were assigned to Cell Block "D." Every prison in every town had a Cell Block "D." It had the worst conditions imaginable: fewer family visits, putrid food, and less outdoor time.

These cells were small and narrow, and there was no room for walking. In spite of this, four women were assigned to each cell.

On Cell Block "D," beatings occurred frequently. One of the most infamous of these attacks occurred on Mother's Day of 1961 when the prison commander suddenly decided to search everyone, thus shortening the family visits of the women in the Cell Block "D" to just a few minutes on such a special day.

Mothers, daughters and sons had been standing in long lines outside the building since before dawn so they could see their daughters or mothers in prison. When the prisoners found out what was going on, they started to protest with a "Golpe de Lata", which consisted of beating the cell bars with any piece of metal they had: plates, empty cans or metal utensils. The noise was unbearable; the guards could not stop it and called the firemen that were standing by in anticipation of such a problem. The firemen came and doused the prisoners with water under high pressure. They concentrated the water attacks on the most sensitive parts of the women's bodies, especially to their breast. One of the women was obviously pregnant, and a fireman intentionally directed the water pressure at her stomach to cause her to abort. A group of prisoners, among them Yara, noticed his plan and got in front of her, saving her and the baby. Some of these women were seriously hurt as they fell on the rough concrete floor.

That day many of the prisoners ended up in the infirmary with all kinds of injuries, bruises and fractures. Yara suffered severe bruises to her right breast. Many years later, a cancerous tumor was found in that breast. In spite of undergoing a lumpectomy, it metastasized to her bones and it finally claimed her life.

That regrettable Mother's Day will forever be an embarrassing stigma on the history of Cuba, but not so for the authorities who participated in that humiliating event because they do not possess any human sentiment, scruples or dignity. How sad it is to think that this horror was perpetuated by Cubans.

On March 10 of 1971, when Yara's prison term was finally completed, she was not released as she expected. Instead, she was taken to the prison office where she was informed that, in order to be freed, she needed to "rehabilitate," the same order she had received at the beginning of her prison term. Yara was told that she needed to say publicly that she was wrong and the Revolution was right and

Yara Borges Guzmán † (1938 - 2008)

that it was good for the people. Otherwise, she would be transferred to a common jail. Women prisoners were assigned to a common jail for heinous crimes. In spite of this threat, Yara categorically refused this "rehabilitation." For the many days that followed, the authorities continued to harass her. They told her of the horror she would encounter at the mercy of the common women prisoners: beatings, sexual violations and even death. She stood firm in her convictions and did not give in. Finally, sixteen days later, on March 26, of 1971, the authorities allowed her to leave the prison but not to leave the country.

Yara's parents were already in the USA in contact with congressmen in Washington, D.C. to negotiate her departure from Cuba. This probably contributed to her release from prison. Yara always considered those last 16 days in prison the worst time in her life.

A year later in 1972 with the help of some relatives that lived in Spain, the Cuban authorities allowed Yara to leave Cuba and fly to Madrid. She stayed in Madrid with those relatives for a year and finally arrived in Miami in 1973.

When Yara left prison, she was 32 years old, having wasted probably the best years of her youth in the hellish cells of Cell Block "D." But instead of complaining or feeling sorry for herself, she decided that it was about time to recoup the lost time.

As soon as she arrived in the USA, she started to work. She kept books for small Cuban businesses. At the same time, she began to study. She graduated with a Master of Science degree from Mercy College. As a self made entrepreneur, Yara encountered much success. She bought a pharmacy and kept it for five years. She founded two large corporations that she ran for over 30 years: CABRINI CORPORATION, which distributed all types of pharmaceutical products, and LEMAX PHARMACEUTICAL, a company that produced and marketed many medications such as Chenocol, Hematonic, Reflex and Pellet-C. These products were approved by the FDA and Yara held the patents.

In 1978 Yara wrote two educational stories for children. She published them in a collectable card format with their albums and posters. The first one, "The Ruler," was based on the story of the legendary lost continent of Atlantis. The second one, Kalkulkin, for pre-school children, is the story of a talking miniature horse.

Near the end of 1992 when she saw the terrible destruction that hurricane Andrew caused, Yara founded B-SAFE, INC., a company dedicated to the production of different types of storm protection devices, by special orders. These panels were constructed surpassing construction code demands that were instituted after Andrew.

In 1994 she founded Unicorn Enterprises to make specialty stained glass for doors and windows in churches, temples, as well as luxury yachts and residences.

EXCLUSIVE was another successful company Yara founded. This company created trophies, plaques and awards of all kinds for educational institutions, sport teams and associations, and other businesses.

For Yara Borges Guzman, there was no impossible project, no unsolvable problem. Every problem was a challenge that she confronted with passion until she was able to master it. Of a competitive nature and a determined temperament, she had the gift to know how to measure any situation, regardless how unexpected or difficult it was, and find the best and quickest solution. She was able to supervise and handle all the companies she founded, some of which are still in operation. It is quite sad to think that so much talent was wasted for so many years in the filthy jails of the Castro regime.

The Communist government of Fidel Castro stole from Yara her country, ten years and sixteen days of enjoying the Cuban sky, which was as brightly blue as her eyes and ten years and sixteen days of watching the majestic royal palms, as straight and tall as her ideals. But the tyrant was never able to break Yara's spirit, to damage her intellect, or to destroy her dreams.

Perhaps the following poem that Yara wrote in 1971, shortly after being released from prison, explains the philosophy, the sensitivity and the purity of feelings of this extraordinary human being.

Yara Borges Guzmán

I am just a new- born to half of my existence
With my soul naked to pain and happiness
I want to enjoy a new morning as much as
to place a smile in every tear I see.
I want to exude love from each pore in my body
and to be born again without barriers or prejudices
I want to open my arms to Life
and, rather than belonging to her, make her mine.
I want my feet to transform themselves in wings,
to go over all of the roads I have walked
contemplating in every sunset a sunrise
and starting each day a new road at dawn
so, when I arrived to my place of resting
have my hands full of all that I lived.

—

"The soul exists. It is the spiritual heart of our bodies. At the same time, it is the brain, pure, innocent and wise, that allows that each of our senses listen, see, touch, feel, and perceive the most delicate and beautiful creations of this marvelous planet that God has given us. Each piece of art not only represents the plastic facility of the artist, but it is also, at the same time, a sample of his eternal soul, which makes itself concrete in a piece of canvas, in a pen, in a musical instrument, in a piece of marble, or stone, or clay….and, also, in a smile, in a caress, in a kiss when these are given with love."

Pedro Ramiro Machín

Memories of a Political Prisoner

Pedro Ramiro Machín

Do not put me in the dark
to die like a traitor;
I am good, and like a good man
I will die facing the sun.
JOSÉ MARTÍ

CASTRO'S REVOLUTION

As a young guerrilla fighter, I was mentally prepared to give my life for Cuba to liberate the island from what we considered then "the tyranny" of Batista. Unfortunately, I never suspected that I was fighting for the benefit of the communists; that my patriotism and loyalty to the Revolution would cost me eighteen years as a political prisoner and my father's life.

It all started in the year 1952, a few months before the general elections, when Fulgencio Batista overthrew the government of Carlos Prio Socarrás, imposing a dictatorship that the country detested. The corruption and abuse of authority was obvious. Cuba longed for democracy and the freewill to elect its representatives.

The university students, young idealists, complained and openly rebelled; they asked for justice for the acts committed by the government. They became heroes for the youth, admired and supported by the country. During that time, I was a teenager and was studying at Havana Military Academy. I was in tune with everything that was happening in the country and was totally for the student movement. At the end of the school year, I went home to Ranchuelo and soon decided to gather a group of friends to join the young fighters in the mountains of Escambray, Central Cuba.

The first step would be to find the firearms. You can't go to war with just the wish to fight. Carefully, we began to visit those people we knew that had firearms, especially the farmers. To avoid looking suspicious, we would go in the dark of night. We would arrive and say, "We are here in the name of the Revolution. We need your arms, whatever you have to help us fight."

Some farmers were afraid of us, but once we explained our mission, they would relax and many of them would even join us. The farmers became our greatest allies. They helped with food, shelter, pistols, revolvers, machetes, and with anything they had.

Once we gathered the necessary armaments, we trekked through the mountains to join the fight. We walked carefully during the entire night without stopping, following our guide. This was especially difficult for me; just a few weeks before, I had undergone an appendectomy, and the long walk was causing me great pain. Each step was like a dagger in my wound. The time came when I could not move my right leg, and I could only keep moving with my friend's help.

Finally, a farmer who lived near the mountains permitted us to rest in his tool shed. That earthen floor seemed like the best mattress in the world! The following morning, after devouring a nutritious breakfast, we started out again. Our patriotism and faith in our mission were more powerful than any pain or fear.

Our destiny was the "Hoyo de Macagual," where the Rebel Camp was situated. To get there, we had to go down the mountains that surrounded the camp. In the middle of the forest, there was no sunlight penetrating the vegetation. The heat and humidity were suffocating. Finally after arriving, we were welcomed by our comrades. There, we experienced innumerable struggles and the inclemency of nature.

Sometimes the enemy was alerted by infiltrators of our operation zone. I remember one morning, we were walking in a line as always; we heard the voice of our guide say, "Plane, plane!" And suddenly, we seemed to be in hell. We threw ourselves on the side of the road to hide in the grass, staying very still. The planes were coming at us, roaring. The machine guns blasted; bombs exploded making the earth move as in an earthquake. My ears were about to explode. Fortunately, we were so high up in the mountains that the clouds became our allies. The planes lacked the needed visibility to find our exact location. It was just a matter of meters, but that space was enough to save our lives.

Gathering our wits and trembling, we ventured forth to observe the damage. A high intensity hurricane could not have caused such destruction…hundred-year-old trees were destroyed, some dead animals, decapitated. It was the typical, cruel war scene.

Until the end of 1959 when Batista left, our days were filled with battles, seeking overnight shelter and trying to finally free Cuba from the claws of tyranny. (If we had only known!) After several incidents, in one of the greatest battles in Las Villas in the center of Cuba, the government of Batista was overthrown.

Triumphantly, we went to the city of Cienfuegos. After everything was under control, and we were intoxicated by victory, we marched to Havana. What joy! - The whole country was out in the streets to support the bearded heroes. They gathered on the sidewalks to see us pass by. The sides of Central Highway were covered with people wanting to greet that handful of men that had been able to overtake a heavily armed government.

THE DISAPPOINTMENT

At first, arriving at the capital, everyone breathed triumph; however, soon the "Chief of our Revolution," disguising his true intensions, began to take power without anyone daring to oppose him. Fidel was not the liberator the country was hoping for. He imposed his absolute power. He influenced the frenetic masses against anyone who would dare to express an opinion opposing his communist plans. He would simply eliminate them! Uturria, for example, was named the first President of the Revolution. When he opposed Fidel's diabolical plans, Fidel ensured that the masses would turn against him, and Uturria had no other option but to go into exile.

During Castro's first speech he ordered us to disarm. He said, "Firearms…what for?" Those who had fought in the mountains, who had truly sacrificed for the supposed liberty of our island, now had to turn in their firearms to the new government and go home. This created discontent and disgust. Luckily for me, by this time I was an officer and was able to keep my gun.

Many officers were sent to Cabaña Fort in Havana under the command of Che Guevara. An army needed to be organized. During a meeting, I mentioned to Che the need to organize the troops, and I offered my military knowledge. Very despotically he responded, "Mind your own business!" and he looked at the rest of the officers with disgust and a threatening expression. I had touched a taboo subject.

Without rest, the communists had begun to decide the chain of command. They were structuring the gears that would move forward and consolidate the Revolution. We began to realize that that was not what we had fought for. We were frustrated. Some of the commanders left the country; others began to conspire against Fidel.

Since the beginning, the government instilled great fear by means of the Paredón (firing wall.) Anyone who opposed the government was executed or put in prison with long-term sentences. The Cabaña was disintegrated, and I was sent to a military post in Varadero. The communists sent their political indoctrinators to this place. I decided it was a good idea to go to a military advancement school to be able to have more control. I wrote a letter to Commander Camilo Cienfuegos explaining what was happening. I asked to be sent to advance training to learn to stop the communist penetration in our troops. How naive! As a reward, I was sent to a school for illiterates and was stripped of my rank.

Soon I found myself taking the necessary steps to fight against the same Revolution for which I had sacrificed so much. A group of old friends and I started conspiring against the government, but in our group was an informant who "squealed" about our operations. One way or another, we were all taken prisoners; some were sent to death row and others received long sentences. I got thirty years in prison.

ISLA DE PINOS

At the beginning of 1961, many of us were sent to the prison at Isla de Pinos. When we landed, there were groups of soldiers armed to the teeth; but, to our amazement, we realized that they were not Cubans. At that time, the Russians were already in Cuba. After humiliating interrogations including verbal and physical mistreatments, we arrived at the Circulars of the Model Prison, which looked like tanks of a petroleum refinery. There were four circular buildings; I was sent to number four. As we entered, there were hundreds of screaming prisoners welcoming us…it looked like the Roman Coliseum. There I found some of the friends with whom I had fought in the mountains.

As time passed, we had no choice but to get used to our circumstances. Every two or three days we were given a bucket of water to drink and to bathe with. We were allowed one visit every six months. I remember the morning of April 17. We awoke to the intense sound of machine guns shooting everywhere. It was a plane from the Bay of Pigs Invasion that was shooting at a boat in the Nueva Gerona River. Our hearts were palpitating full of hopes of being rescued, but the mission failed. Day by day we witnessed truck loads of wooden boxes being hauled into the circulars, followed by the piercing noise of obvious drilling into the foundation. In case of a US invasion, the government was placing over 28,000 tons of dynamite under the foundation of the circulars. The attitude of the guards against the inmates was atrociouis, "If the Yankees come, we will blow this shit with all of you inside," we were informed. We were practically sleeping on a mattress of explosives.

Frequently, a group of guards would come to beat us, humiliate us, and to move us from one circular to another to avoid any structured plans by the prisoners. Of all these so called inspections, there was one that stood out as the cruelest and most barbaric. We called it "The Pacific." On this particular day we were ordered to undress and as they pushed and beat us, we were gathered against a wall on the first floor. We had to place our hands on our private parts to avoid direct contact with the person in front. Those who dared to protest were beaten and taken out and ordered to lie on the ground face down with their arms extended as in a cross and with their mouths in puddles of dirty water.

At that time we had calculated that there were around 1,200 prisoners in a circular that had been built for no more than 500 people. The abuse and atrocities were horrendous. Each day the enemy tried to crush us, humiliate and destroy us physically and morally. One way or another we tried to maintain the morale and our fighting spirit. Among the political prisoners there were many professionals who shared their knowledge by means of conferences, lectures, demonstrations and the like. We all shared whatever we knew. Our goal was to get out of that inferno better than we went in and with something that couldn't be taken from us: an education.

In 1964 a forced labor plan was implemented. We prisoners were sent to break stones at the quarries. The hard labor camp was a living hell. It was a savage plan. The prisoners resisted. We opted for what we called the "turtle step," doing everything as slow as we possibly could and only working when it was forced. The beatings, bayonets and gun shots were very common. On many occasions the guards would get furious, lose control and would savagely stab a defenseless prisoner. We had deaths, mutilations, leg and arm amputations, but we would not give up.

The time came when the work boots wore out. Those of us who did not have a pair of boots to go to work stayed behind in the circulars along with the sick inmates. One day a heavily armed group of guards ordered us to form a line and walk. We had a column of soldiers on each side of us. We walked barefooted on the rocky road, our feet bleeding. We were ordered to jump over barbed wire fence as best we could. Our backs constantly were battered by the bayonets until we arrived at a trench. The soldiers pushed us until we fell in; then they ordered us to clean it. There floated the feces of the entire penal population as well as that of the guard and their families who lived nearby. In this trench drained the waste of thousands of people, and flies were everywhere. Once in a while the bottom was deeper than we expected and we would fall in the rot.

We advanced through that crust of feces until we arrived at the "Pigsty." Now the waste of hundreds of pigs was added to the human filth! It was intolerable. One of our friends, who was malnourished and who had received a horrendous beating the previous day, fainted and fell into that cesspool. The guards threatened to shoot anyone who helped him; but, totally ignoring them, those of us who were near him were able to get him out before he drowned.

After the guards ordered us out of the trench, they took us to the beach. A truck full of food and fresh water arrived, something that we rarely ever got. They were trying to humiliate us even more offering something good to eat when we were sickened and covered in feces. It was obvious that we would not be able to enjoy the food. Even if we were hungry, we also had dignity, so we refused to eat. Later that afternoon we were taken back to the prison.

We entered the circular, battered, wounded, exhausted and walking with difficulty. Our friends had already heard what had taken place that day and received us singing the Cuban National Anthem. That revived us. The guards, frustrated, beat us again while the prisoners were yelling, "Murderers, sons of bitches, bastards" and any other insults they could think of. Finally the doors leading to the showers opened, and we were able to wash the pestilence off our bodies. The infections we suffered in the days that followed required intensive medical care.

The atrocities committed against the political prisoners caused a lot of pressure on the government. In May 1966 a group of soldiers arrived at the circulars carrying lists of prisoners that were to be transferred. They transported us by boat to Batabano, a port on the southside of Havana and later to the Cabaña Fort, an old Spanish Fortress from the colonial period. Along with us in gallery number 7 were death row prisoners and a group of young men who had gone insane and periodically received electroshock treatments. There was no hygiene in the cells and very little water, not even to drink.

Pedro Ramiro Machín, 19 years old

LA CABAÑA FORTRESS

To make our stay even more unforgettable, we had a bed bug infestation. We spent the evenings trying to kill thousands and thousands of maddening insects that would suck our blood like vampires. It was mission impossible! We would finally go to sleep from exhaustion. The next day we would wake up in a terrible state and were forced to run around the patio. Of course, we resisted; we would not run. As a consequence, we received plenty of beatings. Normally the only nourishment of the day was sugar water for breakfast, extremely hot cornmeal for lunch, and broth and bread for dinner; everything was extremely rationed, and we were given a few minutes to eat. When the guard gave the order to get up from the table, whoever would not do so immediately would feel the bayonets hitting him on the back. "Son of bitches, I will beat you to death if you don't obey me! I said...to get up! When I say get up, I mean get up! Stop eating!"

Although we were political prisoners and had lost our human rights, we tried to maintain our dignity. We were insulted to the point that someone would lose control and attack a guard. On many occasions there were big confrontations and fights between prisoners and guards for which we were punished with months of not being able to talk with our loved ones. To avoid our making connections with other prisoners, they would move us from one prison to another. It was like being in a centrifuge. Some prisoners arrived from Isla de Pinos while others were sent to the other 200 Cuban prisons, some of which were more like concentration camps. Before 1959, Cuba only had 14 prisons, and only one was high security.

The soldiers practiced techniques learned from the Soviet Union, creating new forms of physical and mental torture. During the first months of 1967, it was announced that the Isla de Pinos prison would be dismantled and no longer used as a prison. It was also decided that the political prisoners would be transferred to rehabilitation camps which were nothing more than concentration camps.

There were new orders, among them a uniform change. The government wanted to change the yellow khaki uniform, which we had used since the beginning of our political imprisonment, to the blue uniform used by the common prisoners. The political prisoners adamantly refused as we realized they were trying to eliminate our distinctiveness. If we all dressed in blue and were mixed in with the common prisoners, no one would be able to differentiate between political and common prisoners. Since they suspected we might refuse, they brought personnel trained in the martial arts from state security. They used their techniques to force the prisoners to change uniforms. In some prisons, they would tie the prisoners so that they could not take off the new uniforms. This process took several days and resulted in broken arms, legs, fractured skulls, and severe beatings. Some prisoners decided to accept the uniforms and others decided to stay in their underwear, creating a new status. To put pressure on us, some of the naked prisoners were transferred to common prisons.

Some prisoners were able to keep a t-shirt, and others perhaps a towel, but nudity was the common denominator. The officers would offer to transfer us to camps near our homes, to lower our sentence, allow more frequent visits, give periodical passes to our homes, anything in exchange for wearing the common prisoner's uniform. Their objective was to show the world that in Cuba there were no more political prisoners, that they just had delinquents and murderers.

During the first month, many accepted the blue uniform and were transferred. Those of us left, although in our undergarments, enjoyed more space and a larger piece of floor to sleep. By the time the cold north wind arrived, some of us had been able to gather newspapers and some potato sacks to cover ourselves in order to tolerate the cold. It is amazing how much a piece of paper can protect you from the cold.

At the beginning of 1968, we were transferred to a jail in the province of Santa Clara. There were children of eight, nine, and twelve years of age…all ages! The horrific aspect of this situation was that in the same area, among those children, were also experienced delinquents. Those kids were "prison meat," and the victims of all types of aberrations.

We were put in a cage once again and taken to Remedios in Central Cuba. Upon arrival the guards had a small cell ready with beds. We were still only wearing underwear. When we were taken out to do our physiological needs, the common prisoners were not allowed to come near us. Nevertheless, due to the respect that the common inmates felt for us for being political prisoners, somehow they would find ways to give us a few things: sugar, soap, and other luxuries. Some of them even offered for their families to take messages to ours. When our families were finally able to visit us, the guards would try to convince them to talk to us about the advantages of wearing the blue uniform. We were even offered our freedom. Of course the government would not comply with their promises, but some of the political prisoners would accept hoping that could change their families' situations.

Many of the prisoners went on hunger strikes. It was an intolerable situation. Some of the inmates were willing to attack us in exchange for favors offered by the guards; and, as a consequence, there were fights between the prisoners and the guards.

As a result of one of these uproars, we were transferred to the maximum security prison in Manacas, Las Villas, a concentration camp known as "Las Tapiadas de Manacas." Las Tapiadas were large concrete warehouses with windows that blocked the light and air. In these warehouses were lines of concrete cells measuring approximately five by seven feet, built independently from the outer building. Each cell had a window without a view through which the air could not penetrate. The steel doors were narrow with two

Pedro Ramiro Machín & friends

openings, one to pass the meals through and another to inspect what was going on inside. The surroundings were suffocating, humid and unhealthy for our lungs. In one of the corners there was a hole for our bodily needs. Water came in three times a day for only one minute. This was for drinking and all other needs. Although the feces and urine were supposedly cleaned, the smell was part of the environment.

After three months we were taken out of our cells. There were barbers waiting for us. They shaved us and cut our hair. It was a very painful shave. Later we were taken to some showers in the front of the building and given some soap for us to finally bathe. We were very thin, malnourished. The next day, we were transferred back the Cabaña. Our friends were happy to see us and were horrified to find out everything we had gone through. Even though we continued to wear our underwear, the galleries had been refurbished and had beds.

Things had changed for the better; there was more enthusiasm. We were able to get back some of the books that had been taken away. We could read and had group discussions about the books. After a few days, the patio was once again inundated with officers from the Ministry of the Interior. We were taken to one side of the patio, and one of the officers began to speak about the righteousness and generosity of the Revolution. After speaking for a while, he finally said that they had agreed to give us back our khaki color uniform. Now the galleries were opened for a few hours, and we had the opportunity to visit with each other and talk to friends with whom we had not been able to communicate for years. We also had a bath schedule.

Apparently there were no more violent confrontations, and that was worrisome. We were constantly transferred. The government was using more refined methods to divide the political prisoners. They were using the "divide and conquer" tactics.

Many prisoners went on hunger strikes. Some groups of prisoners were transferred to prisons near their families trying to use their families to put pressure on them. Other groups, however, were taken far away from their families and suffered horrible torture. Many of them were put in drawers were they had to stay in the same position for long periods of time. The guards were using cruel torture methods that had been used against the prisoners in Vietnam.

Our group was destined to go to the high security prison in Manacas. We were all from the province of Las villas, so we went near our families. We were put in the same galley. We were allowed to have frequent visits. All of these improvements happened in the year 1969.

December arrived. During the holidays, our families somehow were able to bring us food, so that we could at least have Christmas dinner. We all knew they were doing without so that we could have a good meal. The Cuban government had forbidden the celebration of Christmas, but the country always remembered it with sadness because it was part of our being. During this Christmas visit, the guards were more flexible and allowed for us to have visitors we had not seen for years. It was so good to be able to embrace my parents, my sister and brother, to once again feel the warm touch of the family. Saying goodbye was just as hard, since we did not know when we would see each other again, if ever.

THE EXCRUSIATING PAIN

My father was always in my thoughts. He was always admired by the community, and I loved him very much. Toward the end of the month of March, a friend, who had accepted the outside work plan, asked one of our friends to go get me. When I was near him he said, "I came to warn you, so you can prepare yourself. Your father has been taken prisoner. They are giving him the death sentence." He left very quickly as he was taking a big risk for telling me. It could have been very costly for him.

I spent two or three days full of uncertainty, swallowing my worries and my anguish. During the night, everything floated through my mind. On the evening of the first of April, I threw myself on the rickety old bed. I could not conceive it; I could not accept it. There was no justification for this to happen. There was a whirlwind in my head. Why my father? My mother needed him, so did my brothers; he was a good and loved man who would not harm anyone. Finally, around 2:00 a.m., after many nightmares, I felt a strange peace as if I were being transported to another world. I woke up to the loud sound of my name, "Machin, get ready. You are being transferred."

The next day I was escorted to the provincial jail. The guards did not allow anyone to come near me. Up to that moment no one had said anything to me about what had happened. A political prisoner finally came to me and said, "Look, these things should not be kept from you; your father was executed last night."

The world came crushing down on me! The guards left me near the infirmary. I went in. Most of the inmates there were political prisoners. They told me whatever they knew. I threw myself on a bed not being able to hold back my tears. Even though I was raised under the false concept that men don't cry, I cried. I kept my face on the pillow, trying to hide my emotions. My tears were pouring out; I felt impotent and confused. My world was crushed. My father had been murdered. He was a sugarcane chemist. He was accused of throwing away juice with high levels of sugar. A hand full of sugar was the excuse they used to accuse him of sabotage against the Revolution. He was loved by his friends; people admired and listened to him. He was against communism, against what was happening to the political prisoners, something that the totalitarian dictatorship could not tolerate. He had to be silenced. Afterwards, the guards tried to put me in the galleys with the common prisoners with the excuse that there was no bed for me in the infirmary. They were looking for justification to eliminate me, trying to make it look like an accident, perhaps a prison uproar.

Thank God, Chichi and one of his friends who, due to all the tortures and mistreatments were declared insane, were in the infirmary. They periodically received electroshock treatments. Chichi had been taken prisoner at the same time I was, and he found out about what had happened to my father. He immediately gave me his bed. When he found out that they wanted to put me in with the common prisoners, he started screaming insanely. When he was informed that the problem was that there was no bed for me, he insisted he had already given me his bed and if they took me, "the jail was going to burn!" Everyone, inmates and guards, were afraid of Chichi and his friend, since both were crazy and dangerous. I was able to remain in the infirmary.

MY MARRIAGE

During the time I was in prison, I met Regla, who, along with her sister, had been in the women's prison for ten years as a political prisoner as well. From the time she was freed, she visited me in the different prisons. I proposed to her at the end of 1970 while I was in the Santa Clara prison. She accepted. Due to the circumstances, it was only a "symbolic marriage" since we were not able to be together for many years. She endured the test of time and never stopped visiting me.

It was not easy to obtain permission to get married. The guards thought we were planning an escape, and the security was heightened. On our wedding day, I was ordered to take off all of my clothes, and I was searched thoroughly. I even had to lift my genitalia for inspection; it was the condition they imposed before I was to enter the room where the hazardous wedding was to take effect. Regla was the only person allowed in the room. She signed the papers, and the ceremony was over. The witnesses had to sign outside the prison. Such was our wedding on November 6, 1970.

In December I was transferred to the maximum security camp in Manacas. I was finally allowed to have visits and was able to see family members whom I had not seen for many years. By that time, the communists had progressed in their goal of destroying the political prison. The Ministry of the Interior was putting together the "Progressive Plan" by which the political prisoners could obtain their freedom. The only condition was to work hard.

Some of the prisoners accepted the plan after being reassured of the outcome. After almost two decades of being confined in horrendous and inhumane communist's prisons in Cuba, we accepted with the hope of being free from the misery and the atrocities of the system. As a result of this plan, the "Six Front" was created and we formed construction teams. We were to build four-story school buildings.

The communists were planning to use the farming areas to build schools. This way they could use the students to work the fields. At the same time, the students would be separated from their families, and it would be easier to indoctrinate them with the Marxist-Leninist theories. Their main objective was to have control over the youth by brain washing them. These experimental "Progressive plans" for political prisoners took place all over the country. Of course, we had to learn everything related to construction.

Once we reached certain goals in the construction, sometimes we were given a pass to visit our families for forty-eight hours at the guard's discretion or depending on how long a person had been on the plan. Of course, the government prohibited our contact with the people on the outside because they believed we could influence their opinions.

In 1979 something happened to the full advantage of the Cuban government; Cuban exiles in the United States were allowed to travel to Cuba. This group was known by the name of "the community". The Cuban government permitted the members of the community to express their ideas and suggestions about the political prisoners.

As a result, Jimmy Carter's government and Cuba reached an agreement. Hundreds of political prisoners and their families were allowed to leave the island. That is how I became an exile in 1980 after being imprisoned for 18 years. God blessed me with the privilege of coming to a country full of opportunities where respect for human rights is the law. Every day when I wake up, I thank the Lord for my freedom, the greatest gift and blessing a person can ever enjoy.

Other prisoners, for one reason or another, remained captive on our island. They continue hoping that one day, a free, prosperous and democratic Cuba will come true... once a long time ago, this was also the dream of our national revolutionary hero, José Martí.

P.S. Pedro Ramiro Machín lives in West Palm Beach and is in the process of writing a book about his memories as a political prisoner.

Alex, Debbie, José Manuel & Anabel García.

My Memories of El Mariel

Dr. José Manuel García

A teacher affects eternity he can never tell,
where his influence stops.
HENRY B. ADAMS

In 1980 a busload of Cubans crashed the Peruvian Embassy gates in Havana. Thousands of people rushed to seek asylum and the infamous Mariel Boatlift began.

My father had been a prosperous member of Cuban society. At that time, he was vice-president of a governmental construction company at a national level; however, he did not belong to the Communist Party. Because of a baseless arrest during the Bays of Pigs invasion in the 1960's when he spent three months in jail, my father vowed to leave Cuba. It was not until 1980 when he finally found the opportunity.

I recall that day vividly when a knock on our door led to our departure to the Mariel Port. We had an hour to pack. I was 13, my sister was 11, and we were both scared. As we were about to board the bus, two policemen came by looking for a person whose name they had on a list to be interrogated; it was my father. As the police officers sped away with my father on their motorbikes, I thought I would never see him again. My mother was crying and trying to console us.

Thank God that did not happen. Two things saved my father; we had one of the nicest houses in my hometown in the province of Sancti Spiritus (the home is currently used for The Ministry of Education), and my father had a Spanish passport. If my father were detained, the home would not transfer over to the government. Also, the police did not want to deal with the hassle of a foreign citizenship situation. My father's parents were both Spaniards; therefore, he was automatically granted Spanish citizenship. They let him go; however, he was told by Cuban officials that there was a strong possibility that they would come looking for him later on if any questions came up.

We sailed from El Mariel on a very calm sea without too many incidents. However, as our boat began to approach the Gulf of Mexico, the waves became increasingly higher, and the water that was invading our boat seemed to be reaching our ankles in a matter of minutes. People started crying and screaming that they did not want to die. Shortly after, a Cuban coast guard arrived on the scene. The captain was able to calm everyone by saying that with everyone's help, we would be evacuated into a shrimp boat nearby. One by one we were transferred. We weren't allowed to take anything with us, because even though the boat was bigger, it was also over capacity. This boat was filled with convicts and many other people that suffered from different mental illnesses.

My mother still remembers how a large black man, apparently very strong, fainted as he saw the rescue operation taking place. The Dulce II was pulled away from the shrimp boat and twenty minutes later we saw it submerge into the sea. It was very sad and a horrific sight. We were shaking as we witnessed the boat now heading for the abyss. The shrimp boat must have had over one hundred people on board, and there was barely any sitting room. We were like sardines in a can. Every five minutes we were asked to move from one side to the other to balance the boat. During 18 hours we sat on this boat being rocked by waves. One minute we were on top of a huge mountain, and three minutes later we were on the bottom of a precipice; it was impossible to sleep. Everyone had to urinate and defecate in place. Most of us were hungry and completely dehydrated. In desperation, one man in his early twenties began to scream that he wanted to die, and a fight ensued when he was asked to be quiet or he would be thrown off the boat. A few minutes later he was calm, but then he began to scream again, and they had to tie him to a poll.

As night set in, any sign of life on the open ocean became hopeless. Due to the desolation, every five minutes someone would swear that they had seen lights or land. At 3:00 a.m., we were approached by an American coast guard boat that led us into Key West. A trip that normally took one or two days had taken us almost a week, more than five of those days on the ocean. We were finally in the U.S.

THE UNITED STATES

Once we arrived to the United States, we immediately moved to New York. It was a city full of crime and drugs. My father worked three jobs, and we spoke little English. Nevertheless, during his second year working with Goya Foods, he reached sales of over one million dollars. I attended high school in Washington Heights until my junior year.

Then my father, through sheer determination and hard work, moved our family to an affluent New Jersey suburb. I attended my senior year at a local public school and went on to Montclair State University in New Jersey. I graduated with a bachelor's degree in political science, and a minor in Spanish. I then found my calling and realized I wanted to teach Spanish film and Latin American literature. I received a full scholarship to study Hispanic literature at the University of Arizona where I completed a master and doctoral degrees in Spanish and Latin American literature.

Since 1999, I have been a professor at Florida Southern College. I have taken the department from six or seven majors and minors to forty five. I have created a study abroad program to Spain that averages 50 to 60 students each year. I have added literature and film courses.

I am blessed to have grown up in two cultures and have the ability to be multi-lingual. I am grateful to my father for his perseverance and support in helping my sister and me to realize the "American Dream." I would like to pass on that passion "to get ahead" to my children. I am grateful to my mother, who has also succeeded in the field of real estate, for giving us her support and unconditional love.

I also want to inspire my students to "think outside of the box." Taking them abroad allows them to see other worlds and gives them a new perspective on life. Several of my students have gone on to work abroad or teach Spanish. I am now taking a sabbatical and focusing on writing a book about the Mariel Boatlift. It has been a dream of mine for years.

The immigrant experience is like none other. As all Cuban Americans, we long for that journey to see our homeland, the island that bore us. But I am forever grateful to this country which has boundless opportunities to seize.

Eliezer, Rodolfo, Acela (Carito), Andrew & Osdany Lumpuy

El Dorado, a boat that brought the Lumpuy family to freedom

I Reached My Goal

Acela (Carito) Lumpuy

As long as the storm may be,
the sun will always shine through the clouds.
KHALIL GIBRAN

Our life in Cuba was always very poor, but Communism made it worse. To put food on the table my husband worked in the fields. I ran a variety store for the government where we sold groceries, clothing, and other things. Most of the time, I worked alone and very hard. I do not know how God gave me strength. Weighing only 70 pounds and being 4.5 feet tall, I had to move sacks of brown sugar around that weighed 218 pounds. The days that the petroleum arrived were exhausting. It only came once a month and everybody needed it. The farmers formed long lines to buy petroleum, and I spent hours lifting and selling it. I earned 118 Cuban pesos, which is the equivalent of seven or eight dollars a month. That was not enough.

We were issued ration books in which the government wrote down all the groceries that we could buy. There were four of us in our home. The government gave us 20 pounds of sugar per month, 20 pounds of rice, about 3 liters of oil, and 4 ounces of coffee. Beans were hard to find. That was about all that you could buy in the grocery stores.

In 1980, due to an agreement reached between the President of the United States, Jimmy Carter, and Fidel Castro, political prisoners where freed to go to the United States. My brother was one of them, and my family was able to leave Cuba through the Port of El Mariel, in Havana. All of us were going to leave together, but Immigration did not let me go, so my brother left with my parents. That was heartbreaking for everybody in the family because we had never been apart.

My mother arrived in Miami with high blood pressure, probably because she was sad and worried. Two weeks later, after my family's arrival, there was a party at the house of one of my uncles in Lakeland, Florida. During the celebration my mother went to the bathroom and never came back. Later, she was found on the floor. Three days later my mother went to be with the Lord. The exhaustion from all the travel and anxiety and worry were too much for her.

The news was devastating, not only because we realized that we were not going to be able to see her or feel her affection anymore, but because my mother did not have the chance to enjoy what she came looking for: freedom.

My father had saved a little money from his job as a school custodian. He had to start working again at the age of sixty when he arrived in the United States. He also received a lot of help from our compatriots in Lakeland. Despite the expense of my mother's funeral, my father paid $500 per person to a boat captain to bring my children, my husband and me to the United States.

The days passed with no word about our leaving. Then I called my father and asked him, "Dad, are you going to send for us?" and he answered, "The boat is already in Cuba." The boat had already been in Cuba three weeks, but the government ordered many boats to take the people that they wanted to leave Cuba. These were criminals and people with mental conditions who the government passed off as political prisoners.

On May 13th, I was at the store working on inventory that the government had requested. An officer told me that he knew that I was leaving the country, and if something was missing, they would make me pay. They would not let me go until I paid. Knowing that under any excuse they could make me stay was terrifying.

The same day two policemen went to my house to deliver the permission for us to leave. We had to leave that same afternoon. My children were at the school. Their teachers were my friends, and as soon as they heard, they took my kids to the house to bathe and dress them. I had a small suitcase ready with medicine, clothing, and food for my children. The police took everything out, including a picture of my mother. They left only enough food to last less than one day.

We used to live in Placetas. The police took us to different offices to fill out papers. Then they took us to a hotel in Havana. There were so many people in that hotel that there was not enough space, so my husband, the kids and I had to sleep by the seashore on mattresses they provided. To bathe, we had to use the water from the ocean because the bathrooms were always full and were filthy. My husband and I did not eat. What we got we gave to the children because we did not have enough money.

After we left the hotel, we were taken to a different place, and from there they took us to the Port of Mariel. We had to stay in the port two days due to the size of the flotilla; there were thousands of boats. Some boats belonged to Cubans who were waiting to take their family members out, while others were there to take advantage of the opportunity to make good money. This was the only way to leave the island.

We were put in tents. One by one we were called to go to the boats. Those who left would leave us whatever money they had left. When they finally called for us, an officer said that only three of us were claimed, supposedly I was not on the list.

"What do you mean Acela is not on the list? It is her father who sent for us! He sent for the four of us, and we will leave together!" My husband said in a desperate tone. I felt like dying, I did not know what they were going to do with me, if they were going to make me stay and how long. A gentleman talked to the officer for us, "The purpose for our leaving is for family reunification. Why would you separate this family and leave the mother of those two children behind?" Finally, they let me in.

After hours of paperwork, we got on the boat. It was an old shrimp boat, but still in good shape. Beside us, there were 32 more families. When we finally got ready to leave, a Cuban official informed our captain that he had to take with him 60 undesirables. Among them were common prisoners or people that had been in insane asylums. That was the Cuban government's trap. In order for the boats to transport the families they had been paid to bring, they had to also take scoundrels. Our captain had already brought 200 of those people to the United States, but he did not have another alternative but to accept. His condition was that those undesirable people would go to the highest part of the boat, and he warned them that if something happened to any of his passengers, they would end up in the ocean. Thank God we did not have any problems. Those people behaved and even helped us.

We did not have money. The little that we had left, we gave to the people that were still in the tents in Cuba so they could buy some food. We left Havana on May 18, 1980. I was sad about leaving my country and turning my back on all those people that were staying in poverty. At the same time, I was happy to be going to the United States to be reunited with my dad, my brother and other family members. I could not contain my tears during that mixture of feelings and the uncertainty of the future.

A few minutes before we set sail, the captain told us about the dangers that we could face on our journey. I don't remember everything he said, but I do remember his last warning, "Listen well...if someone falls into the ocean, no matter who it is, you cannot help him. We cannot stop due to the amount of people we have on board. Whoever tries to help someone who falls will drown as well." His words froze the blood in my veins. I knew we were about to face the darkest hours of our lives. I held on to my children and to my God.

Many boats left at the same time we did. I wish I could have filmed those scenes. There were small boats that were carrying over two hundred people. Some fell out of the boats because they did not fit. People were screaming, overwhelmed with desperation. Something really sad. We were all risking our lives, abandoning our island due to the doctrine of a crazy tyrant.

The weather was supposed to be good; however, after an hour of sailing, the storms started. We endured hours of horror: black waves, monumental black waves that covered us. It seemed as if the ocean were going to swallow us. The thunder was deafening and the lightening was incredible. We had to use buckets to get rid of the water inside the boat. The children were crying with terror and many were praying out loud.

Next to me there was an elderly lady that was soaked. I could see her shaking from the cold and fear. I wanted to hug her, protect her, but I had to pay attention to my own children.

Finally the storm ceased. We saw boats that had left full of people, now empty. Some of the passengers on my boat saw sharks attacking people that had fallen into the ocean. I only saw blood in the water.

When we entered U.S. waters, we saw Coast Guard airplanes and helicopters. The airplanes came to check on us. We asked for help. We begged to be rescued. They answered that our situation was not as bad as that of other boats; that there were people in worse conditions with children and elderly people that were dying. They picked up those who were sinking and drowning.

Nearing the Gulf of Mexico, our ship broke down. The crew made us move to another part of the ship. This time it seemed as if we were going to sink. Thank God a ship that was near by us helped us and the engine started. We were calm for a while. All of a sudden people started joyfully screaming, "Look, lights! Look, lights!" It was Key West.

It was dawn; hundreds of boats were arriving at the same time. We had to wait. The Coast Guard asked for us to form a line. The Red Cross was there helping. There were a lot of sick people. In my boat there was a boy suffering from hemophilia. He was taken by the Red Cross, along with the elderly lady that was beside me.

My dad was waiting for us in Miami, but Immigration did not have enough personnel to process that many people there. That is why we went to Key West. The next day, we were sent to a military base in Pennsylvania. We were taken to a two-story house, along with the scoundrels. There were daily verbal and physical fights as well as murders. The situation was so bad that my husband said that he would have preferred to stay in Cuba. Our children were living a horrible experience which could mark them for the rest of their lives.

We stayed in Pennsylvania for a month; waiting was difficult. We had to wait in line for everything, especially to eat. At first, people wanted to eat twice, and they fought to get back in line. My husband had to hold our place in line for breakfast, and immediately he had to form another one for lunch and later for dinner. Thank God we never missed a meal. The crew that worked in the kitchen already knew us, and they gave our kids some treats.

Most of the time, I stayed at the house with my children because it was so cold. My husband would wrap himself in a blanket to go wait in line. We could not even take a shower because the water was freezing. The heater was old and did not work properly.

Finally we were allowed to leave. By then, we had some clothes that the church had given us when we arrived in Pennsylvania. On the plane, everybody was eating except us because we did not have a penny. Next to me there was an older gentleman (May God bless him wherever he is.) That gentleman asked the flight attendant, who spoke Spanish, why we were not eating. I told her that we were coming from a military base, we were Cubans exiles. We did not have money to eat. He paid for our food, and said to bring us whatever we wanted. We accepted his help, without overdoing it.

Finally, we arrived in Lakeland and our sacrifices soon began to pay off.

Since the moment we arrived, we received a lot of support, particularly from the Catholic Church. They gave us money and food. After a few days, we got $200 from the government. Our family also helped. We stayed at my uncle's house where my dad was living.

My first job was working as a nanny. I got enrolled in an upholstery class and in spite of the language barrier, I passed and obtained a certificate.

Immediately, I started working for a company that manufactured boat seats. The work was so hard that my hands used to bleed. I had to resign. I always had two jobs at the same time. I worked day and night cleaning houses and offices. After sometime, I started my own upholstery business that I ran for around five years. It was a good business.

At the same time I started working as a substitute maintenance employee at Southwest Middle School where my father worked. After two years they offered me a full-time position. Since they offered me benefits, I had to close my business. I continued cleaning houses, offices and new constructions during the mornings. I have worked at Southwest Middle School for over 21 years and I have been recognized in several occasions as "Worker of the Year. I am the Maintenance Supervisor, which has given me the opportunity to offer work to many other immigrants. In 2008 the Polk County School Board recognized me as "The Best Employee of the Year." It was a great surprise and an enormous pride for me and my family.

I have always felt the need to give back for the blessing of arriving safe and sound in the United States. The families that I worked for have always given me clothing, furniture and other things that I had been accumulating. With all of that I have been able to help immigrants and others in need. In addition to guiding them, I take them to the doctor, to the Social Security office, and I help them with their paperwork and other things. It is my duty as a human being. My husband and I have gone back to Cuba several times to help our family. We have repaired their house, we have taken them medicines, eye glasses, and we help them as much as we can. We have so much and they have so little.

The Lakeland community has been aware of my efforts. They have always provided help. In 2005, the "Lakeland Magazine" published an article entitled "Everyday Angels" in which I was recognized along with another seven individuals for our community service. My story also appeared in Vision Latina, a local Spanish newspaper. If I had won the lottery, it would not have meant as much to me as receiving all of these recognitions.

We came to the United States to work and to provide a better life for our children. There is no doubt that we have reached our goal. I feel like a millionaire because I have learned how to manage my life. I do not spend money on myself to be able to help others. Our children have followed our footsteps. They work hard and enjoy success in their lives.

My proudest achievement has been helping those who stayed in Cuba and to have brought my parents-in-law to the United States for a vacation. They now know what it is to live in the country of opportunities. They were thrilled to see their grandchildren and great-grandchildren enjoying the life we had always dreamed of.

Carlitos, Carlos, Lidia & Manolo Martínez

My Escape Through Honduras

Dr. Manuel Martínez

Liberty is always dangerous,
but it is the safest thing we have.
H.E. FODICK

A new patient was sitting on my examining table. He was a young, thin man who appeared strong and healthy. His shoes and attire demonstrated he worked in the fields. He was there nervously rubbing his hands together, yet his face seemed expressionless.

"How are you feeling today? How can I help you?" I asked.

Without saying a word and looking deeply into my eyes, my patient reached into his shirt pocket. With his right hand he handed me a picture while putting his left index finger to his lips signaling silence. As I stared at the photo, my hands started trembling and my heart was pumping faster and faster while a cold sweat quickly broke out on my forehead. Finally, the moment I had been waiting for... this man was here to attempt to set me free. I tried to maintain my composure. Putting the stethoscope to his chest I said, "Breath deeply... again," followed by a couple of other loud medical questions. "Take these pills and you should be ok. Come back and see me in a few days." On his prescription I wrote the time and name of the place where we were to meet later that evening.

Concentrating the rest of the afternoon was not easy. I kept looking at the picture in disbelief, but there it was, there was no doubt. My uncle Luis said he would send an obvious sign. My plan was working. I was about to escape from Nicaragua crossing the mountains to Honduras.

Since I was a young man, back in the 60's, my family had tried to escape from communism. My parents had both come from humble backgrounds. With hard work and sacrifices, they were able to achieve a comfortable position in life. In 1959 they owned a very prosperous grocery store, a beauty salon and several rental homes.

After the revolution, all of these symbols of their hard work were confiscated by the government in only one day.

My heart still aches every time I remember one of the saddest days of my life, the day I went to the store with my father and found it closed. An arrogant officer at the door approached us and, in a very stern and officious manner, told my father, "You are no longer the owner of this business! It now belongs to the people!" He meant it now belonged to Fidel Castro. From then on, my father could not go in the store again, not even to get a pencil. At the same time, the government also tried to take away his automobile, but, in spite of the incarceration threats, my father utterly refused to turn in the keys. Afterward, the rest of our properties were expropriated. My parents had no other alternative but to become government employees.

My family made several fruitless efforts to leave for the United States. When my older brother turned military age at fifteen, he was no longer eligible to leave the country. Leaving without him was not an option for us. My uncle Luis and his family emigrated a few years later, leaving a deep emptiness within us. From then on we suffered the regime's anguish and calamities all alone.

I decided to study medicine. It was not easy since the government knew that my family did not agree with the dictatorship. I was constantly threatened to be sent off to the military service with no possibility of entering medical school. Luckily, after plenty of humiliations, I graduated in 1975. I applied to do a specialty in plastic surgery. Unfortunately, I was sent to practice general medicine in a small town in the mountains of Escambray with a salary equivalent to twenty dollars per month. I was the only doctor in the area, working regular hours and always on call.

After a year, feeling totally exhausted, I decided to complain about the work conditions that, in my opinion, were unacceptable. Without any previous notice or agreement, the Directors of Public Health came to my office to let me know that I had been sanctioned for "inappropriate conduct," which was a different way of saying "counter-revolution." After being ordered to gather my belongings, I was transported to a remote area called Meyer. Among the medical professionals, Meyer was known as the "Model Prison." This was the place where the government sent the majority of the doctors and dentists that dared express their opinions about the regime. It was not very accessible, especially during rainy weather, at which times we were totally without communication.

In Meyer, there was plenty of time to think and to study the tactics needed to be free of communism. I decided to be more flexible and live up to the government's expectations. I transformed the Meyer Medical Center into one of the best service medical centers in the area. I was highly congratulated for my initiative and excellent work. At the end of one year, the same "Directors of Public Health" that had sanctioned me asked if I was ready to work for a year as Director of the Trinidad Policlinic, the biggest in the region. I accepted. That was the beginning of my revenge and preparation of my road to freedom. I made sure the Policlinic ran to perfection. I hoped to be "rewarded" by the directors sending me to another country to work as a volunteer doctor... and so it happened!

In the summer of 1979, the new Sandinista government took power in Nicaragua and the Cuban government made me an offer to go work to that country for a period of two years. I happily accepted since it was precisely what I wanted. Along with many other doctors, dentists, nurses and soldiers, I arrived in Ocotal, a small town near the border of Honduras. By the grace of God, everything was going according to my plan. Even though we were under constant surveillance and among us there were members of State Security, I knew that, somehow, I would find a way to escape.

II. THE ESCAPE

After a year, I wrote a letter to my uncle Dr. Luis Vázquez, who lived in Florida, explaining my situation and my desire to go to the United States. I asked for absolute discretion since any suspicion would send me straight to prison in Cuba.

Uncle Luis made several trips to Honduras to try to make contact with someone who could help, but it was all in vain. He was met with only false promises and was swindled out of a considerable amount of money. We lived through several months of sheer frustration. Then a miracle happened! A couple brought their sick child to his pediatric practice in Bartow, Florida. The father was Cuban and the mother Honduran, from a town near the Nicaraguan border called Danli. After establishing a friendship, Luis told them about my situation and asked them if they knew of anyone who would be willing to help me. The child's mother called her brother in Danli and he accepted.

When I least expected it, this young man came into my office pretending to be a patient and handed me the picture. I could not believe my eyes when I saw an old picture of my cousins Tere and Lourdes playing with me in the park in Esperanza, Cuba!

We met at the indicated place, and we decided that he would come back for me in two weeks. On the agreed day, I finished work, asked for authorization to visit some friends and I never, ever came back! I took only the clothes I had on and my medical credentials. Everything else stayed behind. My guide was waiting as agreed. We were able to rent a car under the pretense of going to see a sick friend at Las Manos, a place near the border. I was horribly afraid that someone would see me in the company of a stranger and become suspicious. Leaving the car near the mountains, we started our journey on foot, a very dangerous experience. Well-armed guerrillas and army surveillance units roamed everywhere. We were risking our lives for my freedom.

As we trudged along, it got dark and started to rain. Thunder and lightning made the escape even more stressful, like a horror movie. We could hear voices of men nearby. I was paralyzed with fear... my heart was beating so loudly that I feared it could be heard at a distance. Fortunately, no one saw nor heard us, and we continued walking through the night until my guide pointed to a barbed wire fence and said, "Do you see that fence? That is Honduras!"

The rain would not stop, and we decided to spend the rest of the night at a school nearby. After resting for two or three hours, we continued walking until we found the Pan-American Highway. We cleaned the mud off of us in a creek and kept walking until a truck offered to take us to town. In Danli, Luis had established contact with a Cuban family who was going to take me in.

Immediately, I asked to use the phone and called Luis and Maria Teresa, who started crying when they heard my voice. The next morning, Luis arrived on the first available plane, ready to do whatever was necessary to take me to United States. After talking to several people, and seeing that it was quite difficult, he decided that the best option was to seek help from the United States' Embassy in Tegucigalpa. I will never forget the kindness and disposition the American Consul showed to resolve my case.

After several days of interviews, the American Consul informed us that they did not know how long it would take for me to leave, that the most appropriate thing to do was for Luis to return to the United States, and I was to stay in a hotel in front of the police station so they could offer protection. At the precise moment that Uncle Luis was returning the key to his rental car, he

Liana, Virginia, Omaida, Carlitos, Lindsey & Manolo Martínez

heard his name called over the hotel intercom. It was the Consul. She had received approval for me to travel to the United States of America the next day! No one can imagine the impact that had on me, especially after having come to terms with the idea of staying in Honduras in legal limbo.

We were personally escorted by the United States Consul and her guards to the Tegucigalpa Airport. We arrived at the Miami Airport in 1981with a letter authorizing my entrance to the country for humanitarian reasons. I also received a document authorizing me to live and work in this wonderful country. After living in the oppression of communism for twenty long years, I was finally a free man!

I went to live with my aunt and uncle in Bartow. I did not speak English fluently. Luis taught me how to manage a medical office in this country, how the hospital operated, and even though I was quite limited, he employed me as a medical assistant. He was a great mentor! I studied day and night to prepare for my medical exams and I learned English. I also bought my first car – a used Ford Pinto!

Later I moved to Miami to live with my uncle Ricardo and Aida García. They also gave me their full and unconditional support. I continued studying to reach my final goal. Even though I was a doctor, I could not practice my profession. I was lucky to meet Dr. Velazquez, House Physician Chief for the Miami Hospital, who hired me part time as an assistant, making twelve dollars an hour plus benefits. On February 1984 I passed the State Board and was certified to practice medicine in the State of Florida

It was around that time that I met Virginia, who is now my wife. She managed three weight reduction clinics in Miami. She offered me a job as a physician in her clinics. I accepted and, before long, we fell in love and got married. She taught me all about weight reduction medical practices, which were totally unknown to me. I am very grateful for that. The success I enjoy today I owe to her.

We opened our own office of Family Practice and weight reduction clinic, named Lite Weight, Inc. We have been successful from the beginning. The Lord gave us two wonderful daughters, Liana and Lindsey, and Virginia's son Carlo came to live with us. With time and hard work we have been able to reach every goal we have set for ourselves.

In 1994, we were able to make my parents' dreams a reality. They came to live in the United States. After thirty-four years of living under communism, they are enjoying their retirement years in Miami, in their own home, and with freedom to do as they please.

III. PAY IT FORWARD

My brother Carlos, a neonatal surgeon, and his wife Omaida, a respected pediatrician making the equivalent of about thirty-five dollars per month in Cuba, expressed their interest in leaving the island along with their two sons. The fact that they were both doctors would make it even harder to do it legally. It was virtually impossible! It was then that I remembered what my uncle, Dr. Luis Vázquez, told me when I asked him what I could do to repay everything he had done for me. He said, "I want you to do for someone else what I have done for you. Pay it forward." My wife and I decided to do whatever it took to get my brother and his family out through a third country.

We finally met someone with connections in Venezuela who could get them out of Cuba. He asked for an exorbitant amount of money to make the necessary arrangements. He told us that the easiest way to escape was for my brother and his wife to get divorced and marry Venezuelan citizens. My eighteen-year-old nephew would have to do the same. They accepted this plan as they would have done anything to get out of Cuba. The divorces and marriages took place. At first, everything went according to plan. When they arrived, we all went to Venezuela to greet them at the airport. It was Christmas of 1995 and, finally, we were together again. Priceless!

We returned to the United States with the promise that my brother's family would arrive a few days later. However, this did not happen, and they spent many months in Venezuela. They tried to leave several times. The whole family was even detained by Venezuelan State Intelligence for a while for trying to use false documentation. Finally, one by one, they were able to leave.

Today, most of our family lives in Miami. My parents have been able to enjoy their grandchildren and great grandchildren. My brother Carlos and his wife Omaida have been able to see their sons graduate as electrical engineers and establish wonderful careers. As for me, I am living the life I always dreamed of. I am very proud of my family and my wife for all we have accomplished together. I especially thank God for allowing us to live in freedom.

Camila, Claudia, Carlitos, Carlos & Cristobal Luna

I Will Always Be With You

Carlos Luna

When I die with no country but no master
in my grave I want to have a bouquet of flowers and a flag.
JOSÉ MARTÍ

The memories of my childhood, in a little country town, are the great launching site for my need of expression. In my native town we grow the best tobacco in the world. I am from San Luis, but I grew up Pinar del Río, Cuba. Mine is a town full of characters and colorful stories which are only found in the countryside. The most powerful memory of my childhood is the intense love that my grandmothers infused in me; the love of family, country and my roots, as well as the certainty of where I am from. This has always helped me to know where I am going. I can tell you many stories about my youth.

In my family, especially on the father's side, there has always been a predisposition to be rowdy rebels; perhaps it is the rare mixture of my grandparents who are from the Basque Country and the Canary Islands. The Lunas come from Sephardic Jews, Hebrews who converted to Catholicism, there is also Moorish influence. As a matter of fact, the first famous Luna was a priest who rebelled against the church in the XIV century. He was crucified and burned. On my mother's side, as in most Cuban families, there is Spanish-European influence, and to that we can add African and Asian as well. Because of my ancestry, race, creed and circumstances, I inherited a rebellious spirit.

My mother's side of the family lived off the land in Cuba; they were *Guajiros* (farmers) with a great tradition for growing tobacco. On my father's side, there were also farmers; they had cattle and other businesses as well.

My paternal grandparents lived in Santi Spiritus. My father was the youngest of their children. When Fulgencio Batista took over the country becoming president by means of a *coup d'etat*, like most

Cubans, they were against Batista and began to conspire against him. My father and his brothers joined the movement in the mountains to fight for the country they loved. The family supported the fight in different ways by donating food, money, and clothing - anything they could. This came back to haunt them when Batista's police came to the house and tortured my grandfather until he died in the presence of my grandmother Ramona, who was detained and tortured as well. They left the body there, alone; nobody knows who buried my poor grandfather.

In 1959, when Fidel Castro took over, my father's family realized that he was communist, something they did not support, so they went back to the mountains of Escambray as did many Cubans in the area. This time they went to fight against the dictator who, even today, after more than fifty years, continues taking my country through a systematic process of destruction and total deterioration. His main objective, in my opinion, was to destroy the most powerful base of the country- the family. The family has always been the infrastructure and the heart of Cuban society.

At that time the families who lived in the Escambray area were perhaps the first to suffer the consequences that later would reach the entire country: division of family, intrigue, fights, hatred, tears and being uprooted, which was all part of the inauspicious process of unfairness and pain. There, the agrarian reform was implemented with the confiscating of the private farms, including the homes and adjacent lands, so that Fidel could distribute them at his will. Once my father came back from fighting in the mountains, he went to Pinar del Río to find his family, but he did not find anyone. It was there where he met my mother and married her, creating a family of which I am the first born.

After the first ten years of dictatorship, the majority of the population had learned that the best way to survive in Cuba, was maintaining silence. We had to be careful about what we said, especially if we were going to talk about the government. Everything was hidden; we had to be careful even in the presence of our own families for fear of being turned in. An opinion against the government was and still is a mortal crime.

I grew up in that environment of unfairness, the lack of respect and destruction that my country had become. It was total repression; all dreams, screams, protests, tears and love had to be done silently, cautiously and half-way; all of which contradicts our nature. Those who know the Cuban culture know that we are vociferous and don't know how to do anything in silence, that we have the natural tendency to be loud. We do everything singing and shouting, making our voices heard. I believe that the Lord gave us a special musical patent.

I was raised by my grandmothers. We lacked the basic necessities. If we had toothpaste, we didn't have toothbrushes; if we had rice, we didn't have beans, if we had to go to the bathroom, there was no toilet paper. This system keeps people active... they can't think about the situation because they are too busy trying to survive.

No matter how hard my parents worked, they couldn't solve anything. My maternal grandmother, now ill, would sweetly whisper to me about the greatness of the former Cuba. Her internal fortitude fed my ideals and my rebellious spirit. My parents would plead with her not to do it, afraid that I would get into trouble, something that was impossible to avoid.

There was something that we never lacked in my home: unconditional love, which we all need to grow into a person of character. That love was what kept me strong and gave me the tools to survive to this day. My grandmother taught me to build from what we love as opposed to what we hate. She witnessed how her husband was killed, but in spite of that, she never stopped being a happy woman who smiled at life. She sang and danced while cleaning the house. She was a vivid example of personal strength. She was in love with life in the present, leaving the past where it belongs...in the past. I owe my appreciation for Cuban music and dancing to her.

My maternal grandmother, Juliana Sánchez, was, and still is, my guardian angel. She was my sweetheart during those years, and the Lord gave her back to me when I met Claudia, my wife. It was Juliana who taught me about tradition, pride, and what Cuba was before Fidel. She taught me about José Martí and his love for Cuba, about integrity, responsibility, forgiveness and many things that at that time I didn't understand.

I remember my parents would complain, especially my father, because he knew my nature and what the consequences of those long conversations would be. Nevertheless, today at 41 years of age, and after having three children, my 16-year-old beautiful Camila and my two boys, Carlos 13 and Cristobal 12, I understand the responsibility that my grandmother felt telling me of my family's history to mold my character, as well as that of my parents to protect me. I had many arguments with my father when I was an art student, but now I realize that he only wanted to protect me.

It was to my grandparents Juliana and Genaro that I made a promise which impacted my life forever. I was just nine years old when my grandma made me a coconut custard pie. When I finished the last bite she sat in front of me and said in a very serious but loving tone of voice,

"We have to talk to you."

"Yes, Abuela?"

"Your grandfather and I need you to promise before God, before us. We want you to swear something."

"What?" I asked nervously.

My grandfather held me by the arms, pulled me toward him and said,

"Please, swear that as soon as you have an opportunity, you will leave Cuba. Swear it! Don't look back. You can't look back, you have to leave Cuba."

I did not understand. I still get goose bumps thinking about it. I swore it, I don't know how many times, crying, scared, and nervous. After I had calmed down, Grandma tenderly said, "Now swear that this conversation never happened. You can't tell anyone, not even your parents."

My grandmother's health was already fragile by then, and she died soon after. The day before, from her death bed, she ordered her oxygen be removed, and for everyone to leave the room except for me. She asked me to kiss her and when I did, she took my hands in hers and whispered in my ear, "My boy, don't you worry. I will always be with you; we will both be with you, but don't you ever forget your promise. Swear to me that I can go in peace knowing that you will leave this country."

Her death marked the beginning of my possibility or dream to leave Cuba as my only means of survival. Everything turned hostile and dark for me. I was angry with God and with life itself for taking her from me. I became a difficult child in that complicated mixture of my age and my inner feelings. I fought with everyone about everything; I protested out loud. My parents separated shortly after, making it even worse. During this period, I was already studying plastic arts in Pinal del Rio, and a year later, I went to study in Havana. It was through art, the career I am passionate about, that I started to heal from my internal pain. I found a way to express my feelings; I took total refuge in it.

My school years in a Havana boarding school were not a piece of cake either. Everyone was looking for a way to survive in a country

Carlos Luna

that was quickly deteriorating. During those years, art schools in Cuba were considered "schools of privilege," but they were also a living hell, a jungle where we had to survive. There were hundreds of students; the strongest took advantage of the weakest. We spent our time looking for something to eat because the school food was absolutely horrible, sometimes putrid. We had to be cautious not to do or say anything that could be used by a classmate to squeal on us. There were many students anxious to step on others to get ahead in the system.

I lived on the streets; I ate my meals there. There I had to survive and start to put in practice the possibility of being an independent artist, not tied to anything or anyone. The street was a tough teacher. I learned to work hard. I washed dishes in restaurants, painted homes, planted rice and tobacco, worked in construction. I learned to negotiate and to endure. At the art school I always excelled. I learned the techniques and the history of art; I understood the basics of a career to which I would dedicate the rest of my life.

By 1991, my career as an artist in Cuba had become promising. I had won several important awards, and I was starting to exhibit my work at international museums. It was during that year, by recommendation of a great artist and friend, that I was contacted by a Mexican gallery owner who invited me to Monterrey, Mexico. He was able to get me a visa to go teach at a university for a semester. I had to return to Havana on November 4th to participate in the *Bienal de la Habana,* an international art event every other year. My work was part of the Cuban Exhibit. As usual, my trip to Mexico had been kept as quiet as possible, so the organizers of the Bienal, wondered where I was. "Where is Carlos Luna and his work?."

I finally showed up. Havana was full of people, a lot of movement and vigilance. That was the beginning of the worse internal economic crisis of the government since 1959. Among all of the people who were in Havana, I saw an old classmate who was very integrated in the system; he was an informant, a squealer, someone who usually steps on someone else to get ahead. I met with him and he sarcastically said, *"Luna, I have bad news for you. My brother is the Chief of State Security in this area. On the list of people that are going to be arrested, I saw your name. Let's see how you are going to get out of this one."* Today I think that he shared this information to show me his power and to intimidate me.

In reality, I am grateful because I took immediate action. As a result, today I am free and out of Cuba. I corroborated the information visiting a relative who was totally integrated and highly ranked in the system. The information was true. On December 4th of 1991, I was scheduled to be taken prisoner under who knows what cause, something invented. Anything at all could be interpreted by the government as counter-revolutionary. My relative was sharp and clear, *"Carlos Luna, I can't do anything for you. You should leave the country. I have not talked to you; this conversation did not exist and we have not seen each other. If by 12:00 noon on the December 4th you are still here, you are history. Good luck."*

I didn't understand why, but I didn't have to. Since January 1st 1959, the situation in my country has been more than surreal; full of injustices, where a man has planted hatred in such an immeasurable way that I fear we will suffer the consequences of his actions for many years to come.

Horrified, I ran to the Mexican Embassy. It was the only place that came to mind, but it was also the only place where I could find help. I went in without any difficulty. I found two high powered officials who were friends with the Mexican gallery owner. Their help and the cooperation of a high ranking Mexicana Airlines officer and his personnel were key to my escape. Without their help I would have not been able to leave Cuba. During my flight, one of the Mexican officers who helped me witnessed, in shock, the injustice of the Cuban authorities who even violated international laws. When I arrived in Mexico, he shook my hand and said, "Good luck to you! You know how to contact me. Don't look back...never look back." I continued to Monterrey where I still had a teaching contract.

In Cuba, the only one that knew I was leaving was my mother. She was in Havana the night before I left. I woke her up during the night to let her know. *"Mom, I am leaving Cuba tomorrow. I will not come back; I don't know when I will see you again."* My mother has never told me, but I don't think she was surprised. Mothers have a sixth sense; they know what is going on. I don't know how to describe what I felt at that time; it was a mixture of sadness and happiness. I was saving myself and I had the hope that one day I could help my family emigrate as well. We hugged and I left. After I left, my family suffered hostility and persecution. They underwent interrogations and were even arrested.

After the first few months of uncertainly in the city of Monterrey, I decided to go to Mexico City where other young Cubans were living. I met the woman who would be my soul mate, the mother of my children, my wife, my everything: Claudia Catalina Ramírez. We married on the 6th day of December, 1992. Since then I began to rebuild my life, to feel once again the love of a close family, to enjoy life. It was as if everything in my childhood was coming back to me.

With the arrival of my children, the stories that my grandmothers told me with such passion became more and more vivid in my mind. My Cuban character became stronger as did my love for my countrymen; those marvelous people capable of starting over again and again even on shaky ground. Images of my little country town began to appear: the rooster, the dark-skinned girls, the palm trees, the popular sayings, the guajiro, the music and the themes in which I express my fearless opinion about what I think and feel about my country.

I decided to flee my country. I did not allow its political situation to squash my morale. No obstacle will ever interfere with my efforts to tell the world who I am and where I come from. The years I have been out of Cuba have allowed me a personal and professional growth where I have been able to enjoy total freedom of expression, something that, unfortunately, I could not have experienced in Cuba. Away from my island I chose to start my fight and add my little grain of salt to the identity song that all Cubans have in their hearts.

My work is full of stories that occurred in the little town where I was raised. They may have been told by my grandmothers, or my uncles, my parents or friends, or they could have been my own stories; my travels through Mexico enriched them, made them more powerful. Upon my arrival in United States, this mix settled; the chick broke out of its shell transforming itself into a rooster or the guajiro that so many times I have portrayed in my paintings. It stands tall and proud, knowing where he comes from, and sure of where he is going.

The *guajiro* in my paintings represents all Cubans; in my opinion he is our national hero. He has always been there, in good and bad times. In my work, the *guajiro* is the protagonist of *El Gran Mambo*, he is the one knocking out Fidel Castro in *"1,2,3, Your Count Is Up."* He also sings, dances and falls in love. In my paintings there are also the voices of those who did not live to tell their stories. Now I am in the United States with my wife and children and part of my immediate family (my brother, my mother and her husband). We have traveled the road of rebirth. They have been able to go back to Cuba; my sisters and father still live there. I would love to see them again but only in a free Cuba.

Now I have become an American citizen. This country granted me a EB-1-1 residency given only to those with extraordinary ability; something that fills me with a lot of pride. On the other hand, it is a curious fact that neither my work nor my name have appeared in any art document or book in Cuba since I left twenty years ago, with the exception of the book *"Memories of Cuban Art of the 20th Century"* that was published in the United States. It seems as if they had carefully erased me so that there are no footprints even when my work has been recognized on a global level, academically and professionally and has a solid position on the international art market.

I hope to return to my island to exhibit my art. I want to enjoy and freely share in the land where I was born. I want to reunite with my old friends and relatives. I want to stop remembering Cuba and live it again. Meanwhile, I will continue dreaming and painting for the world my testimony of whom I am proud to be: a free Cuban. I believe that a man without a past is a man without a future, and that a man without memories is nothing.

Before 1959 Cubans in general did not feel the necessity to leave the island; there were problems like there are everywhere, but Cuba was indeed the Pearl of the Caribbean and of a great part of the world. Today we Cuban exiles are disseminated over the planet, highly successful in everything we set our minds to do. We don't allow discrimination, and we have demonstrated who we are, wherever we are. We take our cuisine with us: black beans and rice, roast pork, fried bananas, our *yucca con mojo,* guava pies and our flan. We dance a mambo by Dámaso Pérez or the best *son* by Benny Moré, the *Guajira* by Celina Gonzáles or "La Vida es un Carnaval" by our Queen, Celia Cruz. For over 50 years, Cubans have carried the memories of a small island in the Caribbean in a cup of coffee, while inhaling an exquisite Cuban cigar, as if we were carrying the whole planet in the palm of our hands. Proudly, we have grown and have enriched our culture in exile. We are the uprooted Cubans, the only transplanted population, with the exception of the Hebrews, that for over half a century has not lost their identity.

I have always said that one Cuban is plural; two Cubans, a multitude.

Christian, Yipsy, Eduardo & Nicole Fernández

Everything Was a Lie

Eduardo Fernández

Freedom is the right a person has to act freely,
to think and speak without hypocrisy.
JOSÉ MARTÍ

If I said that freedom of expression and freedom in general were the reasons why my wife Yipsy and I came to the United States, I would be lying. Unlike the Cubans that left the island during the first two decades of the Revolution, we never knew the concept of freedom until we arrived in this country. We are part of a large mass of Cubans born in the seventies, for whom every facet of our lives was planned. From a very early age, our government determined what school to attend, what clothes to wear, what to do or not to do, what to eat, our next step, what career we were going to study, where we were going to work, how much we were going to earn, what we were going to say at an international conference in a business meeting. From birth, we were given a ration book for all the minimal necessities of life. We were not taught to have free will.

The reason we came to the United States was mainly financial; it was the thought of being able to live by our own effort and labor, the thought of owning our own home, building a family and for that family to have a good future. In Cuba "tomorrow" does not exist, it is all for "today." What am I going to eat, and with what resources do I get it? Everybody feels forced to steal from whatever source of goods is available to them, especially from their jobs, in other words, the government. For example, a pharmacist that has access to medication, skims off the top in order to barter with someone else who has access to food or clothing. It has become a way of life. The future is totally uncertain for the Cubans on the island. How is it possible that after going to school for five years a professional's salary is not enough to cover basic nutritional needs? Tragically, even professionals have to rely on their relatives abroad to provide them with financial support.

For years, the Cuban government brainwashed us to believe that our system of equality was the fairest and most perfect in the world. Frankly, the majority of our generation was convinced that the Cuban Revolution was advancing and building a better Cuba. Even when we were going through the worst crisis the country has known, after the fall of the Soviet Union and Socialism in 1990, many of us thought that it was the fault of our "enemy," the United States, who had corrupted the socialist countries. That was the repeated message we heard for years.

The Cuban government demands that students "volunteer" to work in agricultural labor camps to help the country. Depending on the student's overall level of succumbing to the brainwashing and of course, academics, he or she will be eligible to go on to college. We were asked at the age of eighteen, "What five careers would you be interested in?" Of course, at that age, a student hasn't had an opportunity or the exposure to the many career possibilities. But that is OK, since the government will pick one for you anyway.

Since Yipsy and I collaborated with the system, I was assigned a career in economics, and she was sent to veterinary school. Like all males, I was required to serve one year in the armed forces as a condition to study the career the government had chosen for me. In 1994, after finishing military service, I earned the right to finish my studies at the University of Havana. I started a program sponsored by the Autonomous University of Madrid, and I learned something that had not been taught in Cuba for many years: Market Economy and Free Enterprise. This was immediately after the fall of the Soviet Union. Cuba was desperate for economic support and opened free trade with countries like Canada and Spain, encouraging tourism and joint ventures. Supposedly, this program was training us to work in the new mixed companies funded by foreign capital. Many sectors of the economy were being decentralized to give the impression of being more independent and thus attracting foreign investors. The chameleon (Castro) was merely changing colors.

I realized the many lies we had lived. While Fidel and his cronies were living like royalty with luxuries and resources that were unimaginable to me, the rest of the country was living in vile poverty. At that time I thought there was only one road to follow in order to better our lives, to join them and form part of their system. On the other hand, the veterinarian world where my wife was evolving was full of limitations with no prospects for her future. After analyzing our options, we arrived at the conclusion that it would be best to try to get out of the country. Yipsy decided to register in the country's visa lottery. On March 27th, 1997 she was selected to go for an interview at the United States Interest Office in Cuba, and I, of course, went with her.

At that time we began what I called the transitional period. Yipsy and I were now traitors to the system and envied by those who also wanted to leave but did not have the good luck to be able to.

Now we also faced a very important variant to solve: how were we going to get the $2,000 dollars necessary to get out of the country since our salaries were less than $30US a month? There was only one person who could help us, my uncle Dr. Luis Vazquez in Florida, who for many years has been supporting his sister Nonín, my grandmother. I remember we spoke on the phone and he asked me, "Are you sure you want to come? Life is very difficult here…!" I did not believe him. Later, during another conversation he said, "I will help you, but you will have to find your own way, you won't be able to come live in my home." I truly did not understand at that time. In my mind, I needed a guide, someone who would tell me what I had to do, how was I going to do it alone? I really did not appreciate then the value and sacrifice of what this good man and his family were doing for us.

We waited nine months to receive our permission to leave. Professionals in Cuba had to be cleared by the ministry of the department to which they belong. In other words, the government had to verify that Yipsy and I did not have any confidential economic or veterinarian information that would put the national security at risk. On December 21, 1997, we were granted the right to get out of the world's largest prison, Cuba, and we started our new life. In retrospect, we consider that was the best Christmas present ever!

Once in the United States, we had to make many important decisions. With the help of the church, we went to Kentucky where there were more job opportunities than in Miami. From being totally dependent Cubans, now we found ourselves in a labyrinth full of opportunities and with no one telling us what to do next. I believe that God does everything for a reason, and I also believe that old saying, "God only gives you what you can handle." There are always angels that will offer a hand. He sent us Helena and Jeffrey Robbins who gave us our first pieces of furniture for our apartment; they helped us buy our first car and took us in like their very own children.

The biggest shock for a professional in exile is to realize that his degrees are not recognized. In order to put bread on the table, he has to start from zero, in whatever job is available, making minimum wage as a simple worker. It is humiliating, but it makes him stronger and gives him the incentive to advance.

Yipsy started working as a helper to a veterinarian, cleaning the cages, bathing the animals, cleaning the anal glands of canines, and brushing the teeth of cats and dogs. I worked in a freezer, packing beef that would come to me on a conveyor belt. I had to be fast and attentive or it would accumulate and overwhelm me. From never even seeing beef in Cuba, and always yearning for it, now I was covered with it. I grew to hate it! Later we went to work at a factory were we worked 14 hours a day for two years. We went to Jefferson Community College twice a week and tried to speak English with each other. It was something that we really needed to learn. It was then that God gave us another friend, Christina, a wonderful North American lady who we barely understood, but from whom we learned a lot since we were forced to use the language. We watched television in English with subtitles to make sure we understood. Then we worked part time in a department store. There were daily challenges with the language and new things to learn. We worked so hard that if we missed work, the managers would tell us that they missed and needed us.

Time passed and having a better handling of the English language, we decided that one of us had to validate his or her professional degree while the other worked to maintain the home. My wife could study for the Veterinarian State Board, or I could go back to school, which ever was easier. So we took the second choice. I graduated with a Masters in Business Administration from the University of Louisville. We were able to pay for it with our savings. Today I am the Human Resource Manager at JBS USA LLC, while Yipsy works in the Accounting Department of Rescare in Louisville, Kentucky. In time, she plans to validate her doctorate.

Now I finally understand and realize that the key factor of what I consider my success in exile is precisely the fact that my uncle Luis forced me to carve my own future, to walk on my own two feet like he and his family had to do 30 years before me. I will always remember that when we arrived in Miami, I immediately called him from a public phone, "Uncle Luis, we are here; as soon as I start to work I will pay you the money we owe you" to which he and his wife Maria Teresa responded, "No, you don't have to pay back anything. Take it as a gift for you to start a new life without debt." Yipsy and I will always be grateful to them.

I believe that we are a testimony that the American Dream is reachable and attainable to anyone who goes for it. Our success is our family. It is the education that we can offer our two children, Christian and Nicole. It is also to have realized the dream to have built our own home, and honoring the example of "Tío (uncle) Luis," helping those we left behind in Cuba.

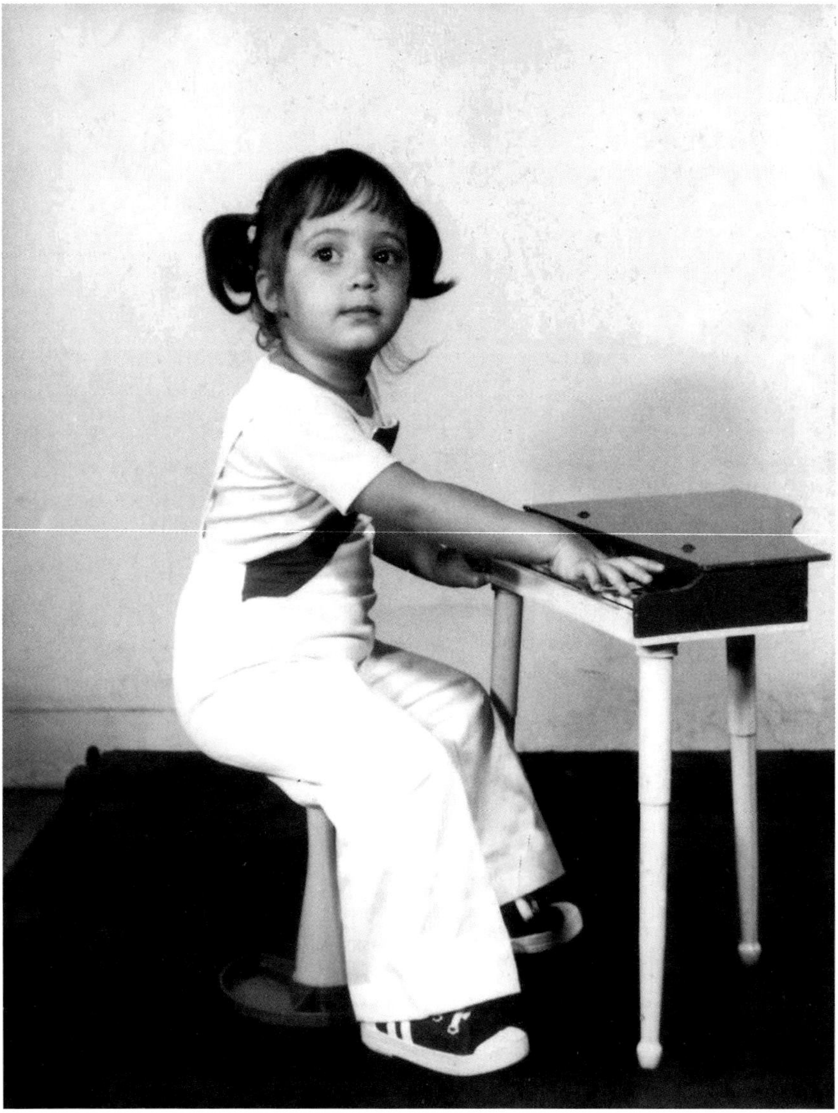

Ivelisse de la Fe

The Soul of the Song

Ivelisse de la Fe

All our dreams can come true,
if we have the courage to pursue them.
WALT DISNEY

I was never sure why my grandmother, Caridad, always nurtured my every opportunity to excel in my musical talent. It began, I think, when I was about one and a half years old and received a toy piano as a gift. While my dad and mom were at work, I remember spending all the time I could with my grandfather and grandmother playing that toy piano. Several years later when my parents decided to move to another house down the street, my grandmother insisted that I continue living with her and grandfather. She used the excuse that the family piano I was now playing was too big to fit into my parents' new smaller apartment. We were only a five-minute walk away, so even though I lived with my grandparents, I was still close enough to my parents and new baby brother who was born shortly after they moved.

It was not a total coincidence that gave me a love of music and a desire to pursue something I was passionate about. My father was very smart and played the guitar by ear. I grew up hearing him play the Beatles' songs. Both of my parents worked in Havana; my father as an electrical engineer and later as an agent for a Spanish equipment company and my mother worked for the electric company. Indeed, I had a goal-oriented, secure childhood, and my musical talents flourished, especially with my grandmother's passionate encouragement and grandfather as a propelling motor. They both would take me to school everyday, and then they sat next to me for hours to listen to me practicing the piano. Although my grandmother had a limited education, she had a huge influence on my life. Later, as an adult, I would understand her passion for my musical success.

When I was five years old, I had to take a test to see if I could qualify to take piano or dancing/gymnastics. Although I passed both tests, I chose to focus on piano and began my studies with a private teacher, Muñeca. Because transportation was a problem in Cuba, I had to walk 10 blocks to her house, yet some of my fondest memories are of staying at Muñeca's house and even taking naps there. Muñeca loved me so much and let me stay as long as I wanted. She was dedicated beyond words to helping me excel in my music. She taught me to study, and to this day I still worry about making the highest grades.

Two years later, I was admitted to the Alejandro García Caturla Conservatory where I received numerous academic and musical recognitions, winning awards in mathematics, Spanish literature, and several piano competitions. My teacher at the Conservatory, Isabelita, was so committed to my achievement in competitions that I actually stayed at her house to practice and prepare for concerts. She is like a second mother to me, and I will always be grateful to her. I was able to maintain the highest GPA in my class on a yearly basis. I achieved the highest award in music, first place in Cuban music competition and special mentions for interpreting the music of Ernesto Lecuona. Upon graduating, I had the great honor of being accepted to the Municipal Musical Conservatory Amadeo Roldán under the tutelage of Professor Jorge Bueno. At the end of four years, I was recognized with the Golden Award in both academics and music, and I graduated with 99.54 out of 100 (4.0 GPA). Upon finishing, I took the entrance exam to enter the Superior Institute of Arts (Instituto Superior de Artes), which represents the whole country and specializes only in the Arts. There, I studied under Professor Danae Ulacia.

In addition to my studies, my spiritual life became very important to me. When I was 14, my mother was lured into the Methodist Church by the music, and the first time I went with her I learned what had been missing from my life. I began to attend services regularly and played the piano with the Praise Band. When I became the church pianist, I knew that I had found a religious home. My brother and grandparents also joined even though Grandmother was a non participating Catholic.

Although traveling to the United States is almost impossible for most Cuban students, I was able to come for the first time in the year 2000 with the worship group. We were invited to play at different churches during the Florida Annual Conference. On my visit to Lakeland, I met several members of the United Methodist Church, among them Brenda and Marty Higgenbotham and Riley and Claire Short. They were extremely nice to me and showed interest in helping me develop my musical talent. In South Florida, I also met another very special couple, the Jhaveri Family, who became wonderful friends of mine. This trip marked my destiny. During one of the performances I met Roberto Michel, a wonderful Christian musician who five years later would become my first boyfriend, the love of my life.

After a month, I returned to Cuba, but in the USA I had found new friends and had made contact with people who could help me. I sent them a video where I interpreted several musical pieces. Even though my whole family was in Cuba, I had the desire to study in a country full of opportunities. As a Cuban national, it was nearly impossible for me to study in the USA. I did not know when or how, but I had faith that the Lord was going to open the door and my dreams would come true.

My friends started trying to get me a scholarship in Florida. In 2002, our worship group returned to the USA, this time invited by the North Carolina Conference, and we played numerous concerts in several churches. We also came to visit our friends in Lakeland, who had already contacted the distinguished piano professor Robert McDonald at Florida Southern College, a renowned Methodist college in this city. After watching my video, he tried to get me accepted

Ivelisse de la Fe

into the college. I went back to Cuba, but kept in close touch with my friends who were helpping me in Florida with my future plans.

Also in 2002, the First United Methodist Church sent a group of missionaries to Cuba. Among them the Higgenbotham and Short families. I had the opportunity to see them and once again express my desire to come to study in the United States. Again, they were wonderful to me, not only offering me their friendship but also helping me reach a goal that seemed impossible. These fabulous people had nothing to gain; they offered their unconditional help. Upon their return, they, along with Rakesh and Milly Jhaveri, did everything possible to gather the money and the necessary paperwork to comply with both countries' requirements, especially Cuba's, which were a lot more complicated.

In March 2003 my dream came true, and I arrived in Florida ready to start classes at Florida Southern College. After living a few months with the Jhaveri family, I arrived in Lakeland where I lived with the Higgenbotham family for awhile and later with the Shorts. I had a full scholarship through the Methodist Church, and a music

Ivelisse de la Fe

scholarship granted by Mrs. Julie Fancelli. Even though I was in my junior year in Cuba, I had to start from zero since I could not transfer the credits, and because I had to study very hard to gain domain of the English language. I had no family in the United States, yet I felt very secure.

I remember the day I arrived, trying to begin to learn English, everything I heard sounded like "Blah, blah, blah." For three days, I had headaches! I could not talk, and I was so frustrated because I am a very talkative person. At night I was turning words over in my mind and actually dreaming in English. Yet during those first days I could not seem to put the words together. Little by little I started to learn. Feeling like an idiot. I would point to an item and ask repeatedly how to say its name in English.

Then I started watching "Who Wants to be a Millionaire?" on TV and I learned phrases and trivia. In the summer of that year I had the opportunity to spend some time at the Methodist Camp in Leesburg, Florida, where I met many young people. One of them Audrey Warren, who became one of my best friends and with whom I could practice my English. I had to conquer English before school started in the fall. I was very dedicated and watched a lot of television. The show "Friends" was also a great help, along with my own friends who never tired of my innumerable questions.

All the while that I was adjusting to life in the USA and for all of my time here, the Higgenbothams have been the greatest blessing of my life. Brenda made sure that I had everything I needed to start school. She and her husband, Marty, bought a house near the college so I would have a place to live, and she decorated it herself, and even included a piano so that I could practice. I can never totally express the pain and sorrow I felt when she suddenly passed away, leaving within me a great sadness and emptiness. She had become my other mother in this country. At her funeral, I was full of emotion, but through my tears, I played two of her favorite piano pieces. The same day the Lord placed two other persons who become very special and important in my life, Susan and Waite Willis. Marty Higgenbotham continued being my own personal angel whom God sent to illuminate my life.

At the end of my first year at Florida Southern College, I received the Phi Eta Sigma Freshman Honor Award given to the student with the highest grades taking the greatest number of credit hours. I was also on the President's Scholar list each semester. It was the least I could do to show my appreciation for those who had worked so hard to bring me here and make my dream come true.

During my second year, I received the Alfred Courty Woodard Memorial Award and the Jack Houts Memorial Award in Music. During my senior year, I had the honor of receiving numerous awards such as the Robert Lee Zimmerman Award for Excellence and the Presser Scholar Award and Who's Who Among Students in American Universities and Colleges. In my years in college, I was a member of honor organizations such as Phi Kappa Phi Honor Society, Omicron Delta Kappa Leadership Society and Sigma Delta Phi. I graduated Summa Cum Laude with a 4.0.

I am very grateful for what the Lakeland community has done for me and I have tried to give back as much as possible, like offering my musical talent for several galas at the college, for Kiwanis Clubs, the Rotary Club, and the Chamber of Commerce. I continue to play at the Contemporary Worship at the First United Methodist Church and play in a praise band with my boyfriend, Roberto, wherever churches need us. I have also been a counselor in church camps.

Following my graduation from Florida Southern, with a degree in Music, I wanted to continue studying. I had met Teresa Martinez, a Cuban compatriot, and we became good friends. Teresa gave me an opportunity to work with her as an interpreter for several law firms for Spanish-speaking clients. I have always been fascinated by the rights and freedom of American citizens. Studying law seemed like a good challenge. I also would be following my grandfather's footsteps who studied law at the Universidad de la Habana.

After taking the LSAT, I was accepted for study at three different universities. I am now attending Stetson University College of Law for its renowned name in Florida and because it is close to home. I am on the Honor Roll. I have not decided what field of law to pursue, but I believe good, honest Christian lawyers are needed in the world.

The Lord has been good to me and has put numerous angels on my path, wonderful people who are part of my success. I share it with them. Aside from those whom I have already mentioned, I also want to thank Angela Higgenbotham, Marcia and Paul Alley, Mary Kay and John Langford and Ingrid McDonald, my church and all the angels who have enlightened my path. I thank my Lord and Savior who has given me and will continue to give me the strength to conquer new goals.

Of course, I am very grateful to my family in Cuba for always being my inspiration and for teaching me that with respect, love and a lot of perseverance I could reach the stars. My grandparents, parents, and brother decided to make me their priority and let me go far from them, for the first time, knowing my capacity for achievement and my strong will. Now, even though the separation and distance is hard, my family is proud of my accomplishments.

On one of my return trips to Cuba, Grandmother Caridad showed me a little theater program from her own youth. She confided to me that in those days of her childhood, the entertainment field was not thought fitting for a young lady, so she and her mother had to sneak out to the countryside little theaters so she could pursue her own love of singing and acting. Now, after all these years, I no longer wondered why she had so fervently supported my journey toward musical excellence, for on that program, across the front page, large letters announced Grandmother Caridad as *The Soul of the Song*.

Eduardo Sarmiento in his studio, Miami 2009

I Come From All Places

Eduardo Sarmiento

Time is the teacher of death.
GASTÓN BAQUERO

To my grandmother Rebeca , who taught me to draw.

I have packed my life in a suitcase on several occasions. At one time, I had a plane ticket from Havana to Mexico City, but my true destination was Miami. It was October 20, 2006 (Cuban Cultural Day). I was wearing a white *guayabera* and my face was breathing semi-hidden behind a dark beard. My luggage was light: a suitcase full of drawings, some pictures and the absolute certainty that a man should never stop before realizing his dreams, even when a knot is piercing his throat.

My name is Eduardo Sarmiento. I was born in Cienfuegos, Cuba in 1980, and I don't know exactly the day I am going to die. I am a plastic artist, illustrator and graphic designer.

At the age of eighteen I went to study in Havana at the Superior Institute of Design (ISDI). When I finished my career, I stayed in the capital living with friends or girlfriends.

My father lives with his wife and my two brothers; my mother with her girlfriend and their dog. My father is an orthopedic doctor and Mom is a gynecologist. Both of their salaries add up to $50 dollars a month. During the first years of my career when I visited Cienfuegos on the weekends, I used my mother's car to provide taxi services. It was hard at times because I was only 20 years old, and my hormones were screaming for parties and sex. In order to help the family's economy, I was illegally transporting prostitutes or tourists, running the risk of getting caught and being fined by the police. When I went home with money in my pocket, I could see my mother's face light up. She knew that her only son was assuming the role as the man of the house. On the other hand, I also saw her sadness for seeing me sacrificing my time in illegal endeavors after she had studied so much, and always been opposed to illegal activities. The fact is that I would make the same amount of money in one night as a taxi driver as my mother would operating and delivering babies during a whole month. It was an enriching experience. I grew quickly (true growth is usually painful). I learned to survive on the street becoming street-wise. I also had a lot of problems and even had to fight on several occasions. Of course, I never told this to my mom.

HAVANA

When I started my third year at the university, I had the opportunity to work as a freelance designer and illustrator for magazines and publishing companies. It was difficult at first, and I was earning very little. However, after several months of tireless work and knocking on all possible doors, I started to earn more or less the same as I did as a taxi driver (still much more than my parents). Those years were exquisite professionally for I met many intellectuals. I was the co-founder of *Camaleón*, a group of artists who worked painting murals, posters, books, and illustrations. I worked and studied, and I was even hired to do designs for clients who had access to US dollars. My finances had taken a turn for the better.

I remember the day I was able to buy my mother her first plastic washing machine. I paid $160 dollars. This was a huge family celebration and my mother could not stop boasting to her friends about her son's gift. I enjoyed the pride she showed, but her financial situation would sadden me (it still does). It was not that I wanted my mother to be a millionaire; I just wished that she was able to buy new tires for her car, with her own money. For the record, it is a pleasure for me to help her. She always offered me much more than she could, and she taught me about love and respect. I feel she gave me much more than I deserved.

CONTRADICTIONS

While I was a student, I believed in the possibility of living in Cuba and doing things for my country, and I enjoyed it a lot until I graduated and the challenges began. Once I graduated I started to work at the *Instituto Cubano del Libro* (Cuban Book Institute) as Art Director and as an Illustrator, teaching illustration and poster design at ISDI and as Art Director for the *National Cuban Ballet* magazine *Cuba en el Ballet.* I also continued doing projects with *Camaleón.* We received several national and international awards.

Professionally I had a privileged life, but my living situation was impossible. While I was studying, I lived at the university or at my girlfriend Themis' house, in Havana. When I graduated, I lived with a friend who offered me shelter in his apartment. Later, I went to live with Rocío, one of the loves of my life. My living situation was disconcerting. A Cuban who decided to live in Havana had no legal way to rent or buy a house or apartment. I arrived at the conclusion that in order to have a roof over my head, I either had to live with Rocío, or kill my grandmother so I could keep her house. Living with my girlfriend was great, while our love lasted; on the other hand, the idea of killing my grandma was only a literary argument!

QUITO

In 2006 my friend, Carlos Zamora, invited me to *La Rosa Gráfica* (The graphic rose) a design event in Quito, Ecuador with all expenses paid. Besides participating in a poster exhibition, I was asked to give a few dissertations about young graphic artists in Cuba. I traveled with a couple who were designers. That was too good to be true. One of my deepest desires was to travel the world. I felt the call to discover other lands. Since I was a member of the *Unión Nacional de Escritores y Artistas de Cuba* (UNEAC – National Union of Cuban Writers & Artists) and my work was cultural, it was not difficult to obtain the necessary papers to travel and represent Cuba in other countries. Quito opened the doors to the world and helped me prove that it was possible to make an honest and professional living off the island. I was tempted to try my luck, to stay in Quito and live there for a while, but I didn't think it was the ideal place to develop my artistic career. By that time, art was starting to dictate my path, and the promise of an inconclusive love was waiting for me back in Cuba.

CAUSES

I returned to Cuba to teach at the university and continued living in my girlfriend's apartment. I even had a room to do my art, but I was not just thinking about the present, I was thinking about the future of my art, the actual possibilities of development on the island and in all my parents' honest hard work, and how little they had to show for it. Days became a torment for me. Everything seemed cloudy, false. I slept with my jaws tightened; I started finding walls instead of bridges. I realized that the majority of the population did not want to do anything to avoid a compromising situation (they

Kassandra, Ella, Evan & Eddy García

He Made It Come True!
The Story of Eddy García

Teresa Vázquez Martínez

"Success-Some people dream of it…
while others wake up and work hard at it.
ANONYMOUS

I will never forget his welcoming hug. I had just left my country, my life as I knew it. My parents, sister and I arrived at the Miami Airport on March 5, 1970, to stay in Hialeah with Uncle Ricardo's family for a while. As I sat in the living room for the first time, he came in and sat on my lap, smiled, wrapped his little arms and legs around me and rested his head on my shoulder. My cousin, Eddy, was just five years old, yet he seemed to know that I was scared and heartbroken.

He was so handsome, so little and yet so strong and energetic; his blonde hair, brown eyes and big smile made him seem like a movie star child, full of stories and goodwill. We were the first family of direct relatives he had ever met, and he was so happy to have us there. I knew then he was a very special person, and I was right!

Aida and Ricardo unselfishly shared their home with us. Eight people happily living under the roof of their three-bedroom, one-bath home. They were the first to leave Cuba, even before communism, looking for a better life. Ricky, the oldest son, was born in Cuba; Eddy was born in New York. My aunt and uncle were factory workers and good parents; their children grew up in a humble and loving home. When I arrived, Ricky was 15, the same age I was, paving the way for me to adapt to my new school. He was very handsome and quite popular, so I was able to ride on his shirt tails. Soon life was easy again; we adapted to life in the United States and Mom and Dad were able to rent their own home in Hialeah. A year later we settled in Bartow, Central Florida.

Eddy would come and visit during the summers. He always brought a few dollars as spending money and went back home with as much money or more than when he arrived. He knew the value of a dollar, and everyone knew he was just not going to spend a dime unnecessarily… Eddy was saving for the future.

When Carlos and I got married in 1975, Eddy was our ring boy, and from then on, he would visit us during the summer. I bought him his first dog, Cookie, and Carlos taught Eddie to hunt, a sport they still enjoy together. He was our pride and joy. We were worried when we realized Eddy had no plans to go to college. We wanted more for him…yet, we should have known better. Eddy always had a plan!

He finished high school, a year before his projected graduation date. He continued living with his parents and saved every penny he made. He went to work for the Coca-Cola® Company, driving a truck and servicing vending machines. He invested in some of those machines, as well. Although he was criticized by the family for making a bad investment, he used his savings to purchase a dilapidated house and worked on it himself on the weekends. He sold it for a large profit and continued to invest in real estate, buying, remodeling and selling homes; making as much as 300% on his investments. It was time to stop working for the Coca-Cola® Company! He went to college and obtained a contractor's license. That was the start of the successes of a life time.

In 1992 he opened the doors of Watermen Properties, a name he adopted because it just sounded prestigious to him. It was a small office within "Worldwide Mortgage Company," his brother Rick's business which was located in Coral Gables, an elite area in Miami. This way they were able to share overhead expenses, and it has an impressive address. The first business card he ever handed a prospective customer got the response of, "I have heard of this company!" – He knew then he had made a good choice of business name! Eddy continued to work with no labor costs or salaries to pay.

One of his friends who was involved in a car accident received a $350.000 settlement. Eddy proposed to go into business together. He had the experience and his friend had the capital. They would go to the courthouse and buy foreclosed homes, remodel them and sell them. They made over $120,000 their first year. During one of the courthouse auctions, Eddy met up with his friend, Marty, who had a mortgage business and they started a new venture. The fierce, vulture-like competition of buying homes at auctions, together with the sadness of knowing that a family had actually lost their home, had started to take its toll. Eddy wanted to get involved in developments, and Marty was the perfect partner.

There was a parcel of land for sale in Hialeah for $750,000. Eddy only had $120,000 in his savings account. It was then that he recruited his high-school buddies, the Ventura brothers, as investors. He also obtained a character loan from his neighborhood community bank.

By then, he was living in a beautiful bachelor pad in South Beach. His life style would have to change considerably to be able to face his financial responsibilities. The development was planned...it would take eighteen months to build sixty-six townhomes. He moved to a small humble apartment, sold his beautiful black Porche convertible, and budgeted $18,000 to live on for eighteen months. Failure was not an option!

Everything was directed from a small trailer without much overhead. In eighteen months the job was finished and it was sold out before it was completed. They made a profit of $1.2 million.

Eddy García, Evan, Ella & Kassandra

Ricky, Janine, Mary & Ricky García

Waterman Development Group continued building many successful projects. The Ventura brothers decided to go work in their family business and Marty and Eddy continued building over 350 homes and shopping centers in Dade County. He became an expert at finding land in urban areas that did not have a for sale sign, avoiding competitive bidding; land and space had become scarce in Dade County.

A friend talked to Eddy about Fort Myers where more land was available at a reasonable price. It was the right place and the right time. Lee County's economy was not moving, and it was easy for someone with Eddy's experience to come and start building new higher-end homes, Mediterranean style...something new in the area. The projects were extremely successful; they would sell even before they were finished. They developed five residential projects and three shopping centers in Lee county. In time, national builders started to come to the area and land deals were harder to find.

Watermen Development Group then became a land development company only. Eddy continued to buy thousands of acres with the help of investors, buying and selling land for several million dollars and making four times the investment.

At the beginning of 2004, Eddy noticed a 125-acre parcel on Daniel Parkway near interstate 1-75 in Lee County. It did not have a "for sale" sign; but he thought it was an ideal site. He investigated and found that it was part of a bankruptcy case. Watermen Development Group purchased it for $16 million. The plan was to develop offices, warehouses and shops on this parcel. He got the city of Ft. Myers to annex the property. It was then that the market took a downturn due to the economy, and everything was put on hold.

In 2009 Lee County was looking for land to build a stadium; Eddy was urged to bid for it. Today his land is the site for the Boston Red Sox Spring Training Stadium. Lee county agreed to pay Watermen Development Group $20 million for the land plus the Boston Red Sox agreed to pay $5 million.

Eddy has been very successful, not only in business but also as a person. He has always maintained an impeccable reputation. His low-key demeanor, straightforward personality, along with a professional and sophisticated image, have earned him the respect of many key people in high places; something that many can achieve, but few maintain.

He still lives in Coral Gables with his wife Kassandra and their two young children, Evan and Ella. The main office of Watermen Development Group is located near his home. He commutes to Fort Myers on a weekly basis.

My cousin Eddy continues to be my pride and joy; a very loving and humble soul who has always worried about the well being of his family. His parents came to the United States for a reason, for a better life...for the American Dream... EDDY MADE IT COME TRUE!

Rick & Lisa García

That Mysterious Island

Rick García

It does not matter how high you reach, never forget your roots.
ANONYMOUS

I was not born in Cuba; my parents came to the United States in 1959 when Batista was still in power. On my mother's last visit to Cuba in 1960, she was pregnant with me. She came back to Miami and neither she nor my father ever returned. My childhood in "Little Havana" was greatly influenced by the Cuban exodus that took place at that time.

My mother is from Camaguey and my father from Havana. My father was an industrious man who owned two businesses: a gift store, where Cuban-made items could be found, and a leather store, where alligator skin purses and belts were manufactured and sold. I started helping him at a young age. I clearly remember the subject that dominated most of the conversations that took place with customers that entered my father's businesses, "The Cuban situation." There was not a day when I would not hear something about everything that was lost in "The Pearl of the Caribbean," the good life that was stolen by a mad man: the blueness of the sea, the whiteness of the sand, the majestic palm trees, the tropical fruit trees and the sugarcane fields. Roosters in Cuba seemed to be braver, their feathers shinier, and the length of their spurs were longer. Food seemed to have tasted better there as well. The *lechón asado,* roasted pork, the yuca, black beans and rice, plátanos fritos and the aguardiente, never could truly compare. There was romanticism about the memories, sadness about family, friends, and the life left behind in the country. There was patriotism in the ambitious conversations of the remote possibility of going back in a courageous rescue…recovering paradise. I grew up feeling as Cuban as anyone on the Island. I always wanted to go see it, to experience it for myself.

When I was fifteen years old, I had the great fortune of being able to take aviation classes as an elective in my high school.

I remember my first field trip to the Miami International Airport and Homestead Air Force Base, where my destiny was set in stone. Avionics was to become my life-long career. The aviation world became my passion.

In 1978 I decided to serve my country and enlisted in the U.S. Air Force. Once I finished my 4 years in the Air Force, I worked for a local avionics company. It was then I realized I wanted to have my own avionics business. I had learned a lot about business from my father; I knew I had the knowledge about the industry, and I was confident that I lived in a country where a man can do anything he sets his mind to do. I asked my father for a $10,000 start-up loan. In the beginning, he did not think I was ready to take on such a responsibility; I was too young and I had a new family to provide for. My father wanted me to learn more about the industry and have more experience before I started a new business. Thankfully, my father taught me another very valuable lesson growing up, PERSISTANCE. After a few months of discussion and my perseverance, my father finally agreed to loan me $10,000.00 with the stipulation that if I was successful, I would pay him back; if I wasn't, I was not to ask for more money. Failure was not an option. I was raised and surrounded by very strong and determined Cuban people in Miami. This was my one shot and I would be successful. I shook my father's hand and Gulf Coast Avionics was born in the garage of my home in Tampa, Florida in 1984.

I worked very hard and believed in myself and my mission. I knew I had been given a strong business foundation. I was fortunate that industry leaders noticed this 24-year-old man working with such a passion and drive. They began to mentor and guide me. I had the satisfaction of paying back my loan in full within six months!

Twenty five years later Gulf Coast Avionics is a multi-million dollar operation with headquarters in Lakeland, Florida with operations in Leesburg, Florida, Portland, Oregon, and Caracas, Venezuela. We sell, install and repair aircraft electronics and flight instruments for customers from all over the world. It has not always been easy, but I did inherit my father's courage. I realize that who I am today I owe to my parents' perseverance, business ethics and fortitude of character. I am grateful for my Cuban upbringing. Being bilingual and bicultural has facilitated international communication and overall understanding.

The memories of those days at my father's shop have continued to influence my life, and I have felt an unrelenting desire to somehow help those on the island. How is it that Cubans are so limited? Is there anything that we could do to help the situation? In 2004 I went to see our mysterious island for myself.

President Clinton had signed a free trade agreement for food and medical supplies with Cuba. I felt I was in a position to assist the U.S. government with this mission. I contracted a consultant to facilitate dealing with the Cuban government, created a trade company, a website, contacted all the necessary agencies and made several trips to Cuba. I met with many government officials. Unfortunately, the rules, restrictions and limitations of 44 years of oppression made it impossible to accomplish my mission. It was, however, an educational experience for me.

All the stories I had heard growing up did not prepare me for this emotional experience. Sitting on the plane I felt the excitement and the anticipation of the other passengers as everyone was looking out the windows, pointing in different directions. I saw tears fill their eyes as the plane landed. Once I went through the customs doors, there I was, in Havana, Cuba. I stood back and watched the other passengers claim their luggage, and I noticed everyone had several huge duffle bags bringing clothing, medicine, and the bare necessities to their families living in Cuba. They were being meticulously

Lisa & Rick García in Cuba

Carlos Luna

Carlos Luna is one of the most prominent Cuban artists of his generation, with a meteoric career and a defined personal style. Born in Pinar del Rio, Cuba, Carlos began his personal training as an artist at a very early age, attending various government art schools for promising young artists. At 16 years of age, his work had been already shown in group exhibitions in Cuba; and internationally a year later. Carlos Luna fled the Communist regime of Fidel Castro, in 1991, taking with him his strong personality, and an insatiable desire for growth in the art field. He immigrated to Puebla, Mexico where his career started a new phase of exploration and success.

After receiving a U.S. EB-1-1 visa for foreigners with extraordinary ability, Carlos emigrated to Miami, along with his wife and three children. Since their arrival in the United States, his work has been received with great enthusiasm and has been exhibited individually and collectively in more than 25 museums and art institutions around the country. It is highly appreciated by connoisseurs and art critics. Carlos Luna's work has expanded in scope to an international audience. His artistic vision and influence has now reached a global scale.

In the past three years, the recognitions that Luna has received from curators and critics have allowed him to increase his number of solo exhibitions in different museums throughout the country, including the *Bass Museum of Art* in Miami Beach; *American University Museum,* Washington, D.C.; *Museum of Latin American Art,* Long Beach, California; *Polk Museum of Art,* Lakeland, FL, as well as the presence of his art in a growing list of collective exhibitions and museum's collections.

Among Luna's many successes, is the Pollo*ck-Krasner Foundation Award* received in 2001. In the same manner, his career reached an important milestone in 2008 with the joint exhibition Pablo Picasso Ceramics | Carlos Luna Paintings, in the *Museum of Art of Fort Lauderdale,* Florida, and in 2009 at the *Cultural University Complex BUAP,* in Puebla, Mexico.

A quemar penas compay / **Burning in hell, my friend**, 2000
Oil on canvas
19 ¾ x 15 ¾ in (50 x 40 cm)
© Carlos Luna

Para un gallo pisador, una mujer elegante (detalle) / **An elegant woman for a horny rooster** (detail), 1999
Oil on canvas
43 x 51 in (110 x 130 cm)

Las cuatro estaciones / **The four seasons**, 1999
Oil on canvas
47 ¼ x 70 ¾ in (120 x 180 cm)

Carlos Luna

Los novios (detalle) / **The lovers** (detail), 2002
Oil on canvas
47 ½ x 59 in (120 x 150 cm)

Pisando tierra / **Touching land**, 2000
Oil on canvas
59 x 47 in (150 x 120 cm)

Isla sola II (detalle) / **An island alone II** (detail), 2007
Gouache and charcoal on amate paper
15 ½ x 47 in (39 x 120 cm)
© Carlos Luna

Isla sola III (detalle) / **An island alone III** (detail), 2007
Gouache and charcoal on amate paper
19 ½ x 53 ½ in (49 x 136.5 cm)
© Carlos Luna

Carlos Luna

BESAME
AHHH

ÉXITO *en el* EXILIO

CINCO DÉCADAS DE HISTORIAS CUBANAS

Teresa Vázquez Martínez

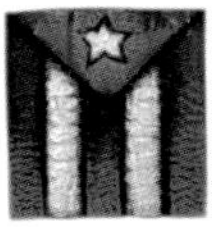

PINTURAS DE
Carlos Luna

Institute of Spanish Communication, Inc.

1ra Edición: Diciembre, 2009

4927 Southfork Drive
Lakeland, Florida 33813
www.instituteofspanish.com
T. 863-646-5141

Todas las pinturas y viñetas: © Carlos Luna
www.carlosluna.com
Edición: Dra. Norma de la Torre, Teresa Vázquez Martínez
y Stephen Osthoff
Dirección de Arte: Eduardo Sarmiento
www.eduardosarmiento.com

Library of Congress
ISBN: 978-0-9825558-0-4

Impreso en China

A mis padres
El Dr. Luis J. Vázquez y María Teresa García de Vázquez

Mis suegros
El Rev. Gerardo Martínez † y Teresa Hidalgo de Martínez

Y Lizette, Alexis, Peter, Lauren, Antonio y Colton
Por ser mi inspiración

Agradecimientos

Ha tomado más de dos años recopilar, editar y traducir las anécdotas en este libro, las cuales han sido la contribución de muchos individuos, familiares y amigos, quienes me han otorgado permiso para publicar y hasta filmar sus historias personales. Es nuestro propósito común el dejar testimonio de nuestro éxodo, para que otras generaciones aprecien la libertad. Mi más sincera gratitud a todos los participantes. Muchas gracias por apoyarme y animarme hasta la recta final.

Quiero darle las gracias a ***Mami*** *y* ***Papi*** *por haber tenido la valentía y entereza de carácter para desarraigar a nuestra familia y traerla a un país libre. Gracias por asegurar que Lourdes y yo, tanto como nuestros hijos, hayamos podido disfrutar del libre albedrío. Ustedes han sido un perfecto ejemplo de lo que es ser buenos padres, seguiremos su ejemplo con nuestros hijos. Este libro es tanto el logro de ustedes, como el mío.*

Mi querido esposo ***Carlos****, gracias por amarme incondicionalmente y proporcionarme todo el apoyo, tanto emocional como financiero, que he necesitado. Gracias por leer todas las historias y darme tu opinión y la atención que he requerido. ¡Eres lo mejor!*

A mis bellas hijas ***Lizette*** *y* ***Alexis****: Gracias por ser mi inspiración, por ayudarme a corregir las historias, por comprender mis compromisos de trabajo y por siempre darme el 100% de su amor, respeto y apoyo. Gracias por ser jóvenes exitosas y autónomas. ¡Estoy muy orgullosa de ustedes!*

Lizette*, mil gracias por obsequiarme el gran tesoro que es* ***Antonio****.*

Mi hermana ***Lourdes****, mi más devota aficionada y cheerleader personal. Gracias por siempre estar ahí, a cada paso del camino, y por pensar que la mayoría de las cosas que yo hago son fantásticas…¡Eres tú la que es FANTÁSTICA!*

Este libro no se hubiera podido terminar sin la ayuda y el continuo apoyo de mi fiel amiga peruana y colega, **Karen Gallardo Heverling**. No hay palabras para expresar mi gratitud por tu dedicación incondicional. Gracias por editar, traducir y revisar cada página. ¡Ahora ya casi eres cubana! Te nombraremos "Cubana Honoraria".

Me gustaría extender una gratitud muy especial a **Gay Finkleman**, Presidente de Ginnie Publishing, Inc. y escritora de historias personales, quien fue instrumental en el lanzamiento de este libro. Muchas gracias mi amiga.

A la **Dra. Norma de la Torre**, mi amiga de toda la vida; mi primera maestra en los Estados Unidos, a quien le prometí escribir este libro hace 38 años. Gracias por darme el regalo de innumerables horas de apoyo. Ha sido un privilegio tenerte a mi lado y trabajar contigo…en persona y por teléfono…hasta altas horas de la madrugada. Gracias por ser tú, pero sobre todo, por la gran influencia que has tenido en mi vida.

A mi queridísimo amigo y colega, el profesor **Stephen Osthoff** por haber sido el corrector de pruebas de todas las historias para asegurar que el inglés no se "cubanizara". ¡Gracias hermanito!

Mi especial agradecimiento a una gran cantidad de amigos y familiares quienes han aportado su tiempo y conocimientos a este proyecto: **Claudia Luna**, **Pam Matheny**, **Sandra Hudson**, **Ami Scroggin**, **Dr. Luis J. Vázquez** y muchos más. A la **Dra. Solange Pendas**, **Mark Kaylor**, **Emily Soto**, **Daniel Stetson** y **Carolyn Jackson**, por sus ideas y sugerencias. Gracias a **Wayne Kline** por siempre cuidarme las espaldas y asegurar mi éxito. A mi diseñador gráfico, **Ed Sarmiento**, por tu talento, amistad y también por haber sido mi GPS personal cuando me perdía en el tráfico del gran Miami.

También quiero mencionar a **Lizette**, **Alexis**, **Ana**, **Alex**, **Abby**, **Maya**, **Isaac** y **Adam Martínez; Ami** y **Sam Scroggin**, **Peter Petriw** y **Lauren Farrell**, tanto como a mi querido amiguito **Nathan Gimness**, por ser nuestra exitosa e independiente primera generación de cubanos, honrando así el sacrificio que hicieron sus abuelos, y sus padres al dejar su patria.

Sobre todas las cosas, le doy gracias a **Dios** por tantas bendiciones que he recibido en mi vida. En este caso en particular, por haber puesto a una persona del calibre del internacionalmente reconocido artista cubano, **Carlos Luna**, en mi camino. Es un honor inefable para mí poder tener tus obras representadas en este libro. **Carlos**, gracias por el privilegio de poner mi nombre junto al tuyo.

Contenido

10 Prefacio • *Dra. Norma de la Torre*

12 Prólogo • *Dr. José Manuel García*

14 Introducción • *Teresa Vázquez Martínez*

22 Mi isla en forma de cocodrilo • *Teresa Vázquez Martínez*

DÉCADA DEL 60

42 Invadidos por nuestra propia gente • *Felipe y Alicia Olivera*

46 No sabía nadar:
Una historia de estoicismo • *Dr. Sergio y Mirtha Vallejo*

52 Lo vi venir • *Dr. Pedro Almazán*

58 Un verdadero acto de amor • *Rosa Delfín Hernández*

64 ¡Yo creo en milagros! • *Dr. Ramón Rodríguez-Torres*

70 Un legado de fe. La historia del Rev. Gerardo
y Teresa Martínez • *Teresa Hidalgo de Martínez*

76 Una lección de patriotismo • *Martha Espinosa Laurent*

86 Tesoros de Cuba • *Ana María Guitérrez Myers*

92 Cinco dólares y una caja de tabacos • *Roberto y Viviana Pedroso*

98 Oportunidades encontradas,
una oportunidad perdida • *Dr. Jorge González*

DÉCADA DEL 70

104 Cinco años de soledad • *Loly Garriga*

110 Edificando el futuro • *Eduardo Tapia*

114 Recuerdos de una heladera • *Dania Frías de Pendas*

120 La juventud truncada
de Yara Borges Guzmán • *Dra. Norma de la Torre*

DÉCADA DEL 80

128 Recuerdos de un preso político • *Pedro Ramiro Machín*

144 Mis recuerdos de El Mariel • *Dr. José Manuel García*

150 Alcancé mi meta • *Acela (Carito) Lumpuy*

158 Mi escape por Honduras • *Dr. Manuel Martínez*

DÉCADA DEL 90

166 Siempre estaré contigo • *Carlos Luna*

176 Todo fue una mentira • *Eduardo Fernández*

DÉCADA DEL 2000

182 El alma de la canción • *Ivelisse de la Fe*

190 Yo vengo de todas partes • *Eduardo Sarmiento*

NACIDOS EN USA

196 ¡Él lo realizó! La historia de Eddy García • *Teresa Vázquez Martínez*

202 Aquella isla misteriosa • *Rick García*

GALERÍA

208 Pinturas de Carlos Luna

Dra. Norma de la Torre

Prefacio

Dra. Norma de la Torre

Por primera vez, y en sus propias palabras, Teresa Vázquez Martínez, nos relata el intenso trauma que sufrió cuando sus padres decidieron irse de Cuba con sus dos hijas: ella, Teresa, y Lourdes, su hermana. También nos cuenta las dificultades que enfrentaron para abandonar la isla; su llegada a estas tierras de libertad, y como su familia fue capaz de reconstruir - con éxito- unas vidas drásticamente interrumpidas por la revolución castrista.

A la vez, la autora incluye en este libro, la odisea por la que atravesaron otras veinticuatro familias que, como la suya, tuvieron que abandonar su país de origen - y todas sus posesiones materiales- para "comenzar en cero", en una tierra extranjera, con idioma, costumbres, olores y sabores diferentes a los de su patria. Cada familia constituye un vivido ejemplo de lo que significa Éxito en el Exilio

La mayoría de estas historias han sido escritas por los propios protagonistas. Otras están basadas en entrevistas grabadas o filmadas por la autora. Todas incluyen fotografías familiares y personales.

En este importante trabajo, Teresa también incluye estadísticas, más otros datos relevantes de lo que fue Cuba antes del gobierno marxista-leninista de Fidel Castro; así como un análisis de los distintos éxodos ocurridos en los cincuenta años de opresión y desgobierno que ha sufrido la isla. Incluye también una bella y colorida galería del arte de nuestro internacionalmente aclamado pintor cubano, Carlos Luna, quien a través de sus obras, nos hace un relato visual de las costumbres de nuestro país, y de la tragedia del cubano.

Esta obra nos demuestra, una vez mas, la ingenuidad y el talento extraordinario de su autora, una ilustre exiliada, que- hoy en día- es una figura prominente de su comunidad, además de constituir un legítimo orgullo para todos los exiliados cubanos, y los exiliados de cualquier otro país, donde quiera que estos se encuentren.

Prólogo

Dr. José Manuel García

Con absoluta franqueza quiero manifestar que este es uno de los libros más interesantes, conmovedores e inspiradores que he leído. Esta importante obra testimonial, que relata la realidad de los exiliados a través de sus propias voces, penetra en lo más profundo de nuestros espíritus haciéndonos reflexionar sobre quiénes somos, qué queremos y a dónde vamos. A la vez nos urge a mirar de forma distinta todo aquello que damos por descontado cuando se vive en un país libre.

Al igual que otros muchos inmigrantes cubanos, mi familia y yo llegamos a los Estados Unidos, como parte del éxodo del Mariel en 1980, escapando de una tiranía y en busca de una vida mejor. Sólo unos días antes de nuestra llegada a estas tierras, mi padre había sido arrestado por los soldados de la dictadura castrista y días después, durante la travesía en aquellas peligrosas aguas, nuestra embarcación se hundía en el estrecho de la Florida, pero nuestro espíritu y nuestros sueños de libertad triunfaron sobre estas vicisitudes.

Teresa Martínez, la autora de este fascinante libro de memorias, también vino a los Estados Unidos escapando de una cruel dictadura que cambió su vida y la de su familia. Su vida es un vivo ejemplo de cómo, a través de la perseverancia y la dedicación, todos los sueños son posibles en esta tierra de oportunidades. Ella, después de una exitosa carrera como educadora, también logró triunfar en el mundo de los negocios y ha dedicado gran parte de su vida a ayudar a la comunidad hispana y a otros inmigrantes a alcanzar sus metas. Teresa es hoy una distinguida figura hispana en el centro de la Florida, donde es la productora/presentadora de un importante y popular programa en la televisión local.

Este libro es la materialización de un sueño de la autora, que indudablemente será una importante aportación al estudio de la inmigración hasta pudiera servir como texto de referencia para los estudios étnicos en los Estados Unidos. La obra en si es otra prueba del

talento de Teresa Martínez, quien demuestra una vez más su compromiso con otros inmigrantes.

Yo, como profesor y Jefe de Cátedra del Departamento de Idiomas de *Florida Southern College* y crítico de la literatura hispana, puedo aseverar que libros como éste son sólo posibles cuando sus autores son parte de esa misma experiencia y necesitan compartirla para que otros también puedan alcanzar sus sueños.

El texto, a pesar de hacer hincapié en la realidad política y económica del exiliado cubano, puede ser una herramienta motivadora para que otros inmigrantes luchen por sus metas y por sus sueños; y para que sus hijos tomen conciencia de los esfuerzos y sacrificios realizados por ellos, quienes abandonando todo, vinieron a esta tierra en busca de mayores oportunidades para brindarles una vida mejor.

Estatua de José Martí. Cienfuegos, Cuba

Estatua de la Libertad. New York, USA

Introducción

Teresa Vázquez Martínez

QUIÉNES SOMOS LOS CUBANOS

Los exiliados cubanos en los Estados Unidos hemos tenido una influencia notable en la economía, la política y el desarrollo social de este país, especialmente en Miami, New Jersey, New York, California y Texas. Sin embargo, los sacrificios han sido muchos. Es por eso que existe la necesidad de dar testimonio de las experiencias vividas para haber podido llegar a donde nos encontramos hoy.

Nosotros estamos orgullosos de lo que se ha logrado como una nación de cubanos en el exilio, de las abnegaciones que hemos hecho para superarnos y asegurar el bienestar y la libertad de nuestras familias.

Los cubanos tenemos el ingreso más alto per cápita de todas las minorías en los Estados Unidos, así como el nivel más alto de educación. Nosotros hemos sido descritos como el grupo de habla extranjera que ha tenido el índice más alto, y el más rápido ascenso a la clase media, en la historia de los Estados Unidos. En el transcurso de los años, hemos hecho una enorme contribución a la cultura americana, para el beneficio de todos.

Los artistas cubano-americanos como Celia Cruz, Gloria y Emilio Estefan, Desi Arnaz, Andy García, Cristina Saralegui, Cameron Díaz, Carmen Electra, Jon Secada, Christina Milián, Willy Chirino, Lissette Álvarez, Albita, Olga Guillot, Enrique Chía, Cachao y muchos más, han ascendido bien alto los escalones del éxito. Otros han estado involucrados activamente en política, incluso elegidos como congresistas de los Estados Unidos, tales como Ileana Ros-Lehtinen, Lincoln y Mario Díaz-Balart, de la Florida y el Senador Robert Menéndez de New Jersey; Bob Martínez, cuarentavo Gobernador de la Florida; el Senador Mel Martínez, primer latino en servir en la capacidad de Director del Partido Republicano en los Estados Unidos, y muchos más.

Tenemos también a Jorge Mas Canosa, un gran activista conocido por su fuerte oposición contra Fidel Castro y por su liderazgo

en la Fundación Nacional Cubano-Americana. Fue considerado por muchos como la figura líder de los exiliados cubanos en Miami, Florida. En el campo de los negocios encontramos a Roberto Goizueta, Presidente, Director y Gerente General de *The Coca-Cola Company,* desde agosto de 1980 hasta su fallecimiento en octubre de 1997; Raúl Alarcón, Presidente y Director General de *Spanish Broadcasting Systems*; Ralph Álvarez, Presidente y Director Operacional de *McDonalds*; la familia Bacardí; la familia Fanjul, y muchos más.

Es importante que nuestra historia sea conocida y compartida. Nosotros venimos de una tierra hermosa; una tierra que, antes que Castro tomara el poder, fue la tercera potencia económica de América Latina. Nosotros somos los hijos de la *Perla del Caribe,* la tierra del azúcar, del tabaco y del ron. Somos carismáticos, innovadores y extrovertidos. Tenemos un espíritu emprendedor, un carácter orgulloso que nos ayuda a superar problemas, y que nos ha situado en posiciones prominentes dentro de la sociedad norteamericana.

Mi agradecimiento más profundo a todas las familias que amablemente me ofrecieron sus historias personales, para asegurar que nuestras nuevas generaciones -quienes gozan del privilegio de haber nacido en libertad- sepan que es importante apreciarla, amar a la tierra que nos recibió como exiliados y, sobretodo, que estén orgullosos de sus raíces. También para que nuestros amigos norteamericanos, tanto como los de otras partes del mundo, sepan de nuestro agradecimiento a los países que nos han acogido, y aprendan por los testimonios en este libro, de lo que le puede suceder a un país que no esté celoso y vigilante de su libertad.

El Éxodo Cubano

Los cubanos que hemos llegado a los Estados Unidos somos conocidos por nuestro progreso, innovación y deseo insaciable de alcanzar el éxito. Además de ser emigrantes, también somos exiliados. Nosotros nos vimos forzados a abandonar la isla, que una vez Cristóbal Colón describiera como "La tierra más bella que ojos humanos han visto". Han transcurrido más de cinco décadas desde aquel fatídico día de año nuevo de 1959, tiempo durante el cual se han destacado cuatro éxodos principales:

PRIMER ÉXODO (1959 - 1962)

La mayoría de los cubanos que primero llegaron a Miami en 1959 fueron los seguidores y miembros del gobierno de Fulgencio Batista. Poco después, comenzaron a llegar los empresarios y profesionales cuyas propiedades y negocios fueron confiscados por el nuevo gobierno de Fidel Castro. Estos veían la situación revolucionaria como algo que no duraría mucho tiempo y pensaban que regresarían en un futuro no muy lejano. Algunos pronto comenzaron a planear la invasión de Bahía de Cochinos, con la ayuda del gobierno americano, la cual resultó en un fracaso total. Poco después, Castro se alineó a la Unión Soviética y se declaró Marxista-Leninista, asegurando así protección rusa para su gobierno.

Dentro de esta etapa también se debe reconocer la *Operación Pedro Pan*, coordinada por el Departamento de Estado de los Estados Unidos, la CIA, la Arquidiócesis de Miami y algunos cubanos exiliados. Mediante esta operación, más de 14,000 niños fueron enviados a los Estados Unidos por sus padres, quienes se oponían al gobierno revolucionario y temían por sus hijos, debido a los insistentes rumores de que éstos serían enviados a campamentos estudiantiles en la Unión Soviética. Con la ayuda del Monseñor Bryan O. Walsh, los niños fueron recibidos por familiares, amigos de su familia, o por familias anfitrionas en este país.

LOS VUELOS DE LA LIBERTAD (1965 - 1974)

El descontento continuaba en Cuba por la falta de libertad de expresión, religión y por las dificultades económicas y políticas. Las pequeñas empresas pasaron a manos del "pueblo" (entiéndase el gobierno) y la propiedad privada dejó de existir. Cada día había más encarcelamientos y ejecuciones, algunas de ellas públicas, a causa del desacuerdo político. Debido a la presión anti-castrista, Fidel abrió el Puerto de Camarioca en 1965, para que aquellos que desearan abandonar el país, pudieran ser rescatados por sus parientes en el exilio. Más tarde, el Presidente Lyndon Johnson inauguró los famosos "Vuelos de la Libertad". Estos vuelos trajeron a cientos de miles de cubanos a Miami. Otros salieron por España y por México. Se calcula que, durante esta etapa, salieron alrededor de 450,000 cubanos de la isla.

La mayoría de estos cubanos tuvieron que salir del país sin sus pertenencias. Sólo pudieron llevarse artículos de primera necesidad y aquello que el gobierno de Castro no les podía quitar: la fe en Dios, el amor por su familia, la educación, la dignidad y la perseverancia. Llegaron sin sus credenciales y sin sus títulos universitarios, los cuales necesitaban ser revalidados. No tenían crédito para obtener préstamos comerciales, ni nada que los acreditara como personas responsables y honradas. Desde los más prestigiosos profesionales y dueños de empresas, hasta los más humildes trabajadores, tuvieron que irse a trabajar lavando platos en restaurantes, como ayudantes en gasolineras, limpiando oficinas o en cualquier trabajo honesto que estuviera disponible. Miles de damas profesionales, o aquellas quienes -debido a su nivel social- nunca habían trabajado en Cuba, ahora se veían trabajando como costureras en factorías, o como sirvientas limpiando casas. Poco a poco fueron reedificando sus vidas y creando lo que hoy describimos como un exilio exitoso.

EL MARIEL (1980)

En abril de 1980, un autobús lleno de cubanos, se estrelló contra las puertas de la Embajada del Perú en la Habana, buscando refugio político. Durante el tiroteo que resultó, dos guardias fueron heridos y Fidel, furioso, dio orden de quitar el puesto de seguridad a la entrada de la embajada. En pocas horas, más de 10,000 cubanos buscaban refugio en el recinto. Frenético, Castro abrió el Puerto del Mariel y anunció que cualquiera que quisiera irse de la isla, podía hacerlo. De inmediato, una flotilla de cubanos-americanos, a la que

se le dio el nombre de "Flotilla de la Libertad", salió en busca de sus familiares, mientras otros iban por la oportunidad de hacer dinero. Se estima que entre abril y septiembre de ese año, llegaron unos 125,000 cubanos a la Florida.

Un gran porcentaje de estos nuevos refugiados eran obreros y campesinos; parte del pueblo por el cual, según Fidel, se había llevado a cabo la revolución. Ya que, durante este tiempo, también se había llegado a un acuerdo con el Presidente Jimmy Carter para liberar a los presos políticos y permitirle salir del país, Fidel aprovechó esta oportunidad para vaciar sus cárceles y manicomios. Ya no era sólo la clase alta la que huía de las garras del comunismo. Aunque entre los *Marielitos* llegaron dignos profesionales y miles de personas honorables, los criminales y enfermos mentales que se encontraban sueltos en las calles de Miami, hicieron daño a la imagen del cubano que existía entre la población norteamericana.

LOS BALSEROS (1993 - 1995)

La economía cubana continuaba empeorando y con el colapso de la Unión Soviética en 1991, llegó a paupérrimas condiciones. Fidel estaba sintiendo la presión de un pueblo descontento y una vez más, en un ataque de furia, declaró que todo el que quisiera irse de la isla podía hacerlo. Ya que no había transporte disponible, miles de personas se tiraron al mar en balsas improvisadas o en cualquier cosa que los mantuviera a flote en alta mar. Millares de cubanos, durante las cinco décadas de comunismo, han preferido correr el riesgo de ahogarse o ser devorados por tiburones, antes de quedarse viviendo bajo la opresión del régimen castrista. El estrecho de la Florida es la tumba de una enorme cantidad de cubanos desconocidos, incluyendo mujeres y niños.

EL ACUERDO

Por fin, se firmó un acuerdo entre los Estados Unidos y Cuba para otorgar visas a 20,000 cubanos por año, la conocida "Lotería de Visas", aún vigente. Todavía hoy, miles de cubanos llegan a la Florida en busca de libertad. Aquellos que salen clandestinamente, a través del océano, solamente pueden quedarse en los Estados Unidos, si logran pisar suelo estadounidense; de lo contrario los guardacostas los devuelven a Cuba. Esto es popularmente conocido como la ley de "Pie Seco o Pie Mojado". Mientras tanto, nunca se oye de nadie, de ninguna otra parte del mundo civilizado, tratando de escapar y buscar refugio político y económico en Cuba.

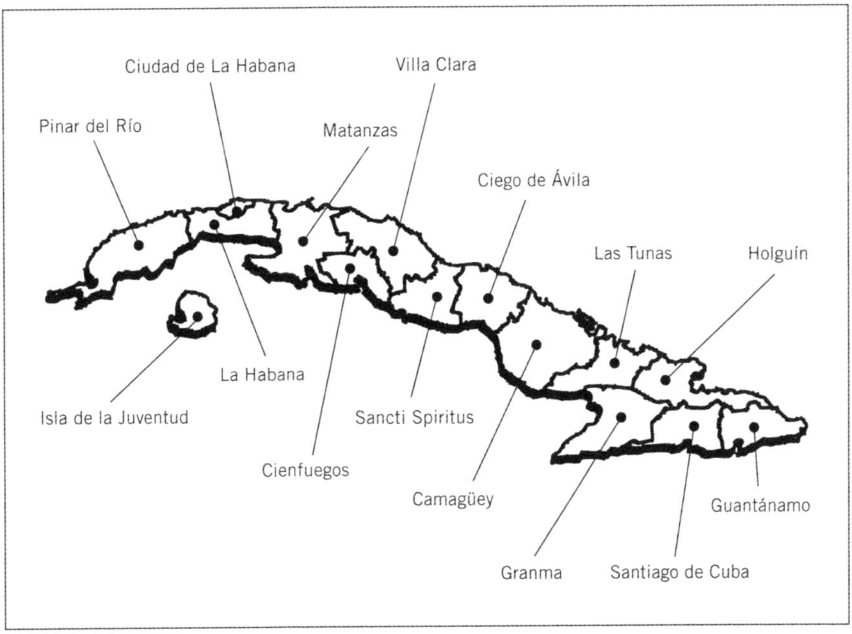

Mapa de la isla de Cuba en la actualidad

ISLA DE CUBA

La República de Cuba es un país asentado en un archipiélago del mar Caribe. Su isla principal, conocida como Isla de Cuba, es la más grande de las Antillas Mayores y se reconoce, a vista de pájaro, por su forma de cocodrilo. También forman parte del archipiélago la *Isla de la Juventud,* la cual se conoció como *Isla de Pinos* hasta 1978, y otros 4,195 cayos o islas pequeñas. Cuba se encuentra cerca de México y de los Estados Unidos, a sólo 90 millas de Cayo Hueso. Tiene más de 11 millones de habitantes, y es la nación isleña más poblada del Caribe.

El nombre de Cuba proviene de la palabra *cubao* en lengua taína que se traduce "Donde la tierra fértil abunda" o *coabana* que se traduce a la lengua española como "Gran lugar".

Algunos Hechos de la Cuba antes de Castro

• En 1958, Cuba era la tercera potencia económica de América Latina por sus reservas de oro, dólares y valores convertible en metales preciosos, después de Venezuela y Brasil. Su inflación era la más baja de la región con 1.4% (la media era de México con 7.8% y la más alta era la de Bolivia con 63%). El peso cubano valía igual que el dólar americano y en ocasiones, lo superó.

• En el campo de la salud, Cuba ocupaba el tercer lugar en Latinoamérica, después de Uruguay y Argentina, con 128 médicos y dentistas por 100,000 habitantes. El nivel de mortalidad infantil era el más bajo de la región.

• En 1958, Cuba era el primer productor de cobalto en América Latina y el segundo de níquel a nivel mundial.

• En cuanto al consumo de pescado fresco, Cuba ocupaba el primer lugar con 5.6 libras por persona, seguida de los Estados Unidos con 5.4. En el consumo de calorías, Cuba ocupaba en América Latina el tercer lugar con 2,682 superada solamente por Argentina con 3,106 y Uruguay con 2,991.

• Cuba disfrutaba de un excelente sistema educativo y un porcentaje impresionante de alfabetismo en la década de los 50. Así mismo, fue el país con el mayor porcentaje de gasto público para la educación.

• Cuba ocupaba el primer lugar en América Latina y el quinto en el mundo en televisores per cápita. Además tenía 58 periódicos en circulación y ocupaba el octavo lugar a nivel mundial en número de estaciones de radio.

• En cuanto al porcentaje de auto por capita, Cuba ocupaba el tercer lugar. Los autos nuevos llegaban primero a Cuba que a Miami.

• La vida en Cuba era comparable a la de los Estados Unidos.

Estos hechos se pueden encontrar en: *UN Statistical Yearbook; the Statistical Abstract for Latin America; and the Bureau of Inter-American Affairs, U.S. Department of State, Contacto Magazine, Cuban Facts, Wikipedia Free Encyclopedia.*

Dr. Luis J. Vázquez y María Teresa García de Vázquez

Mi isla en forma de cocodrilo

Teresa Vázquez Martínez

La libertad, Sancho, es uno de los más preciosos dones que a los hombres dieron los cielos; con ella no pueden igualarse los tesoros que encierran la tierra y el mar: por la libertad, así como por la honra, se puede y debe aventurar la vida.
MIGUEL DE CERVANTES SAAVEDRA

La vida era bella en mi isla… las aguas azules y cristalinas de la Playa de Varadero; las palmas majestuosas orgullosamente erectas en medio de la vegetación tropical de las montañas y valles. Todavía, cuando cierro los ojos, puedo verme junto a mi hermana Lourdes, cruzando el puente de tronco de palma sobre el arroyito de La Guásima (el camino más corto a través del monte tropical) para ir a visitar a Tío Filo y Tía Mercedes en el campo. Su casa, donde creció nuestra madre, era una linda casa de madera, rodeada de árboles de frutas y con un gran pozo del cual se abastecían de agua potable. El aroma de las hojas de tabaco impregnaban las paredes del almacén; recuerdo los campos de caña de azúcar y mi lugar favorito… el "monte", el bosquecillo a donde mi prima Nancy y yo nos escapábamos para ir a sentarnos bajo el árbol de mamoncillo. Allí nos contábamos nuestros secretos y sueños más preciados y profundos. Teníamos entre siete y diez años. Nancy era y es mi prima favorita, mi confidente. De vez en cuando Tío Filo venía en su caballo y nos moríamos de susto. A todos los niños nos gustaba pasar parte del verano en su casa en La Guásima. Era algo así como la Granja del Viejo McDonald, donde había una variedad de animales y teníamos la libertad de correr y jugar en los prados sin ninguna preocupación.

En nuestro pueblo, Esperanza, Las Villas, vivíamos cerca de todo. La mayoría de los familiares más allegados vivíamos en la calle Barnada. Estábamos rodeados del amor de los abuelos, quienes vivían en ambos lados de nuestra casa, y el de los tíos y primos. Por las tardes íbamos de casa en casa para ver quién tenía la comida más sabrosa y

probarla. Por la noche, todos los vecinos se sentaban en los portales a mecerse en los sillones y a saludar a todo el que pasaba. Era un pasatiempo fantástico y, sobre todo, una buena forma de enterarse de las últimas noticias y rumores del pueblo. Papi, el Dr. Luis J. Vázquez, tenía su consultorio adyacente a nuestra casa. Siempre estaba entrando y saliendo, entre consulta y consulta, para ir a tomarse un cafecito, para oler las especias con las que se cocinaba, para averiguar lo que estábamos haciendo, o simplemente para robarle un besito a Mami. Todavía puedo oler el aroma fresco de su traje blanco de médico, del mejor hilo, siempre muy bien planchado y almidonado. Él casi siempre se vestía de blanco al igual que la mayoría de los doctores en la isla. Nuestra casa de estilo colonial tenía un lindo patio de losa en el centro, suficientemente grande para que Lourdes y yo pudiéramos dar vueltas en bicicleta o sentarnos con las amigas a mecernos en el columpio. Cada habitación de la casa daba a este patio, así que Mami o las señoras que la ayudaban siempre podían vernos. La calle Barnada estaba en el centro del pueblo. Allí se encontraba la Iglesia Católica y el Parque Central donde se reunían los jóvenes durante las noches. Había una glorieta en el centro del mismo donde tocaba una banda durante los fines de semana, mientras las damas, vestidas con sus mejores galas, caminaban en dirección opuesta a los caballeros. De vez en cuando alguno paraba a una dama para caminar juntos o para sentarse en un banco a conversar y así comenzar un romance. El parque estaba rodeado de árboles de flamboyán que proporcionaban sombra durante el día. Cuando estaban floridos, las flores anaranjadas parecían llamas de fuego. Siempre había bonita actividad en el parque.

En la esquina de nuestra calle estaba La Central, la tienda mixta de mi tío Carlos, donde se conocieron mis padres. Mami, María Teresa García, era una bella mujer con cuerpo moldeado como un reloj de arena. Papi era un rubiecito delgado que estaba en casa durante sus vacaciones de la escuela de medicina. Mami estaba pasándose unos días con su hermana Lidia y Carlos, ayudando a cuidar a sus sobrinos Carlitos y Manolo. ¡Fue un flechazo! Tan pronto Papi se graduó, se casaron y vinieron a vivir a la calle Barnada. La Central era el lugar donde la gente se reunía, no solamente para comprar los víveres, sino también para tomar un trago, un cafecito o comerse un buen pan con lechón. Siempre había un delicioso olor a puerco asado. Allí hacían los mejores sándwiches y churros calientes del mundo. A la salida del colegio, Manolo y yo íbamos allí a tomarnos una Coca Cola® de botellita y le echábamos dos chicles adentro para ver cómo borboteaba. ¡Qué lástima que sólo pude disfrutar de esas

coca colitas hasta el primer grado! Tía Lidia tenía su peluquería en la misma cuadra y ésta siempre estaba llena de mujeres arreglándose el pelo o las manos, tomando café, contándose algún chisme, etc. Varias peluqueras trabajaban con ella y eran como parte de la familia. En la otra esquina estaba La Maravilla, una tienda de ropa fina donde se encontraba de todo. Era una vida divertida. Nunca necesitamos relojes de alarma pues con las ventanas abiertas nos despertábamos con el ruido de la calle: los vecinos saludándose, el lechero, el claxon de los autos o el canto de los gallos.

Durante el verano, toda la familia iba a la casa de la playa de El Salto. Año tras año nos encontrábamos con los mismos amigos. Nadábamos por las mañanas, almorzábamos pescado fresco y después había que esperar varias horas para volver a nadar, ya que "nadar con la barriga llena" podía hacernos "daño". Jugábamos o nos peleábamos por la hamaca. Por las noches cazábamos cangrejos con Abuelo Joseíto utilizando palos de escobas con una puntilla al final y una linterna. También Mami y Papi nos llevaban a Varadero por una o dos semanas. ¡Eso sí que era playa!

Mi época favorita del año era la Navidad, cuando decoraban el parque y la calle y llegaba el resto de la familia de la Habana. La familia de mi padre se reunía en casa de abuela Rosita para cenar el típico lechón asado. El 25 de diciembre siempre había un baile y el 31 siempre se celebraba en casa de Carlos y Lidia. A las 12:00 de la noche nos comíamos las 12 uvas y tirábamos un cubo de agua por la puerta del frente para empezar el año fresco y limpio. Era divertidísimo. También bailábamos hasta el amanecer.

Yo era muy joven, pero aún así esos recuerdos están frescos en mi mente. Hasta hoy, después de cinco décadas, sigo soñando que vivo allí, en mi Cuba querida. Las flores de mariposa de la casa de abuela Rosita, junto a la mata de hierbabuena, emitían una fragancia muy típica de su patio. El olor de la hierbabuena de los mojitos que tanto disfruto hoy, siempre me transportan al patio de mi abuela.

Siendo niños, no nos dábamos cuenta de la situación política. Después me enteré que estábamos viviendo bajo una dictadura y que la mayoría de los cubanos querían librarse de la opresión del gobierno de Fulgencio Batista. Yo sólo recuerdo que éramos felices, consentidos por la familia y por las señoras que trabajaban en nuestras casas. Teníamos todo lo que queríamos. Yo tenía unos cuatro años cuando Papi se compró su Pontiac. A mí me gustó tanto que fue y me compró un carrito rojo que yo podía manejar. ¡Yo era la niña más mimada de la cuadra!

Mi primer recuerdo de la Revolución fue cuando trajeron a un guerrillero herido al consultorio de mi padre. Poco después, cuando estábamos celebrando el año nuevo en casa de Lidia y Carlos, se supo que Fulgencio Batista se había marchado. Ignorantes de lo que le esperaba al país, la mayoría de los cubanos salieron a las calles para celebrar el año nuevo, el gobierno nuevo, la democracia... en resumen, ¡una libertad ficticia! Esta libertad terminó siendo la destrucción de muchos núcleos familiares y la más grande desilusión de millones de cubanos, quienes, para verdaderamente encontrarla, tuvieron que dejar sus raíces en la isla; muchos para nunca más volver.

En el patio de la casa, mi padre tenía una jaula grande llena de codornices. Bajo la emoción del momento, abrió la jaula y las dejó en libertad: "¡Disfruten la libertad!", les dijo. A la mañana siguiente, la mayoría de las codornices estaban posadas encima de la jaula y había algunas adentro. Parece que fueron más inteligentes que nosotros y entendían mejor la situación.

Un par de días después unos rebeldes vinieron a la casa a pedir las llaves del carro de Papi, diciendo que lo necesitaban para la Revolución. Querían ir a la Habana para marchar en la Manifestación del Triunfo de la Revolución. Cuando Papi se negó a darles las llaves de su nuevo Pontiac, se pusieron insolentes, abusándolo verbalmente y acusándolo de "esbirro" (contrarrevolucionario). Papi les dijo que él era médico y ese carro era para ir a ver a sus pacientes. Además comentó que él había hecho más que ellos por la revolución pues, por años, él había contribuido con dinero y medicinas para los rebeldes en las montañas del Escambray. Él tenía evidencia de sus contribuciones, las cuales había enviado por medio del sacerdote de la iglesia. Bajaron el tono de voz y decidieron llevarse el carro de mi tía Nonín que estaba más viejo. Papi lo encontró unos quince días después, en lamentables condiciones.

Pronto vino la expropiación de la propiedad privada. Fidel tenía una definición muy particular de la palabra socialismo: una sociedad controlada por él. Papi estaba en la Habana cuando los milicianos intervinieron su consultorio médico, las casas de alquiler y todo lo que teníamos. Ese mismo día también confiscaron La Central, la Peluquería Lidia y La Maravilla. A partir de allí, el gobierno se apoderó de todas las propiedades que había en la zona. Todas las puertas fueron selladas. Yo recuerdo a mi tío Carlos, un hombre fuerte y buen mozo, sentado en el sillón de la sala llorando como un niño por horas y horas. Él había creado La Central de la nada, trabajando día y noche, y ahora no había nada más que él

pudiera hacer. Todos tenían que ir a trabajar a donde los mandara el gobierno... no había otra opción.

Papi llegó de la Habana tarde esa noche y Mami no le dijo nada. Ella quería demorarle el dolor lo más que pudiera. Al amanecer, ella le trajo su cafecito, se sentó al borde de la cama y, entre lágrimas, le informó que ya no tenía consultorio ni pacientes para ver ese día y que había un papel pegado en la puerta que decía: "Intervenido, Propiedad del Gobierno Cubano". Papi, muy seguro de sí, le dijo que no llorara que Dios abriría otras puertas. Cuando los milicianos regresaron a informarle a dónde lo iban a mandar a trabajar, él se negó rotundamente:

—Yo no trabajo para comunistas.

—Entonces no trabajará, pero tendrá que hablar con el Jefe de Salud Pública. El jefe le informó que trabajaría veinticuatro horas seguidas un día sí y otro no. Mi padre, enfurecido, le contestó:

— ¿Por qué no sacas esa pistola que llevas en la cintura y me matas con una bala en vez de con esas horas? ¡Me niego a trabajar!

Después nos dijo que cuando iba camino a su carro, le temblaban las piernas pues él sabía muy bien que esa no era forma de hablarle a un oficial del gobierno comunista.

Los clientes de mi padre lo querían mucho y también era muy necesitado en el pueblo. A veces temíamos por su vida, pero los

Alexis Martínez, abuelo Vázquez y Lizette Martínez Candela

milicianos lo dejaron tranquilo. Nunca nos faltó dinero, pues él continuaba viendo pacientes a escondidas. La gente le pagaba clandestinamente; otros le pagaban con pollos o vegetales. Teníamos un patio grande detrás de la casa lleno de pollos, gallinas y gallos. Estos se convirtieron en los juguetes favoritos de mi hermana Lourdes. Ella los había entrenado y les enseñó a quedarse totalmente quietos en el gallinero mientras les leía cuentos. Hasta los hacía caminar "en fila india". Si podía hacer eso a la edad de siete u ocho años, ¡imagínese lo que mi hermanita Lourdes puede hacer ahora!

La escuela privada a la que yo asistía corrió el mismo destino. Recuerdo a una mujer y a un hombre vestidos de verde olivo que vinieron a mi clase para hablar con nosotros:

—¿Ustedes creen en Dios?

—Sí. Dijimos en conjunto.

—¿Alguna vez lo han visto? ¿Lo han tocado? Cuándo le han hablado, ¿Él ha respondido?

—No. Dijimos confundidos.

—Entonces, ¿por qué están tan seguros de que Dios existe? Vamos a hacer una prueba a ver qué pasa. Cierren sus ojitos y vamos a rezar con todas las fuerzas de su corazón para que Dios les mande un helado... ¡Oh, qué lástima! Parece que no rezaron lo suficiente. Vamos a tratar otra vez.

—Yo sé por qué no nos mandó helado, dijo uno de los niños enfáticamente, ¡porque se derrite!

Nos pidieron que oráramos con toda la fuerza de nuestra alma por una galletica, un juguete, etc. Desilusionados, nos dimos cuenta de que nuestro "Señor" estaba ignorando nuestras peticiones; pero éstas fueron rápidamente contestadas por el gobierno de Fidel. ¡Un buen lavado de cerebro! Ese mismo día, nos llevaron marchando a la escuela pública. Los padres se empezaron a preocupar por el control que el régimen estaba ejerciendo en sus hijos, pues temían que los adoctrinaran y les quitaran la patria potestad. Muchas de estas familias no se podían ir del país inmediatamente, así que comenzaron a mandar a sus hijos a los Estados Unidos a través de la Operación Pedro Pan. ¡Yo estaba horrorizada! Esta era una operación coordinada por el gobierno de los Estados Unidos, la Arquidióceses y un grupo de cubanos. Entre 1960 y 1962, más de 14,000 niños fueron enviados de Cuba a Miami por sus padres. Con la ayuda del Monseñor Bryan O. Walsh, los niños llegaron a casas de familiares, amistades o de familias dispuestas a recibirlos, en los distintos estados de la nación. Muchos esperaron varios años antes de ver nuevamente a sus padres.

Para asegurar que toda la isla estuviera vigilada y así evitar ataques contrarrevolucionarios, se formó el Comité de Defensa Revolucionaria (CDR). Cada cuadra, en cada calle del país tenía una familia voluntaria que ofrecía sus servicios para espiar las actividades de sus vecinos. Cualquier movimiento sospechoso era investigado y, si se consideraba inapropiado, se reportaba al Servicio de Inteligencia (G-2). Las actividades no aceptadas incluían, por ejemplo, tener más comida en casa de la que les correspondía por la libreta de racionamiento. Una vez Papi le compró a un campesino un trozo de queso bastante grande. Esa tarde dos policías, con sus pistolas e insignia, vinieron a arrestarlo. ¿Por qué? ¡Porque había comprado un trozo de queso! Estábamos viviendo en un país socialista donde nadie podía tener más que su vecino. Papi se negó a que lo escoltaran a la policía como un criminal común y prometió que iría por sí solo, pero que primero quería que vieran el tamaño del queso. Ya el queso se había dividido en partes iguales para toda la familia y el pedazo que quedaba en el refrigerador era tan pequeño que simplemente le advirtieron que no lo hiciera más.

Mis padres decidieron que era hora de irse del país. Papi comenzó a hablarle a la familia para que todos hicieran los trámites juntos y salieran de Cuba a la misma vez. El papeleo necesario, las fotos para el pasaporte; todo estaba tomando mucho tiempo. Mientras tanto se implementó una ley que decía que los jóvenes entre quince y veintiún años de edad no se podían ir hasta que pasaran por el servicio militar. Cuando por fin presentamos la petición de salida, era demasiado tarde. La mayoría de los profesionales ya se habían ido a otros países lo cual dio lugar a que se creara una ley que exigía a todos los profesionales realizar dos años de trabajo forzado antes de poder salir del país. Pronto después de presentar la petición, dos oficiales vinieron a la casa para hacer un minucioso inventario de todo lo que teníamos en ella. ¡Apuntaron hasta el último detalle! Nos informaron que, a la hora de partida, pasarían lista y si algo faltaba, nos negarían la salida. Esto también incluía el carro que tenía que estar funcionando perfectamente. Por supuesto, las cuentas bancarias tenían que tener el mismo balance que tenían aquel día tan humillante. Éramos "gusanos" (aún nos sentimos orgullosos de ese apodo). Ellos no le debían respeto a los que le viraban la espalda a la ficticia "Cuba, territorio libre de América". Mami tenía una maleta lista con un cambio de ropa para cada uno de nosotros, pues era todo lo que se permitía. Nosotros sabíamos que el permiso no llegaría muy pronto, pero yo no me

puedo imaginar la preocupación que ella tendría, sabiendo que nosotras estábamos creciendo y todo estaba racionado.

Había mucha vigilancia y según tengo entendido, las cosas han empeorado grandemente. Hubo una temporada cuando podíamos oír gente caminando en el techo de nuestra casa durante la noche. Desde allí se podía vigilar fácilmente los movimientos en la casa. Nos aterrábamos. Cuando oíamos los pasos, Lourdes y yo comenzábamos a llorar y a temblar. Paraban por un rato y volvían a empezar. Mis padres preguntaban:

—¿Quién está ahí? Pero nadie contestaba. Papi fue a la estación de policía para expresar su preocupación.

—No se preocupe Dr. Vázquez, esta noche le mandaremos a dos policías para proteger a su familia. No se preocupe.

El supuesto ladrón se fue por un tiempo. Después de unos días, los pasos comenzaron otra vez. Papi fue a la estación de policía por segunda vez. Le ofrecieron vigilancia adicional; pero Papi le dijo al oficial:

—Yo los voy a ayudar a ustedes. Tengo un equipo de rayos X y por lo tanto tengo acceso a electricidad de voltaje de 220. Ya tengo el techo preparado. Si ese ladrón viene esta noche, mañana los llamo para que vayan a buscar el cuerpo. Nunca más volvimos a oír pasos.

Teresa, Carlos, Alexis y Lizette Martínez Candela

La comida estaba racionada a 2 onzas de carne por persona cada dos semanas. La carne costaba $0.40 por libra en las tiendas del gobierno. Pero como en todo país oprimido, existía el mercado negro. Papi iba donde los campesinos y compraba carne de contrabando por $10 pesos la libra cuando era posible. Solamente tenía que tener mucho cuidado de que nuestros inquisitivos vecinos no lo pillaran sacándola del carro a la casa. Una vez, otro doctor le dijo que un guajiro tenía carne de res, pero que tuviera cuidado porque lo estaban vigilando. Papi fue y compró varias libras de carne, pero en el camino a casa lo paró la policía, diciendo:

—¡Pare en nombre de la Revolución! Vamos a revisar el carro y ojalá que no tenga nada. Al descubrir la apetitosa carne, dijeron:

—Usted va preso y tiene que decirnos quién se la vendió.

—Muy bien, —dijo Papi—, pero primero busquen al Jefe de la Policía e infórmenle lo que está pasando. Yo no me muevo de aquí hasta que él llegue.

Unos años antes, el hombre que ahora era el Jefe de la Policía, era un campesino con un ingreso muy limitado. Su hija de siete años de pronto perdió la vista a causa de una enfermedad desconocida. Los médicos habían diagnosticado que nunca volvería a ver. Papi era un pediatra reconocido y muy respetado, así que le trajeron a la niña para que diera su opinión. Él se interesó mucho en el caso. La hospitalizó y pasó innumerables horas al lado de la niña, hasta que ella recobró la vista. No cobró por sus servicios, pues sabía que la familia no tenía dinero.

—La vista de su hija es suficiente pago para mí, dijo Papi.

—Muchas gracias, Dr. Vázquez. Se lo agradezco en el alma. Si algún día yo puedo hacer algo por usted, cuente conmigo.

Ahora, años después, el padre agradecido estaba frente a este "criminal" comprador de carne, el mismo doctor que le salvó la hija.

—Yo a este doctor no le puedo hacer nada.

Se giró a mi padre y le dijo: —Esta vez, usted puede llevarse la carne, pero no vuelva por esta zona. Papi se sintió muy bien retribuido por sus servicios pediátricos.

Ricardo, el hermano de mi madre, ya estaba viviendo en los Estados Unidos desde antes de la Revolución. De vez en cuando nos mandaba un paquetico con algunas cosillas. Una de las cosas que siempre enviaba era chicles, algo que ya no teníamos en Cuba y era simplemente chévere o "cool" masticarlo. Recibir uno de esos tesoros era como ganarse la lotería. A veces recibíamos cartas con uno adentro, pegado con cinta adherente. Lourdes y yo lo cortábamos en

pedacitos y lo guardábamos como una gran fortuna. Lo importante era oler a chicle y que te vieran masticar esta delicia. Y si alguien alguna vez te daba un pedacito de su chicle, entonces sabías que tenías un verdadero amigo.

Mami nunca trabajó en Cuba. A pesar de estar bajo un régimen comunista, teníamos una buena vida gracias a los esfuerzos de mi padre. Se pudiera decir que éramos "gusanos privilegiados". Papi no había trabajado legalmente por seis años. Él era un hombre muy estóico y continuaba negándose a trabajar para el gobierno. Al mismo tiempo, estaba la ley de dos años de trabajo forzado; pero él tenía problemas del corazón, lo que le impedía trabajar en los campos.

Un día, el supervisor del Departamento de Salud Publica le dijo a mi padre que quería ayudarlo, que él sabía que nuestra familia quería irse de Cuba, pero que él no se iba a escapar del trabajo forzado, por lo tanto le iba hacer una buena oferta. Necesitaban un pediatra en el Círculo Infantil de Esperanza. Papi aceptó. Después de unos meses, dos policías vinieron a llevárselo preso. ¿Por qué? Habían oído que Papi había contado un chiste burlándose del gobierno. Cuando lo tenían detenido, uno de los administradores del círculo que pasaba dijo:

—¿Qué le están haciendo al Dr. Vázquez? ¡Él es un buen hombre... suéltenlo! Yo me hago responsable de sus acciones. Papi se dio cuenta de que había sido una táctica para intimidarlo.

Durante todo este tiempo continuamos viviendo bajo el temor de que algo se fuera a romper en la casa o de que alguien se robara algo. Mami seguía preocupándose por tener la maleta lista con ropa que nos sirviera. Todo estaba racionado y solamente podíamos usar la libreta de abastecimiento una vez al año para comprar ropa y zapatos. Cuando llegaba mercancía a las tiendas, la gente hacía colas por días para asegurarse turnos de compra, algo que continúan haciendo hasta el día de hoy.

Todos los años los estudiantes éramos llevados a "La Escuela al Campo", un tipo de campamento donde trabajábamos en los campos y nos entrenaban para la Revolución. Íbamos a un sitio determinado, normalmente bien lejos del pueblo para evitar la interferencia de nuestros preocupados padres. Una vez allí, participábamos en la construcción de nuestros albergues, edificábamos nuestras propias literas de sacos de papa y nuestros baños. Los padres podían visitarnos los domingos, si tenían transporte. Yo recuerdo que, como niños al fin, no nos molestaba mucho la situación. Nos divertíamos de todas formas. Nos levantábamos a la salida del sol, nos poníamos

el uniforme de trabajo y las botas, jurábamos la bandera, marchábamos hacia los campos a cortar caña, a plantar o a recoger melones, marchábamos de vuelta cansados y sedientos, y comíamos un almuerzo nada sabroso. Luego tomábamos una siesta, marchábamos otra vez al campo y después asistíamos a clases. También aprendimos a manejar armas para así poder defender al país. Era un entrenamiento obligatorio de seis semanas de duración. Nuestros padres sufrían porque no sabían lo que estábamos haciendo y porque no tenían control sobre nosotros.

Siendo una jovencita, era difícil para mí pensar en irme de mi tierra, dejar atrás a mi familia, a mis amigos, para nunca más poder volver, ni siquiera de visita. Una vez que nos fuéramos, seríamos expatriados. Ya habíamos estado esperando por ocho años y no parecía que íbamos a recibir la salida. Tenía mi noviecito y no quería ir a un lugar desconocido donde no conocía a nadie. En las escuelas públicas no se enseñaba inglés, por lo que nuestros padres nos hacían tomar clases privadas todas las semanas. El famoso profesor Curí, quien venía a la casa a torturarnos con largas conjugaciones de verbos y repetición de oraciones, siempre vestía traje de tres piezas –aun en pleno verano-, su bastón y sus gafas redondas. También Papi nos hacía sentar para oír la radio de onda corta -lo que era considerado ilegal- pues alcanzaba las estaciones americanas. Lo único que podía entender era: "*Publix, where shopping is a pleasure*".

En febrero de 1970, una señora que de niña había sido paciente de mi padre, vino a casa a buscarlo. Tenía una hija muy enferma y los doctores que la estaban tratando no podían diagnosticar su condición. Cada día la niña empeoraba y la madre estaba desesperada. Al principio Papi le dijo que no podía atenderla. Él sabía que ella estaba casada con un oficial de alto rango y él no estaba autorizado a ver pacientes por su cuenta. Podía ser una trampa. Ella insistió llorando y suplicando su ayuda.

—Tráemela. Haré lo que pueda para ayudarte.

—Muchas gracias. ¡No sabe cuánto se lo agradezco!

La niña tenía una simple neumonía y no tardó en curarse y volver a disfrutar de la vida. La madre agradecida, le preguntó:

—¿Cuánto le debo, doctor, por haberle salvado la vida a mi hija?

—No me debes nada. Es mi deber como médico curar a los enfermos y es un placer ayudarte. Pero la madre insistía.

—Por favor dígame cómo le puedo pagar. ¡Tengo que hacer algo!

Entonces Papi la miró directamente a los ojos y seriamente le dijo:

—Tú sabes lo que yo quiero.

Unos días después, un oficial muy decorado tocó a la puerta a altas horas de la noche. Entró a casa rápidamente, como escondiéndose de ojos imprudentes.

—Le estoy muy agradecido por la salud de mi hija. Ustedes saldrán del país en pocos días. Yo me encargaré de que no le revisen el inventario. Mientras sean discretos, pueden sacar lo que quieran de la casa. ¡Qué tengan un buen viaje!

Aunque Lourdes y yo no nos enteramos de este oficial hasta años después, sí recordamos a Mami, a Papi y a tía Lidia cambiando cosas por el patio durante la noche. Yo recuerdo que cubrieron un colchón con tela oscura para que no se viera y así poder pasarlo a la casa de mi tía. Mami tiraba comida enlatada por la cerca de atrás. ¡Nosotras pensábamos que se habían vuelto locos!

Unas semanas después, el 2 de abril, cuando yo venía de la escuela, paré en el parque para conversar con unos amigos. Mi mejor amiga, Miriam, vino corriendo con lágrimas en los ojos y me dijo:

—¡Apúrate! Están a punto de cerrar tu casa. Te llegó el telegrama. Yo tiré mis libros y empecé a correr. ¡El corazón se me quería salir del pecho! Iba a enfrentarme al momento de la verdad: me iba de Cuba para jamás volver. No nos revisaron el inventario, pero sí le pidieron a mis padres que pagaran $2,000 pesos que habían sacado de su cuenta bancaria el día antes de presentar la petición de salida. Papi los pagó, pero aún así pudo dejarle a su madre más de $20,000 pesos que se había ganado clandestinamente.

Tres días más tarde, parecía que el pueblo estaba concentrado en la calle Barnada para despedirnos. Yo había dormido en casa de tía Lidia, bien pegadita a mi prima Nancy. ¿Cómo decirle adiós a mi prima del alma? Al amanecer oí los llantos profundos de Lidia, preguntándole a la Virgen de la Caridad: —¿Por qué, Virgencita, por qué? Había llegado el momento de decir adiós a todas esas personas con quienes había crecido. Me sangraba el corazón, no podía respirar, me sentía incapaz de abrazar o decirle una palabra a nadie. Le pedí a Nancy que me fuera a buscar algo a casa de abuela, ella sabía que yo no tenía la fortaleza necesaria para despedirme de ella. Ella me miro, se sonrió tristemente y se marchó. Le pedí a Mami que todos subieran al carro y que me dejaran la puerta abierta. Mi plan era salir corriendo de la casa, subir al auto y cerrar la puerta; pero mi abuela María, llorando, me agarró del brazo y dijo:

—¡No te volveré a ver jamás!

Yo simplemente rechacé su abrazo, algo con lo que tuve que vivir por muchos años. Carlos, Lidia y Manolo nos llevaron al aeropuerto

Lourdes Vázquez y sus hijos Peter y Lauren

de Varadero. Nadie dijo nada en el camino. No recuerdo mucho del vuelo excepto que, cuando el avión despegó, vi a Manolo diciendo adiós con una mano y con la otra secándose las lágrimas. Me sentí totalmente entumecida.

Al llegar al aeropuerto de Miami, un arrogante oficial de inmigración nos informó que nos iban a mandar a Michigan. Recuerdo que Papi se enojó y demandó quedarse en Miami:

—Acabamos de salir del comunismo buscando libertad. ¡Si nos van a obligar a ir a Michigan, simplemente regrésenos a Cuba!

Al poco rato saludábamos a tío Ricardo, a tía Aida y a nuestros primos Ricky y Eddy. Era la primera vez que Lourdes y yo los conocíamos en persona, pero pronto se convirtieron en nuestros segundos padres y hermanos. Ellos vivían en Hialeah, en una casa de tres cuartos y un baño. Ahora éramos ocho personas esperando su turno para usar dicho baño todas las mañanas. ¡Qué lío aquel!

Al día siguiente, mi primo Ricky, quien era de mi edad, me invitó a ir a las tiendas con unos amigos. Como de costumbre, le pedí dinero a Papi. Seriamente él sacó tres dólares de su bolsillo y me dijo:

—Aquí tienes un dólar, pero no lo gastes a menos que sea una emergencia. Eso es todo lo que tenemos. Nunca me había hablado tan seriamente. Ese fue el día en el que maduré. Pronto comencé a trabajar y desde entonces no he parado.

Algunos de los pacientes de mi padre, que se enteraron por los periódicos que habíamos llegado, hicieron una colecta y nos trajeron $1,000 dólares. Eso era bastante dinero en aquel entonces. Inmediatamente mi padre compró un maravilloso Ford Falcon por $300 dólares para poder movilizarse. Vivimos muy felices junto a mis tíos y primos por varios meses. Estas acciones de aceptación incondicional, de amor de familia, solamente se pueden pagar haciendo lo mismo por otros.

Mami fue a trabajar, por primera vez en su vida, como costurera a una "factoría". Papi consiguió trabajo en una clínica, pero no como médico, sino como ayudante. Él pasaba cada minuto libre estudiando para pasar los exámenes *Foreign Medical Graduate* y *Medical State Board,* requeridos para poder ejercer en los Estados Unidos. Estaba envejeciendo rápidamente; pero pasó sus exámenes sin problemas, aunque otros médicos tenían mucha dificultad.

En mi primer día de clases en Hialeah Junior High School tuve la suerte de conocer a Emily Alemán, una linda cubanita compañera de clase que aún hoy es una de mis mejores amigas, y a Norma de la Torre, mi maestra favorita y la persona que me inspiró a estudiar magisterio. Fue en 1971 cuando le prometí a Norma que algún día escribiría este libro, lo que ahora estoy haciendo con su ayuda. Hice muchos amigos en Miami. Me sentía feliz.

Una vez que Papi pasó el examen que necesitaba, le ofrecieron un internado en Polk General Hospital en Bartow, Florida. Cuando llegamos al pueblo, noté que no era nada como Miami. Era pequeño,

Abuela María y Teresa Vázquez

Dr. Vázquez, abuela Rosita y familia

con árboles llenos de musgo que parecían estar llorando junto conmigo. Vivíamos en un dúplex de una habitación y un bañito. Nadie hablaba español y el inglés de ellos tenía acento sureño que yo no entendía ni papa frita. Yo odiaba a ese pueblo con toda mi alma. Yo estaba frustrada con la escuela, con todo. La dueña del dúplex, Mary Jane Driesler, me vio llorando un día. Desde entonces, por muchos meses, ella dedicó sus noches a enseñarme inglés y la cultura estadounidense. ¡Otra linda acción de amor incondicional!

Pronto conocimos a otros cubanos, los Almazán, quienes se convirtieron en parte de nuestra familia. Martha, la hija mayor y yo nos hicimos mejores amigas. Años después fui la madrina de su primera hija y ella de la mía. Poco a poco todo cambió. Bartow nos acogió con los brazos abiertos. Nunca podremos olvidar las bondades y lindas acciones de su gente. Papi abrió su consultorio y pudimos reconstruir nuestras vidas.

En 1973 conocí a Carlos Martínez, nada más y nada menos que almorzando con Martha en el nuevo McDonalds de Bartow. El entró con su mejor amigo Steve, ahora el reconocido Dr. Stephen McNutt, quien decidió presentarnos ya que éramos uno de los pocos jóvenes cubanos en el área. Carlos y yo teníamos mucho en común, incluyendo el carro que ambos teníamos, un Chevy Nova. Nos enamoramos y nos casamos a la tierna edad de veinte años en 1975. Hemos sido muy felices prácticamente creciendo, estudiando, trabajando y criando a nuestras dos hijas Lizette y Alexis.

En 1980 ocurrió un milagro. Cuba tuvo problemas con la agricultura y el gobierno decidió permitir que los "gusanos" visitaran a sus familiares por un costo de $1,500 por 15 minutos de vuelo. Mi padre me invitó a acompañarlo. Recuerdo que el avión en el que viajamos tenía la puerta asegurada con una soga. Sentí que mis oraciones fueron escuchadas, iba a tener la oportunidad de despedirme adecuadamente de mis abuelas. Pude volver a ver a mis familiares y amigos, así como volver a hablar por horas y horas con Nancy. Fue difícil ver que mi linda casa ahora estaba en ruinas. De las bellas columnas de estilo romano que adornaban el portal, sólo quedaban las cabillas de soporte. Todo estaba muy destartalado debido a años de negligencia. Las tiendas estaban vacías. Yo hice un comentario sobre la mala situación del país y de inmediato mi prima me mandó a callar:

—Tere, ¡no puedes hablar así! ¿Quieres ir a la cárcel? Recuerda que aquí hasta las paredes tienen oídos.

Se me había olvidado totalmente donde estaba; me había acostumbrado a la libertad de expresión que se disfruta en los Estados

Unidos. Fue bueno volver a mi patria pero, cuando llegamos a Miami, yo quería besar el suelo. Por largo tiempo sufrí depresión y me sentí enormemente culpable por tener tanto cuando mi gente allá tenía tan poco. ¿Por qué tenía tanta suerte yo?

Después de muchos años de trabajo, en el 2008, Papi se jubiló por tercera vez, en esta ocasión como Director Médico del ROHR Home, un asilo de ancianos del Condado de Polk. Ahora Papi tiene 87 años y a veces nos reímos cuando le decimos que empezó en pediatría y terminó en geriatría. Él dice que no hay mucha diferencia.

Mis padres recientemente celebraron su 57 aniversario de boda. Ellos son los orgullosos abuelos de cuatro nietos y bisabuelos de dos lindos bisnietos. Todos hemos tenido la bendición de su influencia y de haber aprendido las lecciones de cómo luchar por la libertad y ser firmes ante lo que consideramos correcto.

Mi hermana Lourdes y yo hemos disfrutado de una vida maravillosa. Ella ha trabajado en la industria cosmética por los últimos 30 años, trabajando con individuos dinámicos en la compañía Estee Lauder. Actualmente ella es la Ejecutiva de Cuentas de la costa oeste de la Florida para la prestigiosa compañía Christian Dior. Ella tiene dos hijos, Peter y Lauren y un lindo nieto, Colton. Yo estudié magisterio, trabajé como maestra y más tarde como empresaria. En 1989, fundé el Institute of Spanish Communication, Inc. que me ha permitido disfrutar del "sueño americano" por más de veinte años. También soy productora y presentadora de Comunidad Viva, un programa de televisión local. Mi esposo Carlos es especialista clínico. Él trabaja con dispositivos médicos para pacientes que necesitan transplantes de corazón. Carlos ha tenido el honor de trabajar con el mundialmente famoso Dr. DeBakey. Nuestras hijas, Lizette y Alexis, son graduadas universitarias y tienen un futuro brillante.

Mis padres pudieron ayudar a mi primo Manolo a escapar mientras trabajaba como médico en Nicaragua. Él, por su parte, pudo traer de Cuba a su hermano y familia, así como a sus padres Carlos y Lidia. Mi querida prima Nancy también pudo escapar, así como otros familiares. Todos ellos disfrutan de una buena vida en los Estados Unidos. Sin embargo, todavía tenemos familiares en Cuba a los que le enviamos ayuda lo más que podemos.

La vida en Cuba se continúa deteriorando. La comida todavía está racionada a 3 libras de arroz al mes por persona, 1 libra de frijoles, 4 libras de azúcar, 1 libra de sal por familia y un pedazo de pan por persona al día. La leche está reservada para los niños recién nacidos hasta los siete años de edad y para los mayores de sesenta y

cinco años, además de los enfermos. La carne es muy escasa: 3 onzas al mes para las personas que están enfermas, casi siempre pollo. El resto de la población disfruta de picadillo de soya de vez en cuando. Las personas que tienen acceso a los "chavitos" pueden comprar muslos y contra muslo de pollo. Me han contado que las pechugas no se ven ni en las tiendas de los turistas. El gobierno necesita la comida para el turismo o para exportación. Los ciudadanos se tienen que sacrificar por la patria. Me imagino que esa es la razón por la cual solamente los que sufren de colesterol alto o diabetes reciben una cuota de pescado de vez en cuando. ¡Permítame mencionar que Cuba es una isla conocida por su pesca!

En cuanto a productos de higiene, la ración mensual de una familia es un tubo de pasta de dientes y media barra de jabón por persona. No hay desodorante, ni papel higiénico, ni champú, sólo diez toallas sanitarias al mes para las necesidades femeninas. Al mismo tiempo, hay tiendas abastecidas con casi todo lo que una persona pueda necesitar, pero a precios accesibles sólo para turistas. Estas tiendas solamente venden en dólares convertidos conocidos también como "chavitos" cuyo valor es sólo el 80% del dólar americano. Por años no se permitió que los cubanos de la isla entraran a estas tiendas, ni a hoteles o restaurantes de turismo en su propia patria. Esto cambió después de que Fidel pasara el poder a su hermano

Giuseppe Candela, Tere, Antonio y Lizette Candela y Carlos Martínez

Raúl. Ya desde el 2009, los cubanos pueden ir a comprar lo que deseen mientras tengan el poderoso dólar.

Otro avance que ha ocurrido en la Isla es que los cubanos ahora pueden tener teléfonos celulares y algunas computadoras. Esto nos trae al tema de los salarios. Según las últimas investigaciones, la mayoría de los profesionales como doctores, ingenieros, abogados tienen un sueldo estándar de menos de $300 pesos al mes. Algunos especialistas ganan de $500 a $700 pesos al mes. Los trabajadores o proletarios pueden ganar unos $150 a $200 pesos al mes. La taza de cambio es de $25 pesos por dólar, haciendo que estos salarios sean de $6 a $30 (dólares) al mes, menos un descuento de 20% para convertirlos en "chavitos". Solamente 1.5% de la población cubana tiene sueldos de $6,000 pesos o más: estos son los altos funcionarios del gobierno. Si los artículos en las tiendas se venden a precios regulares, un paquete de papel higiénico costaría el 10% del salario de un proletario. Por lo tanto, no es común encontrar tal lujo en la mayoría de los baños de los hogares cubanos. (En caso de que usted se pregunte qué utilizan, al Gramma, el único periódico que circula en Cuba, se le ha encontrado un buen uso). Por supuesto, muchos cubanos tienen familia en los Estados Unidos que les envían ayuda. También tienen la oportunidad de ganar dinero mediante el turismo siendo hospitalarios y ayudando a los generosos turistas a disfrutar de la Isla. Una de las oportunidades de ganarse el sustento ha sido cuando se le permitió a los cubanos en la isla trabajar en los restaurantes y hoteles designados solamente para turistas.

Con respecto a la salud, Cuba goza de popularidad por tener un buen sistema de cuidado médico. Muchos doctores están listos y deseosos de irse a trabajar a países del tercer mundo, pues dichos países están en mejores condiciones que Cuba. Estos se esmeran por trabajar bien para que les permitan quedarse y así tener una oportunidad de escaparse a un país libre. Por lo tanto, han adquirido fama internacional positiva.

Cuba tiene hospitales modernos donde los turistas de todas partes de mundo van a recibir tratamientos y cirugía plástica a precios muy reducidos. Al parecer el embargo no afecta a los turistas ni a los dirigentes del gobierno. Tengo entendido que, por mucho tiempo, hubo un médico y dos enfermeras por cada 120 familias. No hay duda que ha habido buena atención al paciente. Lo que no hay es medicinas, ni equipos para examinarlos. La medicina preventiva no existe en Cuba; uno de los países más "avanzados" en las ciencias médicas en Latino América.

Los cubanos tienen que ir a hospitales prehistóricos, poco sanitarios y en paupérrimas condiciones. Uno de mis familiares tuvo que hospitalizarse recientemente pues necesitaba cirugía. Ella tuvo que llevar sus propias sábanas, almohada, pijama, comida, además de un cubo con un jarrito y jabón para poder bañarse y descargar el inodoro. Para llenar el cubo de agua, tenía que ir a la única llave de agua potable que funcionaba en el edificio. Además, ella tuvo que esperar un par de meses a que le mandaran las suturas para que le cerraran la herida. ¿Dónde está la igualdad en este sistema? ¿Cuáles son los avances que han tomado lugar en cinco décadas de comunismo en el sistema médico cubano?

Ahora mi esposo y yo tenemos casi la misma edad que tenían nuestros padres cuando salieron de Cuba. Tenemos dos hijas maravillosas, Lizette y Alexis, quienes han crecido sabiendo que el cielo es el límite, y Antonio nuestro primer nieto quien es nuestra nueva motivación. Hemos tenido éxito a nivel familiar y personal y aún tenemos mucho por hacer. A veces me pregunto qué haríamos si de pronto hubiese un cambio de gobierno y tuviéramos que enfrentarnos a las mismas circunstancias que enfrentaron nuestros padres. No puedo imaginarme dejar todo lo que tengo, irme a otro país con los bolsillos vacíos y empezar de cero en otro idioma. Muchas veces trato de imaginar si nosotros tendríamos la misma valentía, determinación y perseverancia que ellos tuvieron para asegurar nuestra libertad.

Anhelo que un día, no muy lejano, podamos ir de visita a nuestra isla con toda la familia. Quisiera poder llevar a nuestros hijos y nietos para que disfruten de la cultura, de nadar en las aguas cristalinas de Varadero, de cruzar el puente de palma real sobre el arroyo de la Guásima. Me gustaría verlos correr libres por los campos y comer las frutas tropicales de los árboles de tío Filo. Allí verán las palmas majestuosas que han tolerado por siglos el azote de tormentas y huracanes, las brisas del Caribe y, sobre todo, la furia de los Castros. ¡Si las palmas hablaran…!

Felipe y Alicia Olivera

Invadidos por nuestra propia gente

Felipe y Alicia Olivera

Para realizar cosas grandiosas, no solamente debemos actuar, sino también soñar; no sólo planear, sino también creer.
ANATOLE FRANCE

Yo nací en la Habana y vine a los Estados Unidos en octubre de 1961...sola. Eso fue aproximadamente dos años después que Castro tomó control del país. Vine simplemente porque mis padres así lo decidieron. La situación política se estaba deteriorando rápidamente. Yo acababa de comenzar en la universidad y esos años que yo pensé que serían los más felices e importantes en mi vida, fueron abruptamente destrozados. Mi sueño de siempre había sido estudiar arquitectura, sin embargo no pude acabar ni el primer semestre. Todas mis ilusiones y esperanzas se desvanecieron.

Algunos grupos de estudiantes universitarios que no estaban de acuerdo con la revolución castrista, estaban en constante peligro de persecución debido a sus ideas y actividades. Cualquiera que se opusiera era arrestado y encarcelado. Después de un breve juicio era enviado al Paredón de Fusilamiento y ejecutado, sin explicaciones. Este fue el caso del hermano de mi cuñado, un joven veinteañero quien fue ejecutado por el simple hecho de estar involucrado en un movimiento estudiantil que estaba en desacuerdo con el gobierno revolucionario.

Mi familia fue sometida a persecuciones y abusos. Una noche, a las 3:00 de la mañana, la policía secreta del G-2 invadió nuestra casa en busca de evidencia que pudiera conectar a mis padres o a cualquiera de nosotros a este caso; especialmente a mi cuñado, el esposo de mi hermana. Fue una experiencia horrible que jamás olvidaré. Yo era una muchacha joven y los policías, armados con ametralladoras, escandalosamente entraron en mi habitación y me despertaron con sus gritos, como si fuéramos criminales. Entonces fue que comprendí la situación tan peligrosa que estábamos confrontando y a la vez comprendí la decisión de mis padres.

Acepté decirles adiós a ellos y al resto de la familia, suponiendo que sería cuestión de pocos meses y que podría regresar a mi patria en un futuro cercano. Pero esto no ha ocurrido todavía. No sentí miedo al salir de Cuba, pensando que era sólo una aventura. Sin embargo fue muy doloroso decirle adiós a mi abuela. Con lágrimas rodándole por las mejillas y la sabiduría de sus años, me miró a los ojos y dijo: —Nunca más te volveré a ver. Yo no lo creía entonces, pero ella estaba en lo cierto. Ella murió poco tiempo después. Mis padres no pudieron salir de Cuba hasta cinco años más tarde. Esos fueron los cinco años más largos de mi vida.

Yo no recuerdo mucho de mi salida de Cuba. Mi mente ha deseado borrar aquellos dolorosos momentos. Sólo recuerdo llegar a la casa de unos amigos de mis padres en Miami. Yo no los conocía y aunque ellos fueron muy amables conmigo, yo me sentía profundamente triste y sola. Yo era muy joven, en un país extraño, sin familiares ni amigos, porque mi país había sido invadido por mi propia gente...cubanos como nosotros.

Decidí aprender inglés y comencé en la universidad, donde estudié magisterio. Esto no fue nada fácil, gran parte por el idioma, pero yo estaba decidida a lograrlo. Para mi gran sorpresa y felicidad había encontrado una nueva vocación. Trabajé como maestra de español y matemáticas por veinticinco gloriosos años en la ciudad de Lakeland en la Florida.

Aunque no llegué a estudiar arquitectura, Dios me bendijo con mi esposo Felipe, un exiliado cubano como yo, quien, con mucho sacrificio se hizo ingeniero y ha logrado una gran carrera como constructor de residencias de lujo. Felipe salió de Cuba en 1960, inmediatamente después de completar su primer año de ingeniería mecánica en la Universidad de Villanueva en la Habana. Llegó a Miami a los diecinueve años con una visa de turista, una maleta con alguna ropa, un par de libros de ingeniería y cinco dólares en el bolsillo. Felipe también fue el primero de su familia en salir de Cuba.

Al día siguiente de su llegada, se reunió con un amigo que manejaba un camión de entrega de pan a las bodegas. En cada parada, él se bajaba y preguntaba acerca de las oportunidades de trabajo allí. Al final del día, tenía dos ofertas de trabajo. Al día siguiente lo contrataron en un mercado, para limpiar los pisos antes de que abriera la tienda y después como empaquetador de las compras de los clientes. Ese fue su primer trabajo, ya que nunca trabajó en Cuba. Desde entonces, nunca más ha dejado de trabajar.

Comenzó en la Escuela de Ingeniería de la Universidad de Miami y nos casamos después que se graduó como ingeniero mecánico. Unos años después compró un negocio de lavadoras automáticas, el que mantuvo por cinco años. El era el dueño, el que mantenía el local y reparaba las máquinas. Pocos años después, en el año 1972 obtuvo su licencia de Contratista General y comenzó a construir algunas casas, mientras continuaba trabajando como Ingeniero Principal de Proyectos. Después de varios años sosteniendo dos y hasta tres trabajos, Felipe decidió vender el negocio de lavadoras, dejar su trabajo de ingeniería y concentrar todos sus esfuerzos en el negocio de la construcción.

Hoy en día, en sociedad con nuestro hijo y nuestro yerno, la compañía construye unas veinte casas de lujo por año, a especificación del cliente, además de edificios comerciales y profesionales. *Olivera Construction, Inc.*, es reconocida como una de las compañías constructoras más distinguidas del área. Muchas de sus casas han ganado numerosos premios.

El trabajo duro y la honestidad combinados con una vida familiar cristiana en este hermoso país de oportunidades, es lo que ha hecho de nuestra vida un éxito en el exilio. Nuestra familia es nuestro orgullo. Tenemos tres hijos, ocho nietos y familiares y amigos maravillosos. Después de cuarenta y nueve años, considero que los Estados Unidos es nuestro hogar. Ambos, mi esposo y yo, estamos eternamente agradecidos a este país que nos abrió las puertas y nos ayudó a encauzar nuestras vidas de nuevo. Sin embargo, siempre añoramos a nuestra pequeña isla. Los recuerdos son muchos. Amamos nuestra música, nuestra cultura y la manera en que disfrutamos nuestras vidas. Continuamos sintiéndonos muy cubanos y nos encantaría poder visitar y saborear de nuevo todo lo perdido; pero primero, Cuba tiene que ser libre.

Yo pienso que nuestra generación fue la que menos ha sufrido, porque pudimos reconstruir nuestras vidas a través de los estudios, persistencia y muchos sacrificios. Fueron nuestros padres los que más sufrieron ya que para ellos fue un poco tarde el volver a empezar. Aun así, ellos se resignaron y fueron felices pues pudimos de nuevo estar todos juntos, en familia, que es en definitiva, la esencia de ser CUBANO.

Familia Vallejo

No sabía nadar: Una historia de estoicismo

Dr. Sergio Vallejo

Para hacer algo que valga la pena, no debemos pararnos y pensar en las dificultades, sino arriesgarnos y abrirnos paso lo mejor que podamos.
SYDNEY SMITH

En medio de la noche, vestidos de negro y sintiendo que el corazón se nos salía del pecho, nos escapamos de los guardias que, con ametralladoras, patrullaban la costa de Matanzas. Era la noche del 29 de julio de 1968, cuando salimos en una balsa improvisada.

Éramos un grupo de trece personas, incluyendo cuatro niños y cuatro mujeres, tratando de huir de Cuba. Algunos conocidos, otros no. Supuestamente a nuestro encuentro iría un bote que nos esperaría a tres millas de la costa. Algunos de nosotros empujábamos la balsa y otros -con una soga atada a la cintura- halaban de ella mientras nadaban sin mirar atrás.

Una vez en el bote, comenzamos a remar y a luchar contra las olas gigantescas y a sacar el agua que entraba constantemente. Llevábamos un poco de agua para beber, leche condensada y una brújula. Hubo momentos críticos, estábamos agotados, algunos empezaban a alucinar. Nos tomó 30 horas, hasta que llegamos a un banco de arena al sur de Isla Morada, en los Cayos de la Florida. Eran las 3:00 de la madrugada del 31 de julio. Yo no sabía nadar, pero mi desesperación y mi fe en Dios, me dieron las fuerzas para por fin ser libre.

Esperamos el amanecer para poner el bote a flote de nuevo, y empezamos a remar hacia el puente. Los pescadores venían entrando con su pesca; uno de ellos se nos acercó y nos ofreció ayuda. Yo, con el poco inglés que sabía, les dije que éramos un grupo de cubanos que habíamos escapado de Cuba comunista y que teníamos que presentarnos a las autoridades de inmigración de los Estados Unidos.

De Isla Morada nos llevaron a Cayo Maratón en carro de policía y de ahí a las oficinas del refugio en el Aeropuerto de Miami, a la Casa de la Libertad. Teníamos las ropas desgarradas estábamos descalzos. Yo agarraba fuertemente mi maletín de médico, donde traía información sobre el sistema de salud pública en Cuba, mi estetoscopio, mi otoscopio y mis recetarios. Fue lo único que traje conmigo y lo guardo como símbolo del sacrificio que tuve que hacer.

Al día siguiente mi hermano, que vivía en Miami, me fue a recoger al refugio. Enseguida me puse en contacto con otros médicos de Matanzas, que me consiguieron una posición en el Hospital de Winfield en Kansas. Me presenté y pasé el examen del *Foreign Board*, el Board de Kansas y otros más. En 1970, ya con mi esposa e hijos a mi lado, nos mudamos para Lakeland, Florida, donde he practicado medicina desde entonces

No hay día que pase que yo no recuerde mi niñez en Cuba. Éramos cinco hermanos, tres varones y dos hembras. Mi padre trabajó toda su vida en el Banco de Canadá. Con mucho esfuerzo me mandaron a estudiar Medicina a la Universidad de la Habana. En Cuba no importaba tu posición económica, si querías superarte para tener una vida mejor, podías hacerlo. La matrícula de la Escuela de Medicina costaba 60 pesos anuales y si te graduabas con honores del bachillerato, era gratis. Había colegios privados magníficos, pero la educación pública era tan buena como la privada, y al alcance de todos. Cuba era un paraíso que no supimos apreciar.

Con Castro, todo empezó a cambiar. Cuando me gradué como médico, fui enviado a practicar medicina rural. Cuando expresé mi deseo de irme del país, fui informado que mientras necesitaran mis servicios como médico, el gobierno no me daría el permiso para salir. Por haber manifestado mi intención de irme a los Estados Unidos, me consideraban un "gusano" y me castigaron de todas las formas posibles. Era muy difícil soportar las humillaciones, las interminables horas de trabajo, la falta de libertad aún para tratar a mis propios enfermos. Por otra parte, no teníamos las cosas necesarias para vivir: ni suficiente comida, ni zapatos para los niños, ni medicinas. Mi situación se hacía peligrosa ya que me rebelaba diariamente y decía a toda voz lo que pensaba del gobierno comunista. Yo no podía esperar, mi única alternativa era escapar. Aunque estaba consciente de los peligros de la alta mar, sabía que si lograba llegar, seria libre.

Es por eso que yo me fui en una balsa, dejando a mi familia en Cuba, sin saber lo que les iba a pasar. Esa fue la decisión más difícil

que he tenido que tomar en mi vida... pero la mejor. Si me llevaban preso o me fusilaban, entonces no habría esperanza para ellos, como les pasó a muchos que expresaron su opinión contra el régimen.

Dejé mi patria en busca de libertad, para que mis hijos tuvieran la oportunidad de tener lo mejor. Nuestra vida ha sido de completa realización, de éxito y de felicidad. Nuestros hijos han recibido una gran educación, son profesionales respetables. Nuestros nietos también tendrán las mejores oportunidades para desarrollarse plenamente en la vida.

Algún día me gustaría visitar la tumba de mis padres y mi casa en Cuba. Quisiera poder disfrutar nuevamente las playas, ver los campos, los edificios coloniales, las anchas avenidas, la Universidad de la Habana. Pero regresar mientras todavía Cuba este bajo el sistema que destruyó lo que conocimos como *La Perla del Caribe*, jamás.

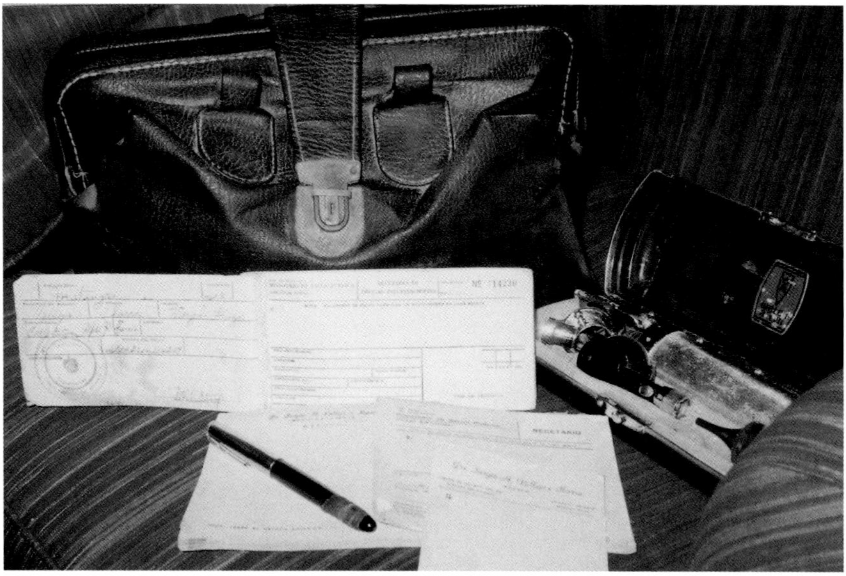

Las únicas posesiones que pudo sacar de Cuba el Dr. Sergio Vallejo

Mirtha Vallejo

Nunca olvidaré aquél día, 29 de julio de 1968. Sergio se despidió de nosotros para irse a trabajar al hospital, como era de costumbre. El trabajaba 48 horas seguidas, así que no lo esperábamos hasta el día siguiente por la tarde.

Ya era hora de que Sergio estuviera en casa; sin embargo el tiempo transcurría y él no llegaba. ¿Qué habría pasado? Empecé a angustiarme. Llamé al hospital y la respuesta fue: "no vino a trabajar". Ya no tenía dudas de lo que había sucedido: Sergio había huído en un bote rumbo a los Estados Unidos. El terror invadió mi cuerpo y sentía que no podía respirar al recordar que él no sabía nadar.

Mi esposo y yo habíamos hablado de la posibilidad de salir de Cuba en un bote; pero los niños tenían 5 y 6 años de edad y me aterraba la idea de exponerlos a semejante peligro y a la experiencia traumática que aquello conllevaba. ¡Tantos cubanos habían muerto tratando de llegar a las costas de la Florida! Sergio trató de convencerme; pero mi posición fue firme. Acordamos que él se iría primero y le pedí que -llegado el momento- que por favor no me lo dijera; yo no quería saberlo. Y así lo hizo.

Las horas seguían pasando, horas de incertidumbre y angustia. Tenía la radio en la estación La Voz de las Américas, cuando de repente apareció en la puerta de la casa un soldado del G2 (Servicio de Inteligencia de Cuba) preguntando por Sergio. Mi reacción fue inmediata: sabía que tenía que convencerlo de que yo no sabía donde estaba mi esposo; si no me acusarían de complicidad. Como era de esperarse, me interrogaron varias veces en las instalaciones del G-2 en las semanas siguientes. Afortunadamente, creyeron mi historia, o simplemente no quisieron hacerme nada, quizás porque tenía a los niños y nadie que los cuidara.

Había mal tiempo y la recepción en el radio era pobre. Las pocas palabras que escuchaba no se entendían. Como a las 10:00 de la noche del día 31, pude oír: "bote procedente de Matanzas, llamado María Josefa, llegó esta madrugada". De inmediato y con mucha alegría salí corriendo bajo la lluvia gritándole a los vecinos:

—¡llegó!, ¡llegó!

Sentí un gran alivio, ¡Sergio era libre! Yo tenía fe que -tarde o temprano- nos reuniríamos con él. Catorce meses después nos encontrábamos juntos en New York. Los niños y yo salimos hacia España donde yo tenía familia. Dos meses más tarde, ya estábamos en

Winfield, Kansas, donde Sergio trabajaba en un hospital. Empezábamos una nueva vida.

En Lakeland, Florida, nuestra familia ha tenido una vida maravillosa, rodeados de amigos cubanos, norteamericanos y de diversos países. Hemos sido y somos muy felices. Sin embargo, nunca hemos olvidado nuestras raíces, nuestra cultura y aquella maravillosa isla, con sus palmas y su prodigiosa tierra, donde las plantas y las flores crecían como por encanto. Nosotros los cubanos sabíamos disfrutar la vida; nos gustaba reír, pasar buenos ratos, bailar, contar chistes. Allí mis padres, con esfuerzo y dedicación, crearon un negocio que nos permitía vivir una vida muy cómoda. Yo pude estudiar leyes, aunque -debido a las circunstancias- nunca practiqué derecho. Viajábamos mucho y tuve el privilegio de conocer una gran parte de la isla antes de abandonarla. Todos los fines de semana nos íbamos a nuestra casa en Santa María del Mar, en la costa norte de la provincia, a disfrutar de la playa más bella, del ardiente sol, de la brisa del mar.

Cuando me preguntan si quisiera volver a Cuba, la respuesta es afirmativa. Como dice mi esposo: Regresaremos el día que Cuba vuelva a ser libre; antes no.

Dr. Pedro y Alicia Almazán

Lo vi venir

Dr. Pedro Almazán

La vida no es la que uno vivió, sino la que uno recuerda y como la recuerda para contarla.
GABRIEL GARCÍA MÁRQUEZ

Nuestra familia se fue de Cuba en 1962, por la misma razón que más de tres millones de nuestros compatriotas lo hicieron. Los cubanos nacimos para ser libres. Nos gusta cantar, bailar y expresar nuestra opinión abiertamente. Somos amistosos, proyectamos alegría, solidaridad, somos carismáticos. Consecuentemente, no nos acostumbramos a vivir oprimidos, subyugados y apagados bajo un régimen encabezado por un hombre que decidió tomar control de la isla y de la mente del pueblo.

Una vez que Fidel Castro tomó el poder, llevó a cabo su plan de ser el único Comandante en Jefe. Pronto se hizo aliado de la Unión Soviética y comenzó a intervenir las propiedades privadas. Tomó control de las fincas, hoteles, restaurantes, escuelas y demás… todo en nombre del "pueblo". Sí, confiscaron todo, empezando por los más ricos hasta los más pequeños. El gobierno se convirtió en la única agencia de empleos. La tragedia más grande, fue que las masas no se daban cuenta del plan del victorioso y carismático líder de la Revolución. Cuando el gobierno comenzó a confiscar las grandes industrias, las masas pensaron que era algo merecido, porque los dueños y los administradores ganaban demasiado dinero. Entonces comenzaron a confiscar las industrias más pequeñas; pero aún esto era apoyado por el pueblo. Los dueños de pequeños negocios pensaban que no iban a ser afectados, que sólo intervendrían a los grandes empresarios. Poco a poco, Fidel se apoderó de todo el sector privado y la gente comenzó a despertar. A eso le llamaban *la Revolución del Callo,* porque nadie protestaba hasta que le pisaban su propio callo. La situación para los que nos dábamos cuenta de lo que estaba pasando, no podía ser más trágica.

Yo me di cuenta que había problemas desde 1959. Tuve mi práctica privada por diez años, después de graduarme en la Escuela de Medicina Veterinaria de la Universidad de la Habana, en 1952. Yo era veterinario de animales de fincas. En esos días, trabajaba para familias que tenían ranchos y ganado. Estos ranchos habían estado en esa familia por años. Pude prever lo que le venía al país porque el gobierno comenzó a confiscar las tierras y los ranchos primero. La gente que vivía y trabajaba en los pueblos y ciudades, no tenía la menor idea de lo que estaba pasando. Pero yo estaba allí, curando a los animales en uno de los ranchos, cuando llegaron cuatro o cinco *Jeeps* llenos de soldados con ametralladoras. Despóticamente, le dijeron a los dueños que su propiedad ahora pasaba a manos del "pueblo" o sea, del gobierno. Como el negocio del rancho se controlaba desde el hogar, los pusieron de paticas en la calle. Ellos suplicaban:

—Por favor, déjennos sacar ropa o algo de la casa.

—No, no pueden sacar nada; todo lo que está adentro ahora pertenece al pueblo.

Recuerdo el segundo rancho que confiscaron mientras yo estaba allí. Les quitaron todo: su hogar, los muebles, la ropa, camiones, carros; absolutamente todo. No les dejaron sacar nada. ¿Por qué dejarlos? Ellos ya habían vivido muchos años ganando demasiado dinero. Eso no era justo. Ahora Cuba era un país socialista donde todos deberían ser iguales... ¡iguales en la pobreza!

Yo estaba trabajando ese día en el rancho de esta desafortunada familia. Cuando me dirigí a mi *Jeep* para irme, los soldados quisieron confiscarlo también. Me enojé mucho, y les comuniqué que ese no era mi rancho. Yo era el veterinario y ellos eran mis clientes. Ese *Jeep* era mi propiedad y ellos no tenían ningún derecho a quitármelo. En tono autoritario, les dije que yo era amigo de Fidel y lo podía llamar para aclarar el asunto. Después de examinar mi identificación cuidadosamente, me dejaron ir. Por supuesto, yo no era amigo de Fidel, ni podría serlo. Me llevé a mis clientes que ahora iban a buscar refugio en casa de unos parientes en Cienfuegos, la ciudad donde yo vivía. Ellos se quedaron sin hogar, castigados por haber tenido éxito.

Una de las razones por la cual el comunismo no prospera, es porque muchos intelectuales no creen en ese tipo de sistema; por eso la mayoría de ellos se fue o trató de irse del país. Sin embargo, muchos cubanos han tenido que quedarse en un sistema que saben es injusto, donde no pueden protestar o expresar opiniones

desfavorables al gobierno, porque se les castiga. Así que se quedan callados y el proceso sigue.

Durante los años 60, Cuba sufrió una "fuga de cerebros". Entonces el gobierno le dio poder a las masas, a esos que no tenían mucha educación. Ahora, de pronto, se veían en una posición mucho más alta; les creció el ego y eran Fidelistas, por supuesto. Ellos gritaban: —¡Viva Fidel! Todo lo que tenían que hacer era estar de acuerdo con el sistema para tener su salario asegurado. No importaba si trabajaban o no, si realmente sabían lo que estaban haciendo o si estaban abusando de su poder. Así es el comunismo.

Por eso yo decidí irme de Cuba. Vi a mis clientes perder sus ranchos donde yo había trabajado por diez años. Eran ranchos y fincas que los abuelos de la familia habían empezado. Después los hijos y toda la familia los trabajaron día y noche hasta convertirlos en un gran negocio. Ellos tenían ganado, plantas y animales. Y ahora la gente de Fidel, que no tenía la menor idea de lo que estaba haciendo, destruía la tierra, plantando algo que no iba a producir en ese tipo de suelo. Era una situación trágica, una destrucción de décadas de trabajo y dedicación.

Yo llegué a casa un día y le dije a mi esposa Alicia: —Prepara todo, nos tenemos que ir de aquí. Yo sabía lo que estaba pasando y lo que venía. Mis amigos de toda la vida en la ciudad, no creían lo que estaba ocurriendo en el campo, lo que yo estaba presenciando con mis propios ojos. Ellos me decían: —No, no, "el caballo" (Fidel) habló anoche y no dijo nada de eso… estás equivocado. No los podía convencer de que Fidel era solamente un buen orador que podía hipnotizar a las masas.

Pronto todos los veterinarios tuvieron que empezar a trabajar para el gobierno. Se formaron cooperativas que pagaban bajos salarios y en las que se cuidaba principalmente del ganado del estado. Yo me negué a trabajar para Castro. No podía cuidar de ganados, así que comencé a cuidar animales pequeños, a las mascotas de familias, y cualquier otra cosa que pudiera hacer para ganarme la vida, mientras hacía los preparativos para salir de la isla.

Nuestra hija Martha tenía siete años de edad cuando en las escuelas comenzaron a lavar el cerebro de los niños fomentando ideas comunistas. Había rumores de que se estaban hasta cambiando los libros para reflejar una versión diferente de nuestra historia. ¡Yo tenía miedo de que pronto fueran a decir que Cristóbal Colón era ruso! Nuestra adorada hija podía terminar siendo una Marxista-Leninista. Pedritín, nuestro hijo de tres años, iría al colegio pronto, y Alicia y yo no tendríamos opciones sobre su educación. Era hora de irnos.

Salimos en uno de los últimos "Vuelos de la Libertad" tres años después de que Castro tratara de tomar control de nuestras vidas. Llegué a Miami con mi esposa y mis hijos con los bolsillos vacios. Yo no tenía ni diez centavos para hacer una llamada, y si los hubiese tenido… ¿a quién iba a llamar?

De pronto, ocurrió un milagro. Encontramos en el aeropuerto a mi ex-cuñado, Rolando González. Él nos vio y nos preguntó con una gran sonrisa:

—¿Qué hacen ustedes aquí?

—¿Qué crees tú?, le dije mientras nos abrazábamos.

Rolando nos llevó a su pequeño apartamento donde nos quedamos por un tiempo. Él nos ayudó y trató de conseguirme un trabajo, pero allí no había oportunidades. Trabajé en Miami por dos meses con un sueldo de $1.15 la hora. Le pedí al gobierno que nos relocalizara en algún lugar del país donde yo pudiera tener un trabajo que me permitiera mantener a mi familia. Nos enviaron al estado de Nuevo México, donde trabajé en una ceba intensiva de ganado, vacunando y enlazando ganado. Yo era un peón; pero era un peón feliz. Era un profesional pasando por una transición, y estaba estudiando para reconstruir nuestras vidas. Sólo era cuestión de tiempo y dedicación.

En 1963, encontré trabajo en el laboratorio del Departamento de Agricultura del Estado de Virginia donde trabajé dos años y a cuyos miembros les viviré eternamente agradecido por su ayuda. En 1965, fui a trabajar con el Gobierno Federal en USDA como veterinario de inspección de carne. Fue en 1966 que pude revalidar mi licencia de veterinario y me convertí en Supervisor de Veterinaria para el Programa de Inspección de Carne. En 1968, USDA me transfirió a Florida para trabajar en *Kaplan Industries* en Bartow, un matadero importante. Tuve varias posiciones durante treinta años, entre ellas la de Presidente de la Asociación Nacional de Veterinarios Federales en 1997 (NAFV, siglas en inglés). Me jubilé en 1999.

Hemos sido muy felices en Bartow. En los años 70, había un grupo pequeño de cubanos en la zona. La mayoría eran médicos que estaban haciendo sus internados en el que fue *Polk General Hospital*; otros eran ingenieros que vinieron a trabajar en lo que era *Davy McKee Corporation*, o simplemente familias que vinieron a esta linda área porque sus familiares o amigos vivían aquí. Nos reuníamos en mi casa y tratábamos de mantener nuestra cultura viva. Bailábamos el cha-cha-cha, la conga, cocinábamos nuestra comida tradicional y nos apoyábamos unos a otros. ¡Cómo nos divertíamos! Nuestros vecinos

estadounidenses admiraban nuestro espíritu. Yo ayudé a organizar la "Noche Hispana" en el *Country Club* de Bartow donde compartíamos nuestra cultura, comida y los bailes típicos con todos los miembros. Esa "Noche Hispana" se hizo muy popular.

Durante las navidades, comencé a iluminar nuestra casa para continuar nuestra tradición y demostrar nuestro agradecimiento de poder celebrar esta época del año. (Los cubanos en la isla ya no podían celebrar esta fecha religiosa). El vecindario me parecía tan oscuro. ¡Decidí cubanizarlo! Comencé a motivar a los vecinos a decorar sus casas, a sincronizar las luces de navidad en la calle y a tocar la música tradicional. Comenzó con dos o tres casas el primer año y gradualmente creció. George Street se le comenzó a llamar "La calle de los árboles de navidad" y la ciudad me nombró "El Papa Noel del Sur de Bartow". La Cámara de Comercio me dio el premio del "Espíritu de Bartow". Hoy, treinta y seis años después, la gente viene de otras ciudades para ver el espectáculo de luces, el cual incluye varios vecindarios. A veces más de mil carros pasan en una noche. Hemos tenido que diseñar una ruta, marcada por flechas verdes, para ayudar a aliviar el tráfico. También tenemos paseos en coches de caballos.

Mi esposa Alicia siempre soñó con tener una boutique, es así que en 1974 se abrieron las puertas de "Alicia's", una tienda de ropa de mujer de alta calidad que ella pudo trabajar y disfrutar por muchos años. Alicia pudo reclamar y traer a la mayoría de su familia a los Estados Unidos. También abrimos "Pedro's" una tienda de sándwiches cubanos, frente a la boutique, en el centro de Bartow.

Ahora disfrutamos de la jubilación. Yo me mantengo activo en la comunidad. Soy el Presidente del Club Republicano Hispano del Condado de Polk. Hemos sido bendecidos con haber tenido la oportunidad de vivir nuestras vidas en un país donde una persona puede hacer cualquier sueño realidad, siempre que esté dispuesto a trabajar duro, con entusiasmo y dedicación. Nuestros hijos Martha y Peter se casaron, y nos han dado cuatro nietos y un bisnieto, todos maravillosos. Estamos muy orgullosos de sus logros y éxitos. Todos los días le damos gracias a Dios. Extrañamos nuestra bella isla, *La Perla del Caribe*, pero encontramos nuestro segundo hogar en los Estados Unidos.

Familia Hernández en Birmingham, Alabama 1998

Un verdadero acto de amor

Rosa Delfín Hernández

Hay dos legados duraderos que podemos dar a nuestros hijos.
Uno es raíces. El otro es alas.
HODDING CARTER, JR.

Hoy comprendo que fue un verdadero acto de amor de parte de mis padres, pero en aquel momento, en 1961, yo estaba enojada y les supliqué una y mil veces; sin embargo no podía hacer nada. Yo tenía diecinueve años cuando mis padres tomaron la decisión de mandar a mi hermano menor, Ramón y a mí a los Estados Unidos.

Nosotros nacimos y crecimos en Cienfuegos, en el sur de la isla, muy cerca de la Bahía de Cochinos. Nuestro padre era co-propietario de Compañía de Seguros y Fianzas, y vivíamos una vida muy cómoda y feliz. Yo nunca había vivido en ningún lugar excepto con mis padres y hermano en nuestra linda casa. Conocía a todos los estudiantes en la escuela, a todos los vecinos y a todo el mundo en la comunidad de la iglesia. Tenía una vida muy cómoda y segura. La simple idea de irnos de nuestro país era aterradora, pero saber que lo haríamos sin nuestros padres se convirtió en una pesadilla. A ellos le era imposible irse de Cuba, así que Ramón y yo teníamos que irnos solos a un país desconocido. Yo no comprendía cual era el peligro que corríamos.

Nuestros padres, Olivia y Ramón Delfín se preocupaban cada día más por nosotros. Decenas de miles de cubanos ya se habían marchado, la mayoría con destino a Miami. En abril de 1961 miles de exiliados de los Estados Unidos, respaldados por la CIA, invadieron la Bahía de Cochinos en un intento de derrocar el régimen de Fidel Castro. El ejército de Castro los venció fácilmente y capturaron a más de 1,100 prisioneros. Este episodio tan aterrador, que tomó lugar tan cerca de mi casa, acabó de convencer a nuestros padres de que tenían que sacarnos del país hacia la seguridad de los Estados Unidos. Entre los exiliados en aquel momento habían muchos

miembros de las órdenes religiosas quienes estaban sintiendo presión bajo un gobierno inspirado por el comunismo, aunque no fue hasta diciembre de ese año que Fidel oficialmente alienó a su gobierno con Rusia y el bloque comunista. Durante el verano de 1961 un grupo de veinte y cuatro monjas de mi escuela, Hermanas del Sagrado Corazón, estaban planeando irse y nos dijeron que tenían espacio y que estaban dispuestas a llevarnos con ellas.

Yo estaba angustiada. Traté de defender mi caso sin éxito alguno. No podía ni imaginar cómo iba a dejar a mi casa, a mis amigos, mis padres. No podía comprender cómo mi madre y mi padre podían tomar la decisión de hacernos abandonar el país. La seguridad siempre había estado en el centro de la familia, en mi comunidad; era imposible entender cómo íbamos a estar más seguros en un país extranjero, lejos de todo lo que era nuestra vida.

El día de nuestra partida desde el aeropuerto de la Habana, yo estaba aterrorizada. Había soldados con ametralladoras por todas partes. Cuando los guardias comenzaron a interrogarme, yo simplemente repetía lo que mi padre y las Hermanas me habían instruido a decir. Cuando me preguntaban una y otra vez: —¿Por qué te quieres ir de Cuba?, yo respondía muy seriamente, aunque el corazón se me partía: —Yo voy a entrar a un convento para hacerme monja. Estaba horrorizada de los soldados. Yo quería llorar, pero no lo hacía. No podía dejar que me vieran llorando. Mi hermano Ramón estudiaba con los Maristas y simplemente dijo que iba con sus profesores para terminar sus estudios y para que yo no me fuera sola. Finalmente nos dejaron pasar y abordamos el avión, exiliados de nuestra patria.

Fue muy difícil acostumbrarnos cuando llegamos a Estados Unidos y fuimos a vivir con unos amigos de nuestros padres en Pennsylvania, un lugar frio y extraño para jóvenes cubanos.

Al año siguiente, cuando estaba estudiando en St. Joseph College en Filadelfia, conocí a un estudiante de la Universidad de Villanova, Andy Hernández, un exiliado quien era de la Habana. Él también extrañaba su hogar, aunque su historia de emigración era diferente a la mía. Andy y uno de sus amigos habían sido arrestados por el G-2 (Seguridad del Estado) en septiembre de 1960 en la Habana porque uno de ellos había dicho que Andy tenía un revolver en el carro. Ellos estaban en un restaurante en las afueras de la Habana donde uno de los trabajadores del campo, a quien ellos le habían hecho el favor de transportar, los chivateó a la policía. Los dos jóvenes, hijos de muy distinguidas familias de la ciudad, pasaron dos días

Residencia de la familia Delfín, Cienfuegos, Cuba

en la cárcel. Después de soltarlos, el amigo fue arrestado otra vez, y la policía comenzó a buscar a Andy. Andy no se arriesgó a regresar a su casa, sabiendo que la policía estaría vigilando. Sus padres no lo enviaron fuera del país, él se tuvo que ir por su propia seguridad. Esa noche él se quedó con algunos familiares y por la mañana fue al aeropuerto, era el 27 de octubre.

En septiembre el gobierno, en un esfuerzo de parar el flujo de personas que estaban abandonando el país, pasó una ley que todos los billetes de avión que se vendieran al extranjero tenían que ser comprados con dinero extranjero. Un agente de viaje, que simpatizaba con la causa del exilio, había sellado cada billete que tenía en la agencia con fecha anterior a la nueva ley. Andy se fue de Cuba, con un billete de ida y vuelta de la Habana a Nueva Orleans, Nueva York, Miami y de regreso a la Habana. El tenía una maleta y $5 en el bolsillo para comenzar su nueva vida.

Nos enamoramos y nos casamos el 5 de septiembre de 1964, dos años después de habernos conocido. Cuando nuestras vidas fueron bendecidas con el nacimiento de nuestro hijo Andy, yo comencé a comprender cuanto un padre puede amar a un hijo, y lo difícil que puede ser tener que tomar decisiones por su bien. Fue en ese momento que yo comencé a sanar emocionalmente y a entender a mis padres.

Con una maestría en ingeniería química, diez años después de su aterrador viaje a los Estados Unidos, Andy tuvo la oportunidad de trabajar en la Florida. Primero trabajó como ingeniero químico, después en ventas y finalmente como Director de Desarrollo Comercial en América Latina. Más tarde, Andy hizo un cambio del mundo empresarial a bienes raíces y se convirtió en

Rosa, Ryan, Nicolás y Andy Hernández

el Presidente de *A.H. Realty*, Century 21 en Lakeland y Winter Haven. Desde 1990 *A.H. Realty* obtuvo el primer lugar en ventas y transacciones, en tres ocasiones diferentes, dentro de las 150 oficinas de Century 21. Andy ha participado como miembro de la Junta Directiva de la Cámara de Comercio de Greater Lakeland, fue Presidente de la Junta Administrativa del Museo de Arte de Polk y de la Imperial Symphony Orchestra, fue Presidente por dos años del Consejo de la Parroquia de la Iglesia Católica Resurrección, es miembro de la Junta Directiva de *Lakeland Regional Medical Center* y *Santa Fe High School.* Después de 19 años como Presidente de *A.H. Realty*, Andy pasó a ser el Presidente de *MidFlorida Real Estate Sales, LLC* el cual es parte de *MidFlorida Credit Union.*

Yo siempre he querido retribuirle a la comunidad que me dio la bienvenida como exiliada. He sido muy activa en muchas organizaciones en mi ciudad, pero mi familia siempre ha sido mi prioridad. Nuestro hijo Andy y su esposa Lisa viven en Carolina del Norte. Nuestros dos nietos Nicholas y Andy, nos llenan la vida de felicidad. Mi familia es lo más importante que tengo.

Yo no me quería ir de Cuba, pero ahora que soy madre, sé que haría lo mismo que hicieron mis padres. Aunque la separación de nuestra familia, fue difícil y dolorosa para Ramón y para mí, yo sé que la decisión que ellos tuvieron que tomar, y la separación fue más difícil para ellos que para nosotros y que fue una buena decisión.

PD: Rosa Delfín Hernández se ha distinguido en la comunidad de Lakeland como voluntaria en diferentes capacidades, sobre todo como Presidenta del Museo de Arte de Polk, con una junta de 36 fideicomisarios. El Museo de Arte de Polk acaba de reconocerla otorgándole el Premio de Harrison-Hooks Lifetime Achievemnet. Ella es miembro de la Florida House Council de Lakeland y es Comisionada de la Junta Directiva de Florida House Council en Washington. Su hermano Ramón Delfín vive en Coral Gables, Florida y es el Director Internacional de Rovina Packing Corporation.

Dr. Rodríguez-Torres y Guly

¡Yo creo en milagros!

Dr. Ramón Rodríguez-Torres

Existen dos maneras de vivir:
puedes vivir como si nada fuera un milagro,
o puedes vivir como si todo fuera un milagro.
ALBERT EINSTEIN

Después de graduarme de la carrera de medicina en la Universidad de La Habana, en el año 1951, y de terminar mi especialización en Medicina Interna y Cardiología en el año 1953, decidí abrir un consultorio para la práctica de estas especialidades en la Habana. Pronto me di cuenta que las organizaciones médicas en Cuba, similares a las hoy conocidas como Organizaciones de Salud Médica (HMO) en los Estados Unidos no aceptaban pacientes de la tercera edad ya que eran considerados como un gran riesgo desde el punto de vista económico. Debido a esto, me impuse la tarea de crear una clínica privada que ofreciera un excelente cuidado médico y aceptara y atendiera a los ancianos. Después de haber conseguido un grupo de médicos de alta calidad científica, quienes compartían mi visión, abrimos la "Clínica F y 25" en el Vedado en 1954. Como éramos el único centro médico con esas características, nuestra clientela aumentó de forma increíble, tanto así que dos años después de la inauguración, tuvimos que construir dos plantas más para servir mejor a nuestros pacientes.

En el año 1957, me gané una beca ofrecida por el Gobierno Británico, (*British Council Scholarship*) para estudiar Cardiología en la Universidad de Manchester y en el *National Heart Hospital* en Londres. Durante mi estancia en Inglaterra, varios de los médicos de la "Clínica F y 25" ayudaron a los guerrilleros de Castro en la Sierra Maestra en Oriente, Cuba. Cuando yo regresé a la isla a finales de 1958, me informaron que la Clínica estaba proporcionando ayuda a los guerrilleros y que uno de nuestros médicos había decidido unirse a la guerrilla en las montañas de la Sierra Maestra.

El primero de enero de 1959, después de la salida de Fulgencio Batista, la guerrilla castrista se estableció como el nuevo gobierno de Cuba. De esta manera, algunos médicos de la Clínica llegaron a ocupar distinguidas posiciones gubernamentales (Vice Ministro de Salud, Jefe del Sistema de Salud de la Ciudad de la Habana por ejemplo.) En ese tiempo, se me ofreció una posición como profesor de la Universidad de la Habana. Aunque siempre había soñado con llegar a ese nivel en mi carrera, no acepté. Esas posiciones siempre se habían ocupado por concurso-oposición y no por favores políticos.

Ese año fue crítico para todos los que teníamos principios democráticos. Miles de cubanos fueron fusilados o sentenciados a muchos años de prisión, sólo por no estar de acuerdo con el régimen dictatorial comunista de Fidel Castro. En febrero de 1960 fui invitado a una cena en casa de una colega, aparentemente ella pensaba que yo era partidario del nuevo gobierno. A las 11:00 p.m. Fidel Castro llegó y explicó a los presentes lo que la revolución iba a crear en Cuba y los cambios significativos que iban a ocurrir en mi país. Yo no podía creer lo que estaba oyendo. Llegué a mi casa alrededor de las 2:30 a.m. y no pude dormir pensando en todo lo que había oído. A la mañana siguiente, cometí uno de los errores más grandes de mi vida. Llamé a una reunión de emergencia a los médicos de la clínica para informarles sobre la necesidad de hacer algo de inmediato, de lo contrario Cuba sufriría por largo tiempo. Al final de mi presentación nadie me hizo preguntas, con la excepción de un médico que era como un hermano para mi quien me entregó un librito rojo y me dijo: "todo lo que tienes que hacer es leerte este libro y cambiarás de idea". El libro era "*La guerra de las guerrilla de Mao Tse Tung*". En ese momento comprendí que mis días en Cuba estaban contados y que debía de irme lo antes posible.

Aunque tuve suerte de que mis compañeros no me acusaran por no compartir su doctrina, a partir de aquel día, comenzaron los registros policiacos en mi hogar a altas horas de la madrugada, con el afán de encontrar cualquier cosa que pudiera ser ilegal para el régimen. Después de muchos meses de tribulaciones, ansiedad y angustia, pude obtener el permiso para salir del país. La decisión de dejar mi patria y perder todo lo que yo había creado, no fue lo más difícil para mí, sino el dejar el resto de mi familia y aquellas personas a las que tanto quería. En el mes de octubre decidimos que yo me iría solo y mi señora, mis dos hijos y mis padres se reunirían conmigo 48 horas más tardes. De esta forma, si las autoridades cambiaban su forma de pensar y no me dejaran salir, Guly no

Rafael, Dr. Rodríguez-Torres, Raymond, Guly y Raúl.

tendría que enfrentar la decisión de irse sola con los niños. En el aeropuerto, Seguridad me quitó todo lo que llevaba, con excepción de $5.00 y dos mudas de ropa.

Yo había decidido irme a Puerto Rico porque en aquel tiempo, el salario a un médico que comenzaba un internado en los Estados Unidos era solamente de $50.00 al mes, mientras que en Puerto Rico

Familia Rodríguez-Torres

era de $150.00. Cuando el avión comenzó el viaje a Miami y de ahí a Puerto Rico, comencé a pensar: "¿Qué voy a hacer con sólo $5.00? ¡No conozco a nadie en ese país! Me preguntaba si debería quedarme a dormir esa noche en un asiento del aeropuerto o en un parque. Finalmente mi avión aterrizó en San Juan a las 9:00 p.m.

Yo siempre he sido cristiano y por lo tanto he creído en milagros. Ese día, Dios me demostró su omnipotencia. Cuando bajaba por las escaleras del avión vi a un amigo inglés quien había conocido en Londres. Nunca se me olvidará la pregunta que me hizo:

—¿Qué haces tú aquí Ramon?". El era un empresario quien estaba trabajando en Puerto Rico con mucho éxito.

Después de explicarle mi situación, me invitó a su casa, donde pasé la noche. A la mañana siguiente, mi amigo me facilitó los medios económicos para rentar una casa, comprar muebles, comida y otras necesidades. Cuando mi señora Guly y los niños llegaran al día siguiente, Guly se encontraría con un hogar esperándoles. Dígame Ud. ahora, ¿cree o no en milagros? ¡Yo creo!

Después de haber hecho las gestiones de renta y equipamiento de nuestra casa, decidí ir al Ministerio de Salud para buscar trabajo. Sabía que sería difícil, ya que para obtener una entrevista con un ministro en cualquier país normalmente lleva meses...si uno es dichoso. Al parecer, yo lo era aquel día pues el Ministro de Salud no sólo me dio audiencia, sino que también me dio una posición en uno de los hospitales del gobierno. Algunos le llamarían a estas coincidencias suerte, yo las llamo: "Milagros".

Un año más tarde nos mudamos a Nueva York, donde obtuve el puesto de Asistente del Director de Cardiología Pediátrica en La Universidad Estatal de Nueva York (New York State University). Cuatro años más tarde, me convertí en el Director de dicho Departamento. Después de doce años asumí el puesto de Jefe de Cátedra y Profesor de Pediatría. Había alcanzado mi meta. Yo había mantenido mis principios y Dios me había dado la oportunidad de vivir en un país libre: LOS ESTADOS UNIDOS DE AMERICA.

Cuando abrió la nueva Escuela de Medicina de Ohio (*Medical College of Ohio*) tuve el honor de ejercer como Jefe de Cátedra y Profesor de Pediatría, con todas las emocionantes oportunidades de empezar y establecer un nuevo departamento.

Cinco años más tarde, y después de haberme ofrecido la posición de Jefe de Cátedra de Pediatría en la Universidad Estatal de Michigan (*Michigan State University*), decidí aceptar la posición de Jefe de la Facultad Médica (*Chief of Staff*) del Hospital Infantil de Miami (*Miami Children's Hospital*) en Florida, posición que ocupé por 15 años hasta mi retiro el 30 de junio de 1996.

En mi trabajo con niños, así como con adultos, he podido tratar a muchos compatriotas. Siempre les he aconsejado lo mismo que les he enseñado a mis hijos: Nunca se aparten de sus principios ni tengan miedo ante la verdad. Las personas que trabajan y luchan alcanzan sus metas, no importa de donde vengan ni adonde los lleve el destino.

Teresa Hidalgo de Martínez y el Reverendo Gerardo Martínez †

Un legado de fe. La historia del Rev. Gerardo y Teresa Martínez

Teresa Hidalgo de Martínez

Pueden quemar las iglesias y las sinagogas, pueden destruir todos los Textos Santos, pero nunca podrán hacer que las abuelas dejen de contar sus historias a sus nietos… para que siempre haya esperanza de libertad.
ANÓNIMO

Mi esposo, el Reverendo Gerardo Martínez, era pastor de la Iglesia Metodista en Guayabo, Mayari en la provincia de Oriente. En el año 1958, fuimos trasladados a la Iglesia de Guantánamo. La casa pastoral estaba al lado de la iglesia y detrás de ella estaba el Cuartel de la Guardia. Desde la cocina podíamos ver a los soldados armados caminado por la azotea del cuartel quienes nos transmitían el estrés y la tensión que se vivía adentro. En una de las calles cercanas había un puesto de policía que casi todas las noches era atacado por los rebeldes quienes asesinaban a los policías y les robaban sus armas. Era un ambiente aterrador, especialmente porque teníamos tres niños y otro en camino.

En aquellos meses se recrudeció la Revolución, todos los caminos y carreteras para llegar o salir del pueblo estaban cortados y algunos dinamitados. A las cinco de la tarde ya nadie podía caminar por las calles y por las noches no se permitía encender las luces en el frente de las casas. Vivíamos asustados. Cuando oíamos disparos, mis hijos y yo nos escondíamos debajo de la cama. Gerardo por su parte, parecía no poner mucha atención a la situación, probablemente para no asustarnos más de lo que la situación ya lo hacía.

Un sábado por la noche, mi esposo estaba en la oficina que daba a la calle preparando su sermón para el domingo, cuando de pronto se escuchó un disparo. La bala atravesó la ventana y fue a dar en la pared un poco más arriba de su cabeza. Rápidamente apagó la luz y se fue a terminar su sermón en el comedor bajo la luz de una lamparita. La situación era cada día más insostenible, la gente tenía

miedo de salir de sus casas y encontrar comida era cada vez más difícil. Pasamos quince días comiendo harina de maíz.

El 28 de diciembre de 1958, nació nuestra hija Rebeca. Yo no podía ir al hospital porque era peligroso salir de casa, además no quería dejar a los niños. Así que una señora, miembro de nuestra iglesia que era enfermera comadrona, se quedó conmigo hasta que nació la niña. Mi esposo fue al mercado para ver si encontraba algo de carne. Lo único que encontró fue un pato. El pobre hombre nunca había cocinado en su vida, ¡mucho menos pelar un pato! Aunque había plumas por todas partes, la comida resultó deliciosa.

El primero de enero de 1959, triunfó la Revolución. Recuerdo que el pueblo estaba celebrando, pensando que esto sería la salvación de Cuba, mientras otros estaban preocupados, entre ellos Gerardo, pues nunca creyó en Fidel y su gente. El tenía razón.

El próximo día los rebeldes entraron en la ciudad y quisieron tomar el Cuartel, el Jefe se negaba a entregarse, y los rebeldes le prometieron que si salían sin oposición les perdonarían la vida. Los guardias se entregaron y los rebeldes los hicieron montarse en la parte de atrás de un camión. El verdadero plan era fusilarlos en el paredón. Los guardias pronto se dieron cuenta del plan y trataron de revelarse, así que los rebeldes comenzaron a disparar y los asesinaron a todos allí en la calle.

Un joven, quien era el presidente de los jóvenes de nuestra iglesia, fue a donde trabajaba mi esposo y con una sonrisa le comentó:

—Pastor, hoy vi como mataron a todos esos guardias, caían al suelo como moscas y yo hasta escupí a uno de ellos.

Mi esposo lo miró con indignación ya que no podía creer lo que escuchaba y le dijo —¿Tú hiciste eso? Pues quiero que ahora mismo renuncies como presidente de los jóvenes.

—Pero ¿por qué?, contestó el joven.

—Porque tú no has demostrado compasión para esos hombres y nadie tiene derecho de quitarle la vida a un ser humano, sólo Dios. El joven se fue molesto.

Como Pastor Metodista, Gerardo no podía estar de acuerdo con esas atrocidades y empezó a predicar en contra de los fusilamientos y las acciones de los revolucionarios. Muchos de los miembros en la congregación que eran fidelistas, se quejaron con el superintendente de la iglesia quien le dijo a mi esposo: "Gerardo, yo sé que tú estás haciendo bien, pero por tu seguridad y la de tu familia, te voy a trasladar". Nos mudamos a Báguanos, una ciudad azucarera, en

junio de 1959. Era un lugar bonito y acogedor y Gerardo tenía que dirigir muchas iglesias en el área.

El administrador de la azucarera era una persona muy educada quien había estado a cargo del central por muchos años, pero no estaba de acuerdo con Fidel. Lo reemplazaron por uno que apenas había completado el segundo grado escolar, pero que estaba totalmente de acuerdo con la Revolución de Fidel. Como consecuencia de esto, la producción de azúcar empezó a disminuir y pronto la central cerró. Un día se apareció el nuevo administrador con dos soldados en nuestra casa para pedirle el Jeep a Gerardo para ir a los cañaverales y ver lo que la gente estaba haciendo. Gerardo les dijo:

—Lo siento, pero ahora mismo voy a salir a un programa de la iglesia. El administrador le dijo a uno de los soldados:

—Apunten ahí que el Reverendo Martínez se niega a prestar su carro. Después de unos meses volvieron a pedir el Jeep para llevar armas a los campos, mi esposo les contestó:

—Lo siento, pero mi carro es de la iglesia y sólo transportamos Biblias, no armas.

Las cosas se estaban poniendo un poquito peligrosas.

Un lunes por la mañana estaba mi esposo en el patio de la iglesia cuando llegaron los soldados, mi esposo les preguntó:

Familia Martínez

—¿En qué los puedo servir?

—Nos han dicho que usted ayer predicó sobre el Tío Sam.

—Yo les dije a la congregación que los misioneros y misioneras habían venido a hablarnos de Cristo, y no del Tío Sam. Si gustan vengan a mi oficina para que lean mi sermón.

Así lo hicieron y entonces se disculparon. En todo este tiempo nosotros nunca habíamos pensado salir del país, pues pensábamos que esta situación era pasajera. La vida agradable y serena de nuestra isla se había convertido en una vida de atrocidades y pesadillas. ¿Cuánto más podría durar?

La iglesia de Báguanos tenía una escuela que enseñaba desde los primeros grados hasta octavo. Una mañana que Gerardo fue a abrir el colegio se encontró con varios soldados armados quienes le informaron que la escuela había sido intervenida y si insistía en abrirla, se lo llevarían preso. Ese fue el día que decidimos que era hora de irnos del país. Nos dimos cuenta que Cuba había perdido toda su democracia y que no había esperanza.

Comenzamos a preparar pasaportes, vacunas y todo lo que requerían. Esperamos mucho tiempo y ya pensábamos que no había esperanzas de salir, hasta que el día 4 de enero de 1962 llegó a mi casa un primo que trabajaba en el correo y nos trajo los telegramas. Nos daban 72 horas para dejar el país. Eran las 10:00 a.m. y ese día Gerardo estaba en Holguín en una reunión de la iglesia. Lo llamé por teléfono y me dijo:

—Prepara todo; nos vamos de la casa esta misma tarde.

Había una señora jamaiquina que me ayudaba en la casa; ella me ayudó a preparar dos maletas con algunas ropas para los seis. A las 3:00 p.m. del mismo día salimos de Báguanos. Nadie de la familia sabía nada. En el camino pasamos por la casa de mis padres. Ese fue el día más triste de mi vida. Mi padre me abrazó y dijo que esa sería probablemente la última vez que nos veríamos. Así fue; él murió unos años después.

Salimos el 6 de enero de 1962 "Día de los Reyes Magos", día en el que se entregan los regalos y nosotros recibimos el regalo de la libertad. Nos mudamos a Chicago, Illinois y fuimos a trabajar con los Laboratorios Abbott. En 1965, Gerardo recibió una llamada del Obispo de la Iglesia Metodista diciéndonos que nos necesitaban en Florida.

Gerardo renunció a su distinguida posición en los Laboratorios Abbot, y fue a trabajar como Pastor en la Iglesia Metodista de Zolfo Springs, Florida. La congregación estaba integrada principalmente

por inmigrantes mexicanos quienes necesitaban un pastor que hablara español. Mientras trabajaba en la iglesia, él también se preparaba para el seminario en la Universidad de Duke en Carolina del Norte durante los veranos. También asistió a la Universidad de Emory en Atlanta, Georgia. Después de graduarse de Teología, la Conferencia Metodista de Florida nos mandó a Nicaragua, donde trabajó como Director de Desarrollo Comunal para Alfalit; una organización sin fines de lucro, la cual basada en la fe, enseña a adultos necesitados a leer y escribir alrededor del mundo. En 1974, nos enviaron a Costa Rica, como Director General de AlFalit Internacional. De ahí, el dirigía a toda América Latina. Viajaba frecuentemente y pudo llevar a cabo la obra del Señor, ayudando a innumerables personas a mejorar sus vidas

En 1979, regresamos a Estados Unidos a trabajar en la Iglesia Metodista de Coral Way en Miami, donde disfrutamos la congregación por 13 años inolvidables. En mayo de 1991, Gerardo se graduó como Elder de la Iglesia Metodista en la Conferencia de Florida, trabajando sus últimos años en la Iglesia Metodista de Tampa y retirándose en 1995 después de 50 años como pastor. Mi esposo pasó a la presencia del Señor el 27 de mayo de 2003, dejándoles a sus cuatro hijos, diez nietos y un bisnieto, un legado de fe cristiana y amor hacia la humanidad.

Estamos muy agradecidos a este país que nos acogió, nos ayudó y nos abrió las puertas a las oportunidades. Nuestros hijos, Santiago, Carlos, Gerardo y Rebeca han podido estudiar sus carreras y desarrollar sus dones como ciudadanos dignos y responsables. También agradecemos a la Iglesia Metodista, a la cual hemos dedicamos nuestra vida.

Todavía soñamos con que un día, no muy lejano, nuestra Cuba sea libre y soberana nuevamente, aunque muchos no alcancemos a verla.

Dra. Madelyn Espinosa Buttler, Miriam Espinosa Martínez y Martha Espinosa Laurent

Una lección de patriotismo

Martha Espinosa Laurent

La enseñanza no es una profesión, es una pasión.
ANÓNIMO

El timbre de la primera clase acababa de sonar. Como de costumbre, por el altoparlante se oyó la voz del director del colegio pidiendo que nos pusiéramos de pie para jurar a la bandera. Mientras en coro decíamos: "Juro lealtad a la bandera de los Estados Unidos de América...", me di cuenta que algunos de mis alumnos no se llevaban la mano al pecho y otros simplemente repetían las palabras por inercia. Decidí entonces tomar unos minutos de la clase de español para enseñarles un poco sobre la historia de mi país de origen, Cuba, con la esperanza de despertar en ellos un poco más de apreciación por el suyo.

—¿Creen ustedes que son seres privilegiados por vivir en un país democrático? Los estudiantes me miraron sin responder.

—¿Cuántos de sus padres tienen su propio negocio? Algunos alzaron la mano.

—¿Alguno de ustedes tiene planes de tener su propio negocio algún día?

—¿Cuándo fue la última vez que disfrutaron de un buen bistec, o pollo, pescado, una hamburguesa, cualquier tipo de carne?

Al ver la seriedad de mi rostro, reinó el silencio en la clase.

—¿Por qué nos hace esas preguntas, Sra. Laurent?

— ¿Por qué? Porque me gustaría compartir algunas de las experiencias de mi juventud con ustedes:

Yo tenía sólo cuatro años de edad cuando mis padres decidieron que teníamos que salir de mi patria. Fidel Castro había tomado el poder y ahora éramos un país comunista donde se suponía que habría una distribución equitativa de riqueza e igualdad social. Sin embargo, esto significó que el gobierno tenía poder absoluto, que se apoderaba de todas las propiedades privadas e incluso de nuestras vidas.

Como a todas las familias que presentaban su petición para salir del país, a nosotros nos hicieron un inventario minucioso de todo lo que teníamos en casa. Los guardias armados les advirtieron a mis padres que cuando llegara el momento de la salida volverían a inventariar la casa. Todo tenía que estar intacto. Así lo hicieron ocho años más tarde cuando nos llegó el ansiado permiso. Los despiadados soldados sellaron nuestra puerta con un papel que decía: "Propiedad del Gobierno Cubano". Jamás volveríamos a entrar en el hogar donde habíamos crecido.

Recuerdo que durante los primeros años del gobierno de Castro, Mami trataba de evitar que mi hermana y yo escucháramos las terribles noticias que provenían de las bocinas de la plaza cerca de nuestra casa: "¡Paredón…Paredón!" Las fuertes voces se oían una y otra vez durante los juicios públicos que sentenciaban a muerte a los supuestos contrarrevolucionarios. Ella nos hacía cubrir nuestros oídos y nos mandaba al dormitorio. Sin embargo, después nos enterábamos por otros adultos o niños que contaban sobre los fusilamientos públicos que se llevaban a cabo por las tardes en la pared que rodeaba el cementerio del pueblo. Esas víctimas: hijos, esposos, padres, hermanos, amigos, llegaron a ser un espectáculo para las masas que andaban sedientas de sangre. El único crimen de los fusilados era protestar contra un gobierno que les estaba quitando sus propiedades o estar abiertamente en desacuerdo con el comunismo.

Uno de los recuerdos más vívidos de mi niñez fue el día que fuimos a visitar a mi tío Oscar a la cárcel. Era un día húmedo y caluroso y mi padre me llevaba de la mano. El guardia que vigilaba a los presos, despóticamente llamó el nombre de mi tío mientras con un tolete le tocaba el hombro: — Oscar, tu hermano y tus sobrinas vinieron a verte. Me acuerdo de la mala impresión que recibí al ver a mi tío en un uniforme de preso que dejaba ver parte de su cuerpo, pues parecía ser varias tallas mas pequeño de lo que él necesitaba.

Los prisioneros vivían con la única ilusión de que les permitieran la visita de sus seres queridos.

—¿Qué hizo tío Oscar?, le pregunté a mi papá.

—Tu tío no hizo nada malo, trató de asegurarme mi papá.

—Un vecino lo delató porque mató una de sus propias vacas… ahora eso es ilegal. La mató para comer y compartir la carne con toda la familia. Tu tío es una excelente persona.

También recuerdo un día, cuando un mar verde de soldados en uniforme de camuflaje entró armado a nuestro hogar gritando:

Martha Espinosa Laurent

—¿Dónde tienen escondido a ese hombre?

Estaban buscando a un amigo de mi padre, que había vuelto a Cuba durante la invasión de Playa Girón y que había escapado de las garras del gobierno. Ellos sabían de la amistad que él había sostenido con mi padre y alguien les había dicho que estaba escondido en nuestra casa. Por esto se sintieron con el derecho de entrar a nuestro hogar y atacarnos verbalmente. Mami estaba entonces embarazada de mi hermana menor, Madelyn. Yo estaba aferrada a su mano, mientras me llevaba con ella hacia el baño para vomitar no por su condición de embarazada, sino por el gran temor que sintió. Los gusanos, nombre que se les daba a las personas que no estaban de acuerdo con el régimen, no teníamos derechos humanos. No merecíamos respeto ni consideración.

El comunismo trajo también el racionamiento a todo nivel. A cada familia se le asignó una libreta de abastecimiento en la que se determinaba la cantidad de comida y provisiones que les correspondía basado en el número y condición de cada persona que formaba parte del núcleo familiar. Por ejemplo, la leche era sólo para niños y ancianos de cierta edad. El gobierno decidió que el resto de la población no necesitaba calcio. El resto de los alimentos se racionó a onzas por persona. ¡Qué diferente a la experiencia de comprar en

Publix! ¡Qué dichosos somos de poder entrar a un centro comercial y comprar lo que nos plazca!

Cuando llegaba un cargamento de zapatos de Rusia, la gente salía en manadas a las calles para hacer cola con la esperanza de poder comprar un par de aquellos zapatos horribles y de malísima calidad. Las personas se aferraban a su preciado lugar en la fila por horas y horas hasta que otro miembro de la familia viniera a reemplazarlo para no perder su sitio. Allí estaban por días, mañana, tarde y noche. La mayoría de las veces, cuando por fin llegaba su turno, ya no tenían su talla. Igual ocurría con los cargamentos de ropa o telas.

Más tarde, decidieron que sería más fácil distribuir los productos de consumo personal a nivel de comités de barrio. Estos estaban encabezados por una familia abiertamente comunista, que asumía la responsabilidad de reunir representantes de familias en un área de tres o cuatro cuadras a la redonda, para decidir a quien asignarle pases para comprar las cantidades limitadas de ropa, zapatos, telas, medias y otros artículos. Yo fui a alguna de estas reuniones con mi hermana mayor y nunca se me olvidará la experiencia de ver a una señora, ya entrada en años, exponer su caso de por qué ella necesitaba una prenda de ropa interior con más urgencia que otra de las vecinas de la cuadra. Aunque estos comités llevaban a cabo esta labor coordinativa, su función principal era vigilar al barrio y reportar al gobierno cualquier movimiento sospechoso que pudiera ser un acto de "contra-revolución".

Yo tenía 12 años cuando finalmente en 1966, después de mucho tiempo de espera, mi familia logró salir de Cuba. Habían sido años que hasta vivir en nuestra propia casa se convirtió en una terrible tensión debido a la preocupación de que alguien nos oyera decir algo contra el gobierno o de que algo se perdiera una vez que el gobierno había hecho el inventario de nuestras posesiones, de lo contrario nuestro sueño de escapar del comunismo se vería truncado.

Nos íbamos vía México, una de las únicas dos vías que se podían tomar para salir del país legalmente. Las visas para México las consiguió mi padre por medio de un cliente y amigo que tenía en dicho país, el cual accedió a visitar al cónsul y usar sus influencias para conseguirnos los ansiados permisos. Por nuestra corta edad, mi hermana Madelyn y yo, pensábamos que nos íbamos de viaje. Pronto descubriríamos que era un viaje eterno. Mi hermana mayor, Miriam, sabía que el viaje significaba decirles adiós al resto de la familia, a sus amistades de la infancia, y a todas las ilusiones que tiene una joven

de quince años. Mis padres dejaban atrás todo por lo que habían trabajado una vida: su casa, que con tanto trabajo habían planeado y construido; sus posesiones; sus ahorros y recuerdos de la familia, a la cual no sabían si algún día volverían a ver. Pero todo lo hacían por nuestro futuro y por tener lo más preciado que tiene un ser humano que es la libertad.

El día de nuestra salida, en el aeropuerto, Madelyn y yo llevábamos cada una, una muñeca. Los guardias nos las quitaron y les arrancaron la cabeza bruscamente para ver si mis padres escondían algo de valor en ellas. Por supuesto, a aquellos milicianos no les importaba el efecto que aquello pudiera tener en nosotras, ni los derechos de nuestros padres quienes iban preparados para que los desnudaran como parte del registro acostumbrado para aquellos que salían permanentemente del país.

Al fin salimos rumbo a México con lo que traíamos puesto, sin prendas ni dinero, sin fotos familiares y con sólo cuarenta libras de ropa. Nos íbamos desterrados.

Durante tres meses, mi padre, el Dr. Jorge Espinosa, mi madre Matilde, Miriam, Madelyn y yo, vivimos en una pequeña habitación del Hotel Pal, un modesto hotel en una modesta colonia de la Ciudad de México. La mayoría de las familias hospedadas aquí eran cubanos en tránsito, sin recursos y que recibían ayuda de sus familiares en los Estados Unidos para poder pagar los costos de vivienda y manutención. Nuestros días en México estuvieron llenos de desasosiego y confusión. Estábamos sobreviviendo lo mejor que podíamos mientras mi padre hacía todos los trámites para nuestra entrada legal a los Estados Unidos.

Dr. Jorge Espinosa † y su esposa Matilde †

Todavía retengo en mi memoria aquel pequeño cuarto del Hotel Pal, el cual incluía un salón que servía de dormitorio para todos por la noche y de sala durante el día; un minúsculo baño y una estrecha cocina. Al poco tiempo de llegar a México, una señora amiga de mi padre, que se había casado con un mexicano y hacía años que residía en México, se llevó a mi hermana mayor para su casa. Como ella sabía de nuestras condiciones y mi hermana ya tenía quince años, le presentaría a otros jóvenes y de ser posible, le buscaría algún trabajo para que pudiera cubrir sus gastos y quizás ayudar algo a la familia. Así fue, y Miriam se fue con la señora Lola a vivir a un barrio muy bonito, donde tenía su propio cuarto. No mucho después de irse, Lola le consiguió un trabajo como extra en una película del famoso Cantinflas, lo cual fue una gran experiencia para ella.

Durante nuestra estancia en México tuvimos la oportunidad de conocer otros cubanos desterrados, pero que no irían a los Estados Unidos porque no tenían familiares que los ayudaran con los

Familia Laurent

trámites o porque les parecía mejor quedarse en un país en el que se hablaba su propio idioma o para seguir la causa de salvar a Cuba del régimen comunista desde más cerca.

Cuando llegamos a Miami nuestra vida cambió. Era hora de madurar. Mi madre se fue a trabajar por primera vez fuera del hogar. Tenía que tomar tres autobuses para llegar a la fábrica donde trabajaba como costurera. Allí trabajaban muchas cubanas exiliadas que, como ella, jamás imaginaron que se verían en tal situación; pero lo hacían con orgullo. Ella trabajaba de lunes a viernes y también traía costura para poder ganar más los fines de semana. Miriam cosía en la casa para la misma fábrica donde cosía mi mamá, y entre ella y yo cuidábamos a nuestra hermana menor, Madelyn. Papi, a pesar de que era veterinario, tomó un trabajo como peón en los Everglades. Salía de madrugada para llegar al amanecer y trabajaba de lunes a viernes. Durante la semana vivía con unos *cowboys* en un tráiler donde también desempeñaba el trabajo de cocinero. De alguna manera se las arreglaba para mantenerse al día con lo que estaba pasando en su profesión. Ya por su edad, le era muy pesado hacer la labor física que era necesaria para trabajar en el rancho, así que cuando oyó de otros veterinarios cubanos en el exilio, que el gobierno federal estaba necesitado de inspectores de carne y había desarrollado un programa para entrenar veterinarios extranjeros, puso mano a la obra y empezó a buscar la forma de entrar en ese programa.

Un día mi padre se llenó de valor, compró un boleto de avión para Tallahassee, y se apareció en la oficina de Hacienda, donde le explicaron lo que tendría que hacer para ingresar a este programa y donde llenó una solicitud. Unas semanas después, le llegó la noticia que esperaba: lo habían aceptado en el entrenamiento intensivo en inspección de carne en California. El curso tomó un par de meses, del cual regresó con su licencia y una plaza de inspector en Sylvester, un pueblito pequeño al sur de Georgia.

Una vez que mi padre emprendió este trabajo, las cosas empezaron a mejorar desde el punto económico, pero no todo fue felicidad, pues la familia seguía en Miami y Sylvester estaba a casi a ocho horas de viaje por carretera, un viaje que él emprendía cada quince días. En uno de esos viajes, recibimos una alarmante llamada de la policía. Mami, que no hablaba inglés, le tuvo que pasar el teléfono a mi hermana mayor, quien pudo entender que Papi había sufrido un grave accidente cerca de Miami. Tuvo la suerte de salir con vida, pero una de sus piernas sufrió varias fracturas que requirieron cirugía. Estuvo en un hospital de Fort Worth por varios días y luego

vino a Miami para pasar unos días de recuperación. Tenía la pierna enyesada hasta el muslo y aunque a duras penas podía ambular, y el médico le recomendó lo contrario, Papi decidió regresar a Georgia para resumir su trabajo. Para él, la presión que sentía de no atender a un trabajo que tan duro le había costado conseguir era mucho más que el dolor físico por su pierna rota. Así estuvo trabajando en el matadero, todo el día parado con sólo muletas como apoyo. La dueña del hotel donde vivía nos decía que la pierna buena de mi padre estaba tan hinchada de noche que a ella le parecía un milagro que pudiera estar de pie, pero poco a poco fue sanando y al fin pudo volver a caminar sin problemas.

Apenas terminó ese año escolar, nos mudamos a Georgia con mi padre. Cuando llegamos a Sylvester, quedamos felices pues Papi había comprado una casita de ladrillos en la cual estaríamos cómodos. Allí vivimos por cinco años, durante los cuales, con mucho esfuerzo, Papi estudió durante sus horas libres y pudo dar su examen de revalidación y obtener su licencia para ejercer como veterinario en el estado de Georgia. Aunque él quería seguir en la inspección de carne, siempre pensó que tener su licencia para trabajar en su giro sería algo útil. Mi madre trabajaba de costurera, pero ahora estaba en casa.

Como vivíamos lejos de la familia en Miami, mi papá pidió que lo transfirieran a una planta en la Florida. Así fue que llegamos a Bartow, donde él fue a trabajar a Kapplan Industries como veterinario inspector de carne y donde posteriormente, también sacó su licencia de veterinario del estado de la Florida. Mi padre fue un hombre brillante, estudioso y aplicado. Estas cualidades fueron las que lo ayudaron a pasar los exámenes estatales de veterinaria tanto en Georgia como en la Florida, los cuales aprobó al primer intento a pesar de que estos son difíciles, incluso para veterinarios de habla inglesa.

En Bartow nuestra vida fue aún más holgada. Compramos una linda casa donde mi madre, aunque siguió de costurera, tuvo más tiempo para ser ama de casa. Papi siempre nos había dicho que él esperaba que nosotras, sus hijas, no paráramos hasta poder obtener una carrera universitaria. Él prometió que haría todo en su poder para facilitárnoslo. A mí, en particular, me dijo que quería que aprendiera a volar con mis propias alas. Gracias a su apoyo y a las oportunidades que hay en los Estados Unidos para todos aquellos que tienen el deseo de aprender y están dispuestos a trabajar, pudimos llegar a la meta que él nos había trazado. Las tres hermanas llegamos a obtener carreras universitarias y postgrados.

Durante el comunismo, mi niñez transcurrió bajo represión, secretismo y miedo; donde ni creer en Dios era aceptado. Todo eso dejó secuelas imborrables en lo más profundo de mi ser. Es por eso que siento que es mi deber como cubana y profesora asegurar que mis alumnos no den por sentado la bendición de vivir en un país libre y democrático, y que cuando juren a la bandera, lo hagan con el más absoluto respeto y conciencia de lo que significa este acto.

Al día siguiente, los alumnos se pararon y llevándose la mano al pecho, fuerte y unánimemente repitieron las palabras:

"Juro lealtad a la bandera de los Estados Unidos de América y a la república que representa. Una nación, bajo Dios, indivisible, con libertad y justicia para todos".

Tal vez cada uno de estos adolescentes de mi clase de español, cuya vida está tan llena de abundancia y libertad, pueda continuar descubriendo el verdadero significado del patriotismo.

PD: Martha Espinosa Laurent es la Jefa del Departamento de Lenguas Extranjeras en Bartow High School, International Baccalaureate School. Martha contrajo matrimonio con John Laurent en 1982. John es Juez de la Corte del Circuito de Polk. Ha sido Senador del Estado de Florida, Distrito 17 y Legislador. Tienen dos hijos maravillosos, John Alex y George quienes, siguiendo el legado de su abuelo y su madre, han aprendido a volar con sus propias alas. Miriam disfruta de una maestría en Administración de Empresas y trabaja como asesora empresarial. Madelyn es Ginecóloga y propietaria de dos clínicas en Tampa y co-fundadora de una en Virginia. Madelyn fue la primera mujer presidenta de la Asociación Médica de Hillsborough y ahora es Presidenta Electa de la Asociación Médica de la Florida. El Dr. Jorge Espinosa y su distinguida esposa Matilde hoy están en la presencia del Señor y dejaron un legado de excelencia profesional, amor familiar y un gran orgullo y agradecimiento a los Estados Unidos de América.

Ana María Gutiérrez Myers

Tesoros de Cuba

Ana María Gutiérrez Myers

La educación consiste en enseñar a los hombres
no lo que deben pensar, sino a pensar.
ANÓNIMO

—¿Qué es lo que nos llevamos de Cuba hoy?, preguntó mi papá.

Estábamos en el aeropuerto de la Habana y él estaba tratando de distraernos a mi hermana de doce años, a mi hermanito de ocho y a mí de catorce. ¿De qué? Pues de los milicianos y de sus ametralladoras que iban y venían, y de los altoparlantes que retumbaban -al parecer- cada cinco minutos, para que algunas familias que esperaban, al igual que nosotros, se dirigieran a la jefatura, amenazando así la posibilidad de salir de Cuba.

Nosotros nos reímos de su absurda pregunta, pensando que, como siempre, estaba bromeando. Pero le hicimos caso.

—Nada, dijo mi hermana, abrumada, mirando alrededor de nosotros, dándose cuenta de la obvia falta de maletas. Ella llevaba puesto un traje de gabardina de lana roja, con una falda plisada y una blusa de seda blanca, hecha por nuestra costurera copiando un viejo patrón de Vogue. Mami había guardado por mucho tiempo todas nuestras tarjetas de racionamiento de telas en anticipación a nuestra salida, y con éstas había comprado la mejor lana y seda china que había. Mami quería que se viera que nosotros no éramos -ni actuábamos- como "gusanos", el nominativo favorito de Fidel Castro para los que se iban.

—Ninguno de mis juguetes, dijo mi hermanito, probablemente acordándose de su colección de camiones y su zoológico plástico que se habían quedado en su caja de juguetes en Holguín, nuestra orgullosa ciudad oriental.

—Papi, estás tratando de hacernos reír, dije yo, pensando en mi novio que hacía sólo unas noches me había besado y abrazado tímidamente al despedirse. Él me había dado un bello anillo de plata

que yo tuve que quitarme y dárselo a mi abuela para que me lo guardara. Miré mis manos desnudas.

—No, yo no estoy bromeando. ¡Piensen!, dijo él con gravedad. "Nos llevamos lo más importante con nosotros", y volvió a hacer hincapié en su pregunta. A mí me dio pánico pensar que a Mami y a Papi se les había ocurrido tragarse las joyas y monedas de oro para sacarlas de contrabando. Yo ya había oído a otras familias hacer los cuentos sobre los guardias que registraban los orificios de los niños y de los padres, para después humillarlos exhibiendo sus "tesoros". Yo miré a Mami.

—Él no se refiere a cosas materiales, respondió Mami, como leyéndome la mente. "Nos vamos con la ropa y los zapatos que llevamos puestos. Es todo lo que dejan llevar", dijo ella alzando la voz y mirando alrededor. "Espero que alguien tenga algunas ropas viejas o por lo menos ropa interior limpia, para darnos cuando lleguemos. ¡Vamos a necesitarlas!" Todos nos reímos al verla pincharse la nariz.

—Piensen, insistió Papi. —Todo lo que es importante lo tenemos con nosotros, aquí. Con sus manos, él señaló el espacio alrededor de nuestros asientos en el aeropuerto. Cerca de nosotros, otras familias hablaban y esperaban que no los llamaran para otro interrogatorio agotador.

—Bien, dije yo, mirando alrededor, entendiendo su onda. —Nos tenemos los unos a los otros, nos llevamos a nuestra familia.

—¡Muy bien, Ana María!, me miró con orgullo. Se veía tan guapo con su mejor traje y corbata, y con un pequeño bigote sobre su boca. Me acordé de su cara, dos años antes, en abril de 1961, cuando vinieron a buscarlo en la madrugada para llevarlo a la cárcel, acusado de cooperar con la invasión de la Bahía de Cochinos. Por seis semanas no supimos dónde lo tenían, ni si estaba vivo o muerto.

—¡Pero eso no es verdad!, añadió mi hermana. —¡Se quedan los abuelos, tíos y primos! La imagen del angustiado rostro de Abuela Felisa vino a mi mente y sentí una vez más el desesperado abrazo que me dio el día que nos despedimos.

—Es verdad, asintió Mami, optimísticamente, pero tan pronto tengamos trabajo en los Estados Unidos, podremos mandarlos a buscar. Nos íbamos de Cuba ese día. Nuestros sueños de libertad ya llegaban. Pero, ¿por qué me sentía tan triste?

—Bien, Papi siguió con su juego. —¿Qué más se les ocurre? Mi hermanito estaba inquieto, impacientándose, porque no estaba ganando ningún punto en el juego de Papi.

—No, Papi, ¡dinos ya, por favor!

—Bien, nos vamos todos juntos, repitió. Miró a Mami con orgullo y a nosotros tres, y entonces se le pusieron los ojos pícaros. —Nos escapamos de Fidel y probablemente está furioso, sonrió. También nos llevamos clandestinamente todos nuestros recuerdos. Piensen en todos los días que hemos disfrutado juntos: cumpleaños, bautizos y comuniones en nuestra iglesia; veladas del colegio, navidades con los abuelos, veranos en la playa, días en el bote y viajes. Las memorias, no tan distantes, y los rostros sonrientes de todos los que dejábamos atrás, llenaron mi mente como un desfile, una comparsa de carnaval cubano con canciones, olas, días de sol, con olor a lechón asado, plátanos fritos, churros y ron.

—Nadie puede hacer inventario de esos momentos y exigir que los dejemos aquí; y él se rió con aire de triunfo. Me acordé del último día en Holguín, tan sólo unos días atrás, cuando vi a los milicianos pegando un documento oficial sobre la puerta de nuestra casa. Nuestra casa, muebles, libros y juguetes habían desaparecido para siempre detrás de esa puerta.

Padre, Ana María, Liliam, Madre y Guillermo

No me pareció que Papi estuviera triste al dejar la única vida que habíamos conocido. —Mami, estos niños no saben jugar muy bien. No tienen la menor idea de los tesoros que nos llevamos. A Papi le encantaba bromear con nosotros. —¡Creo que dejaron los cerebros en la casa de Holguín, detrás de la puerta sellada!

—Bueno, el otro tesoro, Mami continuó seria. Ella no quería darse por vencida con nosotros. Nos miró con expectativa. —Es algo que llevamos en la cabeza.

—¡Nuestros cerebros!, gritó mi hermanito, tomando la idea de Papi de hacía unos segundos. Él no pudo esperar a contribuir con el juego. Mi hermana y yo nos destornillamos de la risa.

—Correcto, dijo mi mamá, echándonos una mirada amenazante. Mi hermanito se sentó muy orgulloso en su asiento. —Pero, ¿qué es lo que tenemos su papá y yo en el cerebro que será muy importante en los Estados Unidos?

—Lo que sabemos, lo que hemos estudiado, dijo ella lentamente, después de mirarla en blanco por unos cuantos segundos. —Nuestras carreras. Cuando lleguemos a los Estados Unidos, no vamos a tener ni un centavo. Vamos a tener que depender de otros para poder vivir las primeras semanas, tal vez los primeros meses. Vamos a tener que quedarnos con Tío Carlos en Miami hasta que su padre y yo encontremos trabajo. ¿Pero saben lo que nos va a facilitar encontrar empleo? El que yo sea maestra y su padre farmacéutico. Ese es otro gran tesoro que nos llevamos de contrabando. Se puso las manos alrededor de la cabeza. —¡Es portátil! Nadie nos lo puede quitar. Nuestra preparación va a facilitar que encontremos trabajos que paguen sueldos decentes. Cuando nos paguen, podremos comprar una casa, un carro, comida, ropa y mandar a sacar al resto de la familia que se quedó en Cuba. También podremos mandar a ustedes tres a la universidad en unos años. Al decir esto, sonreía. A mi padre se le llenaron los ojos de lágrimas. Tal vez él recordaba lo orgullosa que Mami siempre había estado de su carrera. La mayor parte de las mujeres en Holguín, no iban a la universidad; y para Mami el tener un título de la Universidad de la Habana, recibir su doctorado y ser una profesora admirada, la habían hecho sentirse satisfecha.

—En los Estados Unidos, dijo Papi casi llorando, tendremos libertad para hacer nuestros sueños realidad. Los Estados Unidos nos darán las oportunidades. Podremos hacer decisiones sobre nuestras propias vidas. Al decir esto, bajó un poco la voz y dijo: —Sin que el gobierno nos diga lo que podemos o no podemos hacer. Eso es lo bello del país al que vamos. Es allí donde seremos libres. Nosotros ya

sabíamos que no debíamos añadir nada a lo que él había dicho. Sospechábamos que había "oídos" por todos lados, y habíamos aprendido que cualquier cosa que dijéramos en contra de la Revolución, podría resultar que Papi y Mami fueran a la cárcel. Continuamos jugando, sin mucho alboroto.

—Hay algo más que nos llevamos sin que nadie lo sepa, dijo mi madre, aprovechándose del silencio. —Es el más importante de todos nuestros tesoros.

Una vez más, no teníamos respuesta.

—Es Dios, añadió simplemente, abrazando el aire que la rodeaba, es nuestra fe. Es lo que nuestros padres nos dieron a nosotros, y es lo que Papi y yo esperamos que ustedes se lleven consigo a los Estados Unidos. Cuando ustedes tengan niños, que la fe sea el regalo que les den a ellos. Sin fe en Dios, no hay nada. Con fe, lo tenemos todo. Y diciendo eso, nos miró amorosamente, y suspiró satisfecha al haber finalizado la lección.

Mientras ella hablaba, me vino a la mente el radio de onda corta que Papi mantenía escondido debajo de su cama en Holguín. Para que no se oyera sus inconfundibles sonidos, Papi siempre encendía el aire acondicionado que tanto ruido hacía. El gobierno había decretado que escuchar cualquier estación de onda corta, era un acto contra la Revolución y el Comité de Defensa de la Revolución delataría a los vecinos que violaran la ley. Nosotros siempre escuchábamos *La Voz de las Américas,* y recordé claramente el programa que hacía poco tiempo había trasmitido el juicio de los jóvenes cubanos acusados de contrarrevolución. El fiscal les pedía que dijeran que habían cometido un error, que estaban de acuerdo con la Revolución. Ellos se negaron y en el momento en el que fueron fusilados gritaron "Viva Cristo Rey" al exhalar su último aliento. Esa era la fe que Mami mencionaba.

Poco después anunciaron nuestro vuelo. No teníamos ningún equipaje, pero lo teníamos todo.

Roberto y Viviana Pedroso

Cinco dólares y una caja de tabacos

Roberto Pedroso

Todos aman la vida, pero el hombre valiente
y honrado, aprecia más el honor.
WILLIAM SHAKESPEARE

La última vez que salí de Cuba fue en el año 1960. La razón por la que digo "última vez" es porque, aun después de estar viviendo en los Estados Unidos, me era posible regresar a Cuba durante los días de navidad y las vacaciones de verano. Sin embargo, el haber tenido que salir de allí bajo coacción, temiendo por mi vida y la de mi familia que se quedaba en el país, fue una experiencia sumamente impactante.

Recuerdo el verano de 1960. Yo estaba trabajando en una planta química en la pequeña ciudad llamada Sagua la Grande, localizada a unos trescientos kilómetros al este de la Habana. La planta había sido confiscada por el gobierno de Castro. Un día, el administrador de la planta, quien había sido nombrado por el nuevo gobierno, vino a mí y me dijo:

—¿Cuándo harás guardia en la planta durante la noche, como hacen otros empleados?

—No sé de qué hablas. Él me lanzó la ametralladora que llevaba y me dijo,

—¡Aquí tienes! Toma esto y déjame enseñarte cómo manejarla, para que puedas hacer guardia esta noche. Dejé que el arma cayera al suelo, y dije:

—No tengo intenciones de cooperar con su gente esta noche, ni mañana en la noche, ni ninguna otra noche.

—Veremos; pero debo decirte que al capitán de la policía de Sagua le llaman Rocky Marciano, porque da unos golpes muy fuertes.

Esa noche, antes de acostarme, me detuve en un pequeño café para tomar un café cubano y fumar un cigarrillo americano. Dicho sea de paso, el café me costó la enorme cantidad de tres centavos y

el cigarrillo dos. Allí me esperaba un hombre con el cual había entablado una amistad en la planta química. Él había participado en la revolución contra Batista, pero estaba muy desilusionado por la dirección que había tomado la revolución. Deseaba advertirme que la policía de Castro estaba esperándome en la casa de huéspedes en la que estaba quedándome, con el propósito de arrestarme y someterme a un interrogatorio. En la Cuba de Castro, nunca se sabía si se iba a soportar, o sobrevivir, un interrogatorio. Me monté en mi auto, manejé hasta la Habana, y tomé el primer avión que salía de Cuba con destino a los Estados Unidos.

Cuando salí de Cuba, llevaba $5 dólares en mi bolsillo, pues ésa era la única cantidad de dinero que permitían sacar del país en esos días. ¡Hoy en día eres afortunado si puedes salir con tu vida! Pero también permitían llevar una maleta pequeña con tres pares de ropa interior, tres camisas, un par de pantalones y un reloj que no fuera muy lujoso porque, si lo era, la policía de Castro lo confiscaba en el aeropuerto. Luego de considerar las alternativas, decidí comprar una caja de tabacos cubanos en el aeropuerto de la Habana. Tan pronto el avión aterrizó en Miami, conseguí transportación a una tienda de tabaco en la ciudad, y vendí los tabacos que había comprado: pagué diez centavos por cada uno y los vendí a dólar. Así fue como comencé en este país: con cincuenta dólares que gané vendiendo una caja de tabacos cubanos.

Salí de Miami tomando transportación con varias personas diferentes hasta llegar a Atlanta. Allí encontré empleo y continué mis estudios de ingeniería. Sobra decir que tuve que trabajar al mismo tiempo que efectuaba mis estudios universitarios, pues no tenía a nadie que me ayudara o apoyara. Mi trabajo era mi única fuente de ingresos.

Mi educación universitaria se vio brevemente interrumpida por mi participación en la fallida invasión de Bahía de Cochinos contra Fidel Castro. Yo pasé los días de las navidades del 1960 con mis padres, que para ese entonces vivían en Miami. Ellos salieron de Cuba en octubre del 1960 porque sufrían constante acoso de la policía de Castro debido a que yo me negaba a cooperar con la revolución comunista. Un amigo cubano me preguntó durante la víspera de año nuevo si yo tenía planes de unirme a los campos de entrenamiento para la invasión de Cuba. Le respondí que no tenía la más mínima idea de que existieran tales planes; pero que lo tomaría en consideración. Lo pensé y decidí que me uniría a los campos de entrenamiento.

Fui de regreso a Atlanta, recogí todas mis pertenencias, y regresé a Miami. Mis padres se sorprendieron al verme de regreso en

Miami y me preguntaron por qué había regresado. Cuando les hablé de la decisión que había tomado, se descorazonaron y trataron de convencerme para que no participara en esa actividad. Les dije que Cuba necesitaba soldados para liberarla, y luego ingenieros para poder reconstruirla.

Me enlisté en una pequeña oficina en Miami que era operada por cubanos y por una agencia del gobierno de los Estados Unidos. Me preguntaron qué estaba haciendo, y respondí que había estado estudiando ingeniería. Luego me preguntaron si conocía y entendía vectores (la dirección de una fuerza), y les contesté que sí. Entonces me preguntaron si sabía nadar, y les respondí que sí podía nadar bien y que era capaz de nadar distancias largas. Entonces me informaron que sería el navegante de uno de los botes que participarían en la invasión, y que dentro de poco tiempo sería transportado a uno de los campos de entrenamiento. Me advirtieron que, si me capturaban las fuerzas armadas de Castro durante la invasión, "el Secretario negará tener cualquier conocimiento de tus acciones". Como una semana después, me llevaron a un motel en Big Pine Key. Allí, junto a otros compatriotas cubanos, fuimos entrenados por "Tom, Dick y Harry". "Tom" nos enseñó a utilizar el armamento, "Dick" nos enseñó navegación, y "Harry" nos trajo cada semana alimento y otros artículos esenciales desde Key West. A cada uno nos dieron un revólver calibre 45 y también una Thompson, o una ametralladora M-1. También nos dieron un rifle sin retroceso (*recoilless*) de 57 mm.

Viajamos dos veces a Cuba en un barco de rescate, sin identificación, perteneciente al gobierno americano. Este barco tenía como equipo dos ametralladoras de calibre 50 y lo utilizamos para arrojar armamentos envueltos en tela impermeable en ubicaciones específicas del mar Caribe. En una ocasión, también viajamos a la bahía de la Habana para transportar a dos hombres que infiltrarían la isla para sabotear las instalaciones de Castro. Finalmente, el 19 de abril de 1961, viajamos a la costa norte de Cuba para recoger a algunos invasores que habían escapado la persecución que surgió al fallar la misión. Yo no sufrí daño, ni fui capturado, así que regresé a Atlanta a continuar mis estudios de ingeniería en *Georgia Tech.*

Esa fue la última vez que salí de Cuba. Desde entonces, mi esposa Viviana y yo hemos vivido en los Estados Unidos, aunque también vivimos en Venezuela durante cinco años por razones de trabajo. A lo largo de los años, mi trabajo me ha llevado a muchas otras partes del mundo, y he podido apreciar que no hay otro país como éste:

una tierra de oportunidades en la que es posible trabajar duro y lograr algo en la vida.

Aunque soy ahora ciudadano americano y tengo una gran deuda de gratitud con la gente de los Estados Unidos, continúo amando a mi país natal. Es inevitable que el futuro traiga cambios, y espero que éstos resulten en una Cuba unida, próspera y feliz.

Viviana Pedroso

Cuando me preguntan: "¿Cuál fue la parte más difícil de tener que salir de Cuba?" contesto que fue el tener que dejar atrás una manera de vivir que atesoraré para siempre.

Durante mi niñez, mi familia y yo vivíamos en la casa de mis abuelos, una vieja mansión en la zona de El Vedado. La casa no sólo tenía muchas habitaciones, sino que siempre estaba llena de familia, gozo y amor. Durante mi adolescencia, nos mudamos a la urbanización Biltmore. Allí mis padres, abuelos y todos mis tíos compraron las casas de una cuadra completa, de manera que todas colindaran y tuviéramos un patio trasero común.

En Cuba, mi padre era médico y también profesor en la Universidad de la Habana. Él era un hombre que amaba a su patria y creía apasionadamente en la democracia. Su conciencia no le permitía ignorar la súplica de sus estudiantes, algunos de los cuales eran parte de la contrarrevolución contra Castro. Ellos buscaban su ayuda, ya fuera para curar las heridas resultantes de torturas infligidas por los hombres de Castro, o debido a su desesperante necesidad de escapar de la isla.

Por dos años, Papá pudo escapar del enemigo y ayudar a la causa. Sin embargo, desde enero del año 1960, los hombres de Castro, armados con ametralladoras y rifles, vinieron varias veces a nuestro hogar buscando a mi padre. Papá escapó de Cuba el 13 de marzo de 1960. Mamá se unió a él en junio. La situación en Cuba seguía deteriorándose más cada día; y por lo tanto se comenzaron a hacer planes para que mi hermana y yo nos uniéramos a ellos en Nueva York.

El 8 de noviembre de 1960, mi hermana y yo llegamos al aeropuerto de Idlewild, ahora JFK, en Nueva York. Yo tenía quince años de edad, y acababa de separarme del resto de mi familia, sin saber si volvería a verlos otra vez. Lloré durante todo el viaje, desde el momento que el avión despegó de Rancho Boyeros hasta que aterrizó

en Idlewild. La peor parte fue la agonía de la espera al pasar por Inmigración. Sin embargo, cuando al fin sentí el abrazo de mis padres, comprendí el significado de la frase inglesa "*Home is where your heart is*" (El hogar es donde esté nuestro corazón).

A pesar del dolor y la tristeza que sentía nuestro corazón, por habernos separado de los demás miembros de nuestra familia, pudimos sobrevivir ese período de tiempo en Nueva York, gracias a la fe, perseverancia y actitud de nuestros padres. Ellos eran unas personas maravillosas… Nos enseñaron a reír ante las adversidades de la vida, a sonreír como si de verdad quisiéramos hacerlo; a cantar como si nadie en el mundo pudiera oír lo mal que sonamos, a bailar, bailar, bailar como si fuera el último día de nuestra vida; a llorar como si fuéramos un río; a amar, como si nunca se nos hubiera lastimado; y a esperar la llegada del futuro con la misma pasión que sentimos por el día de hoy.

Mi esposo y yo, al igual que nuestras familias, llegamos a este país como exiliados, pero nos sentimos bienvenidos desde el comienzo. Se nos han dado muchas oportunidades; las mismas que se ofrecen a cualquier persona nacida aquí.

Aunque las razones por las que se llega a los Estados Unidos son diferentes, para tener éxito ¡hay que trabajar! Por eso, la frase favorita de los inmigrantes de Cuba al llegar aquí es: "¡No es fácil!" Sólo la fe, esperanza y determinación, permiten lograr el éxito. Sólo el agradecimiento y el trabajo duro, permiten vencer las desilusiones. Nunca olvidemos que este país nos ha recibido con los brazos abiertos: hemos recibido más de lo que probablemente merecemos.

Ya de adulta he llegado a comprender que mi confianza en mí misma, mi fe y mi estado de ánimo positivo se deben al amor y cariño que recibí de mis padres. El éxito es una travesía, no un destino... y este viaje es nuestro esfuerzo.

Familia González

Oportunidades encontradas, una oportunidad perdida

Dr. Jorge González

Cuando pierdes una oportunidad, ganas una lección.
ANÓNIMO

El sol de la mañana brillaba a través de la ventana de la sala de nuestra nueva y modesta casa. Papá siempre se aseguró que nuestra casa tuviera una piscina, por lo menos desde que me dio la poliomielitis cuando era un niño pequeño y los médicos recomendaron que hiciera ejercicios en el agua. Esta casa nueva estaba en Miami y el año era 1963. Yo tenía diez años de edad y mi hermano doce. Los dos nos tendíamos en el suelo para ojear el *Miami Herald* de los domingos, deseando que Papá contuviera sus ganas de discutir sobre política y eventos mundiales, hasta que nosotros hubiéramos terminado de leer todas las noticias deportivas que nos interesaban.

—Ah ja—, yo tartamudeaba, conforme mi hermano mayor y yo respetuosamente mirábamos a nuestro padre que estaba interrumpiendo nuestra lectura. A él le encantaba leer el periódico de los domingos de principio a fin antes que nosotros, los niños, nos levantáramos, para poder hablar sobre política y la vida en general con nosotros. Desafortunadamente, nosotros éramos muy jóvenes para apreciar esa oportunidad. Conforme pasaba el tiempo, aprendíamos más y más acerca de nuestro padre, de sus sueños y de su valentía.

Aunque disfrutábamos de nuestra vida en Miami, yo siempre me acordaba de mi infancia en Cuba. Recordaba nuestra hermosa casa en Biltmore, una subdivisión moderna en el Malecón, la Habana, donde teníamos nuestra enorme casa con una piscina y un área de servicio. En mi mente puedo ver a nuestra madre ayudando a nuestra ama de llaves, a preparar el desayuno, y dando la bienvenida a nuestra abuela y tía, que vivían al lado de mi casa, y a mi tío que vivía cerca. Nuestra casa siempre estaba llena de actividades, familia y visitantes compartiendo comida y alegría en la

tradición latina. Mis tres hermanas menores siempre estaban en medio de la actividad también.

En Cuba, mi papá había administrado una exitosa ferretería. Temiendo los disturbios y la violencia que se estaba viendo en Cuba, envió a mi madre con los cinco niños —mi hermano, mis tres hermanas y yo— a la Ciudad de México, a vivir en un apartamento cerca de su hermana. Papá se quedó en la Habana, administrando el negocio que había heredado de su padre. Poco después de la invasión de la Bahía de Cochinos, llegó un *Jeep* militar a la tienda. Un capitán y cuatro militares se acercaron a mi papá y le preguntaron quién era el dueño del negocio. Papá contestó que él era, y el capitán inmediatamente le dijo que el gobierno estaba confiscando el negocio; pero que él podía quedarse como administrador.

—Si yo no soy el dueño, no me quedo, dijo Papá, y el capitán le pidió las llaves y la combinación de la caja fuerte. Castro había estado apoderándose de negocios, una categoría a la vez, comenzando con los medios de comunicación. Ahora era, aparentemente, el momento de apoderarse de la industria de materiales y de herramientas de construcción. En menos de cinco minutos, y sin ninguna compensación en lo absoluto, Papá perdió todo por lo que él y su padre habían trabajado.

Afortunadamente, Papá había mantenido vigente su visa para México; así que regresó a la casa de la Habana, la cerró y voló a la Ciudad de México, para estar con todos nosotros. Por supuesto, él tuvo que dejar todas nuestras posesiones materiales y sabía que nuestra casa pronto sería saqueada y confiscada, como una nueva propiedad del gobierno.

Recuerdo otra ocasión, cuando el gobierno tomó la casa de alguien. Un día, cuando yo tenía seis años de edad, Mamá sugirió salir para ver de qué se trataba el alboroto. Había una caravana de autos dirigiéndose hacia la casa de nuestro vecino. Anteriormente este vecino, un general del ejército de Batista, había desaparecido prácticamente en medio de la noche, después de que Castro tomó el poder. Como si hubiera un letrero de "Todo Gratis," la gente de áreas vecinas venía a robarse las cosas de esta casa abandonada. Ahora el gobierno era el dueño de la casa y la caravana traía al nuevo presidente ruso, Mikoyan, para que se quedara allí. Yo pude ver a Castro y a su guarda espaldas, cuando salió del auto para escoltar a su camarada invitado a lo que era ahora una inmensa casa para invitados perteneciente al gobierno cubano.

Nosotros salimos de Cuba en 1960. En la Ciudad de México, mi padre se aventuró en varios negocios. El era inteligente, tenía buen

sentido de negocios y era multilingüe. Su padre —mi abuelo— era español, y cuando Papá terminó la secundaria, fue enviado a Inglaterra a una escuela de negocios por un año, de manera que también pudiera aprender inglés. Cuando mi abuelo murió, mi padre, sus hermanas y su madre heredaron su lucrativo negocio. El siempre fue el Gerente General y pudo desarrollar otros negocios exitosos.

En 1962 la familia se mudó a Miami. Con un socio, mi padre dirigió un criadero de pollos en la República Dominicana. Compraba los huevos en Miami, los enviaba a la República Dominicana y luego vendía los pollitos a los agricultores. El vendió su parte del negocio a su socio y se embarcó en otra empresa en la República Dominicana. Se trataba de comprarles maíz a los agricultores, descascararlo, y vendérselo otra vez a los agricultores, como pienso. Durante este tiempo, en el verano de 1969, Papá tuvo un terrible accidente de auto en la República Dominicana, en el cual se fracturó ambas piernas. El había estado viajando entre Miami y la República Dominicana; pero, debido a su larga y pesada recuperación del accidente, dejó de viajar y en 1971 se mudó para Miami permanentemente. Allí, Papá abrió un negocio de suministros y herramientas para la construcción, como el que teníamos en la Habana. Después de varios años de arduo trabajo, el negocio se convirtió en un éxito.

Mientras Papá trabajaba duro en su negocio de Miami, yo trabajaba arduamente en mi primer año escolar en los Estados Unidos. Se me hacia dificultoso aprender inglés. No sé por qué, pero tal parecía que mis hermanos aprendían inglés fácilmente y yo tenía mucho problema. Sin embargo, en sexto grado tuve una profesora maravillosa, la Señora Shefsky, quien tomó un especial interés en ayudarme a aprender el idioma. Ella incluso venía a mi casa convirtiéndose en una buena amiga de la familia y hasta ayudó a mi mamá a empezar un negocio de cosméticos desde casa.

Aunque había estado estudiando en un buen colegio público, en octavo grado empecé a ir a un colegio católico y en noveno me matricularon en un colegio católico para varones. Este fue un gran sacrificio para mis padres; pero nuestra educación y la habilidad para tener éxito, era muy importante para ellos. Después de la secundaria, asistí a la Universidad de Miami y luego me gradué de la Escuela de Medicina. Más tarde asistí a la Universidad de Alabama en Birmingham, donde hice una residencia en Medicina Interna y terminé con un título en Cardiología.

Otra maravillosa bendición de haberme ido a Birmingham fue conocer a mi esposa. Leah es Americana y se acababa de graduar

como enfermera registrada. Nos conocimos mientras ella estaba trabajando en el mismo hospital donde yo estaba trabajando para obtener mi residencia en medicina interna. Mi plan había sido regresar a Miami a dejar mi huella, con una combinación de investigación y carrera académica. Sin embargo, esto era a principios de los 80, y mi esposa tenía dudas de mudarse a Miami para empezar una familia, debido a la mala reputación de la ciudad por la cantidad de crímenes. Además, Leah sentía que mudarse a Miami era como mudarse "al extranjero" Ella había crecido en Birmingham, una ciudad sureña muy conservadora. La posibilidad de mudarse a Miami, lejos de casa, no era algo que ella quisiera considerar. ¡La preocupación de mi esposa fue una bendición!

Afortunadamente para ambos, una oportunidad se presentó por sí misma. Durante mi especialidad en Cardiología, el Dr. Henry McIntosh de *Watson Clinic* en Lakeland, Florida, estaba reclutando médicos reputables para que se unieran a la clínica. Aceptar esta oferta resultó ser la mejor decisión para nosotros. Me mudé lejos de lo académico y de la investigación, para unirme a *Watson Clinic* en 1985 como cardiólogo. En los últimos doce años, he sido el Director Médico de la clínica.

En mi trabajo practico la medicina la mitad del tiempo y la otra mitad está dedicada a reclutar a los mejores cardiólogos para nuestra clínica. Cuando me preguntan cuál es la tareas más difícil de mi profesión, debo admitir que es el ser despertado de un sueño profundo en medio de la noche para ir al hospital por una emergencia; luego tener que regresar a casa para poder dormir un par de horas, y después tratar de tener un día normal; es difícil. Por supuesto, las cosas que más me gustan de mi profesión son la emoción de realizar un diagnóstico correcto y la satisfacción de que un paciente en realidad ha hecho lo que le aconsejé, verlo mejorar su salud y recibir su gratitud.

Fuera de mi trabajo, gozo manteniéndome al día con eventos mundiales y viendo noticias y comentarios políticos serios. No debo de tener una sangre muy latina porque nunca he tenido oído para la música. Mi verdadero amor, es ver a los niños participando en deportes y ver los deportes en la televisión. Ha sido un gozo de toda la vida ser un padre aficionado en las escalinatas y haber podido asistir a eventos deportivos en los que mis tres hijos participaban. Criar a nuestros hijos ha sido uno de los placeres de mi vida. Estoy muy orgulloso de ellos. Actualmente, mi hijo mayor, Nicholas, está estudiando ingeniería de sonido en Full Sail University en

Orlando; nuestro segundo hijo, Phillip, es estudiante del segundo año en la Universidad de Notre Dame en South Bend, Indiana, decidiéndose entre medicina y negocios; y nuestro hijo menor, Brian, está en el *International Baccalaureate* en Bartow.

Pienso en mis padres cuando veo a mis hijos crecer. Aunque todo por lo que mi familia trabajó en Cuba se perdió, mis padres han inculcado en cada uno de nosotros que la clave para el éxito, es la educación profesional. Ellos nos recordaban que la vida es frágil y si nosotros fuéramos a estar en una situación similar a la que ellos estuvieron, nadie podía quitarnos nuestra educación.

Mis padres están siempre en mis pensamientos. Los admiro; ellos fueron mi ejemplo a seguir de cómo comportarme y tener éxito en la vida. Papá y Mamá fueron muy respetados. Mi padre amaba las matemáticas y la economía. Cuando mi hermano trajo a casa una nueva calculadora de mano, una novedad a finales de los 60, Papá estaba orgulloso de poder calcular la respuesta en su cabeza antes de que la nueva calculadora de mi hermano mostrara la respuesta. Papá era un hombre culto y aunque callado, era gracioso. El era la roca de la familia. Su familia, amigos y socios siempre buscaban su consejo.

Mamá fue una dama bella y agradable, la vida de las fiestas y la compañera perfecta para mi papá. Ellos se llevaban muy bien. Mi madre era toda una dama. Nunca tuvo miedo a los retos de la vida, y estaba apta para lidiar con cualquier problema que la vida le presentara. En sus últimos años, ella cuidó de su propia mamá quien estaba incapacitada. Después de que mi papá tuvo el accidente de auto, ella lo cuidó muy bien durante todo ese tiempo y más tarde cuando él desarrolló Alzheimer. El murió en 1991, cuando yo tenía solo 38 años. Mi mamá falleció a la edad de 86.

Si pudiera pasar un día con alguien vivo o muerto, definitivamente sería con mi padre. Yo tenía 35 cuando, debido al Alzheimer, ya no era posible sostener una verdadera conversación con él. El ya no podía hablar sobre política y sobre la vida con nosotros. Papá tenía una visión amplia del mundo, una gran perspectiva de la vida y yo daría lo que fuera por tener una conversación más, ya de adulto, con él. Siempre recuerdo que la vida ha sido buena conmigo y con mi familia, en gran parte debido a su amor, su trabajo duro y su influencia. Me gustaría decirle eso, poder recapturar esa oportunidad perdida.

Loly y Dr. Alex Garriga

Cinco años de soledad

Loly Garriga

El tiempo es muy lento para los que esperan,
muy rápido para los que temen, muy largo para los que sufren,
muy corto para los que gozan; pero para quienes aman,
el tiempo es eternidad.
HENRY VAN DYKE

Los cubanos, todos, tenemos nuestras historias acerca de las circunstancias relacionadas con la salida de nuestra querida Isla. Podríamos llenar miles de páginas acerca de ellas: las experiencias vividas, los motivos, el dolor y el costo de querer vivir en libertad, pues, sin excepción alguna, todos pagamos un precio. Pero hay también miles de historias que quedarán en silencio y olvidadas. Esas son las más trágicas y costosas, pues fueron pagadas con la propia vida de los cubanos, que nunca llegaron a saborear su libertad para poder narrarlas. Para ellos: nuestras oraciones y admiración.

Mi familia es una de las afortunadas. Esta es nuestra historia:

Aeropuerto de Varadero, agosto 28 de 1969. Alex y yo llegamos a la entrada principal, donde habíamos sido citados. Era una calurosa tarde de verano y, aunque eran las seis de la tarde, el sol aún brillaba en lo alto de nuestro cielo azul. Sudábamos copiosamente debido al intenso calor que sentíamos y al nerviosismo que nos invadía. Nuestras dos hijas, Beatriz de quince meses y Vivian de cinco años, percibían nuestra ansiedad y sus caras reflejaban incertidumbre y miedo.

Los cuatro pasamos a una sala ancha donde, detrás de un mostrador, dos milicianos revisaban meticulosamente nuestra documentación. El calor era aún más intenso dentro del local, pues carecía de ventiladores o aire acondicionado. La impaciencia se iba apoderando de nosotros mientras esperábamos, angustiados, la decisión de las autoridades. Por fin el miliciano, con los papeles en sus manos, se dirigió a Alex.

—¿Es usted médico?

—Sí

—¿No sabe usted que el que abandona el país, como lo está haciendo usted, es considerado un traidor a la Revolución?

Alex y yo intercambiamos miradas, sin saber qué contestar. Una vez más el tono hiriente del hombre se dejó oír:

—Usted no puede irse. Su salida no ha sido autorizada por la Regional Provincial de Salud Pública.

Alex trató de explicar que sí había recibido el permiso de Salud Pública Nacional y que eso debía ser suficiente. El miliciano no podía disimular su disgusto por la insistencia de Alex al decir que sí estaba autorizado para salir. El miliciano se dirigió al que estaba a su lado y, pasándole todos los papeles, dejó que los revisara. Dirigiéndose a Alex, le dijo despóticamente:

—De aquí no puedes salir, y si quieres que tus hijas y esposa se vayan, firma este poder.

Las manos de Alex temblaban al tomar el papel. Nos miramos tratando de buscar fuerzas y apoyo el uno en el otro. Mis ojos se iban llenando de lágrimas, mientras le suplicaba a Alex que me dejara esperarlo para así salir todos juntos. Pero él ya había tomado la decisión de que saliéramos nosotras, pues él quería que estuviéramos a salvo. Una vez firmado el poder, lo entregó. El miliciano nos ordenó con sarcasmo:

—Dense el consabido beso y despídanse ya.

Nos miramos profundamente... su imagen se fue haciendo borrosa a causa de las lágrimas que insistían en salir. Nuestras hijas nos miraban sin poder entender lo que sucedía. Teníamos que controlar nuestras emociones por ellas. Ni el llanto, ni los sollozos iban a cambiar nuestra situación; debíamos ser fuertes y afrontar las consecuencias. Nos abrazamos muy fuerte, su cuerpo y el mío casi fundidos en uno. No podía creer que en sólo unos instantes quedaría ese vacío, esa ausencia del ser querido, que duraría por una eternidad.

—No me olvides, me dijo Alex casi sin poder hablar.

—Prométeme que no harás una locura, que no tratarás de irte en un barco, clandestinamente -lo miré seriamente- ¡Prométemelo, por favor!

—Lo prometo, no te preocupes...pronto estaremos juntos otra vez. Sé fuerte. Yo no me iré del área hasta que salga el avión...si me ves en la distancia, pásate la mano por el cabello, no digas nada para que las niñas no sufran más. Nos besamos una vez más mientras el miliciano nos observaba.

—Bueno, bueno -dijo el miliciano ya molesto- usted tiene que salir ya, ¡vamos! y escoltó a Alex fuera del salón.

La desesperación se apoderaba de mí y, sin poder evitarlo, comencé a sollozar. Las niñas, al oírme, también empezaron a llorar. No había pasado un minuto cuando un miliciano, agarrándome del brazo, me advirtió: —¡Al patio hasta que se les pase el histerismo! Todo a nuestro alrededor era oscuridad; sólo las luces de los carros que pasaban cerca alumbraban brevemente el patio. Allí nos quedamos un largo rato, hasta que al fin nos mandaron a entrar para revisar nuestro equipaje. No llevábamos mucho; pero todo fue revisado minuciosamente; hasta palpaban las costuras y dobladillos para estar seguros que nada iba oculto en ellas. Las prendas que llevábamos habían sido previamente inventariadas; pero no obstante las volvieron a examinar. Yo llevaba mi anillo de bodas, el cual me quitaron. No sé de dónde saqué fuerzas y valor; pero le pedí al hombre que me lo devolviera, pues como joya no tenía gran valor, pero sí como recuerdo. Creo le ablandé el corazón al hombre, que, sin pensarlo, me lo devolvió.

La noche se hizo interminable, así como mis pensamientos. No dejaba de imaginar qué nos aguardaría al siguiente día. Una nueva vida comenzaba para nosotras en un país extraño y lejos de todo lo que más queríamos: nuestra tierra, costumbres, seres queridos... Ése era el precio que debíamos pagar a cambio de la libertad que tanto anhelábamos. Ése era el castigo que se nos imponía. Al amanecer, salimos a la pista, a lo lejos, tras la cerca de alambre estaba mi amado esposo. Me pasé la mano por el cabello y abordamos el avión.

Nos instalamos en Nueva York. Mis padres vivían allí y así tendríamos el apoyo y refugio de la familia. Fueron años de lucha, inestabilidad y tristeza. Cada día nos hacía más falta la presencia del padre y esposo. Trabajaba duro para mantener mi hogar funcionando normalmente. No quería que mis hijas fueran víctimas de traumas emocionales; quería que sus vidas se desarrollaran lo mejor posible dentro de las circunstancias.

Después de cinco largos años de espera, Alex logró salir de Cuba. El 24 de agosto de 1974, en el aeropuerto John F. Kennedy de Nueva York, nos reunimos todos para recibirlo. ¡Sus ojos brillaban cuando nos abrazó! La emoción nos embargaba a todos: ¡el momento tan ansiado había llegado! Nuestras vidas volvían a tener sentido, los años de separación nos habían hecho más fuertes, sabios y maduros para apreciar lo que de verdad era importante en nuestras vidas: la familia, nuestros valores y el amor que logró hacer que saliéramos vencedores de la dura prueba que se nos impuso.

Aún quedaba mucho terreno por recorrer. Habíamos vencido la primera etapa de nuestro trayecto y ahora comenzábamos la lucha por progresar y alcanzar la meta ansiada de que Alex obtuviera su licencia para practicar medicina en este país. Afanosamente Alex buscaba cualquier oportunidad para conseguir trabajo. Todos sus conocimientos eran relacionados a su carrera. Él era anestesiólogo y pronto nos dimos cuenta que, una vez que le preguntaban acerca de su experiencia y les comunicaba que era médico, era rechazado pues estimaban que estaba más calificado de lo que la posición requería.

Alex decidió que lo más importante era dedicarse a practicar el idioma inglés. Se matriculó en un curso intensivo. También consiguió trabajo en una fábrica que se dedicaba a confeccionar collares. Por las noches toda la familia se sentaba para ayudar con la producción de lindos collares. No ganaba mucho, pero se sentía útil sabiendo que contribuía a los gastos del hogar. Una vez terminado el curso de inglés, comenzó a reunir materiales y libros que le ayudarían a prepararse para tomar el examen de reválida de su título. Estudiaba largas horas en la sala de nuestro pequeño apartamento en Queens. Para poder concentrarse, requería silencio y tranquilidad, así que tuvimos que pedirles a las niñas su cooperación. Cuando llegaban del colegio tenían que encerrarse en el único cuarto desocupado de la casa, que era el dormitorio. Allí hacían sus tareas y se entretenían hasta la hora de comer, y después iban de vuelta a la "celda" a dormir hasta el día siguiente. Pasamos muchas semanas en esa rutina hasta que una llamada de un compañero de la universidad lo convenció de que debía trasladarse a Miami, donde había cursos preparatorios y oportunidades para conseguir trabajo.

En septiembre de 1975 nos mudamos a Miami. Yo conseguí un trabajo de secretaria médica y Alex de asistente médico en un hospital. Él trabajaba los fines de semana y estudiaba el resto del tiempo.

En marzo de 1977, Alex se presentó a tomar el Examen Médico del Estado de Florida, el cual le otorgaría el derecho a practicar su profesión. Semanas más tarde recibió su licencia de Doctor en Medicina: trece años después del momento en que había tomado la decisión de abandonar a su querida Isla de Cuba. La tierra de las oportunidades ahora nos había abierto sus puertas al futuro.

Hoy, treinta y dos años más tarde, después de una larga trayectoria en su campo, el Dr. Alex Garriga aún practica medicina. Hemos encontrado en este país todo lo que soñábamos: libertad, felicidad, prosperidad y éxito.

Mi Cuba de Ayer

Loly Garriga

Mi Cuba de ayer, la que yo recuerdo.
La que alegre el son canta en mi corazón.
La del cielo azul y su sol candente,
Y claras noches de luna sobre el malecón.

La de eternos veranos y fragantes primaveras,
Donde las flores siempre están de estación.
Para el enamorado ofrendar a su amada,
Como muestra pura de su inmenso amor.

La de serenas playas de blanca arena,
Sus cristalinas aguas pintadas de azul.
Donde las olas acarician la orilla y las
Gaviotas revolotean bajo el brillante sol.

La de las altas palmeras que majestuosas se elevan,
Queriendo alcanzar al distante sol,
Que con sus cálidos rayos abraza la verde campiña,
Inundándola de cubano calor.

Como me invade la nostalgia en este cruel destierro,
Lejos de la patria que me vio nacer,
Y veo morir mis anhelos de regresar a mi tierra,
Pues la Cuba que aún recuerdo, solo vive en el ayer.

Familia Tapia

Edificando el futuro

Eduardo Tapia

Educad a los niños. Educadlos en la tolerancia, en la solidaridad. Transmitidle lo más importante que tenemos: la herencia cultural.
JOSEFINA ALDECOA

En el año 1968, al ver que el régimen comunista nos oprimía, mi esposa Zenia y yo decidimos salir del país con nuestras hijas Jacqueline, Patricia y Zenia. Las niñas eran muy pequeñas, una de ellas recién nacida, y queríamos que crecieran en un país libre donde reinara la democracia. Yo era ingeniero y sabía que, si quería salir del país, tendría que someterme a un mínimo de dos años de trabajo forzado. Este era uno de los precios que los profesionales tenían que pagar si querían salir de Cuba. En mi caso fueron cuarenta y nueve meses, durante los cuales solamente podía visitar a mi familia de vez en cuando.

Mi trabajo forzado fue en el campo: cortando caña, sembrando, y fertilizando las plantas. Era un tipo de campo de concentración, donde nos obligaban a trabajar doce horas al día. Los jefes nos levantaban antes del amanecer y nos transportaban hasta el lugar de trabajo en carretas de caballo, como si fuéramos animales. Regresábamos después del atardecer, unos cuatrocientos hombres cansados y sudados, a esperar nuestro turno para utilizar una de las cuatro duchas. La comida era pésima y había muy poca. Si no hubiésemos comido de la misma caña que cortábamos, o de las frutas del campo, hubiéramos muerto de hambre. Nuestros maltratados cuerpos pedían descanso; pero en estos albergues sólo había literas de hierro de tres niveles que causaban aún más dolor y, al atardecer, los mosquitos nos enloquecían.

El maltrato era evidente. Sólo nos permitían ir a casa cada dos semanas, y permanecer allí por menos de treinta horas, únicamente si cumplíamos con todos nuestros deberes y -principalmente- si no protestábamos. Muchos de mis compañeros fueron castigados, suspendiéndole las visitas a su familia o retrasándoles su salida del país.

Este trato contra los profesionales era muy abusivo, pues su único delito era querer vivir en un país donde su familia pudiera tener libre albedrío. Era un alto precio el que había que pagar.

Después de estar unos dos años en esta situación abrumadora, el gobierno tuvo la osadía de ofrecerme un buen puesto de trabajo como ingeniero, si renunciaba a mis deseos de salir de la isla. Por supuesto, ¡me negué rotundamente! Un día, cuando llegamos de trabajar, había un camión del ejército esperando por mí. En cuanto bajé de la carreta, uno de los guardias me dijo que recogiera todas mis pertenencias, porque sería trasladado. Me llevaron a una cárcel de presos comunes en una zona remota. En poco tiempo vino el militar que era jefe de la prisión y, en tono déspota y humillante, me dijo —Me han informado que eres ingeniero. Nos construirás un comedor para los presos y no te irás de aquí hasta que lo termines. Asignaron a dos presos a trabajar conmigo y me permitieron dormir en la enfermería. Afortunadamente no pasé mucho tiempo allí pues, cuando completé los cimientos, se acabaron los materiales de construcción y me enviaron de regreso al albergue anterior.

Por fin, en 1972, recibimos el permiso para salir del país vía España. Juntos como familia, y más decididos que nunca, partiríamos a un país donde no conocíamos a nadie; pero confiábamos en Dios, quien nunca nos ha fallado. Recuerdo muy bien ese viaje a Madrid. Nos habían quitado todo en el aeropuerto, hasta el anillo de bodas de mi esposa. ¿Dónde dormiríamos esa noche? Por suerte, un amigo que leyó mi nombre en el periódico estaba esperándonos.

Comencé a buscar trabajo en cuanto llegamos, y a los tres días ya trabajaba en una empresa de ingenieros. Un año más tarde estaba a cargo de un grupo de veinticuatro ingenieros. Tuve mucho éxito durante estos años. Trabajé con dedicación y devoción, y tuve la oportunidad de viajar y continuar mis estudios universitarios. Aunque éramos felices en España, nuestros padres y hermanos habían ido a vivir a los Estados Unidos y querían tenernos cerca.

En 1974 llegamos al aeropuerto de Nueva York. Mi hermano me había dicho que estaría esperándonos allí; pero, al no verlo, me puse muy nervioso y comencé a sudar copiosamente. Un trabajador que hablaba español notó mi ansiedad y me preguntó: —¿Tiene algún problema? Necesitaba hacer una llamada, pero no tenía los diez centavos para el teléfono, ya que no había podido cambiar dinero español a US dólares. El buen hombre me los proporcionó.

En poco tiempo llegó mi hermano, y me dijo que ya había mandado mi currículum vitae a varias compañías. *Wellman Lord*, una

compañía de ingeniería en Lakeland, Florida, esperaba mi llamada. No hablaba inglés muy bien, pero aún así llamé, y me preguntaron cuándo podía venir para una entrevista. —¡Mañana mismo!, contesté. Trabajé allí por diez años. Después trabajé en el Departamento de Obras Públicas del Condado de Hillsborough, por más de veintitrés años, donde ocupé los cargos de Director de Desechos Sólidos, Ingeniero del Condado, y Gerente de Aguas Torrenciales.

En 1977 la compañía *Tapia Construction*, un negocio familiar, abrió sus puertas en Lakeland. Desde entonces hemos construido más de quinientas casas de lujo de acuerdo con las especificaciones del cliente. En más de diez ocasiones diferentes, hemos tenido el honor de recibir el premio "Casa del Año" debido a nuestro estilo, belleza y originalidad. Creo que mi éxito se ha debido a que siempre tuve la vocación de ingeniero. ¡Ahora me pagan por hacer algo por lo que siento gran pasión! Además, cada vez que pienso en el pasado, me doy cuenta de que las experiencias que viví durante mis últimos años en Cuba, hacen que todo lo demás parezca muy fácil hoy.

Estoy muy agradecido de poder vivir en los Estados Unidos, un país donde el trabajo duro y honesto sigue siendo el eje del progreso personal y social. Por esta razón, todos los inmigrantes tenemos la responsabilidad de ayudar con parte de lo que se nos ha dado.

En cuanto a mí, tengo el honor de ser canciller de los Caballeros de Colón y presidente del Club Hispano de Lakeland, cuyo objetivo principal es recaudar fondos para ayudar a familias necesitadas, ofrecer becas a estudiantes destacados, y propagar la cultura hispana. El Club Hispano ha otorgado veintitrés becas durante los últimos diez años.

Siempre digo a los inmigrantes, que ésta es una gran nación, llena de oportunidades. Todos llegamos aquí sin nada, sólo con el deseo de prosperar y trabajar duro. Al principio puede ser difícil, pero si trabajamos y sobresalimos, pronto recibiremos nuestra recompensa.

Mario Pendas, Solange, Danita y Dania Frías de Pendas

Recuerdos de una heladera

Dania Frías de Pendas

El porvenir de los hijos es siempre la obra maestra de su madre.
NAPOLEÓN

—*I want a chocolate ice cream, please.* (Quiero un helado de chocolate, por favor).

—*I want a vanilla cone and a strawberry stick for my sister.* (Y para mí, uno de vainilla y una paleta de fresa para mi hermanita).

Los niños siempre corrían sonrientes al oír la típica música de mi carrito. Algunos me hablaban en español; pero la mayoría me hablaban en inglés. Yo de inmediato me aprendí todo el vocabulario necesario para comunicarme con ellos sin problema alguno.

Los cubanos que llegamos a este país al principio de la Revolución, no mirábamos atrás. Nos olvidábamos del buen pasado y aceptábamos cualquier trabajo que consideráramos digno y así ganarnos la vida honestamente. Yo compré un carrito de helados y salía a vender por las calles de Tampa, satisfaciendo los antojos de cientos de niños, y a la vez, asegurando el porvenir y la educación de los míos.

Día tras día, manejaba por la misma ruta, sonriéndole a la gente y recordando mi juventud en la Habana, época en la que nunca pensé que trabajaría fuera de casa. Mis planes siempre habían sido criar a mis hijos y estar todo el tiempo en casa para ellos. Yo había sido la niña mimada, la más joven de nueve hermanos. Cuando yo era estudiante de secundaria, ya algunos de mis hermanos eran exitosos profesionales y dueños de negocios. Poco a poco fueron abriendo restaurantes en la Habana hasta llegar a tener once *Mi Buchito Oriental.* A mí me encantaba ir a comer el famoso arroz frito, respirar los olores de especias que salía de la cocina, el olor a pan caliente, y el aroma del café colando. En todas las cafeterías siempre había un ambiente cordial y amistoso de los fieles clientes, quienes venían a tomarse su cafecito y a compartir las novedades del día con sus amigos. Aquellos eran días prósperos y felices; parecíamos tener el futuro asegurado.

Desafortunadamente, lo único constante en la vida es el cambio, y el gobierno de Fidel se encargó de cambiar nuestras vidas radicalmente. A principios de los años 60, comenzó a apoderarse de todos los restaurantes. Una por una, el gobierno se apoderó de todas nuestras propiedades, y tomó control hasta de nuestro destino. Si queríamos trabajar, podíamos hacerlo siempre y cuando trabajáramos para Fidel, por un sueldo miserable. Ahora éramos un país comunista, donde se disfrutaba de la igualdad: Todos éramos igualmente pobres, todos estábamos a la merced de un genio diabólico que controlaba y continúa controlando las masas.

"Tenemos que irnos todos a Estados Unidos" repetía yo diariamente. Recuerdo las reuniones familiares en las que planeábamos la forma de escaparnos de aquella pesadilla. Mario y yo acabábamos de casarnos y no estábamos dispuestos a separarnos. Mario no tenía quien lo reclamara de inmediato. El plan era que mis hermanos se fueran primero, y así nos pudieran reclamar. Algunos de mis hermanos pudieron irse legalmente. Felipe, Rafael y Fernando no pudieron salir en aquellos tiempos. Siendo jóvenes llenos de orgullo y valentía, se atrevieron a tratar de escapar en una lancha. Los descubrieron y los mandaron a la cárcel como presos políticos.

Cuba entera se convirtió en una cárcel. No se podía salir del país libremente. El simple hecho de parecer estar en contra de los ideales comunistas, era razón suficiente para ser sentenciado a años de prisión, incluso al paredón de fusilamiento. Los comunistas comenzaron a abrir cárceles por doquier, tenían que controlar a la oposición.

Mis hermanos fueron a la prisión de La Cabaña donde los presos políticos vivían en deplorables condiciones. Este lugar era las ruinas de un fuerte construido por los españoles en la época colonial. No había ni agua potable. Una vez al mes, el gobierno nos permitía llevarles una bolsa con algunas cosas que estaban aprobadas por el régimen como: leche en polvo, guayaba en barra y chicharritas, entre otros. Los presos sufrían de estreñimiento debido a la mala nutrición que recibían. Una de mis hermanas que vivía en Estados Unidos nos envió un laxante (Ex-Lax) en forma de chocolate. Ya que esto no estaba entre las cosas aprobadas, mis otros dos hermanos y yo decidimos descoser el borde de la bolsa de comida, poner las tabletillas de Ex-Lax adentro y volverlo a coser. El día que llevamos la bolsa los guardias decidieron hacer una revisión minuciosa y, desafortunadamente, se dieron cuenta de nuestro plan. ¡Ojalá que se hayan comido todo el "chocolate"!

Nos quitaron las bolsas que con tanto esfuerzo habíamos llenado y castigaron a mis tres hermanos presos como si ellos hubiesen

sido culpables de nuestras acciones. De inmediato, yo me identifiqué como la responsable de haberlas cosido y dije que Ciro y Ramón, quienes iban conmigo, no tenían ni la menor idea de lo que yo había hecho. Ellos ya estaban reclamados y en lista para viajar a Estados Unidos; cualquier acusación les podía costar la salida de Cuba. Debido a mi "crimen", pasé 12 horas presa en un sótano, totalmente incomunicada, sin saber que iba a pasar con mi vida, pensando en cuándo volvería a ver a mi familia, si esto afectaría el trabajo de mi esposo y otros miles de pensamientos inquietantes. Gracias a Dios, Mario, quien en aquellos momentos tenía una buena posición construyendo la CUJAE (Ciudad Universitaria José Antonio Echeverría), tenía conexiones en el gobierno, rogó en nombre de nuestras hijas, y pudo hacer que los guardias me dejaran ir a casa. De ahí en adelante, estaba señalada y tenía que cuidar mis pasos.

Después de innumerables torturas sicológicas y físicas en la Cabaña, mis hermanos fueron separados. A Felipe lo mandaron a uno de los campos de concentración, Mijial, en Oriente. Rafael fue a Puerto Boniato y terminó siendo uno de los presos que, por no querer trabajar ni ponerse el uniforme azul de preso común, en vez del amarillo que los distinguía como presos políticos, sólo usaba calzoncillos. A estos presos se les conocía como "los plantados". Fernando fue a Tacotaco en Pinar del Río, donde lo podíamos visitar una vez al mes. No era fácil ir a verlo, ya que no había transporte hasta la cárcel y había que cargar con bolsas de comestibles, a pie, por aquellos caminos de tierra, a veces enfangados por la lluvia, con la incertidumbre de si los guardias nos dejarían pasar las pocas cosas que podíamos conseguir con mucha dificultad. No se permitía llevar comida cocinada a la prisión. La comida era atroz y mi hermano estaba sufriendo de desnutrición.

Yo estaba embarazada con mi hija Solange cuando tuvimos la oportunidad de comprar carne de res "en bolsa negra" (la carne de res normalmente no se podía -ni se puede- comprar con la libreta de abastecimiento), cosa que si se descubría, podría costarnos hasta 30 años de cárcel, tanto para el comprador como para el vendedor. Como yo vestía ropa de maternidad, me arriesgué a hacer algo insólito: durante una de las visitas, llevé tres bistecs cocinados y cortados escondidos en mi ajustador. Yo vigilaba a los guardias y cuando se descuidaban, me sacaba un pedazo de bistec y se lo ponía en la boca a mi hermano. El tenía que dejar de masticar cuando los guardias miraban. Si lo descubrían, automáticamente le prohibirían las visitas y yo iría presa. Ahora cuando lo recuerdo, me doy cuenta de lo que nosotros nos atrevemos

a hacer por los seres queridos, sin pensar en las consecuencias. Si me hubiesen descubierto, Solange hubiera nacido en la cárcel.

Después de dos años, mis hermanos obtuvieron su libertad y pudieron salir del país. Eventualmente, nosotros también salimos reclamados por ellos. Nos fuimos a España con sólo la ropa que llevábamos puesta y un cambio para nuestras hijitas Danita y Solange. Recuerdo que estaba nevando; y el frío que sentíamos era también por la soledad. ¿Adónde íbamos a ir ahora?, ¿De dónde vendría la próxima comida para las niñas? No teníamos nada ni a nadie en España. No teníamos dinero ni para un vaso de leche. Estábamos totalmente a la merced del Señor.

—¡Mayito!... ¡Mayito!..., me pareció oír la voz de alguien llamando a mi esposo al llegar al aeropuerto de Madrid.

—¡Mayito, alguien te está llamando! –dije con voz llena de sorpresa a mi esposo.

—Estás alucinando, ¿quién me va a llamar aquí? No conocíamos ni a un alma en España, y sólo su familia y amistades más cercanas le llamaban "Mayito"; los demás lo conocían por Mario. Era evidente que estaba alucinando, como un alma sedienta en el desierto, cree ver un oasis.

—¡Mayito, Mayito! Esta vez la voz era más fuerte, más clara.

—Sí Mayito, oigo una voz que te llama, ¡escucha, escucha!... ¡No son locuras mías!

—¡Mayito, soy yo, tu prima Marta. Gracias a Dios los he podido encontrar! ¡Bienvenidos a España!

¡Tal parecía que se nos aparecía la misma Virgen María! Marta estaba en España y no lo sabíamos. Ella había leído en el periódico los nombres de los cubanos que llegaban, entre ellos los nuestros. Era un verdadero milagro de Dios, algo por lo que siempre viviré agradecida. Al día siguiente les compró abrigo a las niñas y nos ayudó a instalarnos.

Pocos meses después, el 31 de diciembre de 1970, estábamos en el aeropuerto de Barajas en Madrid, para salir hacia Costa Rica reclamados por nuestros amigos Pancho y Dulce. Al oír por el alto parlante: "¡Son las doce de la noche, feliz año nuevo!" Nos abrazamos los cuatro y dimos las gracias a Dios por estar juntos y a salvo. Fue un abrazo de libertad, fraternidad y amor.

Pancho y Dulce eran personas de mucha influencia y debido a esto, Mayito consiguió un buen trabajo en ingeniería y, como otro milagro de Dios, también nos ayudaron a hacernos residentes costarricenses en sólo 46 días. Pronto pudimos viajar a los Estados

Unidos con visa de turistas. En el aeropuerto de Miami, a través de los vidrios, vimos a toda mi familia: mi madre, hermanos y otros familiares, dándonos la bienvenida. Fue el momento más emocionante de mi vida, el volver a estar en los brazos de mi madre.

Así es que eventualmente llegamos a Tampa y a mi trabajo de heladera ambulante. El sueldo de mi esposo no alcanzaba para pagar por la educación que yo quería para mis hijas. Yo había estudiado en *La Inmaculada*, un colegio católico en la Habana y quería lo mismo para ellas. Estaba dispuesta a trabajar día y noche para que así sucediera. —¿Cómo van a aceptar a las hijas de una heladera en la escuela Católica, cuando en la lista de espera hay hijos de médicos y profesionales?-, me decían a menudo; pero yo no me rendía ni me cansaba de ir al colegio para tratar de matricularlas. Por dos semanas me senté en el piso frente a la rectoría del colegio *Saint Laurence*, hasta lograr mi meta. Después de graduarse de *Tampa Catholic High School*, mis hijas continuaron sus estudios universitarios mientras nosotros nos dedicábamos al negocio de joyería desde nuestro hogar. Este negocio nos permitió tener una buena posición económica y estar en casa mientras mis hijas crecían. También pudimos invertir en varios apartamentos y casas, de cuyos alquileres vivimos hoy.

Danita, mi hija mayor, se graduó de ingeniera eléctrica a los 20 años de edad y obtuvo su grado de máster con los más altos honores a los 23. Trabajó para la compañía *General Electric* por varios años hasta que tuvo a su primer hijo. Hoy disfruta de los más altos reconocimientos como agente de bienes raíces, vendiendo más de veinticinco millones de dólares en *Florida Central* durante el 2008, a pesar de una economía decadente.

Solange, hoy la Doctora Pendas, es Cirujana Oncóloga y la Directora del Departamento de Cáncer de Mamas en *Lakeland Regional Cancer Center*. Su labor ha hecho que esta distinguida institución haya sido reconocida por el Centro Nacional de Acreditación de Programas de Cáncer de Mamas, como uno de los dos "Centros de Excelencia" en el Estado de la Florida. Ella ha estudiado y trabajado con los mejores maestros en su campo y ha publicado numerosos estudios de investigación sobre su búsqueda incansable por la cura.

Todos mis hermanos han logrado alcanzar el sueño americano en Miami, todos volvieron a triunfar, esta vez en el exilio. Yo he podido ganarme la vida desde mi hogar, asegurando la educación y la influencia familiar que siempre quise para mis hijas; disfruto de su éxito y soy la orgullosa abuela de cinco nietos maravillosos, a quienes, de cuando en cuando, les compro un heladito cuando por casa pasa una heladera.

Yara Borges Guzmán, dos meses antes de caer presa

La juventud truncada de Yara Borges Guzmán

1938 - 2008

Dra. Norma de la Torre

No hay en la tierra, conforme a mi parecer,
contento que se iguale a alcanzar la libertad perdida.
MIGUEL DE CERVANTES SAAVEDRA

Abruptamente, en medio de la presentación de uno de los catedráticos de la Escuela de Medicina de la venerable Universidad de la Habana, se abrieron las dobles puertas del recinto. Esto resultaba inaudito para los presentes. Una vez que se cerraban las puertas de un aula universitaria, no se volvían a abrir hasta que concluyera la clase o en caso de extrema emergencia. Todos los alumnos se quedaron pasmados, sin atreverse ni a susurrar. Estrepitosamente irrumpieron en el aula los temidos guardias de la milicia del gobierno revolucionario. Sin pedir permiso, sin preámbulo alguno y sin dirigirse a nadie en particular, uno de ellos pregunto quién era Yara Borges Guzmán. Ella se puso de pie y dijo: —Soy yo. Inmediatamente dos guardias se colocaron uno a cada lado de ella y tomándola por debajo de los brazos la sacaron del aula, sin ni siquiera excusarse con el catedrático que estaba a cargo de la clase. Los guardias llevaron a Yara a la Estación de Policía Central, donde fue encerrada en una celda. No le avisaron a sus padres ni a ningún otro familiar. Ellos se enteraron por algunos compañeros de clase, los cuales tuvieron la entereza de informales lo que había sucedido, a pesar de los riesgos que esto les podía conllevar. Los padres de Yara fueron a la estación, pero no les fue permitido verla, ni les dieron información sobre por qué estaba detenida. Pocos días después, Yara y otras personas arrestadas en diferentes "redadas", fueron presentadas frente a un Tribunal Revolucionario para ser juzgadas por el delito de "Contra-Revolución", un cargo genérico aplicado a cualquiera que no estuviese de acuerdo con los postulados de la revolución castrista. Así, sin ningún testigo de cargo y sin el beneficio de abogados defensores (¿Quién se hubiese atrevido?) procedieron a juzgarlos.

Cuando le tocó el turno a Yara, el Fiscal se dirigió álgidamente a ella y la acusó, en tono imperativo, de estar repartiendo propaganda subversiva antirrevolucionaria en el popular parque de atracciones de la Habana llamado *Conney Island.* Cuando le preguntaron qué tenía que decir a estos cargos, Yara respondió:

—Yo no estaba repartiendo ninguna propaganda antirrevolucionaria, ni en ese parque, ni en ningún otro sitio.

—Entonces, ¿qué estaba haciendo allí?

—Jugando con los carritos.

Exasperado y casi fuera de control, el Fiscal se dirigió al Juez diciéndole:

—No tengo ninguna otra pregunta que hacerle a esta mujer.

Sin ninguna otra interacción, el Juez dio un golpe seco con el mazo, diciendo en tono airado:

—Condenada a diez años de prisión.

Y así fue que Yara Borges Guzmán fue condenada - bajo la Causa No. 102/61- a diez años de indescriptibles torturas físicas y mentales, el día 10 de marzo de 1961. Tenía entonces, 22 años de edad, una mente brillante y un futuro prometedor; pero nada prometedor podía existir bajo la cruel tiranía del gobierno fidelista.

Yara nació en la Habana, el 4 de noviembre de 1938. Cursó la enseñanza primaria del Kindergarten hasta el octavo grado en el Colegio del Sagrado Corazón, donde a su vez recibió una sólida base cristiana que la acompañó a través de la vida y posiblemente la preparó para lo que el destino le tenía deparado. Después de pasar el examen de admisión para los estudios del bachillerato, ingresó en el prestigioso Instituto Baldor, del que se graduó de Bachiller en Ciencias. Ingresó a continuación en la Escuela de Medicina de la Universidad de la Habana, donde llegó hasta el tercer año de esta carrera, siniestramente tronchada por el régimen. Durante ese período estudiantil, además de sobresalir en todo lo académico, también se destacó como gran deportista, ganando varios campeonatos de natación en el *Yatch Club* de la Habana y en el de Marianao. Le gustaba escribir y muchos de sus artículos fueron publicados en renombrados magazines, periódicos y otras publicaciones habaneras, entre ellas, la famosa revista *Carteles.*

Ya en la cárcel Yara fue asignada a la galera "D", la más temida de todas las galeras, donde encerraban a las presas políticas que se negaban a "rehabilitarse". La llamada "rehabilitación" consistía en declarar públicamente que uno se había "equivocado", que la Revolución era la salvación de todos y Fidel Castro, el redentor de Cuba.

Las que no aceptaban "rehabilitarse" eran consideradas rebeldes y les llamaban "las plantadas", un término despectivo que utilizaban para indicar que ellas continuaban viviendo en una "época infame y retrógrada que la Revolución había logrado superar".

Durante los diez años y 16 días que Yara estuvo encarcelada, fue trasladada varias veces de una prisión a otra, siendo cada prisión peor que la anterior. Tanto ella como sus compañeras, que trasladaban a la misma vez, eran siempre asignadas a la galera "D" de la cárcel de turno. Las celdas de la galera "D" tenían las más paupérrimas condiciones imaginables, además de menos derechos a visitas familiares, peor comida, y menos salidas al patio, lo cual significaba limitación de oportunidades para respirar aire puro, coger un poco de sol y poder caminar. Estas celdas eran pequeñas y estrechas; pero aun así, asignaban cuatro presas por celda.

En las celdas de la galera "D", las golpizas, por cualquier protesta de las presas, eran frecuentes. Uno de los más infames de estos atropellos fue el del Día de la Madres de 1961, cuando el jefe de la prisión decidió, súbitamente, hacer requisas a los familiares y a las presas de la galera "D", acortando de esta manera el tiempo de la visita precisamente ese día tan señalado. Las madres e hijos habían estado esperando en "cola" desde la madrugada para poder ver a sus seres queridos encarcelados y ahora sólo compartirían pocos minutos.

Cuando las presas se enteraron de la situación con las visitas, comenzaron un "Golpe de Lata", la única forma que ellas tenían para protestar. Esto consistía en coger los jarros, los platos, latas vacías o cualquier objeto metálico que tuvieran para golpear con ellos los barrotes de las celdas, todas las presas a la vez, creando un ruido infernal que retumbaba por los angostos pasillos de la prisión.

Inmediatamente, el jefe de turno, que anticipando problemas había solicitado el respaldo de los bomberos de un puesto cercano, los llamó. Llegaron los bomberos e introdujeron las mangueras entre los barrotes de las altas ventanas y abrieron a toda presión los chorros de agua, atacando con ellos a las indefensas mujeres que, dentro de sus jaulas, no podían escaparse de los fuertes torrentes de agua dirigidos a ellas. Estos hombres, si se les puede llamar "hombres", dirigían la presión del agua a los senos de las presas, porque siendo la parte más sensible de sus cuerpos, les causaría más dolor. Se escuchaba por doquier los gritos de las infelices que los torrentes de agua lanzaban al piso. Una de la presas estaba en avanzado estado de gestación. Con la siniestra intención de hacerla abortar, uno de los guardas apunto la presión del torrente de agua al vientre de la

embarazada. Un grupo de sus compañeras, entre ellas Yara, se percataron de esta maniobra y se pusieron todas delante de la muchacha para interferir el ataque y protegerla. Muchas resultaron lastimadas o heridas por el impacto del agua, por las caídas y por el rodar -una vuelta tras otra- por el áspero cemento del piso de las celdas, con la presión increíble con que salía el agua de aquellas mangueras; pero lograron salvar a la joven y al bebito en su vientre.

Ese día muchísimas de las presas terminaron en la enfermería de la prisión con contusiones, fracturas y lastimaduras de todo tipo. Yara recibió golpes en el seno derecho, donde años después, ya en el exilio, se le formó un tumor canceroso que degeneró más tarde

Yara Borges Guzmán † (1938 - 2008)

en una metástasis ósea y finalmente le costó la vida. Ese funesto Día de las Madres constituirá por siempre un recuerdo doloroso para las madres e hijas que lo sufrieron y una mancha bochornosa en la historia de Cuba. Pero no para la autoridades que participaron en estos acontecimientos, porque ellos no tienen ni sentimientos humanos, ni pudor, ni vergüenza. ¡Qué triste pensar que eran cubanos!

El 10 de marzo de 1971, al cumplirse los diez años de prisión, el tiempo total de la condena que le impusieron, no le concedieron a Yara la libertad inmediata como ella esperaba. En lugar de ello, la llevaron a la oficina del penal donde le informaron que, si deseaba ser puesta en libertad, tendría que rehabilitarse, o de lo contrario, sería transferida a las celdas de las presas "comunes". Las llamadas "presas comunes" eran las que estaban cumpliendo años por crímenes no políticos, tales como asesinatos, asaltos u otros delitos graves. A pesar de las amenazas, Yara se negó rotundamente a la mencionada "rehabilitación". Por varios días continuaron asediándola con amenazas cada vez más insistentes y escalofriantes, porque le advertían de las consecuencias que sufriría en las celdas de "las comunes", tales como violaciones sexuales, abusos de todo tipo y hasta ser asesinada por alguna de ellas. A pesar de todo, Yara se mantuvo firme en sus convicciones y no cedió a las bravatas de las autoridades. Finalmente, dieciséis días después, el 26 de marzo de 1971, autorizaron su salida de la cárcel; pero negándole el permiso para salir del país.

Sus padres ya se encontraban en los Estados Unidos y estaban haciendo gestiones por su libertad, lo cual posiblemente ayudó a que no la enviaran a las celdas de las "presas comunes". Yara siempre consideró aquellos, los peores 16 días de todo el tiempo que paso en la prisión política.

Un año después, en 1972, por gestiones de unos primos que vivían en España, le permitieron salir de Cuba a Madrid, donde permaneció con estos familiares hasta que un año más tarde obtuvo la residencia de los Estados Unidos, llegando a este país en 1973.

Cuando salió de la cárcel Yara ya tenía 32 años de edad, y había desperdiciado, tal vez los mejores años de su juventud en las infernales celdas de la galera "D". En lugar de lamentarse, Yara decidió que era hora de recuperar el tiempo perdido.

Tan pronto arribó a los Estados Unidos, comenzó a trabajar y a estudiar, graduándose con una maestría en Ciencias en el Mercy College. Empresaria por antonomasia, disfrutó de muchos éxitos en todos los negocios en que se involucró. Compró una farmacia que mantuvo durante cinco años. Fundó dos corporaciones que dirigió

por más de treinta años: *Cabrini Corporation*, distribuidora de productos y bisuterías para farmacias y, *Lemax Pharmaceutical* una compañía bajo la cual produjo y patentizó una serie de medicinas muy reconocidas como *Chenocol, Hematonic, Reflex* y *Pellet-C*, entre otras. Estos productos fueron distribuidos por todo el suroeste de los Estados Unidos, gozando de gran aceptación en el campo farmacéutico.

En 1987, Yara escribió dos cuentos infantiles de contenido altamente educativo, que publicó en forma de álbum de postalitas: *The Ruler*, basado en la legendaria Atlántida, y *Kalkulkin*, la historia de un caballito parlante, este último para niños pre-escolares.

A fines de 1992, cuando vio los terribles destrozos que ocasionó el huracán Andrew, Yara fundó *B-Safe, Inc*, una empresa constructora de paneles de protección contra los huracanes. Esta compañía se dedicaba a producir órdenes, por comisión, de paneles que sobrepasaban el Código de Construcción de entonces, y el que aprobaron después de Andrew. Dos años más tarde, en 1994, fundó *Unicorn Enterprises* que fabricaba vitrales para puertas y ventanas de iglesias, así como para residencias y yates de lujo, los cuales les eran comisionados por referencias de otros clientes.

Exclusive fue otra de las empresas, fundada por Yara, que gozó de gran éxito. Esta compañía se dedicaba a crear y fabricar trofeos, placas de reconocimiento, y premios de todo tipo para instituciones educativas, para oficinas ejecutivas, así como grupos y asociaciones deportivas.

Para Yara Borges no existían proyectos ni problemas imposibles: todos eran retos que enfrentaba apasionadamente hasta lograr lo que se proponía. De carácter firme y competitivo, ella tenía la facultad de calibrar cualquier situación difícil o inesperada y encontrarle la solución más rápida y adecuada. Tuvo la facilidad de manejar a la vez, todas las empresas que fundó, algunas de las cuales aún están en operación. Es triste pensar que tanto talento fuese desperdiciado por tantos años en las inmundas celdas de la Cuba castrista.

A Yara Borges el régimen comunista del tirano Castro le robó la patria, además de diez años y dieciséis días de disfrutar del cielo cubano, tan intensamente azul como sus ojos; y de contemplar las majestuosas palmas reales, tan erguidas como sus ideales; pero la tiranía jamás logró doblegarle el espíritu, ni dañarle el intelecto, ni destrozarle los sueños.

Tal vez el siguiente poema escrito por ella en 1971, unos días después de su salida de la prisión política explique la filosofía y la pureza de sentimientos de este ser extraordinario.

Yara Borges Guzmán

Estoy recién-nacida en la mitad de mi existencia,
con el pecho desnudo para alegrías y penas:
Tanto deseo disfrutar de una mañana nueva,
como de poner una sonrisa en cada lágrima que vea
Quiero exudar amor por cada poro mío,
y nacer de nuevo sin barreras ni prejuicios.
Quiero abrirle los brazos a la vida,
y en vez de ser yo de ella, hacerla a ella mía.
Quiero que se conviertan mis pies en alas
y recorrer de nuevo todos los caminos
contemplando en cada anochecer un alba
y emprendiendo en el alba cada día un camino;
para que cuando llegue al lugar del descanso
llevar las manos llenas de todo lo vivido.

—

El alma existe: es el corazón espiritual de nuestro cuerpo. Es, a su vez, el cerebro puro, inocente y sabio, que permite que cada uno de nuestros sentidos, oiga, vea, palpe, sienta y perciba las más delicadas y bellas creaciones de este maravilloso planeta que Dios nos ha regalado. Cada obra de arte, no sólo representa la facilidad plástica del artista, sino que es a la vez una muestra de su alma eterna, la cual se hace concreta en un lienzo, en una pluma, en un instrumento musical, en un pedazo de mármol, o de piedra, o de barro...Y también en una sonrisa, en una caricia, en un beso, cuando estos son entregados con amor.

Pedro Ramiro Machín

Recuerdos de un preso político

Pedro Ramiro Machín

No me pongan en lo oscuro a morir como un traidor;
yo soy bueno, y como bueno, moriré de cara al sol.
JOSÉ MARTÍ

LA REVOLUCIÓN DE CASTRO

Como joven guerrillero, yo estaba mentalmente preparado para dar la vida por Cuba, para liberarla de lo que nosotros considerábamos "la tiranía" de Batista. Desafortunadamente, nunca sospeché que estaba peleando para el beneficio de los comunistas; que mi patriotismo y lealtad a la Revolución me costarían dieciocho años como preso político y también la vida de mi padre.

Todo comenzó en el año 1952, unos meses antes de las elecciones generales, cuando Fulgencio Batista dio un golpe de estado al gobierno de Carlos Prío Socarras, imponiendo así una dictadura que el pueblo cubano detestaba. La corrupción y el abuso de autoridad eran evidentes. El país ansiaba democracia y libre albedrío para elegir a sus representantes.

Los estudiantes universitarios, jóvenes idealistas, se quejaban y se rebelaban abiertamente; pedían justicia por los actos que el gobierno cometía. Se convirtieron en héroes para la juventud, admirados y apoyados por el pueblo. Durante aquellos tiempos, yo era muy joven y estaba estudiando en *Havana Military Academy*. Estaba atento a todo lo que ocurría, y simpatizaba con el movimiento estudiantil. Al terminar el año escolar, regresé a mi casa en Ranchuelo y pronto decidí reunir a un grupo de amigos para unirnos a la lucha en las montañas del Escambray, en el centro de Cuba.

El primer paso sería buscar armas. No se puede luchar sólo con el deseo. Cuidadosamente comenzamos a visitar a todas aquellas personas que sabíamos poseían armas de fuego, sobre todo a los campesinos. Para no levantar sospecha, íbamos a sus casas durante la noche. Llegábamos y decíamos: "Estamos aquí en nombre del

Movimiento 26 de julio. Necesitamos sus armas, lo que tengan, para ayudarnos a luchar".

Algunos nos temían, pero una vez que les explicábamos nuestro propósito, se relajaban e incluso muchos de ellos se nos unían. Los campesinos se hicieron nuestros grandes aliados. Nos ayudaban con comida, albergue, una pistola, un revólver, machetes; con todo lo que podían.

Una vez que obtuvimos el armamento necesario, emprendimos camino hacia las montañas para unirnos a la lucha. Sigilosamente caminamos toda la noche, sin parar, siguiendo a nuestro guía. Esto fue especialmente difícil para mí, ya que unas semanas antes había sido operado de apendicitis, y la larga caminata me causaba un gran dolor. Cada paso que daba era como un puñal en la herida. Llegó el momento en que ya no podía mover la pierna derecha y sólo pude continuar con la ayuda de mis compañeros. Después de varias horas, ya al pie de las montañas, divisamos en la distancia la casa de un campesino, y paramos para descansar en la choza donde guardaba sus instrumentos de labranza. ¡Aquel piso de tierra nos pareció el mejor colchón del mundo! A la mañana siguiente, después de devorar un nutritivo desayuno, reiniciamos nuestra caminata. Nuestro patriotismo y fe en la misión eran más poderosos que cualquier dolor o temor.

Nuestro destino era El Hoyo de Macagual, donde estaba el campamento de los rebeldes. Para llegar allí, tendríamos que bajar una de las montañas que rodeaban el hoyo. Estábamos en medio del monte; no penetraba la luz del sol y sentíamos el calor y la humedad de aquella espesura. Cuando finalmente llegamos, fuimos acogidos con fraternidad. Allí pasamos innumerables necesidades, y vivimos las inclemencias de la naturaleza.

A veces se alertaba al enemigo, quizás por algún informante dentro de la zona de operación. Recuerdo una mañana cuando caminábamos, oímos la voz alarmante del guía: "¡Avión, avión!". De un momento a otro, aquello se convirtió en un infierno. Nos tiramos en la hierba, nos quedamos totalmente quietos. Las ametralladoras tableteaban, las balas silbaban. Estallaban bombas que estremecían la tierra como si fuera el peor de los terremotos. Cada estallido nos levantaba del suelo. Mis oídos parecían reventar. Afortunadamente, en las alturas de las montañas del Escambray, las nubes fueron nuestras aliadas, ya que los aviones no tuvieron la visibilidad necesaria para ubicar nuestra posición. Era cuestión de metros, lo suficiente para salvarnos la vida.

Tratando de recuperarnos, y aún temblando, nos aventuramos a observar la destrucción. Ni siquiera un huracán de alta intensidad hubiera hecho tanto daño: árboles centenarios destrozados; animales despedazados, decapitados. Era la típica escena cruel de la guerra.

Hasta fines del 1959, nuestros días se componían de batallas, buscando refugio para pasar la noche y tratando de liberar a Cuba de las "garras de la tiranía" (¡Si hubiésemos sabido!). Después de varios incidentes, en una de las batallas más grandes en Las Villas -en el centro de la isla- el gobierno de Batista fue derrotado.

Triunfantemente nos dirigimos a la ciudad de Cienfuegos. Después de asegurar su control, y embriagados por la victoria, marchamos hacia la Habana. ¡Todo era alegría! Todo el pueblo salía a las calles para apoyar a los héroes barbudos y se aglutinaba en las aceras para vernos pasar. Una muchedumbre llenaba los bordes de la Carretera Central, para ver a aquel puñado de hombres que habían logrado derrocar a un gobierno fuertemente armado.

LA DESILUSIÓN

Cuando llegamos a la capital, todo era alegría; se respiraba el triunfo. Sin embargo, pronto el Jefe de la Revolución, disimulando sus verdaderas intenciones, empezó a ejercer su poder sin que nadie pudiera interponerse. Fidel no era el libertador que el pueblo esperaba. Él imponía su poder absoluto. Influía en las masas frenéticas contra cualquiera que tuviera la osadía de tener una opinión contraria a sus planes comunistas... ¡Simplemente lo eliminaba! Ejemplo de esto fue Urrutia, el primer nombrado Presidente de la Revolución, quien -al oponerse a los planes diabólicos de Fidel- éste hizo que el pueblo se volcara contra él y tuvo que marcharse al exilio.

Durante su primer discurso Fidel nos mandó a desarmar. Dijo —Armas... ¿para qué? Todos los que habíamos luchado en las montañas, los que verdaderamente nos habíamos sacrificado por la supuesta libertad de Cuba, ahora teníamos que entregar las armas al gobierno e irnos a casa. Aquello creó mucho disgusto y descontento. Por suerte, en aquellos tiempos ya yo era un oficial y pude mantener la mía.

Muchos oficiales fuimos ubicados en la Fortaleza de la Cabaña en la Habana, bajo el mando del Che Guevara. Se necesitaba organizar al ejército. Durante una reunión, le mencioné al Che la necesidad de organizar las tropas y ofrecí mis conocimientos militares. Con un despotismo inaudito me contestó —No se meta en lo que a

usted no le importa, y miró a todos los oficiales con cara de disgusto y aire amenazante. Había tocado un tema que era tabú.

Sin descanso, los comunistas habían empezado a situar sus líneas de mando. Estructuraban el engranaje que movería y consolidaría la Revolución. Comenzamos a darnos cuenta de que aquello no era por lo que habíamos luchado. Estábamos frustrados. Algunos dirigentes se fueron del país; otros comenzaron a conspirar contra Fidel.

Desde el principio de la toma del poder, se creó el terror por medio del paredón de fusilamiento. Toda persona que se oponía al gobierno era fusilada, o puesta en prisión bajo altas condenas. Se desintegró la Cabaña y a mí me mandaron a Varadero. Los comunistas mandaron a sus adoctrinadores políticos a este lugar. Decidí pasar a una escuela de superación militar, para poder tener más control. Le escribí una carta al Comandante Camilo Cienfuegos, explicándole lo que estaba ocurriendo. Le pedí un traslado a una escuela superior para frenar la penetración comunista en nuestras filas. ¡Qué ingenuidad la mía! Como recompensa, me mandaron a una escuela de analfabetos y me quitaron el mando.

Pronto me encontraba en pasos de alzarme contra la misma Revolución por la que tanto me había sacrificado. Un grupo de antiguos compañeros y yo comenzamos a organizarnos para conspirar contra el gobierno; pero en el grupo hubo un infiltrado que "chivateó" nuestras operaciones. De una u otra forma, nos tomaron prisioneros a todos, unos recibieron la pena de muerte y otras altas condenas. Yo recibí treinta años de prisión.

RECLUSORIO NACIONAL DE LA ISLA DE PINOS
LAS CIRCULARES

A principio del año 1961 fuimos enviados a la prisión de Isla de Pinos. Al aterrizar, nos esperaban grupos de militares armados hasta los dientes; pero lo sorprendente de esto es que no eran cubanos. Para entonces, ya había rusos en Cuba. Después de requisas y maltratos verbales y físicos, llegamos a las circulares del Presidio Modelo, que parecían tanques de una refinería de petróleo. Había cuatro circulares, y a mí me pusieron en la número cuatro. Había cientos de personas viéndonos entrar y dándonos la bienvenida a gritos... parecía el Coliseo Romano. Allí encontré algunos amigos con los que había luchado.

Pasaban los días y había que acostumbrarse a las circunstancias. Cada dos o tres días nos llenaban un cubo con agua para

beber y para asearnos. Sólo podíamos recibir visitas cada seis meses. Recuerdo que en la mañana del 17 de abril despertamos bajo el intenso ruido de ametralladoras que disparaban por todas partes. Era un avión de la Invasión de la Bahía de Cochinos, que estaba disparando a una fragata que se encontraba en el Río de Nueva Gerona. Nuestros corazones palpitaban esperanzados, pensando que vendrían a rescatarnos; pero la misión fracasó. Día tras día veíamos llegar camiones llenos de cajas de madera que entraban en los cimientos las circulares, seguidas de los martillazos penetrante de un taladro abriendo huecos en los cimientos. Lo que estaba sucediendo era que, en caso de que hubiese una invasión estadounidense, el gobierno Castrista estaba poniendo más de 28,000 toneladas de dinamita bajo los cimientos de las circulares. La reacción de los militares contra los presos era atroz - "Si vienen los Yanquis, volaremos esta mierda con todos ustedes adentro"-, nos informaron cínicamente. Prácticamente dormíamos en un colchón de explosivos.

Con frecuencia venía un pelotón de militares a golpearnos, a humillarnos, y a cambiarnos de circular para evitar cualquier planificación estructurada. De todas las requisas, hubo una que fue la más bárbara y cruel. Los presos le dimos el nombre de "La Pacífica". En esta ocasión nos mandaron a desvestir y, con golpes y empujones, nos pusieron contra la pared de la planta baja. Teníamos que poner las manos en nuestras partes privadas para no rozar al compañero que teníamos enfrente. Aquellos que osaban protestar, eran sacados a golpes y los hacían ponerse boca abajo, con los brazos abiertos en cruz, y con la boca pegada a los charcos de agua sucia que caía de los pisos superiores.

En aquel momento se calculaba que había alrededor de mil doscientos presos albergados en una circular que había sido construida para no más de quinientas personas. El maltrato y las atrocidades eran insoportables. Cada día el enemigo trataba de aplastarnos, humillarnos y destruirnos física y moralmente. De una u otra manera, nosotros tratábamos de mantener nuestra moral de lucha. Entre los presos políticos había muchos profesionales que compartían sus conocimientos mediante conferencias, lecturas, demostraciones, etc. Todos compartíamos lo que sabíamos. Nuestra meta era salir de aquel infierno mejor de lo que entramos, y con lo único que no nos podían quitar: nuestra educación.

En 1964 se implementó el plan de trabajo forzado. Los prisioneros ahora teníamos que ir a picar piedras en las canteras. El campamento de trabajo forzado era un verdadero infierno. Era un

plan salvaje. Los presos nos resistimos. Optamos por el "paso de jicotea", haciendo todo lo más lento posible, y solo haciéndolo cuando era forzado. Los golpes, los bayonetazos y los tiros estaban a la orden del día. Muchas veces los guardias se enfurecían, perdían control y apuñalaban salvajemente a un preso indefenso. Tuvimos muertos, lisiados, amputaciones de piernas, brazos, etc. Pero no nos doblegábamos.

Llegó el momento en que las botas de trabajo se rompían. Aquellos que ya no teníamos botas comenzamos a quedarnos en las circulares con los que estaban enfermos. Un día apareció un pelotón armado hasta los dientes. Nos ordenaron formar una fila y nos sacaron a caminar, vigilados por una columna de militares a cada lado. Descalzos por aquel pedregoso suelo, nuestros pies se herían. Nos ordenaron saltar una cerca de púas, como mejor pudiéramos. Los sablazos y planazos rebotaban en nuestras espaldas, hasta que llegamos a una zanja. Nos empujaron para que cayéramos en ella y nos mandaron a limpiarla. Allí flotaban los excrementos de toda la población penal, de los militares y de sus familias que vivían cerca del recinto. Esta zanja drenaba los desperdicios de una población de miles de personas, y las moscas pululaban por doquier. De vez en cuando el suelo era más profundo de lo que esperábamos, y nos hundíamos en esa podredumbre.

Fuimos avanzando a través de aquella nata de excremento hasta llegar a la cochiquera. ¡Los desperdicios de cientos de cerdos ahora se sumaban a las inmundicias humanas!...Era algo intolerable. Uno de nuestros compañeros, debido a la desnutrición combinada con una salvaje golpiza que había recibido el día antes, no pudo aguantar más y cayó desmayado en aquella pudrición. Los guardias amenazaron con disparar si lo ayudábamos; pero, haciendo caso omiso, los que estaban cerca de él lograron sacarlo, casi moribundo.

Cuando los guardias decidieron sacarnos de la zanja, nos llevaron cerca de la playa. Entonces llegó un camión lleno de comida y agua fresca, algo que raramente ofrecían. Cínicamente pretendían humillarnos más, ofreciéndonos de comer cuando estábamos asqueados, cubiertos en pudrición. Era obvio que no podríamos disfrutar de la comida. Aunque sí teníamos sed, también teníamos dignidad; así que rechazamos lo ofrecido. Al atardecer nos regresaron a la prisión.

Entramos en la circular, maltrechos, heridos, agotados, y con dificultad en nuestro andar. Ya nuestros compañeros se habían enterado de lo sucedido y nos recibieron cantando el himno nacional.

Pedro Ramiro Machín a la edad de 19 años

Eso nos revivió. Los guardias, frustrados, nos azotaron una vez más, mientras los otros presos gritaban "¡asesinos, hijos de puta, desmadrados!" y otras cosas más. Por fin abrieron las rejas y las duchas, y pudimos quitarnos la pestilencia que llevábamos encima. Las infecciones que sufrimos en los siguientes días requirieron cuidados médicos intensivos.

Las atrocidades cometidas contra los presos políticos llegaron a causar mucha presión en el país. En mayo de 1966 llegó un grupo de militares a las circulares con listas de presos que serían trasladados. Nos llevaron en un barco a Batabanó, un puerto al sur de la Habana, y después a la Fortaleza de la Cabaña, un viejo fortín construido por

los españoles coloniales. En nuestra galera, la número 7, también pusieron a los condenados a muerte y así mismo a un grupo de jóvenes que había perdido la razón y periódicamente recibían electroshock. En aquellas galeras no había higiene alguna, y casi no había agua, ni para beber.

FORTALEZA LA CABAÑA

Para que nuestra estadía fuera aún más inolvidable, teníamos una infestación de chinches. Nos pasábamos la noche tratando de matar a miles y miles de estos desquiciantes insectos que nos chupaban la sangre como si fueran vampiros. Era una misión imposible, y al fin quedábamos dormidos de agotamiento. Al día siguiente, aunque nos levantábamos maltrechos, teníamos que salir a correr una vuelta alrededor del patio. Por supuesto que nos resistíamos; no corríamos. Por esto recibíamos bayonetazos y golpes. Normalmente el único alimento del día era agua con azúcar, para el desayuno; harina de maíz bien caliente, durante el almuerzo; caldo, y pan para la cena todo sumamente racionado y con tan sólo unos pocos minutos para ingerirlo. Cuando el guardia daba la orden de pararse de la mesa, el que no lo hacía de inmediato, recibía golpes de las bayonetas. "¡Hijos de mala madre, los mataré a golpes si no obedecen! ¡Dije que pararan de comer! Cuando yo digo que se terminó, ¡se terminó!", decía el guardia de turno.

Éramos presos políticos que, habiendo perdido nuestros derechos, tratábamos de mantener nuestra dignidad. Nos insultaban hasta el punto en que alguien se desquiciaba y atacaba a un guardia. Más de una vez se entablaron grandes luchas entre presos y carceleros, por lo que pasábamos meses sin tener comunicación con nuestros seres queridos.

Para evitar que hiciéramos conexiones con los otros reclusos, nos movían de una prisión a otra. Era como estar en una centrífuga. Algunos prisioneros llegaban de la Isla de Pinos, mientras que otros salían hacia otra de las doscientas prisiones cubanas, algunas de las cuales eran más bien campos de concentración. (Antes de 1959, Cuba sólo tenía catorce cárceles, y solamente una era de máxima seguridad).

Los militares empezaron a poner en práctica las técnicas aprendidas de la Unión Soviética. Intentaban crear nuevas formas de tortura física y mental. Durante los primeros meses del año 1967, anunciaron que el reclusorio de Isla de Pinos se desmantelaría y que ya no sería usado más como prisión. También se dijo

que los presos contrarrevolucionarios habían sido trasladados a granjas de rehabilitación, que no eran otras cosas que campos de concentración.

Hubo nuevas disposiciones, entre ellas el cambio de uniforme. El gobierno quiso cambiar el caqui amarillo -que se usó desde el comienzo de la prisión política- por el uniforme de color azul que utilizaban los presos comunes. Los presos políticos nos negamos rotundamente, ya que nos dimos cuenta de que ellos estaban intentando eliminar nuestro rasgo distintivo. Si se nos vestía a todos de azul y nos mezclaban con los presos comunes, no se podría diferenciar entre los políticos y los comunes. Como ellos se imaginaron que habría un rechazo a esta medida, trajeron personal, entrenado en artes marciales, de los cuerpos represivos de la seguridad del estado. Ellos utilizaron sus técnicas y fuerza bruta para ponerle el uniforme a cada uno de los presos, y así vestirlos con el uniforme azul. En algunas cárceles amarraban a los presos para que no pudieran quitárselo. Este proceso duró varios días y resultó en fracturas de brazos y piernas, cabezas rotas, y toda clase de golpes. Ante aquel panorama, algunos presos decidieron aceptar el uniforme y otros quedaron en calzoncillos, creando un nuevo estatus. Como experimento, y con el propósito de ejercer presión, algunos de los desnudos fueron trasladados a prisiones comunes.

Algunos presos habían logrado quedarse con una camiseta y otros, quizás, con una toalla; pero la desnudez era común. Los oficiales nos ofrecían traslado a granjas que quedaban cerca de nuestras familias; ofrecían disminución de la condena, visitas frecuentes y pases periódicos para ir a nuestras casas, todo a cambio de vestir el uniforme de preso común. Su objetivo era demostrarle al mundo que en Cuba no existían presos políticos, que solamente había delincuentes y asesinos.

En el primer mes, muchos aceptaron la ropa azul y fueron trasladados. Esto resultó en que pudiéramos disfrutar de más espacio y tener todo un pedazo de piso para dormir. Cuando llegó el aire frío del norte, algunos de nosotros habíamos conseguido periódicos y uno que otro saco de yute para cubrirnos y amortiguar un poco el frío. ¡Es increíble cuanto protege del frío un pedazo de papel!

A principios del año 1968 me trasladaron con un grupo de veintiún presos a la cárcel provincial de Santa Clara. Allí había niños de ocho, nueve, y doce años... ¡de todas las edades! Pero lo terrible de esta situación era que en, el patio donde ellos estaban, también habían otros que no eran menores, sino que eran delincuentes

experimentados. Aquellos muchachos eran "carne de presidio", y eran objeto de todas las aberraciones imaginables.

Más tarde volvieron a montarnos en una jaula y nos llevaron a Remedios, en el centro de Cuba. Cuando llegamos, nos tenían lista una galera pequeña con camas. Allí seguimos en calzoncillos. Cuando nos sacaban para que hiciéramos nuestras necesidades fisiológicas, no permitían que ningún preso común se acercara a nosotros. Pero, debido al respeto y admiración que estos reclusos nos tenían, ya que éramos presos políticos, de alguna manera lograban darnos algunas cosas: azúcar, jabón, etc. Algunos de ellos hasta se prestaron para que sus familias llevaran recados a las nuestras. Cuando por fin comenzaron a permitir que nuestros familiares nos visitaran, trataban de inducirlos para que nos hablaran y convencieran de todas las ventajas que tendríamos si aceptábamos la ropa azul. De hecho, hasta nos ofrecían la libertad. Por supuesto que el gobierno no cumplía sus promesas; pero algunos presos políticos aceptaban con la esperanza de poder solucionar su situación y la de su familia.

Muchos compañeros se declararon en huelga de hambre. Era una situación intolerable. Algunos de los presos comunes se prestaron para atacarnos a cambio de recibir las recompensas que ofrecían los carceleros, y por eso se formaban grandes luchas entre todos los comunes y los políticos.

Debido a una de estas luchas, nos montaron en una jaula y nos trasladaron a la granja de máxima seguridad de Manacas, en las Villas, un campo de concentración. Nos bajaron a un pabellón que era conocido como "Las Tapiadas de Manacas". Las tapiadas eran unas naves grandes de paredes de bloques, con ventanas que bloqueaban la luz. Dentro de estas construcciones, se encontraban en hileras las celdas de concreto de aproximadamente cinco pies por siete pies, construida independientemente del edificio exterior. Cada celda tenía una ventana a través de la cual no se podía ver nada ni dejaba pasar el aire. Las puertas eran estrechas, de acero, con dos ranuras, una para introducir los alimentos y la otra para mirar lo que ocurría dentro de la celda. El ambiente era húmedo e insano para nuestros pulmones. En una esquina, había un hueco en el que hacíamos nuestras necesidades. El agua llegaba tres veces al día por sólo un minuto. El agua era para beber y otras necesidades. Aunque supuestamente se retiraban de la celda las defecaciones y orines, la peste era parte del ambiente.

Después de tres meses nos sacaron de nuestras celdas. Había barberos esperando por nosotros. Nos afeitaron y nos pelaron. ¡Fue

una afeitada dolorosa! Luego nos llevaron a unas duchas que había en la parte delantera del edificio, y nos repartieron algunos jabones para que por fin nos bañáramos. Estábamos delgados, desnutridos. Al día siguiente nos trasladaron en jaulas de regreso a la Cabaña. Nuestros amigos nos recibieron con alegría, ansiosos por conocer todos los pormenores de las cosas que experimentamos. Aunque seguíamos todos en calzoncillos, las galeras ya habían sido nuevamente acomodadas con camas.

Las cosas habían cambiado; había más entusiasmo. Pudimos conseguir algunos de los libros que nos habían quitado anteriormente. Leíamos y comentábamos en grupo algunos de estos libros. Luego de unos días, el patio nuevamente se inundó de oficiales del Ministerio del Interior. Nos llevaron a un extremo del patio y uno de los oficiales comenzó hablar de las virtudes y generosidad de la Revolución. Después de pasar un buen rato exponiendo todo lo que se le ocurría, dijo que la revolución había acordado devolvernos el uniforme amarillo. Ahora se abrían las galeras por algunas horas, y teníamos la oportunidad de visitarnos unos a otros y hablar con amigos con los que no habíamos hablado por años. También se establecieron horarios para el baño.

Aparentemente ya no ocurrían confrontaciones violentas. Eso era algo inquietante. Ahora estábamos bajo una época de provocación psicológica; nos trasladaban constantemente. El gobierno estaba usando otros medios más refinados para crear división en el presidio político. Estaban poniendo en práctica la táctica de "divide y vencerás".

Muchos prisioneros comenzaron a hacer huelgas de hambre. Algunos grupos de prisioneros eran trasladados a prisiones que quedaban más cerca de sus familias en un intento de utilizar a la familia para ejercer presión. A otros grupos, sin embargo, los alejaban de sus familias y los sometían a las más horribles torturas. Muchos de estos prisioneros fueron metidos en gavetas en las que tenían que mantenerse en la misma posición por largos periodos de tiempo. Los militares usaban crueles métodos de tortura, ya utilizadas en Vietnam contra los prisioneros.

Nuestro grupo fue destinado a la granja de Manacas, de máxima seguridad. Éramos todos de la provincia de las Villas, así que nos acercaron a nuestras familias. Nos pusieron a todos en una galera. Nos permitieron visitas más frecuentes. Todo esto sucedió en el año 1969.

Llegó el mes de diciembre. Durante los días de Navidad, nuestras familias se las arreglaron para llevarnos comida, para que -por lo

menos- cenáramos en las Navidades. Todos sabíamos que ellos se privaban de esta comida para podérnosla llevar. Ya en Cuba el gobierno había quitado la celebración de esa fecha; pero el pueblo siempre la recordaba con tristeza porque era parte de ser "cubano". Durante esa visita de Navidad, los guardias fueron bastante flexibles y dejaron que nos visitaran familiares que no habíamos visto por años. ¡Qué bueno fue abrazar a mis padres, a mis hermanos, y sentir nuevamente el calor de familia! Pero fue también muy dura la despedida, ya que no sabía cuando, si alguna vez, los volvería a ver.

EL MÁS DURO DE LOS GOLPES

Yo pensaba mucho en mi padre. Él siempre fue una persona muy admirada, y yo lo quería mucho. Hacia el final de marzo, un amigo, que se había acogido al plan de trabajo, mandó a otro compañero a buscarme. Cuando me vio, me dijo:

—Te vengo a avisar para que estés preparado. A tu papá lo cogieron preso. Le dan pena de muerte.

Se fue rápido, pues estaba corriendo un riesgo al informarme, que podía costarle caro.

Pasé dos o tres días de incertidumbre, tragándome mis penas y mis angustias. Durante la noche, todo navegaba en mi mente. En la noche del primero de abril, me tiré en el camastro. No lo concebía; no lo aceptaba. No había justificación para que sucediera aquello. Era un torbellino lo que tenía en mi cabeza. ¿Por qué mi padre? Mi madre lo necesitaba, y mis hermanos también; él era un buen hombre, muy querido, que no le hacía daño a nadie. Por fin alrededor de las 2:00 a.m., después de un sueño intranquilo, me invadió una gran paz; como si me hubiera transportado a otro mundo. Me desperté al oír el grito de mi nombre:

—¡Machín, prepárate para ser trasladado!

Me llevaron a la cárcel Provincial. Entré escoltado. Los guardias no permitían que nadie se acercara a mí. Hasta aquel momento nadie me había dicho nada de lo que había sucedido. Entonces se me aproximó un preso político y me dijo:

—Mira, con estas cosas no se anda con tapujos... a tu padre lo fusilaron anoche.

¡Se me cayó el mundo encima! Los guardias me dejaron cerca de la enfermería. Entré en ésta. Allí la mayoría eran presos políticos. Me contaron lo que sabían. Me tiré en una cama, sin poder contener mis lágrimas. Aunque fui criado bajo el falso concepto de que los hombres no lloran, ¡sí lloré! Mantuve la cara hundida en la

almohada, tratando de esconder mis emociones. Pero las lágrimas salían. Impotencia. Desahogo. Confusión. Un mundo que se me derrumbaba. Habían asesinado a mi padre. Él era químico azucarero. Lo acusaron de desperdiciar guarapo rico en azúcar: ¡un puñado de azúcar fue la excusa de su supuesto sabotaje contra la Revolución! Era un hombre muy querido, escuchado y que creaba opinión. Estaba en contra de los desmanes de los comunistas; en contra de lo que se hacía con los presos políticos; y eso la dictadura totalitaria, no lo toleraba. Había que callarlo.

Después de esto, quisieron meterme en las galeras de los comunes, bajo la excusa de que no había cama para mí en la enfermería. Eso hubiera sido un gran problema. Estaban buscando una justificación para eliminarme, tratando de aparentar un accidente, quizás una riña tumultuaria. Tal vez pondrían en práctica alguna de sus tácticas eliminatorias, que en muchas ocasiones desarrollaban y ejecutaban con la ayuda de los presos comunes.

Gracias a Dios, allí en la enfermería estaban Chichi y uno de sus amigos, que por todas las torturas y maltratos recibidos, habían perdido la razón. Periódicamente recibían tratamientos de electroshock. Chichi había caído preso al mismo tiempo que yo, y supo lo sucedido con mi padre. Enseguida me dio su cama. ¡Al saber que querían meterme en la galera de los comunes, formó tremendo revuelo! Cuando le dijeron que no había cama para mí en la enfermería, contestó que él me había dado su cama y, si me llevaban, "¡la cárcel iba a arder!" Todos, presos y carceleros, les temían pues eran locos y peligrosos. Allí me dejaron.

MI MATRIMONIO

Durante el tiempo en que estuve en el presidio, conocí a Regla, quien, junto a su hermana, había cumplido diez años en la prisión de mujeres como presa política. Desde que le dieron libertad me visitó en las distintas prisiones a las que me trasladaban. En la cárcel de Santa Clara, finalizando el año 1970, le propuse matrimonio y aceptó. Debido a la situación, era un "matrimonio simbólico", ya que por largos años no pudimos consumar la relación. Ella aceptó aquella dura prueba y nunca dejó de visitarme.

El permiso de matrimonio fue difícil de conseguir. Como los guardias pensaban que estábamos planificando una fuga, extremaron todas las precauciones de seguridad. El día de la boda me desnudaron, me hicieron una minuciosa requisa, y hasta hicieron que me levantara mis partes privadas; fue la condición que impusieron para

entrar en el salón en el que se efectuaría la azarosa boda. Sólo dejaron entrar a Regla. Ella firmó y se acabó la ceremonia. Los testigos y los padrinos tuvieron que firmar afuera de la cárcel. Así fue nuestra boda el 6 de noviembre de 1970.

En diciembre me trasladaron a la granja de máxima seguridad de Manacas. Ahí por fin me permitieron recibir visitas y tuve la oportunidad de ver a otros familiares a quienes no había visto por muchos años. En aquel momento los comunistas habían adelantado en su propósito de destruir el presidio político. En el Ministerio del Interior, se le estaba dando forma a un plan de trabajo, "El Plan Progresivo", por medio del cual los presos políticos podrían obtener su libertad. El único compromiso sería trabajar.

Algunos de los presos dirigentes aceptaron el plan después de exponer sus dudas y aclarar los puntos que pudieran perjudicar a sus ideas. Después de casi dos décadas de estar confinados en las horrendas e inhumanas cárceles del sistema comunista en Cuba, tomaban esta decisión con la esperanza de poder librarse de las miserias y atrocidades del sistema. Como resultado del plan, se creó el "Sexto Frente", y se formaron brigadas de construcción. Íbamos a fabricar complejos de edificios escolares de cuatro plantas.

Los comunistas planeaban utilizar las zonas agropecuarias para construir escuelas. De esta forma podían utilizar a los alumnos para que trabajaran en las labores agrícolas. También, al tenerlos separados de sus familias, les sería más fácil adoctrinarlos con las teorías del marxismo-leninismo. El objetivo principal era tener en sus manos el mecanismo de manipulación y control de la juventud: lavado de cerebro y control. Estos planes de trabajo progresivos experimentales para los presos, fueron implantados en todas las provincias. Por supuesto, al principio hubo que aprender todo lo relacionado con el trabajo de la construcción.

Una vez terminadas ciertas facetas de la construcción, a veces nos daban un pase de cuarenta y ocho horas para ir a visitar nuestra casa. Esto dependía de cuánto tiempo se había estado bajo el plan o de la evaluación que hacían los guardias. Por supuesto, el gobierno evitaba que tuviéramos contacto con el pueblo, ya que ellos decían que nosotros creábamos opinión.

LA LIBERTAD

En el año 1979 ocurrió algo que el gobierno cubano aprovechó al máximo: los cubanos exiliados en los Estados Unidos lograron ser recibidos en Cuba. Este grupo fue conocido por el nombre de "La

Comunidad". El gobierno cubano dejó que los miembros de la comunidad expusieran y plantearan sus ideas sobre los presos políticos.

Esto resultó en que el gobierno de Jimmy Carter y Cuba llegaran a un acuerdo. Se permitió la salida de Cuba a cientos de presos políticos y sus familias. Así fue como llegué yo al exilio, hace ya más de 29 años, después de haber cumplido 18 años de prisión. Dios me otorgó el privilegio de vivir el resto de mi vida en un país lleno de oportunidades y donde el respeto a los derechos humanos es ley. Diariamente, al despertar, doy gracias por el derecho de levantarme y disfrutar mi derecho de ejercer libre albedrío, el éxito y la bendición más grande que un ser humano pueda gozar.

Otros presos, por una razón u otra, tuvieron que quedarse en aquella isla cautiva; y continúan con la esperanza de ver realizado algún día el sueño de ver a Cuba libre, próspera y democrática, como también -una vez en la distancia de la historia- lo soñó nuestro apóstol, José Martí.

PD: Pedro Ramiro Machín reside en West Palm Beach y está en proceso de escribir sus memorias para un libro que publicará en un futuro cercano.

Alex, Debbie, José Manuel y Anabel García.

Mis recuerdos de El Mariel

Dr. José Manuel García

El trabajo de un maestro es infinito,
nunca se sabe hasta dónde llegará su influencia.
HENRY B. ADAMS

En 1980, un autobús lleno de cubanos se estrelló contra las puertas de la Embajada de Perú en la Habana. Miles de personas corrieron a buscar asilo y el infame Éxodo del Mariel comenzó.

Mi padre era un miembro próspero de la sociedad cubana, era vicepresidente de una compañía de construcción del gobierno a nivel nacional; sin embargo no era miembro del Partido Comunista. Debido a su arresto infundado durante la invasión de la Bahía de Cochinos en los años 60 -que lo mantuvo preso por tres meses- mi padre juró irse de Cuba. Pero no fue hasta 1980 que tuvo la oportunidad de salir de la isla.

Recuerdo vívidamente el día en el que la policía llegó a nuestra casa con el permiso de salida. Nos dieron tan sólo una hora para hacer maletas. Yo tenía trece años de edad y mi hermana once, los dos estábamos asustados. Cuando nos disponíamos a abordar el autobús, otros policías vinieron buscando a una persona, cuyo nombre tenían en su lista, para interrogarla: era mi padre. Mientras veía a los oficiales llevándoselo en sus motocicletas, pensaba que nunca más lo volvería a ver. Mi madre lloraba, y a la vez nos consolaba.

Gracias a Dios, eso no ocurrió. Dos cosas salvaron a mi padre: nosotros teníamos una de las casas más bonitas en mi pueblo de Sancti Spíritus (la casa hoy en día es el Ministerio de Educación) y mi padre tenía un pasaporte español. Si lo detenían, la casa no pasaría a manos del gobierno y, por otra parte, la policía no quería tener problemas con ciudadanos extranjeros. Mis abuelos eran ambos españoles, por consiguiente mi padre era automáticamente ciudadano español. Lo dejaron ir; pero con la advertencia de que había una gran posibilidad de ser llamado nuevamente, si tuvieran alguna otra pregunta.

EL VIAJE A EL MARIEL

Al llegar a la Habana, después de largas horas de viaje desde Sancti Spiritus, nos quedamos a pasar la noche en un gran estadio de baseball, a orillas del mar. Había cientos, si no miles, de personas en este lugar durmiendo a la intemperie o en carpas improvisadas rodeadas de montones de basura. Recuerdo claramente que, a pesar de esas tristes circunstancias, el sol y el aroma del océano nos daban esperanzas de una vida mejor. La mayoría de personas, que estaban allí con nosotros, ya llevaban días esperando escuchar su nombre por los parlantes, para poder salir de ese espantoso lugar. Nuevamente la suerte nos acompañó, y unas horas después de nuestra llegada, fuimos llamados. Sin embargo, escuchar nuestro nombre se convertía a la vez en una experiencia tenebrosa, porque podía significar ver a nuestro padre por última vez, si los oficiales del gobierno decidían detenerlo. Otra vez, él tuvo que mentir sobre su profesión, ya que tenía una alta posición con el gobierno y éste no lo quería dejar salir. Nosotros estábamos tan nerviosos y con tal tensión que hasta se podía sentir en el aire.

Felizmente, pasamos la inspección sin contratiempos y nos fuimos en autobús a otro campamento llamado "El mosquito". El chofer nos dijo que si teníamos joyas o cualquier cosa de valor, que nos las quitáramos, pues todo sería confiscado en la próxima parada y que él las aceptaría con mucho gusto. Con lágrimas en los ojos, muchas personas -incluyendo a mi padre- le entregaron al conductor todo tipo de joyas, algunas con valor sentimental. Mi padre se quedó con una cadena de oro que mi abuelo le había dado, la misma que había estado en la familia por generaciones.

Una vez que llegamos al Mosquito, nos dijeron que esa sería la última inspección. El Mosquito también tenía el aspecto de un campamento improvisado, con muchas carpas rodeadas de cercas de púas, y de soldados armados y con perros. Pasamos aproximadamente cuatro horas esperando en línea hasta que nos llamaron. Cada familia tenía que entrar a una de esas casas de campaña y abrir sus maletas para que un soldado las registrara. Los adultos tenían que ir a una carpa separada, donde se tenían que desvestir y entregar cualquier objeto personal de valor. Los policías encontraron y confiscaron la cadena de oro que mi padre había escondido en un lugar secreto de la maleta. No obstante, él estaba contento por no haber sido detenido. Salimos de este campamento con tres maletas que contenían solamente mudas de ropa, y en otro autobús nos fuimos al Puerto del Mariel.

EL VIAJE A CAYO HUESO

El Puerto del Mariel estaba abarrotado con miles de barcos de todo tipo y tamaños. Tan pronto como llegamos, nos escoltaron a nuestro barco: Dulce II. Era un típico barco de vacaciones, de dos plantas con capacidad para aproximadamente 14 personas. A diferencia de los otros barcos, todos los pasajeros del nuestro eran familias con niños. Los otros, una vez abordados por prisioneros quienes por haber recobrado su libertad estaban alborotados, salían inmediatamente. Desesperado, mi padre le preguntó a nuestro capitán cuál era el problema, por qué no zarpábamos. Nuestro barco, al igual que los demás, había sido cargado con el doble de su capacidad. Se nos anunció entonces que, debido a la sobrecarga y al mal tiempo, saldríamos por la mañana.

Al día siguiente, aproximadamente a las 6:00 a.m., comenzamos a navegar hacia Cayo Hueso y veinte minutos después ya no podíamos ver las costas cubanas. De pronto, el motor empezó a fallar y el agua a entrar al barco. Después de unas maniobras, el motor arrancó otra vez; pero el capitán decidió que era mejor regresar hasta que el clima mejorara.

Nos quedamos en el puerto cuatro días esperando a que la tormenta pasara. Durante ese tiempo, el gobierno nos daba una vez al día una cajita de huevos revueltos y arroz blanco para comer. Mi padre sabía que era cuestión de tiempo antes de que lo descubrieran y no estaba seguro de que pudiera irse de Cuba. Cada vez que un guardacostas pasaba, mi padre se escondía pensando que venían por él. Todavía me entristece recordar cómo se tenía que esconder, y a veces pasarse a otro barco, para que no lo encontraran.

Era el 3 de junio de 1980, la tormenta había pasado; pero aún continuábamos con mal tiempo. El capitán aún tenía muchas dudas sobre el funcionamiento del barco; pero un colega suyo ofreció mantenerse cerca en caso de que algo pasara. Ya, para esas horas, estábamos desesperados y las peleas empezaban entre los pasajeros. Algunos niños se habían enfermado por haber estado expuestos a la intemperie y a otros elementos que, mezclado con diferentes olores, hacían la situación en el barco cada vez más difícil. Las raciones de comida se estaban acabando y algunos adultos, entre ellos mi padre, no comían con la excusa de no tener hambre, para así favorecer a los niños.

Salimos del Mariel en un día calmado y sin muchos incidentes. Sin embargo, cerca al Golfo de México, las olas comenzaron a crecer y el agua que entraba al barco nos llegaba hasta los tobillos. La gente lloraba y gritaba que no se quería morir. De pronto, divisamos a un

barco, era un guardacostas cubano que luego se acercó. Nuestro capitán nos calmó diciendo que con la cooperación de todos seríamos evacuados a una embarcación camaronera que estaba cerca. Uno por uno fuimos transferidos. No pudimos traer nada con nosotros porque, a pesar de que ese barco era más grande, también tenía sobrecarga. La mayoría de sus pasajeros eran convictos y personas que, con tan sólo mirarlas a la cara, se podía ver que sufrían de alguna enfermedad mental. Mi madre aún recuerda como un señor de color, aparentemente fuerte, se desmayó cuando nos estaban rescatando. Dulce II fue remolcada por el barco camaronero por unos veinte minutos; para después hundirse en el mar. Fue una escena triste y horrenda. Nosotros temblábamos de sólo pensar que habíamos estado abordo de aquella embarcación que ahora se perdía en las profundidades del océano.

El barco camaronero tenía más de 100 personas a bordo y no había espacio ni para sentarse. Estábamos como sardinas en lata. Cada cierto tiempo nos pedían que nos moviéramos de un lado a otro para mantener el balance. Estuvimos por más de 18 horas en el vaivén de las enormes olas: en un minuto estábamos como en la cima de una gran montaña y en el otro al fondo de un precipicio; era imposible dormir. Todo el mundo tenía que orinar y defecar en su sitio. La mayoría de nosotros nos moríamos de hambre y estábamos completamente deshidratados. Desesperado, un muchacho de unos 20 años comenzó a gritar que se quería morir y se armó un pleito cuando le dijeron que se callara o lo tirarían del barco. Se calmó por unos minutos, pero de pronto comenzó a gritar otra vez y lo tuvieron que amarrar a un poste.

Cayó la noche y ya no había esperanzas de vida en el gran océano. Debido a la desolación, cada cierto tiempo alguien juraba que había visto luces o tierra. Finalmente, a las 3 de la mañana, se nos acercó un guardacostas americano que nos guió hasta Cayo Hueso. Un viaje que normalmente toma de uno a dos días, lo hicimos en casi una semana, ya que pasamos cinco días en medio del océano. Al fin estábamos en los Estados Unidos.

Una vez en tierras norteamericanas, nos fuimos de inmediato a New York. Era una ciudad llena de crimen y drogas. Mi padre tenía tres trabajos y casi no hablaba inglés; sin embargo se convirtió después en el primer vendedor de la compañía *Goya*, en alcanzar ventas por un millón de dólares en su segundo año de trabajo. Yo asistí al colegio de *Washington Heights* hasta el onceavo grado. Luego nos mudamos a un suburbio próspero en New Jersey gracias a la

determinación y a la actitud incansable de mi padre ante el trabajo. Estudié en un colegio público durante el doceavo grado y luego fui a la Universidad de Monclair en New Jersey. Me gradué con un titulo en Ciencias Políticas y Español. Después me di cuenta que quería enseñar Cine y Literatura Latino Americana. Recibí una beca para estudiar Literatura Hispánica en la Universidad de Arizona, donde hice mi maestría y doctorado en Literatura Española y Latinoamericana.

He sido profesor en *Florida Southern College* desde 1999. Mi departamento ha pasado de tener entre seis y siete estudiantes que se han graduado en la carrera de Español -o que la han tenido como segunda especialización- a 45. He creado un programa de estudios en el extranjero que me permite llevar un promedio de 50 a 60 estudiantes a España cada año. He añadido cursos de literatura y cine.

Me siento afortunado de haber crecido en dos culturas y tener la habilidad de ser multilingüe. Le agradezco a mi padre por su perseverancia y apoyo brindado a mi hermana y a mí para realizar nuestro "sueño americano". De igual forma, quiero transmitirles a mis hijos esa pasión de progresar en la vida. También le doy gracias a mi madre -quien ha alcanzado el éxito en el campo de bienes raíces- por haber estado a nuestro lado dándonos su apoyo y amor incondicional.

A la vez quiero inspirar a mis estudiantes a conocer otras tierras. Llevarlos al extranjero les da la oportunidad de ver otros mundos y de tener nuevas perspectivas en la vida. Muchos de mis alumnos han ido a trabajar al extranjero, o a enseñar español. Ahora estoy tomando un año sabático, para escribir un libro sobre el *Éxodo del Mariel*, el cual es un sueño que he tenido por años.

La experiencia del inmigrante no tiene comparación. Todos los cubanos-americanos anhelamos viajar para ver a nuestra patria, la isla que nos vio nacer. Pero yo estoy eternamente agradecido a este país que nos ofrece infinitas oportunidades.

Eliezer, Rodolfo, Acela (Carito), Andrew y Osdany Lumpuy

El Dorado, barco en que la familia Lumpuy arrivó a los Estados Unidos

Alcancé mi meta

Acela (Carito) Lumpuy

Por muy larga que sea la tormenta,
el sol siempre vuelve a brillar entre las nubes.
KHALIL GIBRAN

Nuestra vida en Cuba fue siempre muy pobre y el comunismo la empeoró. Mi esposo se dedicaba a sembrar para poder traer la comida. Yo administraba una tienda mixta en la que se vendía víveres y ropa, entre otras cosas. La mayoría del tiempo trabajaba sola y muy duro. No sé de dónde Dios me daba la fuerza; pero con sólo 70 libras de peso y 4.5 pies de altura, tenía que acomodar los sacos de azúcar prieta de 218 libras. Los días que llegaba el petróleo eran agotadores; como estaba escaso, sólo llegaba una vez al mes y todos lo necesitaban. Los campesinos hacían largas colas para poder comprarlo y yo me pasaba horas y horas levantando y vendiendo petróleo. Ganaba 118 pesos cubanos, que vendrían a ser más o menos ocho dólares al mes; ese dinero no alcanzaba para nada.

Teníamos libretas de abastecimiento donde se anotaba lo que nos tocaba comprar para comer. Como nosotros éramos un núcleo familiar de cuatro personas, nos daban 20 libras de azúcar al mes, 20 libras de arroz, alrededor de 3 litros de aceite y 4 onzas de café. Frijoles, no había mucho. Eso era lo único que se encontraba en las tiendas.

En 1980, debido a un acuerdo entre el Presidente Norteamericano Jimmy Carter y Fidel Castro, los presos políticos fueron liberados y enviados a los Estados Unidos. Siendo mi hermano uno de ellos, mi familia pudo salir de Cuba a través del Puerto del Mariel en la Habana. Íbamos a salir todos juntos, pero emigración no aceptó mi salida; así que mi hermano viajó sólo con mis padres. Eso fue un golpe muy duro para todos nosotros pues nunca antes nos habíamos separado.

Mi mamá llegó a Miami con la presión alta, probablemente por la pena de dejar el país y la preocupación de dejarnos atrás. Dos semanas después de la llegada de mi familia, se hizo una fiesta en

casa de uno de mis tíos de Lakeland, Florida. Durante la reunión, mi mamá fue al baño y no regresó. Más tarde la encontraron tirada en el piso. A los tres días pasó a la presencia del Señor. La trayectoria y las emociones habían sido demasiado para ella.

La noticia fue devastadora, no sólo por saber que no la volvería a ver o sentir su ternura, sino también porque mi madre no llegó a disfrutar de aquello que vino buscando: Libertad.

Mi papá ahorró un poco de dinero trabajando como conserje en un colegio. Él había tenido que comenzar a trabajar de nuevo, a los 60 años, cuando llegó a los Estados Unidos. También recibió mucha ayuda de nuestros compatriotas en Lakeland. A pesar de que tuvo muchos gastos por la muerte de mi mamá, aún así pudo pagarle $500.00 por persona al capitán de un barco para que nos trajera a mis hijos y a mi esposo a los Estados Unidos.

Estábamos esperando; pero los días pasaban y no recibíamos noticias del barco. Llamé a mi papá y le pregunté:

—¿Pero Papi, no nos vas a mandar a buscar?

—Sí hija, ya el barco está en Cuba.

El barco ya tenía tres semanas en el puerto; pero el gobierno hacía que los barcos se llevaran primero a la gente que ellos querían sacar. Estos eran los criminales y gente con problemas mentales, a los cuales el gobierno los hacía pasar como prisioneros políticos.

El 13 de mayo yo estaba en la tienda entregando los últimos papeles de un inventario, que el gobierno me había pedido. Un oficial me había dicho que él sabía que yo estaba por irme, y que si algo faltaba me lo harían pagar. No saldría del país hasta que lo pagara. Esa situación me puso muy nerviosa. El simple hecho de pensar que -por cualquier excusa- me podían hacer quedar, era aterrador.

Ese mismo día llegaron dos policías a traernos el permiso de salida. Nos teníamos que ir esa misma tarde. Mis hijos estaban en la escuela. Sus maestras eran amigas mías y apenas se enteraron llevaron a los niños a casa para bañarlos y vestirlos, mientras yo llegaba de la tienda. Yo ya tenía un maletín preparado con medicina, ropita y comida para mis hijos. Los policías me sacaron casi todo, incluso una foto de mi mamá. La comida que dejaron, no nos duró ni un día.

Nosotros vivíamos en el interior de Placetas. Los policías nos llevaron a diferentes oficinas a llenar papeles y después a un hotel en la Habana. Éramos tantas personas en aquel hotel, que no había espacio para todos, y nosotros tuvimos que acostarnos a la orilla del mar, en unos colchones que nos proporcionaron. Para asearnos teníamos que usar el agua del mar, porque los baños siempre estaban

llenos y extremadamente sucios. Mi esposo y yo no comíamos; lo que conseguíamos se lo dábamos a los niños, porque no teníamos suficiente dinero.

Cuando nos sacaron de ese hotel, nos llevaron a otro lugar y de allí al Puerto del Mariel. En el puerto estuvimos casi dos días debido al tamaño de la flotilla; había miles de barcos. Algunas embarcaciones pertenecían a cubanos que trataban de llevarse a su familia; y otros estaban allí aprovechándose de la oportunidad para ganar buen dinero. Esta era la única forma de salir del país.

Nos pusieron en unas carpas. Llamaban a familia por familia para ir a los barcos. Las que iban saliendo, dejaban el poco dinero que tenían. Cuando por fin nos llamaron, un oficial nos dijo que solamente habían reclamado a tres de nosotros, de hecho yo no aparecía en la lista.

—¿Cómo que Acela no aparece? ¡Es el padre de ella quien nos reclama! ¡Nos reclamó a los cuatro juntos, así que salimos juntos!, dijo mi esposo en tono de desesperación.

Yo sentía que me moría; no sabía que iban a hacer conmigo; si me iban a hacer quedar y por cuánto tiempo. Un señor habló con los milicianos por nosotros y les dijo: —Se trata de reunificación de familias, ¿por qué quieren dejar a la madre de esos dos niños atrás? Finalmente me dejaron pasar.

Después de horas de papeleo, subimos al barco. Era un viejo barco camaronero, aún en buenas condiciones. Junto con nosotros venían otras treinta y dos familias Cuando ya íbamos a salir, un militar del gobierno cubano le informó al capitán que tenía que traer a 60 personas indeseables, es decir presos comunes o personas que sacaban de los manicomios. Esa era la trampa del gobierno cubano; para que los barcos pudieran transportar a las familias pedidas, tenían que llevarse primero a las personas de mal vivir y a los locos. Ya nuestro capitán había traído a los Estados Unidos más de 200 de esas personas; pero no tenía otra alternativa que aceptar. El capitán puso como condición, que los indeseables tenían que viajar en la parte superior de la nave, y les advirtió que si agredían a alguno de sus pasajeros, terminarían en el mar. Gracias a Dios, no hubo ningún inconveniente; aquellas personas se comportaron bien e incluso ayudaron en los momentos difíciles.

No teníamos dinero; lo poco que nos sobró, se lo dimos a la gente que quedaba en las carpas, para que pudieran comprar algo de comer. Partimos de la Habana exactamente el 18 de mayo de 1980. A mí me dio mucha pena dejar mi tierra y darle la espalda a aquellos que

se quedaban en la pobreza. Al mismo tiempo, me sentía feliz de salir para los Estados Unidos y reencontrarme con mi padre, mi hermano y otros familiares. No podía contener las lágrimas frente a aquella mezcla de sentimientos y la incertidumbre de lo que traería el futuro.

Al partir, el capitán nos informó de los muchos peligros que podíamos afrontar en nuestra travesía. No recuerdo todo lo que dijo; pero sí su advertencia final: "Escuchen bien... si alguien cae al mar, sea quien sea, no lo pueden ayudar. No podemos parar por la cantidad de personas que llevábamos a bordo. El que trate de salvar a alguien, se ahoga también". Sus palabras helaron la sangre de mis venas. Sabía que nos esperaban las horas más oscuras de nuestras vidas. Me aferré a mis hijos y a mi Dios.

Junto con nosotros salieron muchos barcos, era una flotilla inmensa. ¡Cómo me hubiera gustado haber podido grabar aquellas escenas! Había barcos pequeños cargando más de doscientas personas. Algunas se caían al mar porque no cabían. La gente gritaba y la desesperación era muy grande. Algo realmente triste; todos estábamos arriesgando la vida, abandonando nuestra bella isla, debido a las doctrinas de un tirano loco.

Aunque se había pronosticado buen tiempo, a una hora de camino comenzó a tronar y pronto llegaron las tormentas. Vivimos horas de terror: inmensas olas negras que nos cubrían. Parecía que el mar nos quería tragar. Los truenos ensordecían y los relámpagos electrificaban el ambiente. Comenzamos a sacar el agua con cubetas para no hundirnos. Los niños lloraban aterrorizados, y muchos oraban al Señor. Al lado mío venía una ancianita, que estaba toda empapada. Yo veía como temblaba de miedo y de frio; quería abrazarla, protegerla; pero tenía que poner atención a mis propios hijos.

Por fin, la tormenta amainó. Vimos embarcaciones que habían salido repletas de gente, ahora vacías. Algunos de los pasajeros en mi embarcación vieron tiburones atacando a las personas que habían caído al océano. Yo solamente vi sangre en el agua.

Ya en aguas norteamericanas, vimos aviones y helicópteros de la guardia costera. Los aviones venían a chequearnos. Nosotros les gritábamos que nos salvaran, les suplicábamos que nos llevaran a tierra. Ellos contestaban que nosotros no estábamos tan mal y que había gente en condiciones más precarias; que había niños y viejitos que se estaban muriendo. Ellos recogían a la gente que se estaba hundiendo, que se estaba ahogando.

El motor se descompuso varias veces. Esta vez, la tripulación nos movía de un lugar a otro porque parecía que nos íbamos a hundir.

Gracias a Dios, el capitán de un barco cercano nos ayudó y el motor arrancó. Agarramos una brecha muy tranquila y llegó la calma. De pronto, la gente empezó a gritar con alegría: "¡Miren las luces, miren las luces!". Era Cayo Hueso.

Era de madrugada, cientos de barcos llegaban a la vez y había que esperar. Los guardacostas nos ponían en filas. Allí estaba la Cruz Roja ayudando. Había mucha gente enferma. En mi barco venía un niño hemofílico que estaba bastante grave y la Cruz Roja se lo tuvo que llevar, al igual que la abuelita que venía a mi lado.

Mi papá estaba esperándonos en Miami. Pero el Departamento de Inmigración no tenía personal suficiente para procesar tanta gente allí y por eso fue que llegamos a Cayo Hueso. Al día siguiente, nos mandaron en avión hacia una base militar en Pensilvania. Nos pusieron en unas casas de dos pisos, todos juntos, incluyendo los indeseables. Todos los días había peleas verbales y físicas y hasta hubo asesinatos. Era tan triste la situación, que mi esposo decía que hubiera preferido no haber salido de Cuba. Nuestros hijos estaban viviendo una experiencia horrible que los podía marcar por el resto de sus vidas.

Nos quedamos en Pensilvania un mes y esperar fue difícil. Había que hacer cola para todo, sobre todo para comer. Al principio algunos querían comer doble y se peleaban y golpeaban. Mi esposo se iba a hacer la cola para el desayuno, desayunábamos y de inmediato se tenía que ir para hacer la cola del almuerzo y después para la cena. Gracias a Dios nunca nos quedamos sin comer. La gente del comedor ya nos conocía, y le daban a mis niños algunos dulces para comer.

La mayor parte del tiempo, yo me quedaba en el albergue con los muchachos, porque hacía mucho frío. Mi esposo se iba envuelto en una frazada para hacer las colas. Ni siquiera nos podíamos bañar porque el agua estaba congelaba. La calefacción que tenían era antigua y no calentaba lo suficiente.

Finalmente nos pudimos ir. Para entonces ya traíamos una caja de ropa que la iglesia nos había dado cuando llegamos a Pensilvania. Ya en el avión todos comían menos nosotros, porque no teníamos ni un centavo. A mi lado venía un señor de edad (que Dios lo bendiga donde esté). Ese señor le preguntó a una aeromoza que hablaba español por qué nosotros no comíamos. Yo le dije que nosotros veníamos de una base militar, que éramos cubanos refugiados y que no teníamos dinero para comer. Él pagó por nuestra comida y dijo que nos trajeran todo lo que pidiéramos. Nosotros aceptamos, pero sin abusar.

Al fin llegamos a Lakeland y nuestros sacrificios pronto comenzaron a dar fruto. Desde el momento en que llegamos hemos recibido mucha ayuda, particularmente de la Iglesia Católica. Nos dieron dinero y comida y al cabo de unos días, el gobierno nos mandó $200. También nuestra familia ayudó. Nos quedamos a vivir con mis tíos, donde también estaba mi padre.

Mi primer trabajo fue de niñera. Entré a clases de tapicería, en la que, a pesar del idioma, logré buenas calificaciones y me dieron un certificado. Inmediatamente comencé a trabajar y estuve dos meses en una fábrica que hacía asientos para embarcaciones. El trabajo era tan duro que las manos me sangraban y lo tuve que dejar. Siempre mantuve por lo menos dos trabajos a la vez. Trabajaba mañana y noche limpiando o haciendo lo que fuera. Al cabo de un tiempo inicié mi propio negocio de tapicería, el que mantuve por cinco años aproximadamente. Fue un buen negocio.

Al mismo tiempo, empecé a trabajar como empleada sustituta de mantenimiento del *Southwest Middle School*, donde también trabajaba mi padre. Después de dos años, me dieron un puesto fijo. Debido a que allí me ofrecían beneficios, tuve que dejar mi negocio. Continué con la limpieza de casas, oficinas y de construcciones por las mañanas. He trabajando en *Southwest Middle School* por más de 21 años. En varias ocasiones he sido reconocida como "La trabajadora del año". Soy la supervisora de mantenimiento, lo cual me ha permitido llevar a trabajar conmigo a muchos otros inmigrantes que han necesitado trabajo al llegar. En el 2008, la Junta Directiva del Departamento de Educación del Condado de Polk me otorgó el premio de "La Mejor Trabajadora del Condado de Polk". Aquello fue una sorpresa enorme y un gran orgullo tanto para mí como para mi familia.

Yo siempre he sentido la necesidad de retribuir la ayuda que se nos ha dado, tanto como la bendición de haber llegado a los Estados Unidos sanos y salvos. Las familias para las que he trabajado siempre me han regalado ropa, muebles y otras cosas que yo he ido acumulando. Con todo eso, he podido ayudar a otros inmigrantes, así como a cualquier otra persona necesitada. También he tratado de orientarlos, llevarlos al médico, ayudarlos a obtener su seguro social, a hacer sus papeles, y demás. Es mi deber como ser humano. Mi esposo y yo hemos viajado varias veces a Cuba para ayudar a la familia. Les hemos arreglado la casa, les llevamos medicinas, espejuelos y los abastecemos lo más que podemos. Nosotros tenemos demasiado y ellos no tienen nada.

La comunidad de Lakeland, enterada sobre mis esfuerzos, siempre me ha proporcionado ayuda. En el 2005, la Revista de Lakeland publicó un artículo titulado "Ángeles de Todos los Días" en el que se me destacó, junto con otras siete personas, por mi labor en la comunidad. Mi historia también salió en Visión Latina, un periódico local en español. Si me hubiese ganado la lotería, no hubiera significado tanto para mí, como lo han sido todos estos reconocimientos.

Nosotros vinimos a los Estados Unidos a trabajar, a luchar por una vida mejor y para sacar a nuestros hijos adelante. No cabe duda que hemos alcanzado nuestra meta. Yo me siento millonaria porque he sabido administrar mi vida. No gasto en mi persona para poder ayudar a otros. Nuestros hijos han seguido nuestro ejemplo y también son hombres emprendedores, quienes gozan de éxito en sus trabajos.

El orgullo más grande que tenemos, es haber ayudado a los nuestros en Cuba y haber traído a mis suegros, aunque fuese sólo por vacaciones. Ellos ahora saben lo que es vivir en el país de las oportunidades y han tenido la satisfacción de ver a sus nietos y bisnietos gozando de la vida con la que siempre soñamos.

Carlitos, Carlos, Lidia y Manolo Martínez

Mi escape por Honduras

Dr. Manuel Martínez

La libertad es siempre peligrosa,
pero es asimismo, nuestra garantía más segura.
H.E. FODICK

Un nuevo paciente estaba sentado en mi mesa de reconocimiento. Era un hombre joven, delgado, de apariencia fuerte y saludable; sus zapatos y vestimenta daban a conocer que trabajaba en el campo. Él estaba allí, frotándose las manos nerviosamente; sin embargo su rostro no tenía expresión alguna. Me senté y rodé mi asiento hacia él.

—¿Cómo se siente hoy? ¿Qué puedo hacer para ayudarlo?

Sin decir una palabra y mirándome fijamente a los ojos, mi paciente metió su mano izquierda en el bolsillo de su camisa y me entregó una foto al mismo tiempo que se ponía el dedo índice derecho sobre sus labios en señal de silencio. Al mirar la foto, me comenzaron a temblar las manos y el corazón me latía cada vez más rápido, mientras que el sudor me brotaba por la frente. Al fin, el momento que yo había estado esperando… este hombre había venido para intentar liberarme. Traté de mantener la compostura. Mientras le ponía el estetoscopio en el pecho, le dije:

—Respire profundo… otra vez. Seguido por un par de preguntas médicas hechas en voz alta.

—Tómese estas pastillas y se mejorará. Regrese a verme en unos días.

En la receta le escribí la hora y el lugar donde nos podíamos reunir más tarde esa noche.

No me fue fácil concentrarme durante el resto de la tarde. Seguía mirando la foto sin poder creerlo, pero ahí estaba, ¡no cabía duda! Mi tío Luis me había dicho que me mandaría una señal que fuera obvia. Mi plan estaba funcionando. Estaba a punto de escaparme de Nicaragua, cruzando las montañas hacia Honduras.

Desde que yo era un jovencito, allá en los años sesenta, mi familia había tratado de escapar del comunismo. Mis padres eran de procedencia humilde, pero con trabajo y sacrificios habían llegado a tener una posición acomodada. En el año 1959 eran dueños de un próspero comercio de víveres, una peluquería y varias casas de alquiler. Después de la revolución, todos estos símbolos de su esfuerzo fueron confiscados en un solo día por el gobierno.

Aún me duele el corazón cada vez que recuerdo uno de los días más tristes de mi vida: el día en que acompañé a mi padre a su tienda de víveres y la encontramos cerrada. Un militar arrogante se nos acercó y, en tono serio y oficial, le dijo a mi padre: —¡Ya usted no es el dueño de este negocio! ¡Ha pasado a manos del pueblo! Es decir, de Fidel Castro.

De ahí en adelante mi padre no pudo volver a entrar a la tienda, ¡ni siquiera a sacar un lápiz! Al mismo tiempo, el gobierno trató de quitarle el automóvil; pero mi padre se negó rotundamente a entregar las llaves, a pesar de las amenazas de encarcelamiento. Después, nos expropiaron el resto de las propiedades. Mis padres no tuvieron otra alternativa que trabajar como empleados del gobierno.

Mi familia hizo varios intentos infructíferos de salir hacia los Estados Unidos. Cuando mi hermano cumplió la edad militar, a los quince años, ya no se le permitía salir del país. Tuvimos que quedarnos viviendo bajo opresión sin esperanzas de irnos de Cuba. La familia de mi tío Luis, de quienes habíamos sido vecinos mientras crecíamos, emigró a los pocos años, dejando un gran vacío en nuestro corazón. Ahora teníamos que sufrir solos las calamidades de ese cruel régimen.

Decidí estudiar Medicina. No me fue fácil, ya que el gobierno sabía que mi familia no simpatizaba con la dictadura. Constantemente era amenazado con que iba a ser reclutado para el servicio militar, sin posibilidad de entrar al Colegio de Medicina. Con suerte, y después de muchas humillaciones, me gradué en 1975. Solicité para continuar estudiando una especialidad en cirugía plástica. Desafortunadamente, fui enviado a practicar medicina general a un pueblecito en las montañas del Escambray, con un sueldo equivalente a veinte dólares por mes. Yo era el único médico en la zona, trabajando largas horas y siempre de guardia.

Después de un año, me sentía totalmente exhausto, y decidí quejarme de las condiciones de trabajo que, en mi opinión, eran inaceptables. Sin acuerdo o aviso previo, los dirigentes de Salud Pública llegaron a mi oficina para dejarme saber que había sido

sancionado por "conducta inapropiada", lo que era otra manera de decir "contrarrevolución". Después de ser obligado a empacar mis pertenencias, me transportaron a un lugar remoto llamado Meyer. Entre los profesionales de la medicina, Meyer se conocía como el "Presidio Modelo". Este era el lugar a donde el gobierno mandaba a la mayoría de los doctores y dentistas que se atrevían a expresar su opinión contra el régimen. No era nada accesible, especialmente durante la temporada de lluvia, durante la cual estábamos totalmente incomunicados.

En Meyer, tuve suficiente tiempo para reflexionar y estudiar la táctica a seguir para poder librarme del comunismo. Decidí entonces ser más flexible y cumplir con las expectativas del gobierno. Transformé el centro médico de Meyer en uno de los mejores centros de servicios médicos de la zona. Fui felicitado por mi iniciativa y excelente trabajo. Al cabo de un año, los mismos dirigentes de Salud Pública que me habían sancionado, me preguntaron si estaba dispuesto a ejercer por un año como director del Policlínico de Trinidad, que era el centro médico más grande de la región. Yo acepté. Ese fue el comienzo de mi venganza y de la preparación de mi camino hacia la libertad. Puse todo mi empeño para que el Policlínico funcionara a la perfección. Mi esperanza era ser "premiado" por los dirigentes siendo enviado a trabajar como médico voluntario en otros países... ¡y así sucedió!

En el verano de 1979, el nuevo gobierno Sandinista tomó el poder en Nicaragua. El gobierno cubano me ofreció ir a trabajar a dicho país por dos años. Acepté con gusto, ya que era precisamente lo que yo quería. Junto con muchos otros médicos, dentistas, enfermeros y militares, llegué a Ocotal, un pueblito cerca de la frontera con Honduras. Por obra de Dios, todo estaba saliendo de acuerdo a mis planes. Aunque estábamos bajo vigilancia constante y entre nosotros había miembros de la Seguridad del Estado, yo sabía que algún día encontraría la oportunidad de escapar.

II. EL ESCAPE

Después de un año, le escribí una carta a mi tío, el Dr. Luis J. Vázquez, quien vivía en Florida. Le expliqué mi situación y le conté mi deseo de irme a los Estados Unidos. También le pedí discreción absoluta, ya que cualquier sospecha resultaría en que fuera a parar directamente a la prisión en Cuba.

Tío Luis hizo varios viajes a Honduras para tratar de hacer contacto con alguien que pudiera ayudarme; pero todo fue en vano.

Sólo encontró promesas falsas y estafas, que le costaron una gran cantidad de dinero. Vivimos varios meses de total frustración. ¡Entonces ocurrió un milagro! Un matrimonio llevó a su hijo enfermo a la consulta de pediatría de mi tío en Bartow, Florida. El padre era cubano y la madre hondureña, de un pueblo llamado Danlí, que quedaba cerca de la frontera de Nicaragua. Después de hacerse amigos, Luis y María Teresa les contaron sobre mi situación y les preguntaron si ellos conocían a alguien que estuviera dispuesto a ayudarme. La madre del niño llamó a su hermano en Danli y él aceptó.

El día que menos lo esperaba, este joven vino a mi oficina pretendiendo ser un paciente y me entregó la foto. ¡Yo no podía creerlo, cuando vi una vieja foto de mis primas Tere y Lourdes jugando conmigo en el parque de Esperanza, en Cuba!

Nos encontramos en el lugar que le había indicado y decidimos que él volvería por mí en dos semanas. En el día acordado, terminé mi trabajo, pedí autorización para ir a visitar a unos amigos y nunca más regresé. Solamente me llevé la ropa que llevaba puesta y mis credenciales médicas. Todo lo demás se quedó atrás. Mi guía estaba esperándome según habíamos acordado. Pudimos alquilar un carro con la excusa de que tenía que ir a ver a un amigo enfermo en Las Manos, un lugar cerca de la frontera. Yo tenía un miedo horrible de que alguien me viera en compañía de un desconocido y sospechara algo. Dejamos el carro cerca de las montañas y comenzamos a caminar a pie, una experiencia muy peligrosa. Había guerrilleros muy bien armados y unidades de vigilancia del ejército por doquier. Estábamos arriesgándonos la vida por mi libertad.

Mientras caminábamos, se hizo de noche y comenzó a llover. Los truenos y relámpagos hacían la fuga más angustiosa, como una película de horror. Podíamos oír las voces de hombres en las cercanías. El miedo me paralizaba... el corazón me latía tan fuerte que temía que se pudiera oírse en la distancia. Afortunadamente, nadie nos vio ni oyó, y continuamos caminando durante la noche, hasta que mi guía apuntó a una cerca de púas y me dijo:

—¿Ves esa cerca? ¡Eso es Honduras!

La lluvia no cesaba y decidimos pasar el resto de la noche en una escuela cercana. Después de descansar unas dos o tres horas, continuamos caminando, hasta encontrar la carretera Panamericana. Nos limpiamos el fango en un arroyo y continuamos caminando hasta que un camionero se ofreció a llevarnos al pueblo. En Danli, Luis había establecido contacto con una familia cubana que iba a alojarme.

Liana, Virginia, Omaida, Carlitos, Lindsey y Manolo Martínez

Inmediatamente les pedí usar el teléfono y llamé a Luis y María Teresa, quienes comenzaron a llorar de alegría al oír mi voz. A la mañana siguiente, Luis llegó en el primer avión disponible, listo para hacer lo que fuera necesario para llevarme a Estados Unidos. Después de hablar con varias personas y ver que se hacía muy difícil, él decidió que la mejor opción era buscar la ayuda de la Embajada de los Estados Unidos en Tegucigalpa. Nunca podré olvidar la amabilidad y disposición que mostró la Cónsul norteamericana para resolver mi caso.

Después de varios días de entrevistas, la Cónsul nos informó que no sabían cuanto tiempo demoraría mi salida, y dijo que lo más apropiado era que Luis regresara a los Estados Unidos y que yo me hospedara en un hotel ubicado frente a la estación de policía para así poder darme protección. En el preciso momento en que mi tío Luis estaba entregando la llave del carro que había rentado, lo llamaron por los altoparlantes del hotel. La llamada era de la Cónsul. ¡Ella había recibido aprobación para que yo viajara a los Estados Unidos de América al día siguiente! Nadie puede imaginarse el impacto que esa noticia tuvo en mí, especialmente porque ya me había hecho la idea de que estaría en Honduras por tiempo indefinido en un limbo legal.

La Cónsul de los Estados Unidos y sus guardias, nos escoltaron personalmente al aeropuerto de Tegucigalpa. Llegamos al aeropuerto

de Miami, con una carta que autorizaba mi entrada al país por razones humanitarias. También recibí un documento que me autorizaba a vivir y a trabajar en este maravilloso país. ¡Después de vivir bajo la opresión del comunismo por veinte largos años, era al fin un hombre libre!

Fui a vivir con mis tíos en Bartow. Yo no hablaba inglés con fluidez. Luis me enseñó a administrar una oficina médica en este país y me enseñó cómo funcionaban los hospitales, y a pesar de que yo estaba algo limitado, me ofreció trabajo como asistente médico. Mi tío fue un gran mentor. Yo estudié día y noche para prepararme para el examen estatal de medicina y aprendí inglés. También me compré mi primer carro... ¡un Ford Pinto de segunda mano!

Más tarde me mudé a Miami para vivir con mis tíos Ricardo y Aida García. Ellos también me dieron su apoyo incondicional. Continué estudiando para alcanzar mi meta. Aunque era médico, no podía practicar mi profesión. Tuve la suerte de conocer al Dr. Velázquez, director médico del *North Miami General Hospital*, quien me contrató media jornada, como asistente, ganando doce dólares por hora además de beneficios. En febrero de 1984 pasé el examen estatal y obtuve mi certificación para ejercer como médico en el Estado de Florida.

Fue durante ese tiempo que conocí a Virginia, quien hoy es mi esposa. Ella era gerente de tres clínicas de reducción de peso en Miami. Me ofreció trabajo de médico en sus clínicas. Acepté y, poco después, nos enamoramos y nos casamos. Ella me enseñó todo lo relacionado con este tipo de prácticas médicas, de las cuales yo no conocía nada. ¡Le estoy muy agradecido! El éxito que disfruto hoy, junto a mi familia, se lo debo a ella.

Abrimos nuestra propia práctica de medicina general y clínica de reducción de peso, *Lite Weight Clinic, Inc.* Hemos tenido éxito desde el mismo principio. El Señor nos dio dos hijas maravillosas, Liana y Lindsey, y el hijo de Virgina, Carlo, vino a vivir con nosotros. Con tiempo y dedicación, hemos podido alcanzar todas nuestras metas.

En 1994, pudimos hacer realidad el sueño de mis padres. Vinieron a vivir a los Estados Unidos. Después de treinta y cuatro años de vivir bajo el comunismo, ahora están disfrutando de su jubilación en Miami, en su propia casa, y con libertad de hacer lo que quieran.

III. HAZ LO MISMO POR OTROS

Mi hermano Carlos, un cirujano neonatal, y su esposa Omaida, una respetada pediatra, quienes ganaban no más del equivalente a treinta y cinco dólares al mes en Cuba, expresaron su interés en

salir de la isla junto con sus dos hijos. El hecho que los dos eran médicos, hacía más difícil lograrlo legalmente. ¡Era prácticamente imposible! Fue entonces cuando recordé las palabras de mi tío, el Dr. Luis Vázquez, cuando le pregunté cómo podía pagarle por todo lo que había hecho por mí. Él dijo —Yo quiero que tú hagas, por otra persona, lo que yo hice por ti. Mi esposa y yo decidimos hacer lo que fuera necesario para sacar a mi hermano y a su familia a través de otro país.

Por fin conocimos a alguien con conexiones en Venezuela que los podía sacar de Cuba. Nos pidió una cantidad exorbitante de dinero para hacer los arreglos necesarios. Nos dijo que la manera más fácil para escaparse era que mi hermano y su esposa se divorciaran y se casaran con ciudadanos venezolanos. Mi sobrino de dieciocho años tendría que hacer lo mismo. Ellos aceptaron este plan ya que ellos estaban dispuestos a hacer cualquier cosa por salir de Cuba. Se efectuaron los divorcios y las bodas. Al principio todo salió como planeado. Cuando ellos llegaron, todos fuimos a Venezuela a esperarlos al aeropuerto. Eran las navidades de 1995 y finalmente estábamos todos juntos de nuevo, ¡un momento inolvidable!

Regresamos a los Estados Unidos con la promesa de que mi hermano y su familia llegarían unos días más tarde. Sin embargo, no sucedió así, y ellos pasaron muchos meses en Venezuela. Ellos trataron de escapar varias veces. La Seguridad del Estado de Venezuela detuvo a la familia entera por un tiempo, por tratar de utilizar documentos falsos. Finalmente, fueron saliendo uno por uno.

Hoy, la mayoría de nuestra familia vive en Miami. Mis padres han podido disfrutar de sus nietos y bisnietos. Mi hermano Carlos y su esposa Omaida, han podido ver a sus hijos graduarse de ingeniería eléctrica y establecer carreras maravillosas. Por mi parte, estoy viviendo la vida que siempre soñé. Estoy muy orgulloso de mi familia y de mi esposa, por todo lo que hemos conseguido juntos. Especialmente le doy gracias a Dios por permitirnos vivir en libertad.

Camila, Claudia, Carlitos, Carlos y Cristobal Luna

Siempre estaré contigo

Carlos Luna

Yo quiero cuando me muera, sin patria pero sin amo
Tener en mi tumba un ramo de flores y una bandera.
JOSÉ MARTÍ

Los recuerdos de mi infancia, en un pueblo de campo, son el gran punto de partida de mi necesidad de expresión. En mi pueblo natal se siembra el mejor tabaco del mundo. Soy de Pinar del Río y me crié en San Luis, Cuba. El mío es un pueblo lleno de personajes e historias coloridas que sólo se encuentran en los lugares de campo. El recuerdo más poderoso de mi infancia es el amor profundo que mis abuelas sembraron en mí, el amor a mi familia, a mi patria y a mis raíces, así como una conciencia clara de donde vengo; esto me ha ayudado siempre a saber para donde voy. Son muchas las anécdotas que puedo contar de mi niñez.

En mi familia, sobre todo en la paterna, siempre hubo una predisposición natural a ser rebeldes e inquietos, tal vez es esa mezcla rara en mis abuelos que tienen de vascos con isleños. Los Luna provienen de hebreos convertidos al catolicismo, judíos sefarditas, también de árabe. De hecho, el primer Luna famoso fue un cura, que se rebeló contra la iglesia en el Siglo XIV al cual crucificaron y quemaron. En la familia de mi madre, al igual que en la mayoría de las familias cubanas, hay de español, de europeos en general, a eso se le suma el africano y el asiático; en fin que de cualquier lugar, raza o credo que haya en mis ancestros y su circunstancias, yo heredé mi condición rebelde.

Mis abuelos paternos vivían en Sancti Spiritus. Mi padre era el menor de sus hijos. Cuando Batista dio el golpe de estado al gobierno de Prío Socarrás y se convirtió en presidente de Cuba, ellos, como muchos otros cubanos, se opusieron a Batista y contribuyeron a conspirar en su contra. Mi familia, estuvo en la sierra apoyando el movimiento que existía en busca de libertad y de mejoras para el

país que amaban. Su apoyo fue de diferentes maneras: apoyaron con comida, dinero, ropa, armas, aportaban todo lo que podían. Esto cobró su factura cuando en su propia casa la policía de Batista torturó a mi abuelo hasta matarlo en presencia de mi abuela Ramona, quien a su vez fue detenida y torturada. Allí no quedó nadie, no se sabe quien se hizo cargo de enterrar a mi pobre abuelo.

En 1959, cuando Fidel Castro tomó al poder, la familia de mi padre se dio cuenta que éste era comunista, algo que ellos no apoyaban; es por esto que regresaron al Escambray. Esta vez se luchaba contra el dictador quien aún hoy, después de más de cincuenta años, continúa llevando a mi país en un proceso sistemático, siniestro de destrucción y deterioro casi total. El objetivo principal del nuevo dictador, en mi opinión, era y es destruir la base más poderosa del país: "La familia". La familia cubana ha sido siempre la infraestructura y el corazón de la sociedad.

En aquellos momentos las familias de la zona del Escambray fueron quizás las primeras que sufrieron la experiencia que después alcanzaría a toda la sociedad cubana: separación familiar, intriga, rencillas, odios, lágrimas y desarraigo, lo cual es parte de todo este proceso nefasto de arbitrariedad y dolor. Allí se implementó la reforma agraria interviniendo las fincas, incluyendo hogares y las tierras privadas para que Fidel las distribuyera a su antojo. Una vez que mi padre regresó de luchar en las montañas, se fue a Pinar del Río a buscar sus familiares. Allí no encontró a nadie. En ese viaje conoció a mi madre y se casó con ella, formando una familia de la que yo soy el primogénito.

Después de los primeros diez años de dictadura, la mayoría de la población había comprendido que la mejor manera de sobrevivir dentro de Cuba era manteniendo el silencio: teníamos que cuidarnos a la hora de hablar, sobre todo si lo íbamos a hacer sobre el gobierno. Todo era oculto, había que cuidarse incluso frente a la propia familia por temor a ser denunciado. Opinar contra el gobierno era y aún es un delito mortal.

Yo me crié en ese ambiente de arbitrariedades, de irrespeto y destrucción que ya era mi país en esos años. La represión era completa; todos los deseos, los sueños, gritos, protestas, llantos y amor debían ser en silencio, cautelosos, a medias; algo bien contradictorio para el que sabe que nosotros los cubanos no sabemos hacer nada en silencio, que tenemos una tendencia natural a hacer ruido, todo lo hacemos cantando y gritando; nos gusta el bullicio, creo que cierta patente musical nos fue otorgada por obra y gracia del Todo Poderoso.

Yo fui criado por mis abuelas, vivíamos llenos de carencias materiales, siempre nos faltaban tres o cuatro cosas a la vez, si había pasta de dientes no había cepillo; si teníamos arroz no había frijoles; si querías ir al baño, no había papel sanitario. Este sistema ha mantenido al cubano ocupado... no pueden pensar en la situación porque están procurando sobrevivir.

Por duro que mis padres trabajaran, no lograban resolver nada. Mi abuela materna, ya enferma, me hablaba en susurros de infinita dulzura de lo que había sido Cuba. Su increíble fuerza interna alimentaba mis ideales y mi rebeldía. Mis padres peleaban con ella, por miedo a que yo me buscara problemas, cosa que fue imposible evitar.

Hubo algo de lo que nunca carecí en mi casa: El amor incondicional, algo que todos necesitamos para crecer como personas de firme carácter. Esto fue lo que me fortaleció y me proporcionó las herramientas para subsistir hasta el día de hoy. Mis abuelas me mostraron posibilidades de cómo sobreponerme al dolor, construyendo desde lo que amas, no desde lo que odias. Mi abuela presenció cómo asesinaron a su marido y sin embargo nunca dejó de ser una mujer feliz que le sonreía al milagro de la vida diaria, barría la casa cantando y bailando. Ella fue un ejemplo viviente de superación personal; de cómo vivir enamorado de la vida, en el presente dejando el pasado donde pertenece... en el pasado. Mi goce por las fiestas, el baile y mi admiración por la música Cubana se lo debo, más que a nadie, a ella.

Mi abuela materna, Juliana Sánchez, fue y sigue siendo mi ángel guardián. Ella fue el amor de mi vida en aquellos años, y que Dios me devolvió cuando conocí y me casé con mi esposa Claudia. Fue Juliana quien siempre me habló de tradición, de orgullo, de lo que había sido Cuba antes del desastre del 59; fue ella quien me habló de José Martí y su amor por Cuba; quien me habló de integridad, del perdón, responsabilidad hacia la familia y de muchas otras cosas que en aquel momento no entendí.

Recuerdo que mis padres se quejaban, sobre todo mi padre porque sabía lo inquieto que yo era y sabía cuáles serían las consecuencias de aquellas largas conversaciones. Sin embargo, hoy a los 41 años y después de tener 3 hijos; una preciosa niña de 16 años, Camila, y dos varones, Carlos de 13 y Cristóbal de 12, comprendo la responsabilidad que sintió mi abuela al contarme nuestra historia para moldear mi carácter, así como la de mis padres de protegerme. Ya siendo un joven estudiante de arte, fueron muchos los desacuerdos

con mi padre; pero después de tener hijos, me doy cuenta que él sólo deseaba protegerme.

Fue a mis abuelos Juliana y Genaro a quienes les hice una promesa en 1979 que marcaría mi vida para siempre. Yo tenía nueve años cuando abuela me hizo un pastel de coco. Al terminar la última cucharadita se sentó frente a mí y me dijo en tono serio y amoroso:

—Tenemos que hablar contigo.

—Sí, abuela.

—Necesito que me jures algo por Dios, por nosotros, por todos.

—¿Qué?, pregunté ya nervioso. Mi abuelo me agarró de los brazos, me paró frente a él y me dijo:

—Por favor júranos que, en cuanto tengas una oportunidad, te irás del país. ¡Júralo! Olvídate de todo. No mires atrás. No puedes mirar atrás, tienes que irte de Cuba.

Yo no entendía nada. Todavía lo cuento y me erizo. Lo juré no sé cuántas veces, llorando, asustado, nervioso. Después de calmarme un poco, mi abuela me dijo tiernamente: —Ahora júranos que esta conversación no existió entre nosotros. No se lo puedes decir ni a tus padres.

Mi abuela, quien ya estaba frágil de salud, murió poco tiempo después de esa tarde. Ya en su lecho de muerte, pidió que le removieran el oxígeno y me dejaran a solas con ella. Me pidió un beso y cuando me acerqué, me tomó de las manos y me dijo muy bajito al oído: —Mi niño, no te preocupes. Siempre, voy a estar contigo; los dos vamos a estar contigo; pero no se te puede olvidar lo que prometiste. Júrame que me puedo ir tranquila. Ella murió al día siguiente.

Su muerte marcó el comienzo de mi posibilidad de salida del país o soñar con irme como mi única vía de subsistir. También todo se volvió hostil y oscuro para mí. Tenía mucha rabia con Dios y con la vida por quitármela; me volví un muchacho conflictivo en aquella mezcla difícil de edad y sentimientos. Me peleé con todo, protesté contra todo. Mis padres se separaron al poco tiempo haciéndolo más doloroso. Durante este período ya estudiaba la carrera de artes plásticas en Pinar del Río, y al año siguiente continué mis estudios en la Habana. Fue por medio del arte, la carrera que me apasionaba, que comencé a sacar todo aquel dolor interno, encontré vías para expresar mis sentimientos, y me refugié totalmente en ella.

Los años de estudio interno en la Habana, tampoco fueron una pera en dulce; todo el mundo estaba buscando la manera de sobrevivir en un país en franco deterioro. Las escuelas de arte en Cuba, en esos años, eran consideradas "escuelas privilegiadas", también

eran un infierno, una jungla de sobrevivencia. Había cientos de estudiantes, el más fuerte abusaba del más débil. La pasábamos buscando algo para comer porque la comida en la escuela era horrenda, muchas veces pútrida. Teníamos que ser cautelosos para no hacer nada que pudiera dar motivo de que algún compañero lo informara como actividad sospechosa. Había muchos estudiantes ansiosos por delatarte para de esa forma escalar dentro del sistema, a costa de la desgracia del otro.

Yo viví en la calle y comí en ella. Allí tuve que subsistir y comenzar a poner en práctica la posibilidad de hacer una carrera independiente, sin estar atado al gobierno ni a nadie. La calle fue dura, cruda, estricta y exigente. Aprendí a trabajar duro, lavé platos, pinté casas, sembré arroz y tabaco, trabajé en construcción; negocié mucho y aprendí a sobrevivir. En la escuela siempre me destaqué, tuve altas calificaciones, fui muy aplicado. Aprendí las técnicas y la historia del arte; entendí las bases de una carrera en la que me desarrollaría el resto de mi vida.

Ya para 1991, mi carrera en Cuba, como artista, se había vuelto prometedora, tenía una serie de premios importantes y comenzaba a presentar obras en eventos internacionales. Justo ese año, por recomendación de un gran artista cubano y buen amigo, me puse en contacto con un galerista mexicano que hizo las gestiones para obtener una visa para viajar a Monterrey, México. Él me consiguió la visa mediante una universidad donde yo fui a enseñar por unos meses. Las buenas relaciones con el cuerpo diplomático mexicano en la Habana facilitaron una salida pronta y sin dificultad. Tuve que regresar a Cuba el 4 de noviembre, para participar en la Bienal de la Habana, un evento internacional que se celebra cada dos años. Mi trabajo formaba parte de la exhibición cubana. Siguiendo el denominador común de Cuba, de mantener todo en silencio, no se sabía que yo había estado en México. Los dirigentes culturales comenzaron a indagar, "¿Dónde está Carlos Luna y su obra para la Bienal?"

Finalmente hice acto de presencia. La Habana estaba llena de gente; mucho movimiento y mucha vigilancia. Era el principio de la peor crisis económica interna del sistema desde 1959. Entre toda la gente que estaba en la Habana, me encontré con un ex-compañero de estudios que estaba muy integrado en el gobierno, era un informante, un chivato como decimos los cubanos; alguien que ganó su posición a costillas de desgraciarle la vida a otros. Me reuní con él y mirándome seriamente me dijo: *—Luna, tengo una mala noticia que darte. Mi hermano es el Jefe de Seguridad del Estado de esta área. En la lista*

de gente que van a detener está tu nombre. A ver qué haces porque de esta no te libras. Hoy pienso que el ponerme sobre aviso fue un alarde de su parte y una manera de mostrar su poder de intimidación.

En realidad, ahora se lo agradezco, porque tomé acción inmediata y como resultado hoy vivo libre fuera de Cuba. Corroboré la información al ir a visitar a un familiar totalmente integrado al gobierno y con un alto rango. La información era verídica. El 4 de diciembre de 1991 me detendrían bajo quien sabe qué cargo, algo que habían inventado, cualquier cosa podía ser un acto de contrarrevolución para ellos. Mi pariente fue claro y tajante: —Carlos Luna yo no puedo hacer nada por ti. Debes irte del país y yo no he hablado contigo. Esta conversación no existió y nosotros no nos hemos visto. Si a las 12:00 del día del 4 de Diciembre estás aquí, eres hombre muerto. Buena suerte.

Yo no entendía el por qué, pero tampoco había que entenderlo. Desde el primero de enero de 1959 mi país ha sido más que surrealista, lleno de arbitrariedades donde un hombre ha sembrado odio de una manera tan desmedida que quizás por muchos años sufriremos sus secuelas.

Salí corriendo aterrado hacia la embajada de México, al primer lugar que se me ocurrió ir, pero además era el único sitio donde encontraría ayuda. Entré sin mayor dificultad. En la embajada me encontré con dos amigos que tenían un puesto alto y que eran muy amigos del galerista que me había invitado a México. La ayuda de ellos y la de un alto funcionario de Mexicana de Aviación y su personal en el aeropuerto de la Habana, fueron fundamentales para mi escape; sin ellos no hubiera podido salir de Cuba. En mi vuelo de salida el alto oficial de la embajada Mexicana que me había ayudado fue testigo, con gran estupor, de la preponderancia y la arbitrariedad de las autoridades cubanas del aeropuerto, incluso violando leyes internacionales. A mi llegada a la Ciudad de México el oficial mexicano me dio un fuerte abrazo y me dijo:

—¡Mucha suerte! Ya tienes todos mis datos. No mires atrás... nunca mires atrás. Yo seguí a Monterrey donde aún me esperaba mi contrato.

En Cuba, la única que supo que yo me iba fue mi madre. Ella estaba en la Habana conmigo, la noche antes de mi salida, la desperté de madrugada para darle la noticia: "Mamá, me voy de Cuba mañana a primera hora. Ya no regreso más, no sé cuando te vuelva a ver". Mi madre nunca me lo ha dicho pero creo que a ella la noticia no la sorprendió; las madres tienen ese sexto sentido de saber que

está pasando. Yo no sé como describir lo que sentí en ese momento; era una mezcla de tristeza y alegría al mismo tiempo. Lograba salvarme y conmigo llevaba la esperanza de que un día los míos tendrían también la posibilidad de emigrar. Nos abrazamos y yo partí. Después de mi salida, mi familia no tuvo descanso de la hostilidad y hostigamiento gubernamental, fueron sometidos a interrogatorio y hasta fueron detenidos.

Después de los primeros meses de incertidumbre en la ciudad de Monterrey, decidí irme a la Ciudad de México donde yo sabía que vivían más compatriotas de mi generación. Fue entonces que conocí a la mujer que iba a ser mi compañera, la madre de mis hijos, mi esposa y mi todo: Claudia Catalina Ramírez. Nos casamos el 6 de Diciembre de 1992, a partir de ahí comencé a reconstruir mi vida, a sentir nuevamente el calor de una familia muy unida, a disfrutar la vida; fue como si los recuerdos y las vivencias de mi infancia vinieran de vuelta poco a poco.

Muchas veces pienso en las palabras de mi abuela antes de morir: "Siempre estaré contigo", es como si ella me hubiera ayudado a escoger a mi esposa Claudia, una mujer con los mismos sentimientos, espíritu y fortaleza que ella. Es en México y particularmente en Puebla, donde fui a vivir, que la tradición cultural viene desde el mundo prehispánico hasta hoy, donde hay incalculable riqueza cultural por todas partes. Es ahí donde comencé a poner en práctica la fortaleza de mi carácter y la riqueza de mi cultura. A medida que me sumergía en la tradición mexicana, más dueño y orgulloso me sentía de mi tradición cubana.

Con la llegada de mis hijos también fueron saliendo todas aquellas historias que mis abuelas me contaron con tanta pasión, se fortaleció aquel carácter pujante típico de los cubanos; aquel amor por un país de gente maravillosa y luchadores que son capaces de levantarse aún en el terreno más inhóspito. Comenzaron a aparecer imágenes que me llevaban a mi pequeño pueblo de campo, aparecieron los gallos, las mujeres morenas, las palmas, el refranero popular, el guajiro, la música y también los temas en que expreso mi opinión sin ningún reparo de lo que pienso y siento sobre la situación de mi país.

Yo tome la decisión de abandonar mi patria, no permití que su situación política me aplastara. Ningún obstáculo detendría mi laboriosidad de contarle al mundo quien soy y de donde vengo. Los años fuera de Cuba me han permitido un crecimiento personal y profesional donde me he expresado en total libertad, algo que

desafortunadamente no hubiera sido posible en mi Cuba. En el extranjero elegí hacer mi lucha y aportar mi granito de arena al canto de identidad que llevamos dentro todos los cubanos.

Mi trabajo está plagado de historias que sucedieron en el pequeño pueblo donde me crié o de algún otro pueblo de la isla, o me las contaron mis abuelas o mis tíos, mis padres o un amigo, o son las mías propias; mi recorrido por México las enriqueció y las fortaleció y la llegada a los Estados Unidos hizo que el caldo fraguara, el pollo salió del cascaron y se trasformó en el gallo o el guajiro que tantas veces he pintado, altivo y orgulloso de saber de dónde viene y muy seguro de saber a dónde va.

El guajiro de mis cuadros, somos todos los cubanos, en mi opinión es el verdadero héroe de la historia nacional, siempre ha estado ahí, en el peor y en el mejor momento. En mi obra, el guajiro es tanto el protagonista del *"El Gran Mambo"*, como el que le da un *"knock out"* a Fidel Castro en la obra *"1, 2, 3, Se Acabó tu Conteo"* o el que canta, baila o se enamora. En mis cuadros también están las voces de todos aquellos que no pudieron contar su historia. Actualmente en los Estados Unidos con mi esposa e hijos y parte de la familia de Cuba (mi madre con su esposo y mi hermano) hemos recorrido un camino de renacimiento. Ellos han podido regresar a Cuba; allá me quedan mis hermanas y mi padre a quienes deseo volver a ver… en tierras de Libertad.

Hoy vivo en los Estados Unidos y soy ciudadano americano por naturalización, este país me otorgó la residencia EB-1-1 reconociéndome por habilidades extraordinarias; algo que me llena de orgullo. Por otra parte, es curioso que mi trabajo y yo no aparezcamos en ningún libro ni documento cubano desde mi partida hace ya 20 años, con excepción del libro *"Memories of Cuban Art of the 20th Century"* que se publicó en los Estados Unidos. Tal parece que me hubieran borrado cuidadosamente para que no quedara ningún rastro, aun cuando a nivel mundial, mi obra ha alcanzado reconocimientos en espacios académicos e institucionales y una posición sólida en el mercado del arte internacional.

Espero un día poder regresar a mi país y exhibir mi trabajo, compartir y disfrutar libremente en la tierra que me vio nacer, poder reencontrarme con mis familiares y viejos amigos; quisiera dejar de recordar Cuba y vivirla de nuevo. Mientras tanto continuaré volando y dándole testimonio al mundo mediante mi arte de lo que soy: un cubano libre. Pienso que un hombre sin pasado es un hombre sin futuro y un hombre sin memoria, no es nada.

Antes de 1959 el cubano en general no tenía necesidad de abandonar la isla, había problemas como en todas partes; pero también es cierto que Cuba era la Perla del Caribe y de buena parte del mundo. Hoy los cubanos en el exilio andamos diseminados por todo el planeta, destacándonos al más alto nivel en todo lo que nos proponemos; no nos dejamos discriminar y en todas partes hemos demostrado la fibra increíble de la que estamos hechos; los cubanos llevamos nuestras tradiciones a donde vamos: el arroz con frijoles, el lechón asado, con tostones o maduros, la yuca con mojo, los pastelitos de guayaba y el flan. Bailamos lo mismo un mambo de Dámaso Pérez Prado que el mejor son de Benny Moré, La Guajira de Celina Gonzáles, que "La Vida es un Carnaval" de la reina Celia Cruz.

Por más de 50 años, el cubano ha llevado en una taza de café y en el goce de un buen habano, todos los recuerdos de una pequeña isla en el Caribe, como si fuera el planeta entero; con orgullo hemos crecido y engrandecido nuestra raza en el exilio. Somos los cubanos del destierro, la única población en el mundo trasplantada, que por más de medio siglo no ha perdido su identidad, con excepción de los hebreos. Siempre he dicho que un Cubano es plural, dos cubanos… una multitud.

Christian, Yipsy, Eduardo y Nicole Fernández

Todo fue una mentira

Eduardo Fernández

La libertad es el derecho que tienen las personas de actuar libremente, pensar y hablar sin hipocresía.
JOSÉ MARTÍ

Si yo dijera que la libertad de expresión y la libertad en general fueron la razón por la que mi esposa Yipsy y yo vinimos a los Estados Unidos, estaría mintiendo. A diferencia de los cubanos que salieron de la isla durante las dos primeras décadas de la Revolución, nosotros nunca conocimos el verdadero significado de la palabra libertad hasta que llegamos a este país. Nosotros somos parte de una gran masa de cubanos que nació en los años setenta, a quienes el gobierno les planificó todos los ámbitos de la vida. Desde muy pequeños el gobierno nos determinó a qué colegios íbamos a asistir, cómo nos íbamos a vestir, qué hacer o no hacer, qué comer, el próximo paso a dar, qué carrera íbamos a estudiar, dónde íbamos a trabajar, cuánto íbamos a ganar, qué decir en una conferencia internacional o en una reunión de negocios, etc. Desde que nacimos se nos dio una libreta de abastecimiento para las más mínimas necesidades. No se nos enseñó a tener libre albedrío.

El por qué vinimos fue principalmente una razón económica, era la ilusión de poder vivir de nuestro propio esfuerzo, de nuestro trabajo, el poder tener un hogar propio, hacer una familia y que esa familia tuviera un buen futuro. En Cuba no existe el mañana, sino el hoy. Cada cual tiene la misma preocupación: qué como y cómo lo consigo. Todos se sienten forzados a robar de cualquier fuente de abastecimientos a los que tengan acceso, principalmente en su lugar de trabajo, es decir, del gobierno. Por ejemplo, un farmacéutico que tiene acceso a medicamentos, trata de retener mercancía para intercambiar con alguien que tenga acceso a comida, ropa, etc. Esto se ha convertido en una forma de vida. El futuro es totalmente incierto para los cubanos de la isla. ¿Cómo es posible que a un profesional

después de cinco años de estudios no le alcance el sueldo ni para comprar la canasta básica de alimentos? ¿Cómo es posible que los familiares que están en el extranjero tengan que mantenerlos?

Durante años, el gobierno cubano nos educó e inculcó que nuestro sistema de igualitarismo era el más justo y perfecto del mundo. Francamente, la mayoría de nuestra generación estaba convencida de que la Revolución Cubana iba avanzando y construyendo una Cuba mejor. Incluso, cuando entramos en la peor crisis del país, después del derrumbe de la Unión Soviética y el campo Socialista en 1990, muchos pensábamos que todo era culpa del "enemigo," los Estados Unidos, que había corrompido a los países socialistas. Ese fue el mensaje que se nos repitió por años.

En el curso de toda la vida escolar, el gobierno exige al estudiante a asistir "voluntariamente" a realizar labores agrícolas para ayudar al país, y según la actitud del estudiante al respecto, será elegible para la educación universitaria o no. A la edad de dieciocho años nos decían: "Nombren cinco carreras en las que estén interesados". Por supuesto, a esa edad, un estudiante no ha sido expuesto a las diferentes oportunidades profesionales. Pero no importa, ya que el gobierno la seleccionará por ti. Por haber colaborado con el sistema, a mí se me asignó seguir la carrera de Economía y a Yipsy, mi novia en aquel entonces, la de Medicina Veterinaria. Yo por ser hombre, tendría que servir un año en las Fuerzas Armadas, como condición previa para estudiar la carrera que el gobierno había escogido para mí.

En 1994, después de terminar el Servicio Militar, me gané el derecho a terminar mis estudios en la Universidad de la Habana. Comencé en un programa auspiciado por la Universidad Autónoma de Madrid y aprendí algo que no se había enseñado en Cuba por muchos años: la economía de mercado, la libre empresa. Cuba estaba desesperada por apoyo económico y abrió el mercado libre para países como Canadá y España, atrayendo así el turismo y asociaciones de negocio con Cuba. Se suponía que este programa nos estaba formando para trabajar en las nuevas empresas mixtas, con capital extranjero. Muchos sectores de la economía se estaban descentralizando, aparentemente para hacerse ver más independientes y atraer capital extranjero. El camaleón sólo estaba cambiando de color.

Me di cuenta de muchas de las mentiras en que habíamos vivido. Mientras Fidel y su cúpula vivían como magnates, con lujos y recursos inimaginables para mí, el resto del país experimentaba una situación totalmente distinta. En aquel momento pensé que había

sólo un camino para mejorar nuestras vidas: hacer lo que convenía, ser partidario y formar parte de aquel sistema. Sin embargo, el mundo donde mi esposa se desarrollaba como veterinaria estaba lleno de limitaciones y sin perspectivas para ella. Después de analizar nuestras opciones, llegamos a la conclusión de tratar de irnos del país. Yipsy decidió inscribirse en el sorteo de visas y el 27 de marzo de 1997 fue seleccionada para entrevistarse en la oficina de Intereses de Estados Unidos en Cuba y yo, por supuesto, con ella.

Iniciamos entonces una etapa a la que yo le llamo de transición, pues te conviertes en una persona mal vista por el sistema y envidiada por los que quieren irse pero no tienen la opción de hacerlo. El mundo se te dificulta mucho más.

Ahora también había una variante muy importante que solucionar: con qué dinero íbamos a pagar los dos mil dólares necesarios para salir del país ya que nuestro sueldo era menos de US$30 al mes. Sólo una persona podía ayudarnos, mi tío Luis Vázquez en Florida, quien por años ha estado ayudando económicamente a su hermana Nonín, mi abuela. Recuerdo que hablamos por teléfono y me preguntó: — ¿Estás seguro de que quieres venir? Mira que esto es muy duro! Yo no le creí. Después en otra conversación me dijo: —Te voy a ayudar, pero debes tomar tu propio camino, no vas a poder venir para mi casa. De veras no lo entendí entonces. En mi mente yo necesitaba de un guía, alguien que me dijera lo que tenía que hacer, ¿cómo lo iba a hacer yo solo? Realmente no apreciaba en aquel momento el valor y el sacrificio que hacía este buen señor y su familia por nosotros.

Esperamos nueve meses para recibir el permiso de salida. Los profesionales en Cuba tienen que ser liberados por el ministerio del departamento al que pertenecen, es decir, que el gobierno tenía que verificar que Yipsy y yo no manejábamos información confidencial, económica o veterinaria que pusiera en peligro la seguridad nacional. El 21 de diciembre de 1997 nos dieron la libertad para salir de la cárcel más grande del mundo, Cuba, y comenzamos nuestra nueva vida. (En retrospectiva, ese fue el mejor regalo de Navidad que jamás hemos recibido).

Una vez en los Estados Unidos tuvimos que tomar muchas decisiones importantes. Con la ayuda de la iglesia católica, nos fuimos a Kentucky donde había más oportunidades de trabajo que en Miami. De ser cubanos totalmente dependientes, ahora nos encontrábamos en un laberinto lleno de oportunidades, sin nadie que nos dijera que hacer. Yo creo que Dios hace las cosas por alguna razón

y también creo en el dicho que dice: "Dios aprieta pero no ahorca", siempre hay ángeles que ofrecen su mano. Dios nos mandó a Helena y Jeffrey Robbins quiénes nos dieron los primeros muebles para nuestro apartamento, nos ayudaron a comprar el primer carro y nos acogieron como sus hijos.

El golpe más duro para un profesional en el exilio es darse cuenta de que al principio los estudios no cuentan y que para ganarse el pan de cada día se tiene que empezar de cero en el trabajo que sea y ganando un salario mínimo como simple trabajador. Es humillante, pero te curte y te estimula a avanzar.

Yipsy comenzó a trabajar ayudando a una veterinaria, limpiando las jaulas, bañando los animales y lavándole los dientes a perros y gatos, y lo que es peor, limpiándole las glándulas anales a los caninos. Yo trabajaba en un congelador, empacando carne de res que llegaba por un carril. Tenía que ser rápido y poner mucha atención pues si no se acumulaba y me abrumaba. De nunca ver carne de res en Cuba y siempre anhelarla, ahora estaba cubierto de ella. ¡Ya no la quería ni ver! Después nos fuimos a una fábrica donde trabajamos durante dos años por más de catorce horas diarias. Asistíamos dos veces a la semana a *Jefferson Community College* y tratábamos de hablar inglés hasta entre nosotros. Era algo que necesitábamos aprender. Fue entonces que Dios nos dio otra amiga, Christina, una norteamericana maravillosa a la que no le entendíamos ni una cuarta parte de lo que decía, pero aprendimos mucho con ella ya que nos veíamos obligados a usar el idioma. Solamente veíamos televisión en inglés con subtítulos para comprender mejor. Después encontramos trabajo a medio tiempo en una tienda de departamentos. Todos los días había retos con el idioma y cosas nuevas que aprender. Trabajábamos tan duro, que si faltábamos al trabajo, los gerentes nos decían que nos extrañaban y que nos necesitaban.

Transcurrido un tiempo y dominando mejor el inglés, decidimos que uno de los dos tenía que revalidar su título profesional mientras el otro trabajaba para mantener el hogar. Mi esposa podía estudiar para el examen estatal de Veterinaria o yo podía hacer una maestría, lo que era más viable. En dos años me gradué de la Universidad de Louisville con una Maestría en Administración de Empresas. Lo pudimos pagar al contado con el dinero de nuestros ahorros. Hoy dirijo el Departamento de Recursos Humanos en JBS USA, LLC mientras Yipsy trabaja en el Departamento de Contabilidad en Rescare en Louisville, Kentucky. Con el tiempo, planea revalidar su doctorado.

Ahora por fin entiendo, me doy cuenta de que el factor clave de lo que yo considero mi éxito en el exilio, es precisamente el hecho de que mi tío Luis me obligó a labrar mi propio futuro, a caminar con mis propios pies como lo hizo él y su familia 30 años antes. Siempre recordaré que cuando llegamos a Miami, de inmediato lo llamé desde un teléfono público:

—Tío, ya estamos aquí, en cuanto empiece a trabajar te pago el dinero que me mandaste.

—No, no tienen que pagarnos nada, —respondieron él y su esposa María Teresa— tómenlo como un regalo para que comiencen una nueva vida sin deudas. Siempre le estaremos agradecidos.

Creo que nosotros somos testimonio de que el sueño americano es viable y lo puede lograr cualquier individuo que se lo proponga. Nuestro éxito es nuestra familia. Es la educación que le podemos brindar a Christian y Nicole, nuestros dos hijos. Es también el haber podido edificar nuestra propia casa y honrando el ejemplo del "tío Luis", ayudar a aquellos que dejamos en Cuba.

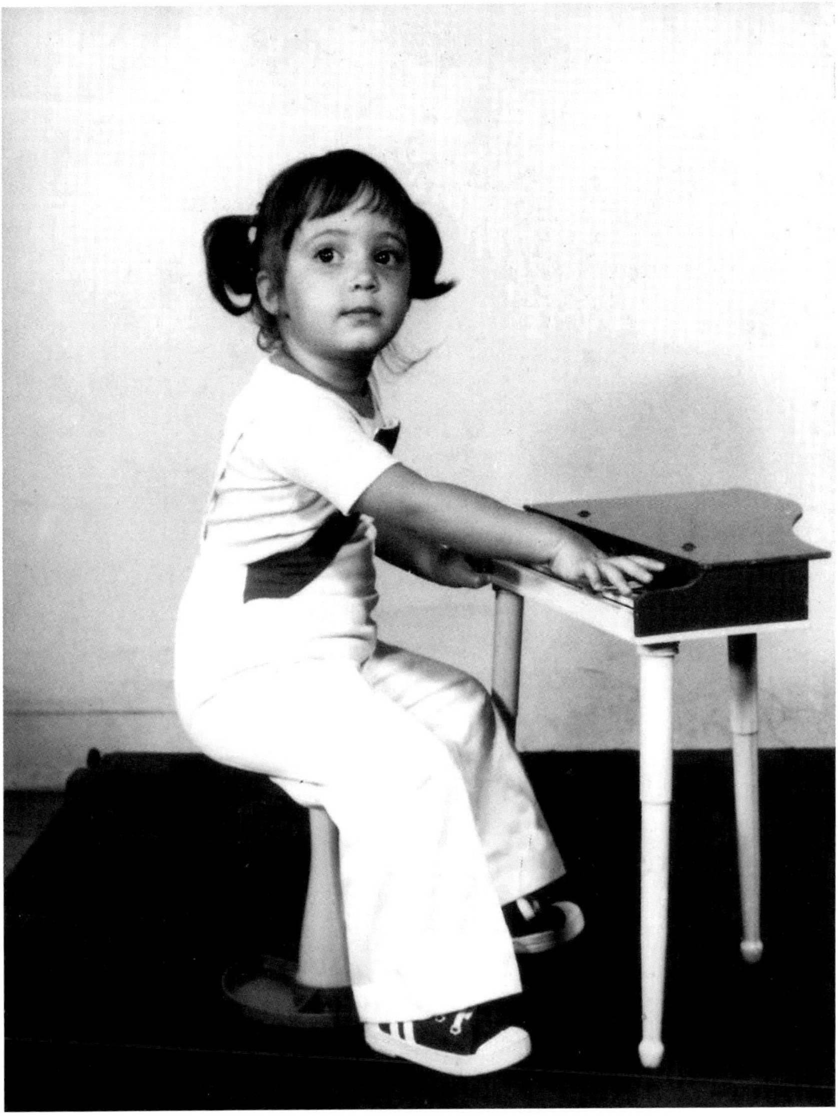

Ivelisse de la Fe

El alma de la canción

Ivelisse de la Fe

Todos nuestros sueños pueden convertirse en realidad,
si tenemos el coraje de perseguirlos.
WALT DISNEY

Nunca supe realmente por qué Abuela Caridad siempre me animó a aprovechar todas las oportunidades para que mi talento musical se destacara. Creo que todo comenzó cuando yo tenía como un año y medio y me regalaron un pianito. Recuerdo que mientras mami y Papi estaban en el trabajo, yo me quedaba con abuela y abuelo tocando aquel pianito. Varios años después, cuando mis padres decidieron mudarse a otra casa, abuela insistió para que yo siguiera viviendo con ella y con abuelo, con la excusa de que el piano de la familia, en el que yo practicaba, era demasiado grande y no cabía en el pequeño apartamento. Eran sólo cinco minutos de distancia a pie de una casa a la otra, así que aunque yo me quedé viviendo con mis abuelos, siempre estuve cerca de mis padres y de mi hermanito quien nació poco después de que mis padres se mudaran.

No es casualidad que yo ame la música y haya querido aprender algo que me encanta. Mi padre era muy inteligente y tocaba la guitarra de oído. Yo crecí oyéndolo tocar las canciones de los Beatles. Mis padres trabajaban en la Habana; mi padre era ingeniero eléctrico y luego trabajó como agente de una compañía española, mi madre trabajaba para la compañía de electricidad del gobierno. No hay duda que yo tuve una niñez segura donde se alcanzaban las metas; por lo tanto mi talento musical floreció, especialmente con la pasión alentadora de mi abuela y el motor impulsor de mi abuelo. Ambos me llevaban a diario a la escuela y luego se sentaban por horas a mi lado para escucharme practicar en el piano. Aunque sus estudios eran limitados, abuela tuvo una influencia enorme en mi vida. Ya de adulta, yo descubriría el por qué de su pasión por mi éxito musical.

Cuando tenía cinco años, tuve que tomar un examen para ver si calificaba para tomar clases de piano o baile/gimnasia. Aunque pasé ambos exámenes, decidí enfocarme en el piano y comencé a estudiar con una maestra privada, Muñeca. Como en Cuba había problemas con el transporte, yo tenía que caminar 10 cuadras para ir a su casa, aún así algunos de mis recuerdos favoritos son de los ratos que pasé en casa de Muñeca, donde incluso tomaba siestas. Muñeca me quería mucho y dejaba que me quedara en su casa todo el tiempo que yo quisiera. Ella estaba totalmente dedicada a mis estudios musicales y a mi éxito. Aprendí a estudiar con ella y hasta el momento, me preocupo por alcanzar las notas más altas posibles.

Dos años más tarde, me matriculé en el Conservatorio Alejandro García Caturla donde recibí numerosas distinciones académicas y musicales, ganando premios en Matemáticas, Literatura Española y en varias competencias de piano. Mi maestra en el Conservatorio, Isabelita, estaba empeñada en que yo ganara las competencias y hasta me quedaba en su casa para practicar y prepararme para los conciertos. Ella es como una segunda madre y siempre le estaré agradecida. Año tras año pude mantener el promedio escolar más alto de toda mi clase. En Música, recibí el premio de más alta distinción, el Primer Lugar en la competencia de Música Cubana y menciones especiales por interpretar la música de Ernesto Lecuona. Al graduarme, tuve el honor de ser aceptada en el Conservatorio Musical Municipal Amadeo Roldán bajo la tutela del Profesor Jorge Bueno. Al cabo de cuatro años, me reconocieron con el Premio de Oro en ambos ámbitos, académico y musical, y me gradué con un promedio de 99.54 de 100 puntos. Tomé el examen de ingreso del Instituto Superior de Artes, el cual representa a todo el país y se especializa en Arte. En dicho instituto estudié con la Profesora Danae Ulacia.

Además de mis estudios, mi vida espiritual también era importante para mí. Cuando yo tenía 14 años, mi mamá sintió una gran atracción por la música de la Iglesia Metodista, y la primera vez que fui con ella, me di cuenta de inmediato lo que le faltaba a mi vida. Comencé a asistir a los servicios regularmente y a tocar el piano con la Banda Alabanza. Cuando acepté ser la pianista de la iglesia, supe que había encontrado mi hogar espiritual. Mi hermano y mis abuelos se hicieron miembros también, a pesar de que abuela era católica no practicante.

Aunque viajar a los Estados Unidos es casi imposible para la mayoría de cubanos, yo pude venir por primera vez en el año 2000 con un grupo de alabanza. Fuimos invitados para tocar en diferentes

iglesias durante la Conferencia Anual de Florida. Durante mi visita a Lakeland, conocí a varios miembros de la Primera Iglesia Metodista Unida, entre ellos a Brenda y Marty Higgenbotham así como a Riley y Claire Short. Ellos fueron extremadamente amables conmigo y demostraron interés en ayudarme a desarrollar mi talento musical. En el Sur de la Florida, también conocí a una familia muy especial, los Jhaveri, quienes se hicieron mis buenos amigos. Este viaje marcó mi destino. Durante uno de los conciertos también conocí a Roberto Michel, un maravilloso músico cristiano quien cinco años después sería mi primer novio, el amor de mi vida.

Regresé a Cuba después de un mes, tiempo en el cual había encontrado nuevos amigos y había hecho contactos con personas que me podían ayudar. Les envié un video donde interpretaba varias piezas musicales. Aunque toda mi familia estaba en Cuba, yo tenía el deseo de estudiar en un país lleno de oportunidades. Siendo cubana, no tenía la posibilidad de estudiar en los Estados Unidos. Yo no sabía cómo ni cuándo, pero tenía fe en que el Señor me iba a abrir las puertas y que mis sueños se harían realidad.

Mis amigos comenzaron a tratar de conseguirme una beca en Florida. En el 2002, nuestro grupo de alabanza regresó a Estados

Ivelisse de la Fe

Unidos, esta vez invitados por la Conferencia de Carolina del Norte y dimos muchos conciertos en varias iglesias. También vinimos a visitar a nuestros amigos en Lakeland, quienes ya se habían puesto en contacto con el distinguido profesor de piano Robert McDonald de *Florida Southern College*, una famosa universidad metodista en esta ciudad. Después de ver mi video, el profesor McDonald hizo todo lo posible para que me aceptaran. Regresé a Cuba, pero me quedé en contacto con mis amigos quienes se convirtieron en mis manos y pies en Florida.

También en el 2002, la Primera Iglesia Metodista Unida envió un grupo de misioneros a Cuba, entre ellos las familias Higgenbothan y Short. Allá tuve la oportunidad de verlos y una vez más expresar mis deseos de venir a estudiar a los Estados Unidos. Otra vez fueron muy amables conmigo, no sólo me ofrecieron su amistad, sino también continuar ayudándome para alcanzar una meta que parecía imposible. Estas fabulosas personas no tenían nada que ganar, su ayuda era incondicional. Una vez que regresaron a los Estados Unidos, junto con Rakesh y Milly Jhaveri, hicieron todo lo posible para

Ivelisse de la Fe

reunir el dinero y el papeleo necesario para cumplir con los requisitos de ambos países, especialmente los de Cuba que eran mucho más complicados.

En marzo del 2003, mi sueño se hizo realidad. Llegué a Florida lista para empezar las clases en *Florida Southern College*. Después de pasar los primeros meses con la familia Jhaveri, llegué a Lakeland donde fui a vivir con la familia Higgenbotham y después con los Shorts. Tenía una beca completa otorgada por la Iglesia Metodista y otra beca musical otorgada por la Sra. Julie Fancelli. Aunque yo estaba en el segundo año de la universidad en Cuba, tuve que comenzar de cero ya que no podía transferir los créditos cubanos y también porque tenía que estudiar muy duro para dominar el idioma inglés. Yo no tenía familia en los Estados Unidos, sin embargo me sentía muy protegida.

Recuerdo el primer día de mi llegada, tratando de aprender inglés, todo lo que oía me sonaba como "bla-bla-bla". ¡Me dolió la cabeza por tres días! No podía hablar, lo cual me frustraba porque yo soy una persona muy habladora. Por las noches las palabras daban vueltas en mi mente y hasta soñaba en inglés, pero durante el día, no podía ni formar una oración. Poco a poco fui aprendiendo, sintiéndome como una idiota al señalar las cosas para saber cómo se decían en inglés.

Empecé a ver el programa de televisión "*Who Wants to be a Millionaire?* (¿Quién quiere ser Millonario?) y así aprendí frases y trivia. Durante ese verano tuve la oportunidad de pasar algún tiempo en el Campamento Metodista de Leesburg, Florida, donde conocí muchos jóvenes, entre ellos Audrey Warren quien se convirtió en una de mis mejores amigas y con quien practicaba inglés. Tenía que dominar el inglés antes de que la universidad comenzara en el otoño. Estaba totalmente dedicada a ello y veía mucha televisión. El programa "*Friends*" (Amigos) también me ayudó mucho, junto con mis propios amigos quienes nunca se cansaron de mis innumerables preguntas.

Desde que llegué a los Estados Unidos y especialmente durante el período de adaptación, los Higgenbothams han sido mi mayor bendición. Brenda se aseguró de que yo tuviera todo lo que necesitaba para comenzar la universidad. Ella y su esposo Marty compraron una casa cerca de *Florida Southern College* para que yo tuviera un lugar donde vivir y ella misma la decoró, incluyendo un piano para que yo practicara. Nunca podré expresar el dolor que sentí cuando, de pronto, ella murió dejándome con una gran tristeza y enorme vacío en mi vida. Brenda estaba el lugar de mi madre en este país. En su

funeral, llena de emoción y cubierta de lágrimas, toqué dos de sus canciones favoritas. Ese mismo día el Señor puso en mi camino otras dos personas muy especiales e importantes en mi vida, Susan y Waite Willis. Marty Higgenbothan continúa siendo el ángel de mi guarda que Dios eligió para iluminar mi vida.

Al final de mi primer año en Florida Southern College recibí el premio de Honor de Phi Eta Sigma Freshman por haber sido la estudiante con las notas más altas y con la mayor cantidad de créditos en la universidad. También me mantuve en la lista de Honor del Presidente todos los semestres. Era lo mínimo que podía hacer para demostrar mi gratitud a aquellas personas que habían trabajado tanto para traerme y hacer mis sueños realidad.

Durante el segundo año, recibí el Premio en Memoria a Alfred Courty Woodard así como el Premio Musical en Memoria a Jack Houts. Durante el último año, tuve el honor de recibir numerosas distinciones como el Premio de Robert Lee Zimmerman por Excelencia, el Premio Erudito de Presser y Quién es Quién entre los estudiantes de Universidades Americanas. Fui miembro de Sociedades de Honor como Phi Kappa Phi, La Sociedad de Liderazgo Omicron Delta Kappa y Sigma Delta Phi. Me gradué Summa Cum Laude con un promedio de 100 (4.0 GPA).

Vivo agradecida de lo que la comunidad de Lakeland ha hecho por mí y trato de retribuir sus acciones ayudando en todo lo posible, como ofreciendo mi talento musical en numerosas Galas de la universidad, para el Club de Kiwanis, el Club de Rotary y la Cámara de Comercio. Continúo tocando en el Servicio Contemporáneo de la Primera Iglesia Metodista y en una banda de alabanza con mi novio, Roberto, donde quiera que las iglesias nos necesiten. También he sido consejera en los campamentos de la iglesia.

Después de graduarme en el *Florida Southern College*, con un título en Música, quise continuar mis estudios. Para entonces, había conocido a Teresa Martínez, una compatriota con quien había entablado una linda amistad. Teresa me dio la oportunidad de trabajar con ella como intérprete para varios abogados y sus clientes hispanos. Siempre me han fascinado los derechos y la libertad de los ciudadanos americanos y estudiar leyes me pareció un desafío. A la vez estaría siguiendo los pasos de mi abuelito quien estudió derecho en la Universidad de la Habana.

Tomé el examen de ingreso (LSAT) y me aceptaron en tres universidades. Decidí estudiar en la Universidad de Derecho de Stetson por su fama y por estar cerca de casa. Estoy en la lista de Honor. No

he decidido qué rama de Derecho voy a practicar, pero creo que en este mundo se necesitan abogados honestos y cristianos.

El Señor ha sido muy generoso conmigo y ha puesto muchos ángeles en mi camino, personas maravillosas que han contribuido para que alcance el éxito y con quienes lo comparto. Además de los que ya he mencionado, quiero dar las gracias a Angela Higgenbotham, a Marcia y Paul Alley, a Mary Kay y John Langford, a Ingrid McDonald, a mi iglesia y a todos los que han iluminado mi camino. Le doy gracias a mi Dios y Salvador quien me ha dado y me sigue dando la fortaleza para conquistar nuevas metas.

Por supuesto, mi agradecimiento inefable para mi familia en Cuba por ser siempre mi inspiración, por enseñarme que con respeto, amor y mucha perseverancia se puede alcanzar las estrellas. Mis abuelos, padres y hermano decidieron darme prioridad y me permitieron irme lejos de ellos, por primera vez, confiando en mi capacidad y compromiso con el triunfo y en la fortaleza de mi carácter. Ahora, aunque la separación y la distancia son difíciles de sobrellevar, mi familia está orgullosa de mis éxitos.

Durante uno de mis viajes de visita a Cuba, Abuela Caridad me enseñó un programa de un pequeño teatro al que iba durante su juventud. Me confesó que en aquellos días, el campo del entretenimiento no se consideraba aceptable para una jovencita, así que ella y su mamá tenían que escaparse para ir a los teatros de pueblos pequeños para que ella pudiera ejercer su talento y expresar su amor por la música y la actuación. Ahora, después de todos estos años, por fin entendía por qué ella había apoyado mi carrera musical tan fervientemente. En aquel programa, a lo largo de la portada y en letras bien grandes, se anunciaba a mi Abuela Caridad como "*El Alma de la Canción.*"

Eduardo Sarmiento en su estudio, Miami 2009

Yo vengo de todas partes

Eduardo Sarmiento

El tiempo es el maestro de la muerte.
GASTÓN BAQUERO

A mi abuela Rebeca, quien me enseñó a dibujar.

He metido mi vida en una maleta en varias ocasiones. Esa vez tenía un ticket de avión Habana-Mexico D.F., pero mi verdadero destino era Miami. Era el 20 de octubre del 2006 (Día de la Cultura Cubana), vestía una guayabera blanca y mi rostro respiraba semioculto tras una barba negra. El equipaje muy ligero: una maleta cargada de dibujos, algunas fotos y la absoluta certeza de que un hombre no debe detenerse en la realización de sus sueños; aún cuando tenga un nudo rajándole la garganta.

Mi nombre es Eduardo Sarmiento. Nací en Cienfuegos, Cuba, en 1980, y no sé exactamente el día en que voy a morir. Soy artista plástico, ilustrador y diseñador gráfico.

A los 18 años me fui a estudiar a la Habana, en el Instituto Superior de Diseño (ISDI), y cuando terminé de estudiar me quedé en la capital viviendo en casa de amigos o de mis novias.

Mi padre vive con su esposa y mis dos hermanos, mi madre con su novia y su perro. Mi papá es ortopédico y mi mamá es ginecóloga. El salario de ambos suma $50 dólares al mes. Durante los dos primeros años de la Universidad, los fines de semana que iba de visita a Cienfuegos me dedicaba a manejar el carro de mi mamá y hacer de taxista. Algunas veces era un poco molesto porque tenía 20 años y mis hormonas gritaban pidiendo sexo y fiestas; entretanto, yo andaba transportando putas o turistas -a escondidas de la policía y a riesgo de que me pusieran una multa- para ayudar con la economía familiar. Cuando regresaba a casa con algún dinero, veía en el rostro de mi madre la alegría de ver a su único hijo asumiendo los roles del hombre de la casa. También podía ver su tristeza de verme sacrificando mi tiempo en aquellas labores prohibidas, después de

ella haber estudiado tanto y oponerse siempre a las cosas ilegales. En una noche, como taxista, ganaba lo mismo que mi madre en un mes, operando mujeres y haciendo partos. Aquella experiencia fue muy enriquecedora; crecí rápidamente (casi todo crecimiento verdadero es doloroso) y aprendí los códigos de la calle. También me busqué problemas y hasta tuve que pelear en varias ocasiones, esto por supuesto nunca se lo conté a mi madre.

LA HABANA

Al empezar el tercer año de la Universidad tuve la oportunidad de comenzar a trabajar como diseñador e ilustrador *freelance* para revistas y casas editoriales. Al principio me costó trabajo y me pagaban poco; pero después de varios meses trabajando incansablemente y tocando todas las puertas posibles, comencé a ganar más o menos igual que como taxista (el doble o el triple que mi madre). Profesionalmente, aquellos años fueron exquisitos; conocí muchos intelectuales. Fui cofundador de "Camaleón", un grupo de artistas quienes hicimos murales, carteles, libros, ilustraciones. Trabajaba y estudiaba, y hasta comencé a hacer trabajos de diseño para clientes con plata. Mi economía creció notablemente.

Recuerdo el día que le compré a mi madre una lavadora plástica que costó 160 dólares; aquello fue un acontecimiento familiar y mi mamá no paraba de hacer el cuento a los amigos cercanos. Disfrutaba aquellas peripecias; pero me entristecía mucho (y aún me entristece hoy) la situación económica de mi madre, y no es que quiera que sea millonaria; pero me gustaría que cuando el carro no tuviera gomas, ella misma pudiera comprarlas; y que conste, que para mi es un placer ayudarla, pues siempre me ofreció mucho más de lo que pudo y me educó con respeto y amor.

CONTRADICCIONES

Mientras estudiaba, creía en la posibilidad de vivir en Cuba y hacer cosas por mi país y lo disfruté mucho hasta que me gradué y comenzaron las contradicciones. Al graduarme comencé a trabajar en el Instituto Cubano del Libro, como Director de Arte e ilustrador, impartiendo clases de ilustración y cartel en el ISDI y como Director de Arte de la revista del Ballet Nacional de Cuba "Cuba en el Ballet". También con "Camaleón" continué haciendo proyectos, obtuvimos varios premios nacionales e internacionales.

Profesionalmente mi vida era privilegiada; pero la situación de la vivienda era imposible. Mientras estuve estudiando viví becado en

la Universidad o en casa de Themis, mi novia habanera. Al graduarme, viví con un amigo que me ofreció su apartamento como guarida. Otra vez, me fui a vivir a casa de mi nueva novia Rocío, uno de los amores de mi vida. Aquella situación de la vivienda me desconcertaba, pues no existía la forma legal de alquilar un apartamento a un cubano que decidiera vivir en la Habana. Llegué a la conclusión de que tenía que vivir con mi novia en su apartamento o asesinar a mi abuela y quedarme legalmente con su casa: la idea de vivir con mi novia fue genial, mientras duró el amor. Por otra parte, matar a mi abuela era sólo un argumento literario.

QUITO

En el 2006 me invita mi amigo Carlos Zamora a un evento de diseño en Ecuador, con todos los gastos pagados. Se llamaba "La Rosa Gráfica" y además de participar en una exposición de carteles, debía impartir algunas charlas sobre la gráfica joven en Cuba. Compartí el viaje con una pareja de amigos diseñadores. Aquello fue demasiado bueno para ser real; deseaba con mucha fuerza conocer el mundo; me sentía llamado a descubrir otras tierras. Como era miembro de la Unión Nacional de Escritores y Artistas de Cuba (UNEAC) y trabajaba para la cultura, no me fue tan difícil gestionar los permisos para representar a Cuba en otros paises. Quito me abrió las puertas del mundo y me ayudó a comprobar que era posible una vida honrada y profesional fuera de mi Isla. Estuve tentado a probar suerte y vivir por un tiempo en Quito; pero no creí que fuera el mejor lugar para desarrollar mi obra artística, ya en aquellos momentos el arte comenzaba a dictar mis pasos; además, me esperaba la promesa de un amor inconcluso.

CAUSALIDADES

Regresé a Cuba, impartía clases en la Universidad, vivía en el apartamento de mi novia y disponía de un cuarto para pintar; pero yo no pensaba sólo en aquel tiempo: pensaba en el camino de mi obra artística, las posibilidades reales de desarrollo dentro de la isla y en todo lo que habían trabajado honestamente mis padres para recoger muy poco. Los días se convirtieron en un tormento y casi todo me parecía turbio, falso. Dormía con las mandíbulas apretadas; empecé a encontrar paredes donde debían haber puentes. Comprendí que la mayoría de las personas no querían hacer nada para no comprometerse (de todas formas iban a ganar lo mismo, y en nombre de la Revolución te podían

destruir). En Cuba lo intrascendente puede convertirse en algo notorio, sólo por ser tangente a la palabra "revolución", incluso los revolucionarios le temen a esa palabra, pues es un estado en si misma, un pretexto para muchos, una excusa para otros. Me desilusioné, estaba agotado de trabajar y ver la mayoría de mis proyectos de diseño empolvarse en una gaveta, y cómo en cambio, se le asignaban proyectos a los más brillantes mediocres. Fue entonces cuando reafirmé que lo más importante en la vida es ser consecuente con uno mismo, y que cada hombre tiene el derecho a decidir su camino.

Medité muy bien y decidí que Miami sería mi mejor opción, pues tenía tíos y primas que me apoyarían en el inicio de la travesía. Viajé a México invitado a un evento de diseño aquel 20 de octubre, sabiendo que iba a cruzar la frontera de los EEUU. No me gustaba la idea de hacer algo tan riesgoso e ilegal; pero mis deseos de vivir eran más fuertes. Después de ocho horas de entrevistas en la frontera entré a los EEUU por Matamoros y la primera noche dormí en el piso de la terminal de ómnibus, tapado con una caja de cartón, esperando que saliera el próximo ómnibus destino a Miami. Así fue la primera noche de mi segunda vida.

EL TÍO PEPE

Al llegar a Miami descubrí que nada era como me imaginaba (demasiados mitos y desinformación) ni mejor ni peor, sencillamente una ciudad donde se respeta al que trabaja y donde cada uno llega hasta donde le permiten sus propios límites. Aquí conocí al tío Pepe, el que se fue de Cuba en el 61; el que se cambió el nombre a la edad de 7 años para llamarse José, como Martí. Él es un hombre de bien y ama a su tierra más que nadie; pero nunca estuvo de acuerdo con el gobierno revolucionario; por ello le dijo adiós a su isla para siempre.

LAS RAÍCES

Cuando alguien se va de Cuba tal parece que no hubiera existido, ni tan siquiera que halla muerto. En Miami he conocido a muchos poetas, artistas y otros profesionales que hicieron mucho por su tierra, y que en Cuba se les ha arrojado sombra sobre su nombres, sólo por el hecho de haber decidido vivir en otro país. Es una pena que se castigue a alguien por ejercer su derecho a escoger una ciudad donde vivir. Nos afectamos todos, los de ambas orillas; pues los puentes son débiles y muchas raíces quedan truncadas. A mi no me

molesta que miles de cubanos decidan vivir en Cuba (aunque pueda discrepar radicalmente). ¿Por qué a algunos cubanos les molesta que otros decidamos vivir fuera de la isla? ¿Qué los hace acreedores de tal derecho?

MIS ABUELOS

La historia de mi abuelo paterno, Eulogio Sarmiento, es la típica historia de un hombre honesto y trabajador, enamorado de su esposa hasta el fin de sus días, quien de cocinero pasó a ser el propietario del hotelito donde trabajaba, el mismo hotelito que le quitó la Revolución en 1965. Mi abuelo recordaba ese día con profundo sufrimiento y decía: "No me dejaron llevarme nada; ni tan siquiera el dinero de la caja registradora". Pero lo peor fue que el hotel era no sólo el sustento, sino también la casa de mi abuelo, porque allí vivía con su esposa y sus hijos.

En cambio, mi abuelo materno, Fausto Portero, trabajó para la policía de Batista y ganó el respeto de sus vecinos porque no maltrataba a nadie y avisaba a los revolucionarios cuando tenía noticias de que iban a ser apresados. Después del triunfo de la Revolución, se convirtió en chofer de una grúa y bebedor por excelencia. Envió a sus dos hijas a estudiar en la Universidad y nunca les permitió que trabajaran hasta que culminaron sus estudios. Lamento no haber podido terminar nunca una botella de ron con mi abuelo, acompañados de sendos tabacos cubanos; pero me alberga la alegría de haberlo hecho muchas veces en su nombre, celebrando su existencia. No puedo estar más orgulloso de la sangre que impulsa estas palabras.

MIAMI

Ahora vivo en Miami, esta ciudad maldita que abrió sus piernas para recibirme y darme calor. Trabajo como director de arte en un estudio de diseño, hago ilustraciones y pinto obsesionado hasta el agotamiento.

Han pasado tres años desde aquel 20 de octubre del 2006. Todavía conservo la guayabera blanca, aunque ya casi no la uso. La barba permanece insistente como hierba en primavera. Me acosan preguntas más contradictorias y complejas que las que me impulsaron a partir de la Habana; pero estoy disfrutando mi viaje por la vida, empleando mi tiempo a mi manera y compartiendo esas preguntas que tal vez sean las respuestas de otros.

Kassandra, Ella, Evan y Eddy García

¡Él lo realizó! La historia de Eddy García

Teresa Vázquez Martínez

El éxito: algunos sueñan con alcanzarlo…
mientras otros se levantan y trabajan duro para lograrlo.
ANÓNIMO

Nunca olvidaré su abrazo de bienvenida. Acababa de dejar atrás mi país, mi vida como hasta aquel momento la conocía. Mis padres, mi hermana y yo llegamos al Aeropuerto de Miami el 5 de marzo de 1970, para quedarnos en Hialeah con la familia de mi tío Ricardo. Cuando me senté en la sala por primera vez, él vino inmediatamente y se sentó en mis piernas, sonrió, puso sus bracitos y piernas alrededor de mi torso y la cabeza en mi hombro. Mi primo Eddy tenía sólo cinco añitos, sin embargo parecía darse cuenta que yo sentía miedo y que tenía el corazón partido.

Era tan guapo, tan pequeño y sin embargo muy fuerte y enérgico. Su pelo rubio, sus ojos café y su gran sonrisa lo hacían lucir como un niño estrella de cine; lleno de cuentos y buena voluntad. Nosotros éramos los primeros miembros de la familia que él conocía y estaba encantado de tenernos allí. Yo supe entonces que él era una persona muy especial, ¡y tenía razón!

Aida y Ricardo generosamente compartieron su hogar con nosotros. Éramos ocho personas viviendo felices bajo el techo de una casa de tres cuartos y un baño. Ellos habían sido los primeros en irse de Cuba. Salieron antes del comunismo en busca de una mejor vida. Ricky, su hijo mayor, nació en Cuba; Eddy nació en New York. Mis tíos trabajaban en factorías, eran buenos padres. Sus hijos crecieron en un hogar humilde y lleno de amor. Cuando yo llegué, Ricky tenia quince años, mi misma edad, lo cual facilitó que yo me adaptara fácilmente a la escuela aquí. Él era muy buen mozo y muy popular, así que yo pude aprovecharme de su buena fama. Pronto la vida se hizo fácil otra vez, nos adaptamos a la vida en los Estados Unidos y mis padres pudieron alquilar su propia casa en Hialeah y un año después nos establecimos en Bartow, en el centro de la Florida.

Eddy venía a visitarnos los veranos. Siempre traía unos cuantos dólares para gastar y regresaba a su casa con la misma cantidad de dinero o más. Conocía el valor de un dólar y todo el mundo sabía que él no gastaría ni un centavo innecesariamente... Eddy estaba ahorrando para el futuro.

Cuando Carlos y yo nos casamos en 1975, Eddy fue nuestro "*ringboy*". Yo le compré su primer perro, Cookie, y Carlos le enseñó a cazar, un deporte que aún disfrutan juntos. Él era nuestro orgullo y alegría. Nos preocupamos cuando nos dimos cuenta de que no tenía planes de ir a la universidad, queríamos más para él... sin embargo, debimos haberlo sabido, Eddy siempre tuvo un plan.

Terminó la secundaria un año antes de lo normal, trabajó duro, vivió con sus padres y ahorró cada centavo que ganaba. Trabajó para la Coca-Cola® manejando un camión y llenando las máquinas dispensadoras, en las que después invirtió. A pesar de las críticas de su familia de que sería una mala inversión, utilizó sus ahorros para comprar una casa en ruinas en la que trabajó los fines de semana para repararla. La vendió por un buen precio y continuó invirtiendo en casas, comprándolas, remodelándolas y vendiéndolas, ganando hasta el 300% sobre su inversión. Era tiempo de dejar de trabajar para la Coca-Cola®. Fue a la universidad para obtener la licencia de contratista. Ese fue el inicio de una vida llena de éxitos.

En 1992, Eddy creó *Watermen Properties*, un nombre que él adoptó porque le sonaba prestigioso. Su oficina era pequeña y estaba situada en el mismo local de *"Worldwide Mortgage Company"*, el negocio de su hermano Ricky en Coral Gables, un área élite de Miami. Así pudieron compartir gastos. La primera tarjeta de presentación que entregó tuvo como respuesta: "Yo he oído de esta compañía"... ahí supo que había escogido bien el nombre del negocio. Eddy continúo trabajando sin costos laborales o salarios que pagar.

Uno de sus amigos, que tuvo un accidente de auto, recibió $350,000 de indemnización. Eddy le propuso hacer negocios juntos. El tenía la experiencia y su amigo el capital. Ellos iban a la corte y compraban casas en ejecución hipotecaria, las remodelaban y las vendían. El primer año ganaron más de $120,000. Durante una de las subastas en la corte judicial, Eddy se encontró con su amigo Marty quien tenía un negocio de hipotecas y se hicieron socios. La competencia feroz, parecida a la de un bando de buitres comprando casas en las subastas, junto con el dolor de saber que una familia había perdido su hogar, habían comenzado a afectarlo. Esto le hizo

tomar la decisión de comenzar a desarrollar urbanizaciones, para lo cual Marty era el socio perfecto.

Había una parcela a la venta en Hialeah por $750.000. Eddy sólo tenía $120.000 en su cuenta de ahorros. Fue entonces cuando reclutó a sus amigos de la secundaria, los hermanos Ventura, como inversionistas. También obtuvo un préstamo, basado en su crédito, del banco comunitario de su vecindario.

Para entonces, él estaba viviendo en un lujoso apartamento en South Beach. Su estilo de vida tenía que cambiar considerablemente para poder afrontar sus responsabilidades financieras. La urbanización se planificó; tomaría dieciocho meses para construir sesenta y seis casas. Él se mudó a un apartamento pequeño y humilde, vendió su hermoso Porche negro convertible e hizo un presupuesto de $18,000 para sus gastos personales durante dieciocho meses... El fracaso no era una opción viable.

Eddy García, Evan, Ella y Kassandra

Ricky, Janine, Mary y Ricky García

Todo se dirigió desde un pequeño tráiler sin muchos gastos. En dieciocho meses el proyecto se terminó y se vendió incluso antes de terminarse. Tuvieron una ganancia de $1.2 millones.

Watermen Development Group continuó teniendo éxito en todos sus proyectos. Los hermanos Ventura decidieron irse a trabajar en el negocio de su familia. Marty y Eddy continuaron construyendo más de 350 casas y centros comerciales en el Condado de Dade. Eddy se convirtió en un experto encontrando tierras en zonas urbanas las cuales no estaban a la venta, evitando así la competencia en subastas; pero la tierra y espacio estaban escaseando en el Condado de Dade.

Un amigo le habló a Eddy sobre Fort Myers donde había más tierra disponible a un precio razonable. Era el lugar preciso en el momento preciso. La economía de Fort Myers no se estaba moviendo y era fácil para alguien con la experiencia de Eddy venir y comenzar a construir casas lujosas, al estilo mediterráneo...algo que era nuevo en el área. Los proyectos tuvieron mucho éxito; se vendían hasta antes de estar terminados. Fabricaron cinco proyectos residenciales y tres centros comerciales en el Condado de Lee. Con el tiempo, otras compañías de construcción nacionales comenzaron a llegar al área y se hizo más difícil encontrar parcelas de tierra a buen precio.

Watermen Development Group se convirtió en una compañía dedicada exclusivamente al desarrollo de tierras. Eddy continuó comprando y vendiendo miles de acres en distintos condados de la Florida con la ayuda de inversionistas. Compraba tierras por varios millones de dólares y las vendía al cuádruple de la cantidad invertida.

Al principio del 2004, Eddy vio una parcela de 125 acres al lado de Daniel Parkway, cerca de la interestatal I-75 en el Condado de Lee. No tenía ningún letrero de a la venta, pero a él le pareció un sitio ideal. Eddy investigó y descubrió que era parte de un caso de bancarrota. *Watermen Development Group* la compró por $16 millones. El plan era edificar oficinas, almacenes y tiendas en esta parcela. También consiguió que la ciudad de Fort Myers la hiciera un anexo. Fue entonces que el mercado bajó debido a la economía y el plan se puso en espera.

Recientemente, el Condado de Lee comenzó a buscar una parcela de tierra para edificar un estadio. Le pidieron a Eddy que pusiera su oferta. Ahora su terreno es el lugar donde se construirá el estadio de entrenamiento de los Boston Red Sox durante la primavera. El condado de Lee estuvo de acuerdo con pagarle $20 millones. Los Boston Red Sox también acordaron pagar $5.5 millones.

Eddy ha tenido mucho éxito, no sólo en el negocio, sino también en su vida personal. Siempre ha mantenido una reputación impecable. Su carácter mesurado, su personalidad franca y honesta, junto con una imagen profesional y sofisticada, le han ganado el respeto y la admiración de muchas personas claves en altas posiciones; algo que muchos pueden alcanzar, pero pocos pueden mantener.

Él aun vive en Coral Gables con su esposa Kassandra y sus dos hijos, Evan y Ella. Las oficinas principales de *Watermen Development Group* están muy cerca de su hogar. El viaja frecuentemente a Fort Myers.

Mi primo Eddy continua siendo mi orgullo y alegría, un alma cariñosa y humilde que siempre se ha preocupado por el bienestar de su familia. Sus padres vinieron de Cuba hacia los Estados Unidos por una razón: buscando una vida mejor… el sueño americano... EDDY LO REALIZÓ.

Rick y Lisa García

Aquella isla misteriosa

Rick García

Por más alto que llegues, nunca olvides tus raíces.
ANÓNIMO

Yo no nací en Cuba. Mis padres llegaron a los Estados Unidos en 1959 cuando Batista todavía estaba en el poder. En la última visita que mi madre realizó a Cuba, en 1960, ella estaba embarazada de mí. Ella retornó a Miami y ni ella ni mi padre volvieron a regresar. Mi niñez en "Little Havana", fue influenciada totalmente por el éxodo cubano que ocurrió en aquel tiempo.

Mi madre es de Camaguey y mi padre de la Habana. Mi papá fue un hombre muy trabajador que tuvo dos negocios: una tienda de regalos, donde se podía encontrar artículos cubanos y una tienda donde se fabricaban y vendían carteras y cinturones de piel de cocodrilo. Yo empecé a ayudarlo de muy joven. Recuerdo claramente el tema que dominaba la mayoría de las conversaciones con los clientes que entraban a las tiendas: "La situación de Cuba". No había día en el que no escuchara algo sobre todo lo que se había perdido en "La Perla del Caribe": la buena vida que les había sido robada por un loco, el azulísimo mar, la blancura de la arena, las majestuosas palmeras, los árboles de frutas tropicales y los inmensos cañaverales. Parecía que los gallos en Cuba eran más aguerridos, su plumaje más brilloso y sus espuelas más largas. También parecía que la comida sabía mejor allá: el lechón asado, la yuca, los frijoles negros con arroz blanco, los plátanos fritos y el aguardiente eran incomparables. Había un romanticismo en los recuerdos y una tristeza por los familiares, amigos y la vida que dejaron atrás. Había patriotismo en las conversaciones ambiciosas sobre la remota posibilidad de regresar en un rescate valeroso para recuperar el "paraíso perdido". Crecí sintiéndome más cubano que cualquier otro nacido en la isla. Siempre quise ir a verla, a experimentarla por mí mismo.

Cuando tenía quince años de edad, tuve la gran fortuna de tomar clases electivas de aviación en la escuela secundaria. Recuerdo

mi primera excursión al Aeropuerto Internacional de Miami y a la Base de la Fuerza Aérea de Homestead, donde mi destino quedó sellado. La aviación se convertiría en mi carrera y en mi pasión.

En 1978, decidí servir a mi país y me uní a la Fuerza Aérea. Una vez que terminé mis cuatro años, trabajé en una compañía local de aviación. Fue entonces cuando me di cuenta de que quería tener mi propio negocio de aviación. Había aprendido bastante de mi papá sobre el manejo de empresas, sabía que tenía suficiente conocimientos sobre la industria y estaba seguro de que vivía en un país donde un hombre puede hacer todo lo que se proponga. Le pedí a mi padre un préstamo de $10,000. Al inicio, él no creía que yo estaba listo para afrontar dicha responsabilidad, ya que yo era muy joven y ya tenía una familia que mantener. Mi papá quería que aprendiera más sobre la industria y que adquiriera más experiencia antes de que iniciara mi propio negocio. Afortunadamente, él me había enseñado otra lección muy valiosa: PERSISTENCIA. Después de unos meses de conversaciones con mi padre y de perseverancia, finalmente él aceptó prestarme los $10,000 con la condición de que si tenía éxito, le tenía que devolver el dinero y si no lo lograba, no le pediría más. No podía fracasar. En Miami, fui criado y rodeado por gente cubana muy fuerte y decidida. Ésta era mi única oportunidad y tenía que lograrlo. Le di la mano a mi padre y Gulf Coast Avionics nació en el garaje de mi casa en Tampa, Florida, en 1984.

Trabajé muy duro teniendo confianza en mí mismo y en mi meta. Sabía que había recibido una base fuerte sobre negocios. Tuve la suerte de que líderes de la industria notaran a este joven de 24 años de edad trabajando con tanta pasión y motivación. Ellos se convirtieron en mis guías y mentores. Tuve la satisfacción de pagar el préstamo en sólo seis meses.

Veinticinco años después, Gulf Coast Avionics es una empresa multimillonaria con sedes en Lakeland, Florida; Portland, Oregon y en Caracas, Venezuela. Nosotros vendemos, instalamos y reparamos equipos electrónicos para aviones e instrumentos de vuelo para clientes de todo el mundo. No siempre ha sido fácil, pero heredé el valor de mi padre. Sé que lo que hoy soy, se lo debo a la perseverancia, ética empresarial y fortaleza de carácter de mis padres. Estoy agradecido por mi educación cubana. Ser bilingüe y bicultural me ha facilitado la comunicación internacional y el entendimiento global.

Los recuerdos de esos días, en la tienda de mi padre, han continuado influyendo mi vida y he sentido el deseo implacable de

ayudar de alguna manera a los que están en la isla. ¿Por qué los cubanos tienen tantas limitaciones? ¿Hay algo que podamos hacer para ayudar? Es así que en el 2004 fui a ver, con mis propios ojos, nuestra isla misteriosa.

Para entonces, el Presidente Clinton había firmado un acuerdo de libre comercio de alimentos y suministros médicos con Cuba. Sentí que estaba en posición de ayudar al gobierno norteamericano con esta misión. Contraté a un asesor para facilitar el trato con el gobierno cubano, creé una compañía, una página web, contacté a todas las agencias necesarias y realicé diferentes viajes a Cuba. Conocí a varios oficiales del gobierno. Desafortunadamente las reglas, las restricciones y limitaciones de 44 años de opresión, hicieron que fuera imposible lograr mi misión. Fue una experiencia educativa.

Todas las historias que escuché mientras crecía no me habían preparado para esta experiencia emocional. Sentado en el avión, sentí la emoción y la expectativa de los otros pasajeros, mientras miraban por las ventanillas, señalando en diferentes direcciones. Vi como se les llenaban los ojos de lágrimas cuando el avión aterrizó. Una vez que pasamos por las puertas de la aduana, allí estaba yo, en la Habana, Cuba. Me paré y observé a los otros pasajeros recogiendo su equipaje y noté que todos tenían varias bolsas grandes de lona llenas de ropa, medicina y de artículos de primera necesidad para sus familiares. Estos fueron meticulosamente inspeccionados y muchas cosas fueron confiscadas por aduana. Cuando más tarde se abrazaban con sus familiares, se sentía una corriente de emociones indescriptible, una pasión por la familia que es difícil de explicar.

Efectivamente, las palmeras eran majestuosas, el mar era azul como me lo había imaginado y la gente era cálida y extremadamente amigable, como si los hubiera conocido de toda la vida. Pero la infraestructura de la isla estaba en ruinas, especialmente en las áreas que no son frecuentadas por turistas. Faltaba de todo, incluso para las necesidades más básicas. Sentí que el corazón se me partía por la pena de ver al hermoso país de mis padres, en esas condiciones. Me sentí profundamente conectado con la isla.

Tuve el placer de conocer a mucha gente durante mis visitas a Cuba, muchos de los cuales ahora considero como mi familia. He regresado con mi esposa y amigos y hemos sido invitados a sus casas, hemos compartido la poca comida que tenían. Nos han contado sobre sus vidas, su cultura y su preocupación por el mundo de hoy.

He experimentado la calidez de la cultura, me he sentido conectado con mis raíces y he sufrido el dolor de la opresión.

En una de nuestras visitas, mi esposa entró por la puerta del hotel, mientras yo fui detenido por el portero quien me advirtió que no hablara español mientras estuviera dentro del hotel. Yo era cubano, lucia como tal, y los cubanos de la isla no les era permitido visitar los hoteles o restaurantes designados para turistas. Fue en ese momento, uno de muchos, que sentí los muchos años de opresión en el que Castro ha mantenido al que también considero como "mi amado país". Mi esposa Lisa y yo nos sentamos en el vestíbulo del antiguo y majestuoso hotel después de haber caminado por las calles de La Habana y sentimos la historia y los espíritus de hace mucho tiempo, cuando Cuba era libre y la vida era seguramente muy diferente.

Regresar a casa siempre es duro. Mientras entrábamos en el aeropuerto vimos muchas familias, la mayoría de las cuales no tienen transporte; pero que de alguna manera estaban allí, esperando por la llegada de sus seres queridos o despidiéndose de sus visitantes. Toda la familia y amigos vienen al aeropuerto para ver a sus familiares regresar a los Estados Unidos. Cuando estábamos parados en la línea, vimos a un joven con una cámara de video grabando a su abuelo que regresaba a los Estados Unidos. Éste nunca paró, ni por un segundo, de grabar a su abuelo. Vimos al caballero pasar por aduana para luego voltear con lágrimas en los ojos, tirarle un beso a su familia y desaparecer en el otro lado. El muchacho parado detrás del área restringida todavía grababa la puerta cerrada mientras las lágrimas le corrían por las mejillas. Observamos a la familia abrazándose. Salieron del aeropuerto sin saber si volverían a ver de nuevo a su ser amado.

Hay tanta gente maravillosa tratando de sobrevivir en Cuba. Un factor común que descubrí en todos los que conocí, es su tenacidad, su sentido de valores y de familia y lo orgulloso que se sienten de ser cubanos. La palabra libertad tiene un significado poco claro para ellos. Es un concepto desconocido, ya que la mayoría nunca la ha experimentado. Los cubanos en la isla están fascinados por el hecho de que los cubanos-americanos podemos viajar a donde queramos, manejar el tipo de vehículo que escojamos, tener la opción de ser dueños de negocios y de nuestras vidas. Aún así, ellos hacen lo mejor que pueden con lo que tienen. Son acogedores, agradecidos, serviciales y están listos para compartir su música y su cultura. Hay músicos tocando en las calles, artistas mostrando su trabajo y gente lista para tomarse fotos con los turistas.

Le agradezco a Dios por las oportunidades y responsabilidades que me han sido conferidas. Nosotros, los residentes de los Estados Unidos, hemos sido bendecidos al vivir en una tierra donde la esencia de nuestra existencia está basada en el significado de la palabra libertad. Yo deseo y ruego para que nosotros siempre honremos y defendamos nuestra autonomía, para que nunca la tomemos por descontada.

PD: Rick García es un empresario muy respetado quien cree en retribuirle a su comunidad. Él es también un piloto a quien le encanta ayudar a los jóvenes a descubrir el maravilloso mundo de la aviación. Con la ayuda de la Junta Educativa del Condado de Polk, Rick pudo establecer la Academia Aeroespacial de Florida Central en el campus de Sun 'n Fun, donde los estudiantes, a partir del noveno grado, pueden obtener créditos de secundaria o de Polk State College; algo similar a lo que él pudo hacer de joven. Rick García es propietario de varios negocios, incluyendo Sunstate Realty Investments Corp., Polk Home Development Corporation y Allure Salon & Day Spa, que abrió con su adorada esposa Lisa. Rick es el orgulloso padre de Michelle y Rick y sirve a su comunidad en diferentes juntas directivas. Es comisionado de la Junta Directiva de Polk State College, es miembro de Sun 'n Fun Fly-In, Polk Vision, West Area Adult School Advisory Board y the Polk State College Foundation, Polk Museum of Art, entre otros.

Carlos Luna

Carlos Luna es uno de los artistas cubanos contemporáneos más prominentes de su generación, con una carrera meteórica y un estilo personal bien definido. Nacido en Pinar del Río, Cuba, Carlos empezó su entrenamiento personal como artista a una edad muy temprana, asistiendo a varias academias del gobierno para jóvenes artistas prometedores. A la edad de 16 años, su trabajo ya se exhibía en exhibiciones colectivas en museos nacionales por toda Cuba, e internacionalmente un año más tarde. Carlos posee un fuerte espíritu, un deseo insaciable por crecer como artista. Huyendo del régimen comunista de Fidel Castro, Él salió de Cuba en 1991; él emigró a México y luego se estableció en Puebla, donde su carrera entró a una nueva fase de exploración y crecimiento.

Después de recibir la visa EB-1-1 de los Estados Unidos para extranjeros de habilidad extraordinaria, Carlos emigró a Miami junto con su esposa y sus tres hijos. Desde su llegada a los Estados Unidos, su trabajo ha sido recibido con gran entusiasmo y se ha exhibido solo o como parte de una colección en más de 25 museos e instituciones de arte en el país siendo altamente considerado por curadores y críticos internacionalmente. El éxito de Luna ha expandido sus oportunidades de exposición a una audiencia más grande y ha difundido su visión artística e influencia a una escala global.

Una de las características resaltantes del trabajo de Carlos Luna es su contenido político y religioso; en especial su apasionada protesta contra el gobierno cubano y lo que éste ha significado para sus compatriotas.

Entre los numerosos éxitos de Luna está la subvención que recibió en el 2001 de la *Fundación Pollock-Krasner.* Así mismo, su carrera alcanzó un hito importante en el 2008 con la exhibición conjunta Pablo Picasso Ceramics | Carlos Luna Paintings en el *Museo de Arte de Fort Lauderdale,* Florida y en el 2009 en el *Complejo Cultural Universitario BUAC* en Puebla, México.

El gallito bum bum / The little rooster, boom boom, 2007
Oil on canvas
38 x 30 in (96.5 x 76.2 cm)

Árbol grande, guajiro yo (detalle) / **Big tree, peasant me** (detail), 2001
Oil on canvas
70 x 78 in (180 x 200 cm)
© Carlos Luna

Sin título / Untitled, 2009
Gouache and charcoal on amate paper
59 x 47 in (150 x 120 cm)

1,2,3, Se acabó tu conteo (detalle) / **1,2,3, Your count is up** (detail), 2006
Gouache and charcoal on amate paper
47 x 94 in (120 x 240 cm)

Muy linda / Very pretty, 2009
Oil on canvas
47 x 39 in (120 x 99 cm)

Muy lindo / Very pretty, 2009
Oil on canvas
47 x 90 in (120 x 229 cm)
© Carlos Luna